A many-sided theologian demands a many-sided biography, which is exactly what Andrew Hoffecker has provided in this careful, balanced, discerning, and insightful book. Although the volume offers an unusually full treatment of the unusually full life of Charles Hodge, who is universally recognized as one of the leading American theologians of the nineteenth century, Hoffecker also has an argument to make. The argument is that in his long career as the mainstay of Princeton Theological Seminary, Hodge successfully combined a strong commitment to confessional Reformed theology and a winsome practice of humble evangelical piety. . . . Hoffecker's life of Hodge demonstrates conclusively that any fair reading of Hodge must recognize at least three things: a full and well-rounded life of steadfast Christian devotion, a more-than-capable advocacy of classical Calvinist doctrines such as universal original sin and the substitutionary atonement, and a set of intellectual instincts commonplace among Americans in the first two-thirds of the nineteenth century.

—**Mark A. Noll**, Francis A. McAnaney Professor of History, University of Notre Dame, and author of *America's God: From Jonathan Edwards to Abraham Lincoln*

Charles Hodge has for too long been victimized by stereotypes. In this fine biography, Andy Hoffecker sets the record straight. Here we meet Hodge the careful Reformed thinker who nurtured a deep piety. This book gives us a winsome portrait of a theologian who still deserves to be taken with utmost seriousness.

—**Richard Mouw**, President, Fuller Theological Seminary

Andrew Hoffecker's biography of Charles Hodge is a wonderfully entertaining and informative read. Hodge is one of the historic giants of Presbyterianism, combining the virtues of scholarship, churchmanship, and a delightful personality. For those who may have read some of his writings but know little of the man and the professional triumphs and personal tragedies he faced, this book will be a great introduction. To those already familiar with Hodge's life, this book will be welcomed as a twice-told tale that will reinvigorate their interest in the man and his work, and set before them an example to be emulated. Andrew Hoffecker has perhaps done as much as anyone to make Old Princeton attractive to a new generation, and this new work is surely a worthy capstone to his career.

—**Carl R. Trueman**, Professor of Historical Theology and Church History, Westminster Theological Seminary, Philadelphia

Years ago I read Andrew Hoffecker's *Piety and the Princeton Theologians*, a very moving account of the vital spirituality among the founders of Princeton Theological Seminary. That point needs to be renewed in our own day, when some writers are suggesting that it is un-Reformed to find anything good in revival or in pietism. Who better to meet that need than Hoffecker himself, who has now returned with a full-scale biography of Charles Hodge, the great systematic theologian of Princeton. Hoffecker teaches us that Hodge's theology is rooted in the confessional traditions of the Reformed faith, but also in the New Side Presbyterianism that emerged from the revival of the Great Awakening. We learn, too, that Hodge also valued friendships with German scholars of pietistic background and spirit. So Hodge developed a form of Presbyterianism known for its balance, a balance sorely needed in our own day. Although church history is not my normal field of specialization, I could not put Hoffecker's book down. It clearly and vividly presents Hodge's theology and his story. I thoroughly enjoyed my trip to the nineteenth century, with this book as my guide. I pray that God will give it a broad readership and use it to promote balanced Reformed theology in our day.

—**John Frame**, Professor of Systematic Theology and Philosophy, Reformed Theological Seminary, Orlando

In 1981 Andrew Hoffecker published his *Piety and the Princeton Theologians*, creating renewed interest in Old Princeton Seminary and, surprisingly, focusing that interest more on Princeton's piety than on its theology. Now in his biography of the central figure of Princeton's great triumvirate—Alexander, Hodge, and Warfield—Hoffecker has done it again. In his *Charles Hodge: The Pride of Princeton*, he has given us a long-needed biography of Hodge that is properly sympathetic—and critical—with careful attention to the life and thought of this many-sided man. This book provides great reading for Princeton Seminary's bicentennial in 2012.

—**David Calhoun**, Professor Emeritus of Church History, Covenant Theological Seminary

Professor Hoffecker stresses the fundamental significance of Charles Hodge's lifelong adherence to his pietist-confessional upbringing—a determination reinforced by his formative time in Europe as a young man. Treating Hodge's life thematically, as the author does, draws out the many-sidedness of his career as Christian believer, educator, theologian, churchman, evangelical statesman, and controversialist. Those who may associate Hodge only with his *Systematic Theology* (great work though that is) are in for a surprise! Written clearly and accessibly, and thoughtfully and reflectively, and full of interesting detail, this biographical study adds momentum to the flow of recent serious writing on Princeton theology and its theologians.

—**Paul Helm**, Teaching Fellow, Theology and Philosophy, Regent College, Vancouver

There has been a happy little renaissance of attention to Charles Hodge of late (e.g., *Charles Hodge Revisited* and *Charles Hodge: Guardian of American Orthodoxy*)

as we mark the 200th anniversary of the founding of Princeton Seminary, and now Andy Hoffecker has made an essential entry in the current discussion with *Charles Hodge: The Pride of Princeton*. Hoffecker is uniquely qualified and widely respected as a scholar of Hodge and the Princetonians. His presentation of Hodge as combining in his life and ministry both the warmhearted piety of the New Side and the sturdy confessionalism of the Old School is not only historically accurate but deeply relevant to the needs of our own time. But Hoffecker also captures Hodge's fairness to the Old Side, the development of his own views, his instincts as a churchman, his participation in polemics, his engagement with the broader church, and dozens of other aspects necessary to a real appreciation and assessment of Hodge as a theologian and doctor of the church. This is now the first book to read for an introduction to Charles Hodge.

—**Ligon Duncan**, Senior Minister, First Presbyterian Church, Jackson, Mississippi

Andrew Hoffecker's biography of Charles Hodge is a beautifully written, compelling analysis of the theologian whose name is synonymous with Princeton theology. Incisive, appreciatively critical, and refreshingly judicious, Hoffecker's Hodge is neither a rigid rationalist nor an unbridled religious enthusiast but a "man of the center" who combined both the head and the heart—both Presbyterian confessionalism and evangelical pietism—in the ideal of the Princeton tradition. Hoffecker's study, which clarifies the role that Hodge played in the development of American Presbyterian identity and uncovers the relevance of his European sojourn both to his understanding of theological education and to his infamous claim that no new idea ever originated at Old Princeton Seminary, is a masterly examination of the life and ministry of the theological giant who, to the dismay of some and the delight of others, continues to exert a formative influence on the life of the evangelical mind.

—**Paul Kjoss Helseth**, Associate Professor of Christian Thought, Northwestern College, and author of *"Right Reason" and the Princeton Mind: An Unorthodox Proposal*

This is a first-rate work by a seasoned historian of American religion. Hoffecker's treatment of the towering figure of nineteenth-century American Presbyterianism is both sympathetic and constructively critical. Hoffecker helps us grasp why Hodge had such enduring influence beyond his life. One cannot understand the nineteenth century without taking Hodge seriously, nor can one understand the Reformed tradition in America without seeing Hodge as its foremost advocate. Hoffecker has reminded us throughout of both these realities. This is a masterly biography, lacking any traces of hagiography while warmly appreciating the larger theological project that motivated Hodge. Hoffecker's Hodge is a mediating figure in an age of increasing polarities.

—**Richard Lints**, Andrew Mutch Distinguished Professor of Theology, Gordon-Conwell Theological Seminary

Charles Hodges' magisterial *Systematic Theology* has rightfully earned its place on bookshelves for the last two centuries. Thanks to the skillful work of Professor Andrew Hoffecker, now you can get to know the man behind this work. In *Charles Hodge: The Pride of Princeton*, you'll find Hodge waxing anxious over his Greek as a college student, and you'll see him standing valiantly for truth in times of conflict. Ultimately, you'll see a theologian in the service of the church. Professor Hoffecker has already set the record straight on the Princetonian constellation; now he helps us fully appreciate the legacy of its North Star.

—**Stephen J. Nichols,** Research Professor of Christianity and Culture, Lancaster Bible College

While several prominent evangelists led by Charles Finney and a handful of princes of the pulpit, most notably Henry Ward Beecher and Phillips Brooks, had a tremendous influence on the nineteenth-century American religious scene, arguably the impact of Princeton Seminary professor Charles Hodge surpassed them all. In his masterly biography of Hodge, Andrew Hoffecker describes the theologian's many contributions: his educating of 2,500 Presbyterian ministers, editing one of the nation's religious journals for more than half a century, writing a three-volume systematic theology, engaging in debates over the direction of the Presbyterian church and Darwinism, and serving as the leading voice of Reformed theology. Hoffecker clearly shows how Hodge combined a powerful intellectual defense of Reformed orthodoxy with evangelical piety. He carefully situates Hodge in the changing religious and theological world of nineteenth-century America and Europe. Hoffecker makes Hodge come alive as a person, controversialist, apologist, and professor. Hodge led Princeton Seminary in training pastors to be rigorous scholars, careful exegetes, solid preachers and teachers, and spiritual guides.

—**Gary S. Smith,** Chairman, Department of History, Grove City College

In his carefully researched and beautifully written study, Andy Hoffecker has opened for specialists and nonspecialists alike the fascinating nineteenth-century world of Charles Hodge—one of the true intellectual giants of America. With seasoned judgment, Hoffecker examines Hodge's many contributions as educator, churchman, and scholar throughout his long and distinguished career on the faculty of Princeton Theological Seminary. *Charles Hodge: The Pride of Princeton* is a feast for the mind and a joy to read.

—**Garth M. Rosell,** Professor of Church History, Gordon-Conwell Theological Seminary

Charles

HODGE

American Reformed Biographies

D. G. Hart and Sean Michael Lucas
Series Editors

Robert Lewis Dabney: A Southern Presbyterian Life
John Williamson Nevin: High Church Calvinist
Cornelius Van Til: Reformed Apologist and Churchman
James Petigru Boyce: A Southern Baptist Statesman
Charles Hodge: The Pride of Princeton

Charles HODGE

The Pride of Princeton

W. Andrew Hoffecker

P U B L I S H I N G
P.O. BOX 817 • PHILLIPSBURG • NEW JERSEY 08865-0817

Page design by Lakeside Design Plus

Printed in the United States of America

Library of Congress Cataloging-in-Publication Data

Hoffecker, W. Andrew, 1941-
Charles Hodge : the pride of Princeton / W. Andrew Hoffecker.
p. cm. -- (American Reformed biographies)
Includes bibliographical references (p.) and index.
ISBN 978-0-87552-658-4 (pbk.)
1. Hodge, Charles, 1797-1878. 2. Presbyterian Church--United States--Clergy--Biography. 3. Princeton Theological Seminary--Faculty--Biography. 4. Theologians--United States--Biography. I. Title.
BX9225.H6H64 2011
285.092--dc23
[B]

2011037268

For Pam
Fellow writer
Mother of our three sons, Drew, Scott, and Timothy
Soulmate
Wife of 48 years

Contents

Foreword

MARK A. NOLL

Francis A. McAnaney Professor of History, University of Notre Dame; author: America's God: From Jonathan Edwards to Abraham Lincoln *(2002)*

A many-sided theologian demands a many-sided biography, which is exactly what Andrew Hoffecker has provided in this careful, balanced, discerning, and insightful book. Although the volume offers an unusually full treatment of the unusually full life of Charles Hodge, who is universally recognized as one of the leading American theologians of the nineteenth century, Hoffecker also has an argument to make. The argument is that in his long career as the mainstay of Princeton Theological Seminary, Hodge successfully combined a strong commitment to confessional Reformed theology and a winsome practice of humble evangelical piety. Well-read scholars will thus recognize a theme that the author developed in his fine study from 1981, *Piety and the Princeton Theologians: Archibald Alexander, Charles Hodge, and Benjamin Warfield*. The general point he made there is reaffirmed with much greater detail here for the greatest of the theologians from nineteenth-century Princeton.

Regarding Hoffecker's argument, which was developed so helpfully in the earlier book and now appears even more persuasively in this biography, it is only proper that I declare an "interest." Through study that now stretches back over four decades, I have been a much-interested reader of works by and about Charles Hodge. I am grateful that Andrew Hoffecker has seen fit to make use here of some of the things I have published on the Princeton theologian. Hoffecker's first book was critically important for me, since I fear I was once among those who tended to interpret Hodge as primarily a rational theologian in thrall to a mechanical, pseudo-scientific theological method. *Piety and the Princeton Theologians* showed that, given the enduring commitment of the main Princeton theologians to practical evangelical piety, such a view was impossible. Now Hoffecker's life of Hodge demonstrates much more conclusively that any fair reading of Hodge must recognize at least three things: a full and well-rounded life of steadfast Christian devotion, a more-than-capable advocacy of classical Calvinist doctrines such as universal original sin and the substitutionary atonement, and a set of intellectual instincts commonplace among Americans in the first two-thirds of the nineteenth century.

In my judgment, Hoffecker is absolutely convincing that Hodge cannot be fairly assessed without giving full attention to each of these three. The only remaining question that I would still like to discuss with Professor Hoffecker is how well Hodge's life ministry integrated these three commitments into a cohesive whole. On this one point, I am not as convinced as Hoffecker seems to be that Hodge's piety, theology, and method functioned smoothly together. But since I have been so well instructed by *Piety and the Princeton Theologians* and now by *Charles Hodge: The Pride of Princeton*, I am more than open to further instruction from all those, like Andrew Hoffecker, who have done the rigorous homework that qualifies their opinions as essential for ongoing discussion.

Readers should not be misled by the preceding paragraphs into thinking that this biography wanders off into exotic or recondite theological thickets. Rather, Hoffecker offers his assessment of Hodge's work unobtrusively in the course of a lively narrative about a long and eventful life. Especially effective are Hoffecker's use of manuscript material for Hodge's early life and his two-year European sojourn in the 1820s, and his assiduous perusal of the scores of articles that Hodge wrote for his seminary's influential quarterly, the *Princeton Review*. The result is a compelling account of contact with a host of notables in the broader theological world, including Nathaniel W. Taylor and Moses Stuart from New England; Hodge's long-time friend but also nemesis John W. Nevin; European mentors and friends, especially E. W. Hengstenberg and F. G. A. Tholuck; and, preeminently, Hodge's colleagues at Princeton Seminary and the College of New Jersey (later Princeton University), who were in a real sense his family.

While keeping his focus on Hodge, Hoffecker also manages to communicate a very great deal about the theological debates and institutional developments of an entire era. Because Hodge, especially in his editorial labors for the *Princeton Review*, was so deeply engaged with such a wide array of contemporary affairs, readers of the biography will learn a great deal about Calvinism versus Arminianism, revivalism, church boards, Roman Catholicism, the nature of baptism, the book of Romans, the nature of language, slavery, the American Civil War, nineteenth-century scientific developments, and much more. As befits a volume published by P&R Publishing, there is also much illuminating material on the main Presbyterian schism of the mid 1830s and the reunion of northern Presbyterian churches in the late 1860s. Above all, at the center of the book, as also of Hodge's career, is his dedication to theological education, which extended for more than half a century, during which time he personally instructed more candidates for the Christian ministry than any other teacher of his era.

One of Hodge's activities that I was particularly pleased to see fully treated in these pages was the regular meditations he offered for seminary students on Sunday afternoons. Ever since reading some of the outlines that Hodge prepared for these "conferences," a few of which were published after his death, I have thought that they represented the best examples of Hodge's biblical, theological, and devotional commitments functioning in harmony with each other. As readers discover for themselves how these "conference" meditations tied Hodge's far-ranging concerns together, and why Andrew Hoffecker justly gives them a prominent place, they, too, will come to a much greater appreciation of a theologian who has been more often caricatured (as heroic paragon or negative exemplar) than understood. Only the right kind of understanding lies in store for those who pick up this book and read it.

It remains to comment on a curiosity. In 1880 Charles Hodge's son, Archibald Alexander Hodge, published a substantial biography of his father, shortly after the latter's death. Subsequently, there have appeared a great number of articles, dissertations, anthologies, and essays on various aspects of Charles Hodge's theology. But no full-scale biographies appeared until this year, 2011. And now there are two of them. In early 2011, Oxford University Press brought out Paul Gutjahr's *Charles Hodge: Guardian of American Orthodoxy*. Like Hoffecker, Gutjahr, who is a professor of English at Indiana University, did the requisite digging in Hodge papers and comprehensive reading in the vast Hodge corpus. Also like Hoffecker, Gutjahr is sympathetic to the main concerns of Hodge's life. The main difference in the two books is that Hoffecker aims his story at those who already have heard about Hodge and who may already be interested to some degree in the Reformed and Presbyterian themes of his life, while Gutjahr is writing more for the general student of American history who may know nothing at all about Hodge. The result is two fine studies, complementary to each other, rather than competitive. In fact, as someone who has been privileged to read both volumes, I can wholeheartedly recommend them both as together providing, really for the very first time, the kind of full-scale attention that Charles Hodge has long deserved but, as a faithful Calvinist himself, never sought.

Series Preface

"All history is biography," Ralph Waldo Emerson once remarked. Emerson's aphorism still contains a good deal of truth. History is the memory and record of past human lives, thus making biography the most basic form of historical knowledge. To understand any event, period, or text from the past, some acquaintance with specific persons is crucial.

The popularity of biography among contemporary book buyers in America supports this insight. Recent biographies of John Adams and Ben Franklin have encouraged many—who fear for America's historical amnesia—to believe that a keen and formidable interest in history still exists among the nation's reading public. To be sure, the source of this interest could be the stature and influence of the subjects themselves—the founding fathers of the United States. Still, the accessibility of biography—its concrete subject matter, intimate scope, and obvious relevance—suggests that the reason for the recent success of these biographies is in the genre of writing itself.

American Reformed Biographies, coedited by D. G. Hart and Sean Michael Lucas, seeks to nurture this general interest in biography as a way of learning about and from the past. The titles in this series feature American Reformed leaders who were important representatives or interpreters of Reformed Christianity in the United States and who continue to be influential through writings and arguments still pertinent to the self-understanding of Presbyterian and Reformed theologians, pastors, and church members. The aim is to provide learned treatments of men and women that will be accessible to readers from a wide variety of backgrounds—biography that is both sufficiently scholarly to be of service to academics and those with proficiency in American church history and adequately accessible to engage the nonspecialist. Consequently, these books are more introductory than definitive, with the aim of giving an overview of a figure's thought and contribution, along with suggestions for further study.

The editors have sought authors who are sympathetic to Reformed Christianity and to their subjects, who regard biography not merely as a celebration of past accomplishments but also as a chance to ask difficult questions of both the past and the present in order to gain greater insight into Christian faith and practice. Thus, American Reformed Biographies is designed to make available the best kind of historical writing—one that yields both knowledge and wisdom.

Acknowledgments

My acquaintance with Charles Hodge and Old Princeton began in my sophomore year of college, when I was the lone student in an advanced Greek class that met three times a week—inappropriately, I might add, immediately after lunch. My professor and I labored through the Greek text of Paul's book of Romans. I found myself frequently drawn, among other sources, to Hodge's *Commentary on the Epistle to the Romans*. Between 1962 and today, many people have encouraged and assisted me, as a student and then professor, contributing to the successful completion of this study of the prominent Princetonian.

Key to the culmination of this project and paradoxically my greatest encourager and critic is my wife of forty-eight years, Pam. Although her writing career ended years ago, throughout this project she has guarded my time and fought the temptation to be like Job's impatient wife. When the light at the end of the tunnel came into view, she read the manuscript and offered words that impelled me to finish strongly.

Scholarship on Hodge would be impossible without the assistance and cooperation of the Speer Library at Princeton Theological Seminary and the Firestone Library at Princeton University. Steve Crocco and his staff at the seminary and Ben Primer and his staff of the Rare Books and Special Collections Department at the university made letters and papers available from numberless boxes and folders courteously and in a timely manner.

My family has been kind enough to approach me about the book project gingerly. In phone conversations and in face-to-face contexts, immediate and extended family would query about my progress. When writing went well, they were rewarded with: "Looks good; thanks for asking." In down times, they heard: "Don't ask and I won't tell." The family breathed a collective sigh of relief when I relayed to them on New Year's Day, "It's submitted!" No one had to ask what "it" was.

Faculty, staff, and students at Reformed Theological Seminary remained optimistic that *Charles Hodge* would see the light of day. I am especially grateful that the seminary offered help in the form of TAs. At various stages they wandered the stacks of the library, retrieved journal articles, combed through the seemingly endless issues of the *Biblical Repertory and Princeton Review*, and wrote succinct reports on their labors. Andy Jones, Brent Evans, Warren Bennett, and Jeff Spanogle aided the birth of this book by their research.

D. G. Hart, Sean Lucas, and John Muether were kind enough to read the manuscript at the worst time of the year—late December 2010—and made suggestions that strengthened the final product. John Muether did double duty by also preparing the index, as he has done for other books in the American Reformed Biographies series. By a happy coincidence, John also has an ancestral connection to Charles Hodge as a first cousin six-times removed. For all of these reasons, I offered to concede a couple of points the next time we meet on the tennis courts.

In the patience department, P&R Publishing personnel have gone above and beyond to hasten the manuscript to press. Marvin Padgett and Barb Lerch, in Phillipsburg, New Jersey, and John Hughes, in Whitefish, Montana, have been indispensable. Karen Magnuson performed the often thankless but nevertheless essential task of copyediting with consummate skill. She has reduced in number whatever may remain the shortcomings of this work.

Introduction

The year 2012 marks the bicentennial of the founding of Princeton Theological Seminary. Propitious events such as beginnings of major institutions like Princeton occasion thoughtful looks backward at their origins and prominent individuals associated with their early years. Ironically, in 1997 scholars celebrated another bicentennial—that of the birth of Princeton's most famous figure in the nineteenth century, Charles Hodge. The results of that three-day conference were published in the highly acclaimed *Charles Hodge Revisited: An Appraisal of His Life and Work*. Since until recently the only biography of Hodge was the one written by his son A. A. Hodge, *The Life of Charles Hodge* published in 1880, scholars have lamented the absence of critical studies of Hodge and his writings. This volume attempts in a small way to fill that vacancy. Although Hodge was not a founding professor of Princeton, he joined the school in its very infancy. Hodge's contributions to nineteenth-century Presbyterianism and his writings are of such magnitude in both quantity and importance that a volume of this size could not hope to be comprehensive in scope. Therefore, it focuses on his contributions as educator, churchman, and scholar.

These three dimensions were no small matter. Unlike the twentieth century, when theological scholarship and ecclesiastical activity became sharply bifurcated, in the early nineteenth century denominational participation and scholarship more frequently than not were closely allied. To borrow from Bruce Kuklick, it was an era of churchmen and philosophers. Hodge occupied a prominent position in those ranks. Since the seminary had originated so close to his involvement, and Hodge was one of its earliest graduates, he became an ardent supporter of both its Reformed perspective and its specific goals in educating ministers in the Presbyterian church. He labored as strenuously to maintain the seminary's model of theological education as he did to continue the Reformed tradition that it had been founded to propagate. For him, the two went hand in hand. From his earliest days until he died in 1878, Hodge manifested a piety and belief that reflected a unique combination of Presbyterian New Side piety and confessional belief.

Many contemporary scholars remember Hodge chiefly for his hefty *Systematic Theology* and therefore recollect his stout defense of Calvinism as framed in a scholastic mold. Such analyses so steadfastly fastened on what are considered by modern standards antiquated methods and conclusions that Hodge lay buried under a barrage of negativism. At the other end of the spectrum, conservatives so revere his Calvinist orthodoxy that it prevents any genuine criticism. Undoubtedly Hodge greatly respected every previous era's attempts to trumpet the achievements of Reformed theology. As *Charles Hodge Revisited* illustrates, a nuanced analysis of his life and work has emerged. Adding to the difficulty of assessing Hodge's ample body of work, however, recent thinkers who might otherwise be expected to be sympathetic to Hodge have—in the name of postconservativism—mounted strong criticism of his theological method. In the midst of this complexity, the present work attempts an appreciatively critical study that takes into account details of his entire life, his vast correspondence with family and associates, and the breadth of his contributions to American religious life in the first half of the nineteenth century.

Our study unfolds in six parts. Part 1 examines Hodge's roots. His familial and churchly affiliations, conversion, college and seminary education, early attempts at ministry, and initial years as seminary professor molded Charles Hodge as a person and formed the prominent features of his thinking that he apparently never seriously doubted.

While despite his objections to the contrary he changed his mind on theological and historical matters, his patterns of thought and habits of life remained remarkably constant.

In part 2, Hodge's extended study abroad is rehearsed in rather great detail. Previous reflections on his two-year hiatus have relatively downplayed this experience because it occurred so early in life that it seemed to bear no real significance when viewed against the broader context of his mature years. I argue, however, that his European experience did in fact "broaden" him as he formed relationships with Germany's evangelical and mediating theologians. But more importantly than expanding his intellectual horizons, it afforded him firsthand experience with a new model of theological education that stood in stark contrast to that of Princeton Seminary. Hodge would return to America not only with a confidence he had previously lacked but also with a renewed vigor for maintaining what had led to Princeton's founding. He brought back a vision for the strongest academic preparation possible characteristic of German scholarship without its professional and philosophical trappings.

Hodge's advocacy of Old School Presbyterianism forms the heart of part 3. His emergence both in denominational discussions and in the field of religious journalism constitutes the primary thrust of these chapters. Numerous issues disrupted the unity of the Presbyterian denomination in the early nineteenth century. Old Schoolers and New Schoolers differed—sometimes radically—on topics ranging from union with Congregationalists to biblical and theological interpretation, voluntary societies, abolitionism, and revivalism. Hodge used both his pen and his penchant for debate at General Assemblies to forge distinctive Princeton positions as a moderate Old Schooler distinct from the two larger factions within the denomination.

While bearing affinities with part 3, the fourth division of this study examines Hodge as Old School controversialist and churchman. Rather than his opposition to narrow issues that divided Old School from New School views, I focus on his interaction involving issues that distinguished his unique Reformed perspective from others with whom he usually agreed. I consider his views on religious experience, evangelicalism, education both parochial and public as well as his surprising support of Roman Catholic baptism, and conflicts with the Mercersburg school of theology and Southern Old Schoolers. Again, Hodge utilized both his journal and the General Assembly floor to express his views.

The shortest section of this work, part 5, "Interaction with Europe," harks back to Hodge's interest in intellectual currents emerging from the Continent. Deeply appreciative of his Protestant heritage emanating from the old country, Hodge continued his alertness to contemporary European biblical and theological scholarship. He vented frustration that rather than Europe's scholars' returning to previously held orthodox views, new movements emerged or old views continued unabated in an unorthodox direction. Hodge viewed Anglicanism's Oxford movement and German transcendentalism as potential threats—and, in the case of transcendentalism, an already realized menace to American religion. In this context, chapter 31 also explores Hodge's poignant response to a longtime friend dating back to Hodge's 1826–28 sojourn in Germany.

The final section, part 6, narrates Hodge's contributions in the last decades of his life. He weighed in with great gusto on the reunion of Northern Old School and New School factions and struggled to keep his emotions under control over the tragedy of the Civil War and its aftermath. He also displayed his heartfelt relation with evangelicals outside the Reformed tradition, as he had when writing his earlier popular theology, *The Way of Life*. Our final topics are Hodge's fascination yet growing concern with modern science and the celebration of his jubilee—fifty years of seminary teaching.

Hodge emerges from this study a vigorous voice for nineteenth-century Reformed thinking. He was a child of his times and thus powerfully influenced by the various contexts in which he was educated. Hodge and his colleagues manifested a coherence in thought and activity that distinguished Princeton as an Old School institution. Though Hodge did not originate that tradition, his contributions were without parallel in the various venues in which he participated.

Abbreviations

BAB	David H. Kelsey, *Between Athens and Berlin: The Theological Education Debate* (Grand Rapids: Eerdmans, 1993)
BH	*A Brief History of the Theological Seminary of the Presbyterian Church, at Princeton, New Jersey: Together with Its Constitution, Bye-Laws, &c.* (Princeton, NJ: John Bogart, 1838)
BS	*Bibliotheca Sacra*
CHP	Charles Hodge Papers, 1773–1930, collection no. C0261, Firestone Library, Department of Rare Books and Special Collections, Princeton University
CHPC	Charles Hodge, *The Constitutional History of the Presbyterian Church in the United States of America*, 2 vols. (Philadelphia: Presbyterian Board of Publication, 1851)
CHR	John W. Stewart and James H. Moorehead, eds., *Charles Hodge Revisited: A Critical Appraisal of His Life and Work* (Grand Rapids: Eerdmans, 2002)
Dissertation	*A Dissertation on the Importance of Biblical Literature, by Charles Hodge, A.M. Teacher of the Original Languages of Scripture, in the Theological Seminary of the Presbyterian Church at Princeton* (Trenton, NJ: George Sherman, 1822)

"Journal"	"Charles Hodge: Journal of European Travels," Special Collections, Princeton Theological Seminary
JPH	*Journal of Presbyterian History*
LCH	Archibald Alexander Hodge, *The Life of Charles Hodge* (New York: Charles Scribner's Sons, 1880)
LSAP	D. G. Hart, *The Lost Soul of American Protestantism* (Lanham, MD: Rowman & Littlefield, 2002)
MTC	John W. Stewart, *Mediating the Center: Charles Hodge on American Science, Language, Literature, and Politics* (Princeton, NJ: Princeton Theological Seminary, 1995)
PAI	Glenn T. Miller, *Piety and Intellect: The Aims and Purposes of Ante-Bellum Theological Education* (Atlanta: Scholars Press, 1990)
PR	*Princeton Review* (also encompasses former names of this publication: *Biblical Repertory*, *Biblical Repertory and Theological Review*, and *Biblical Repertory and Princeton Review*)
PS	David B. Calhoun, *Princeton Seminary*, 2 vols. (Carlisle, PA: Banner of Truth, 1994, 1996)
"Retrospect"	Charles Hodge, "Retrospect of the History of the Princeton Review," *PR*, Index vol. (1871)
RRPM	Paul Kjoss Helseth, *"Right Reason" and the Princeton Mind: An Unorthodox Proposal* (Phillipsburg, NJ: P&R Publishing, 2010)
RWLRA	Immanuel Kant, *Religion within the Limits of Reason Alone* (New York: Harper, 1960)
SABC	D. G. Hart and John R. Muether, *Seeking a Better Country: 300 Years of American Presbyterianism* (Phillipsburg, NJ: P&R Publishing, 2007)
ST	Charles Hodge, *Systematic Theology*, 3 vols. (New York: Charles Scribner's Sons, 1872–73)
UCRC	Paul K. Conkin, *The Uneasy Center: Reformed Christianity in Antebellum America* (Chapel Hill, NC: University of North Carolina Press, 1995)

WID	Charles Hodge, *What Is Darwinism? And Other Writings on Science and Religion*, ed. Mark A. Noll and David N. Livingstone (Grand Rapids: Baker, 1994)
WOL	Charles Hodge, *The Way of Life* (Philadelphia: American Sunday-School Union, 1841)
WTJ	*Westminster Theological Journal*

PART 1

Roots

The Presbyterian church in the nineteenth century exercised an influence on American life out of proportion to its numerical strength. While other denominations transplanted from Europe maintained their connection with a mother church in Europe, Presbyterians began and eventually prospered without support from their predecessors in the old country. Lack of a bond with Presbyterians in Scotland did not prevent them from leaving a significant imprint on American ecclesiastical life and the larger culture as well. In fact, at the conclusion of the century, historian Robert Ellis Thompson attributed the measure of success the denomination enjoyed to "services it has rendered to theological science, the interest it has maintained in Christian doctrine, the high standard of intelligence it has set up for both its ministry and its people, its capacity to develop strength of character, its superior family discipline, and its conservative influence upon the national life."[1] Thompson's description of the Presbyterian denomination could also be ascribed to Charles Hodge, arguably the church's most dominating figure in the first half of the century. Through the seminary where he taught, the journal he edited, and the service he rendered in the courts of the Presbyterian church, Hodge also left a legacy out of proportion to what might be expected given his background. Left fatherless as a child and raised through the thriftiness and ingenuity of his mother, Hodge overcame hurdles that could have easily prevented his achieving the stature he had by the time of his death in 1878. In a clearly discernible trajectory, his family heritage, devout religious habits, education at Princeton College and Seminary, and early ministry provided a platform from which he later exercised enormous influence in American life. Firmly planted in twin emphases of early Presbyterianism—New Side piety and confessionalist traditions—Hodge imbibed and embraced practices and beliefs that would propel him to, by every measure, a remarkable ministry spanning more than fifty years.

1

New Side Confessionalist

Charles Hodge was born, raised, and educated in the Presbyterian church, where he carried out an influential ministry for over half a century. He did so during the formative and arguably the most tumultuous period in American history. The nation was less than twenty-five years old when he was born on December 28, 1797. By the time of his death in 1878, his beloved country would have witnessed seismic shifts in its political, cultural, and social life. It would emerge from the larger Enlightenment era with its own distinctive intellectual traditions, solidify its national identity by the appearance of new political parties, experience rapid westward expansion and dramatic changes in demographic patterns, and eventually undergo the violent upheaval of a massive civil strife that almost severed the country in two.

No less a transformation would convulse his church. Formed in Philadelphia in 1706 by Francis Makemie and seven other pastors, American Presbyterianism was less than a hundred years old at Hodge's birth, yet had already suffered its first schism and reunion over revivalism and would experience intense debates over a wide range of biblical and theological issues and two more debilitating divisions and one subsequent reunion before Hodge died.

No passive bystander in the midst of these events in decades of sweeping change, Hodge emerged not only as one of the most significant religious and educational figures of his era, but also as a prodigious intellectual voice commenting on issues and ideas across a wide cultural horizon. From religion in general to detailed biblical, theological, and denominational disputes, from fine points of American political and electoral debates to the latest developments in science, from the intricacies of Civil War strategy to discussions on the monumental issue of slavery, Hodge's probing, thoughtful analysis gained many followers. Hardly an issue in American public life escaped his notice. His meticulously crafted views became a significant theological force, shaping opinions throughout American culture.

While known primarily for his conservatism, his staunch advocacy of Old School Calvinism, and his remark that a new idea never originated at his seminary, Hodge also launched into uncharted waters. He bridged the gap between the First Great Awakening's revivalism, the engine that drove much of American religion from its inception, and the zenith of Old School confessionalism that dominated the Presbyterian denomination in the first half of the 1800s. He helped initiate the trend of American theologians' venturing to Europe to shore up deficiencies in their scholarship and to ensure that their schools graduated pastors fully apprised of the latest biblical and theological studies. His founding of Princeton's *Biblical Repertory and Princeton Review* helped to inaugurate the heyday of nineteenth-century religious journalism. Training more pastors than all other seminaries in his era combined, Hodge extended Presbyterianism's influence by fleshing out one of the most compelling, coherent worldviews of all his denominational peers. His explication of the core ideas and values of what became known as "The Princeton Theology" established a legacy within his denomination that lasted into the twentieth century.

Hodge traced his ancestral lineage in an autobiographical section of A. A. Hodge's biography of his father. Charles focused on his family's religious heritage, their economic prosperity, and their manifold contributions to American public life. The Hodges came from solid

Presbyterian stock that extended back to the early 1700s in northern Ireland. Following their parents' deaths, William, Andrew, and Hugh Hodge immigrated to America in 1730. They settled in Philadelphia, which boasted several churches, among them the Presbyterian church, which constructed its first building in 1704. The Hodge brothers not only prospered as Philadelphia merchants but established strong attachments to the Presbyterian denomination. Their involvement with the church intensified during the upheaval of the revival led by George Whitefield in 1743. Hannah Hodge, whom everyone knew as "a mother in Israel," wife of the youngest son, Hugh, was a child of a Huguenot refugee who had left France at the revocation of the Edict of Nantes in 1685, and along with other refugees helped to found First Presbyterian Church on Market Street in Philadelphia.[1]

In enumerating the backgrounds and occupations of his forebears, Hodge rehearsed their successful careers. While many were merchants, he listed physicians and surgeons, lawyers, a congressman, several United States senators, and a Supreme Court clerk. He took special notice of those who had served in the military, which included his father, Hugh. A graduate of the College of New Jersey in 1773, Hugh trained in medicine and served as a surgeon with the Pennsylvania troops in the Revolutionary War. British forces captured him and held him prisoner in November 1776, but he obtained release after several months through the efforts of George Washington. Hodge paid tribute to his father's courage in ministering to victims of the yellow-fever epidemics of 1793 and 1795. In describing his family background, Hodge commented, "These family details are of interest to those whom they concern." But he continued immediately with words that could easily summarize an emphasis that dominated his life: "I wish, however, that those who come after me should know that their ancestors and kindred were Presbyterians and patriots." Regardless of particular vocation, Hodge's family served both their church and their country.[2]

Besides historical details, Hodge also revealed the earliest religious influences in his family, which reflect the interplay between evangelical pietism of the First Great Awakening and traditional confessionalism as represented by the Old Side–New Side division that roiled Presbyterians and the New Light–Old Light separation among Congregationalists in the eighteenth century.[3] The Hodge family became enmeshed in the dispute over revivalist piety and its role in religious experience. As a result of "religious excitement" that attended George Whitefield's preaching, Hodge noted that two parties formed the Presbyterian church: those who favored the revival (the New Side) and their opponents (the Old Side). Both groups affirmed the doctrines of the Westminster Confession, but they differed so sharply over the role of religious experience or piety that the denomination split in 1741. The New Siders stressed evangelical conversion resulting in a life of pious living as essential to identifying oneself as a Christian and thus among God's elect. In contrast, the Old Siders disparaged revivals and the enthusiasm that often accompanied them as a spurious form of religion. They claimed that since God's election of believers resides in his mysterious decree, the only sure sign of his choosing lies not in a testimony of a radical conversion experience but rather in a person's adherence to the doctrinal teaching of the Bible and the Westminster Confession. Hannah, Charles's grandmother, joined First Church in the mid-1730s, but it was predominantly confessionalist in its sympathies. Since she attributed her conversion to the ministry of Whitefield, she left First Church with other New Side converts. A throng of 160 communicants formed Second Presbyterian Church in 1743 as a New Side congregation pastored by Gilbert Tennent, who gained notoriety for his fierce denunciation of Old Side Presbyterians as unregenerate Pharisees in his famous sermon "Dangers of an Unconverted Ministry."[4]

In 1745 Hannah married Hugh Hodge, also a founder of Second Church, who served as deacon until his death. The Hodge family established a pattern of denominational loyalty that survived for generations. Their home became the center of New Side activity, gaining fame as "the resort of clergymen and the centre of religious meetings." Hodge expanded on Hannah's religious influence and independent spirit by noting that her house after her husband's death was "the home of several old and infirm ladies, supported in great measure by her bounty; and here also originated the weekly meeting for prayer and religious instruction observed still in the Second Church, and in most of the other Presbyterian Churches of the city." Still more telling, Hodge relates the successful outcome of the meetings and the barely disguised disdain of denominations that did not share their revivalist sympathies: "The crowd [of people gathering in their home was] often so great as to fill, not only the parlor and kitchen but even the back garden, close up against Christ Church ground, and much to the offence of our Episcopal brethren, who called them 'Those conventicles held by Mrs. Hodge.'" The term *conventicles* was the name given by seventeenth-century Anglicans to small nonconformist or dissenting groups meeting illegally or in secret for religious worship. They met for fellowship and Bible study. The Hodge family had a history of pietist activity within the church. They remained active in Second Church through successive generations down to Charles's elder brother Dr. Hugh Lenox Hodge, who served as ruling elder. Thus Hodge grew up an heir of evangelical piety, familiar with its religious enthusiasm and activism.[5]

Hodge, however, also recounted other practices reflecting that in addition to pietism, his family retained important elements of Old Side confessionalism, an alternative and somewhat antagonistic expression of religious experience from that of New Side evangelicalism.[6] Confessionalist Presbyterians, like their counterparts in Lutheran and Episcopalian denominations, explained religious experience primarily in terms of doctrinal faithfulness to church confessions and participation in the sacraments and corporate worship over against revivalist-inspired piety that characterized the Great Awakening. They stressed catechetical instruction and participation in congregational life under careful oversight of the clergy, which stood in contrast to the privatism and individualism of revivalism. Charles Hodge's theological perspective and deepest religious convictions as well as his teaching, publishing, and participation in denominational affairs mirrored his family's background in the internecine quarrels of these two rival traditions that competed in forming the identity of American Presbyterianism from the mid- to late eighteenth century.

Occasionally the tension between these two traditions has been summarized as the struggle between ardor (the evangelical zeal of New Siders) and order (the ecclesiastical and liturgical emphases of Old Siders). The former stressed personal holiness and devotional fervor manifested in keeping diaries of religious experiences and other expressions of personal devotion as indispensable qualities for effective ministry. Old Siders, however, demanded theological precision and strict subscription to the Westminster Standards as more important. Thus, in the early decades of American Presbyterianism, the denomination experienced a heightened tension over its very identity. This conflict constitutes the background for interpreting the life of Charles Hodge.

Both elements play prominent roles in shaping his early life. Isolating these two strands in Hodge's experience and subjecting them to probing analysis as autonomous entities is possible—but only in the abstract. The thesis of this study is that Charles Hodge manifested the attributes associated with Calvinistic confessionalism (strong adherence to creedal religion, liturgical forms, and corporate worship) as well as the characteristics of evangelical pietism (the necessity of vital religion marked by conversion, moral activism, and individual pious practices). That he should be raised in Philadelphia, the cradle of American Presbyterianism, an originally staunch Old Side territory that had given way to New Side influences during the First Great Awakening, only strengthens the notion that these two strands could be combined in a figure that loomed so large in the Presbyterian church. But as the nineteenth century unfolded and new factions developed within the denomination, Hodge became one of the prominent leaders of Old School Presbyterianism. Hodge never relinquished his eighteenth-century New Side heritage, though he criticized its revivalist excesses. It not only shaped his early years but remained an integral part of his belief and practice throughout his life. But he also became firmly convinced that as Presbyterianism developed in the nineteenth century, Old School traditions held stronger claims than the New School to the origin of American Presbyterianism and what constituted its identity in both belief and practice. This study narrates Hodge's role in substantiating those claims.

2

Early Religious Experience

The unique combination of confessionalism and pietism characterized Charles Hodge's spiritual life from the cradle to the grave. Scholars have emptied many pens trying to reconcile this seeming contradiction. The problem of interpreting Hodge on this point stems not from lack of comment by Hodge, his family, and other contemporaries, friends as well as opponents. Because of the centrality to Hodge's life of the two perspectives, we have almost unlimited materials from which to draw, from his earliest years to his death. His reflections on his early childhood, his journal narrating his itinerant ministry in 1819–20, and his correspondence with family and friends vividly depict how confessionalism and pietism combined to shape his religious life up to his graduating from Princeton Seminary and ordination into the Presbyterian ministry. While at times the two strands seem to vie for dominance in his experience, Hodge never thought them in essential conflict with each other. Rather, we see him expressing ideas and attitudes that seem to alternate in his experiences without significant ill effect.[1]

Hodge's descriptions of his early home life reflect warmhearted piety and an equally prominent zeal for the trappings of confessional Presbyterianism. Both of these traits grew out of a closely knit family supported by the ministry of the local church. Several personal tragedies shaped the Hodge family, and its members drew strength from their Presbyterian convictions. In 1793 and 1795 Hodge's parents witnessed the deaths of their first three children, two daughters and a son, from yellow-fever epidemics. Charles was the younger of two surviving sons. When Dr. Hugh Hodge died, Charles was but six months old and his brother a year and a half older. Mary Blanchard Hodge shouldered the responsibility of raising the boys with courage and ingenuity. What little financial resources she received from her husband's estate vanished with the onset of the War of 1812, just at the time the boys went to college.[2] Before that loss, she manifested industry and strength of character by distributing soup and groceries either as donations to those less fortunate than herself or by selling goods at wholesale prices. She also helped to found the "Female Association for the Relief of Widows and Single Women of Reduced Circumstances," an organization that survived in the network of the Philadelphia voluntary societies well past the 1850s. In order to supplement her income further, when the family moved to Princeton, Mrs. Hodge took in boarders, young relatives of the family or close associates who were preparing for admission to the college. These measures, combined with a strict economic regimen, enabled her to put both sons through college and professional school—Hugh studying medicine at the University of Pennsylvania and Charles pursuing the ministry at Princeton Seminary. Echoing a sentiment of many a nineteenth-century Protestant, Hodge summarized his debt to his mother as "beyond all estimate." He wrote, "To our mother, my brother and myself, under God owe absolutely everything. To us she devoted her life. For us she prayed, labored and suffered."[3]

Despite significant physical demands and the financial burden of being sole parent of two sons, Mary Hodge did not ignore their moral and spiritual welfare. She laid the foundation for their religious life by using traditional Presbyterian means. Charles stated matter-of-factly that "our early training was religious." He added immediately, "Our mother was a Christian," and he spelled out the ramifications of that fact by detailing how she educated her sons: she "carefully drilled us in the Westminster Catechism." Attendance at weekly worship was nonnegotiable.[4]

Mrs. Hodge did not labor alone in the task of nurturing her children in the Presbyterian faith. The family benefited from the support of the local church, the same Second Presbyterian Church that Hannah Hodge had joined over a century earlier. Their pastor, Dr. Ashbel Green, would figure prominently in Old School Presbyterianism in the early nineteenth century. Not only did he catechize Hodge and his brother, but as president of Princeton he also taught Charles the Bible when he matriculated at Princeton and preached frequently in the seminary chapel.

Green was one of Philadelphia's most popular preachers for twenty-five years. In carrying out his pastoral responsibilities, he closely adhered to Presbyterian "old measures" by instructing his congregation in matters of spiritual maturity. "Old measures" were the traditional means of grace by which believers under the leadership of their pastors deepened their Christian faith or advanced in their sanctification—practices such as diligence in private devotion as well as public worship, prayer, studying Scripture, participation in the sacraments, and living a disciplined moral life. These and other practices were followed by denominations committed to the First Great Awakening in the eighteenth century to maintain the vitality of the spiritual life.[5] Green's catechizing of his young charges in Philadelphia formed just a small part of his ministerial duties in Presbyterian confessional polity. His pastoral efforts reinforced in the congregation what the parents practiced at home in teaching the Shorter Catechism. Green added to the boys' memorization of the Shorter Catechism by systematically expounding its meaning from the pulpit. Upon successfully learning and repeating answers to the 107 questions, Charles and Hugh then attended a weekly Bible class taught by the pastor in his study.[6]

Green's practice of certifying children's learning the Shorter Catechism resulted in publishing the lessons he used to instruct the children in the meaning of the catechism. The Presbyterian Board of Education published them in 1841 as *Lectures on the Shorter Catechism of the Presbyterian Church in the United States of America Addressed to*

Youth. Archibald Alexander, who became surrogate father to Hodge, reviewed Green's *Lectures* in one of the earliest editions of the *Princeton Review*[7] and displayed the Princeton attitude toward catechizing that so profoundly influenced Hodge's confessionalist perspective. Alexander praised catechizing as a means of instructing children in the "solid" doctrines of the faith. He lamented that young readers often neglected the Bible and catechisms. Catechisms were in danger of "being cast aside like old-fashioned furniture"—in favor of "the religious novel and the religious newspaper." While he did not oppose reading novel literature per se, Alexander noted that only the "ripe fruits of profound spiritual knowledge, and of deep practical experience," would be able to offset "shallow, showy, bustling active piety." Genuine piety therefore rested on the solid base of "creeds and catechisms."[8]

Alexander then emphasized two prominent points in Princeton's confessionalism associated with catechizing. First, he stressed that Presbyterians, and specifically Scotch Presbyterians, "have been distinguished above all people in the world, for a correct and thorough knowledge of the tenets of their own church. No people on earth are so well indoctrinated in the principles of religion, and in the proof of the doctrines believed, as the Scotch and their descendants in Ireland and America." While Lutherans and other confessionalist denominations might take umbrage at Alexander's exclusive claim, its very boldness illustrates a refrain that would underlie Princeton's Old School positions and Hodge's role in those debates. Princeton consistently championed the doctrinal tradition of Reformed theology. Christian truth was not peripheral to Christianity but something to be studied, preached, elucidated, and applied to life.[9]

Second, Alexander extolled the incalculable benefits of such catechizing. By such instruction the young mind was fortified, and while it might not always resist temptation, the truths "which had been early inculcated, and long forgotten, will revive in the memory, and serve to guard the anxious mind from those enthusiastic errors into which ignorant persons are so prone to fall." Alexander closed his review by encouraging pastors to work with elders in carrying out the duties of their spiritual office.[10]

This structured Presbyterian upbringing produced lasting results. It left a permanent impression on the young Hodge in the form of a reverent respect for the truths of his Reformed faith that anchored his vital religious experience. In the autobiographical sketch included in *LCH*, Charles followed his comments about his mother's training and Green's teaching with a description of his early religious experiences. While his account is somewhat self-deprecating, it clearly evidences a positive outcome of his early instruction:

> There has never been anything remarkable in my religious experience, unless it be that it began very early. I think that in my childhood I came nearer to conforming to the apostle's injunction: "Pray without ceasing," than in any other period of my life. As far back as I can remember, I had the habit of thanking God for everything I received, and asking him for everything I wanted. If I lost a book, or any of my playthings, I prayed that I might find it. I prayed walking along the streets, in school and out of school, whether playing or studying. I did not do this in obedience to any prescribed rule. It seemed natural. I thought of God as an everywhere-present Being, full of kindness and love, who would not be offended if children talked to him.[11]

Hodge compared his prayerful ejaculations with the birds' worship of God by their singing. He called his habits a "mild form of natural religion." While these remarks portray a somewhat sentimental, romantic, idealizing exercise, Hodge clearly embraced his spiritual life as an integrated whole. The routine of worship and being "drilled" in catechism existed concurrently beside an affective belief and way of living. They established a pattern of devotion that Hodge not only never rebelled against but also conscientiously affirmed as the modus operandi for his entire life. In what must approach a unique claim for any era, he attributed to his early religious habits his having sworn but once in his life, and that at the tender age of "thirteen or fourteen years old": "I cannot recollect that I ever uttered a profane word, except once . . . I was walking with my brother, and struck my foot against a stone, and said: 'D__n it.' My brother was shocked and exclaimed, 'Why Charles!!' I cannot tell why I said it. I was not hurt, neither was I angry. It seemed to me to be an effect without a cause. I felt like a very,

very small Paul, when he said: 'It was not I who did it, but something dwelling within me.' "[12]

Hodge's family associations and pastoral instruction indelibly shaped his entire life. He admitted that his sensitivity to spiritual matters had begun early as a part of his own predisposition. These reflections on his childhood indicate that Hodge had internalized an appreciation of what constituted New Side piety as a way of life—the value of prayer as conversing with God, articulating a sense of dependence on God as a matter of daily experience and a moral consciousness sensitive to the presence of sin. Religion was a matter of life itself in all its aspects. Alongside and supporting that piety existed an equally firm reliance on confessional practices that provided an objective foundation that held his experience within clearly orthodox bounds of thought and behavior.

3

From Philadelphia to the College of New Jersey

Education formed the core of Charles Hodge's life. It began in humble circumstances, continued in Princeton at the college and the seminary, and broadened in postgraduate studies in Europe. Hodge then spent the remainder of his life teaching at Princeton Seminary. He proved himself an able student, intellectually curious and willing to expend energies to further his knowledge in all disciplines, not just his areas of special interest. Desiring to show himself competent, yet occasionally conscious of his deficiencies, Hodge began his education in Philadelphia in a private home and continued his studies at a classical academy at Somerville, New Jersey, and in Princeton Academy. Mrs. Hodge moved the family to New Jersey so that Hugh could enroll at the college. Studying Latin at Somerville and adding to his progress in Greek at the academy qualified Charles to enroll at Princeton as a sophomore in September 1812, a few months shy of his fifteenth birthday.[1]

Matriculating with advanced standing at such a young age reveals the state of academic standards prevalent in American colleges at the time. Entrance requirements developed slowly and conservatively at Princeton. The 1746 charter of the College of New Jersey mentions its first president Jonathan Dickinson's requirement that one be "hopefully pious." Dickinson, a New Side pastor, played a prominent role in framing the Adopting Act of 1729, which established the theological criteria for admission into the Presbyterian ministry. Dickinson's comment reflected the primary purpose of the institution to provide an educated ministry for the Colonies in keeping with its New Side roots in William Tennent's Log College in Neshaminy, Pennsylvania. Early records of the College of New Jersey, the forerunner of Princeton, speak vaguely of candidates' being "suitably qualified." Only in the nineteenth century did more specific criteria emerge: reading Virgil in Latin, translating English into grammatical Latin, and rendering any portion of the four Gospels into Latin or English. To be admitted, Hodge had to demonstrate his proficiency in each of these areas via oral examination conducted by the president and his colleagues. With these requirements for admission, youths such as Hodge who had received advanced instruction in the classics applied at the tender ages of thirteen or fourteen and were admitted with sophomore standing if they demonstrated sufficient proficiency in Latin and Greek.[2]

The curriculum under which Hodge studied reflected the quality of the entrance requirements. The course of studies developed just as slowly and conservatively. Little information survives about the curriculum under presidents Jonathan Dickinson and Aaron Burr, but Princeton basically followed Yale's lead by demanding a thorough comprehension of the classics. John Witherspoon's arrival from Scotland in 1768 to assume the presidency of Princeton brought changes influenced by his advocacy of Scottish Common Sense Realism as the philosophical foundation for the curriculum. The introduction of chemistry and natural science occurred during Samuel Stanhope Smith's administration (1795–1812). Hodge entered Princeton under the "Laws" of 1802, which listed the following curriculum:

Freshman	Sophomore	Junior	Senior
Greek Testament	Xenophon	Algebra	Natural Philosophy
Sallust [Roman historian]	Homer, Cicero	Geometry	Moral Philosophy
Lucian	Horace	Trigonometry	Chemistry
Cicero	Roman Antiquities	Practical Geometry	History
Mair's "Intro to Making Latin"	Geography	Conic Sections	Criticism
	English Grammar and Composition	Natural Philosophy	Chronology
	Arithmetic	English Grammar and Composition	Logic
	Algebra		Classics
			(Review)*

*Collins, *Princeton*, 296. Wertenbaker severely criticized the college's academic offerings under Ashbel Green (Hodge's former pastor) and James Carnahan, the college's eighth and ninth presidents, as "Princeton's Nadir." Wertenbaker opined, "As for the curriculum, it remained a hodgepodge of poorly related subjects—Greek, Latin, astronomy, belles-lettres, navigation, logic, geography, mathematics, physics, philosophy, chemistry, religious history—which every student had to take regardless of his tastes, desires, and future career." He contrasted Princeton with advances in curriculum design under Thomas Jefferson at the University of Virginia that did not narrowly limit study to one prescribed list of courses but allowed students to choose according to their vocational interests. Wertenbaker, *Princeton*, 88. Wertenbaker's negative connection between the religious emphasis and its "nadir" that made the college the "step-child of the church" is softened by Mark Noll's statement that Princeton attempted to balance its commitment to "science, reason, and philosophy" with "piety, faith and revelation." Mark A. Noll, *Princeton and the Republic, 1768–1822: The Search for a Christian Enlightenment in the Era of Samuel Stanhope Smith* (Princeton, NJ: Princeton University Press, 1989), 256.

Hodge paid tribute to several professors for their impact on him. Hodge listed the courses taken under Dr. Green—belles-lettres, moral philosophy, and logic, as well as lessons from the Bible. He lamented that he had had but one course in logic, but he also reported an old saying, "The best way to make a logician is to set him to study Euclid, or . . . as any old student of Princeton Seminary would say, set him to study Turrettin [*sic*]"—a saying that Hodge would gladly embody in his teaching![3] He paid tribute to excellent instruction in Greek under Philip Lindsley, tutor and later vice president of the college. The most significant gap in Hodge's college education, considering his eventual vocation in graduate education, was modern languages. While amply prepared in Greek and Latin, he had no courses in French and German, a significant factor in his decision to study abroad in 1826. Hodge commented very little about his college curriculum but bemoaned that he had had but six months of Greek under his belt before his enrollment at the college, while some of his classmates had actually been teaching Greek before they enrolled.[4]

Hodge's comment about his inferiority in Greek reflected both the expectation he felt from his family and the demands he placed on himself to succeed academically. His older brother Hugh graduated as one of four in 1814 who earned first honors. Perhaps more significant than his brother's success, Charles labored under the watchful eye of his mother, who had contributed so much to her two sons and in turn exerted pressure on him to excel in life. In a letter to Hugh of January 23, 1815, Mary reported that Charles "did himself justice" in a speech on conscience. While these words might indicate one of many remarks by a proud yet biased mother's high opinion of her offspring, A. A. Hodge notes in a revealing footnote that these words of praise stood alone in all her correspondence regarding Charles: "She had a high conception of Charles' talents, but a very dissatisfied estimate of his diligence, ambition, or power of concentrated and sustained effort. Her tendency was to self-repression, and to the expectation of disappointment." A. A. Hodge concludes the footnote tellingly: "[Charles's] natural disposition was easy, and to the gratification of his tastes. Sense of duty and love for the cause of Christ were the springs of his subsequent life-long labors. But up to the day of her death, when he had been professor for ten years, the mother lamented that Charles would 'never do himself justice.'" Doubtless Hodge felt the weight of such judgment and, typical of his age's respect for elders, bore this disparagement silently.[5]

While the academic milieu may have suffered during Hodge's undergraduate days, Princeton experienced a resurgence of spiritual life under Ashbel Green's leadership. Green began his term as president of Princeton with the express aim of returning decorum to a campus that had experienced student riots during the presidency of Stanhope Smith. Likewise, Green committed himself to reinvigorate the college with a firm dose of religious devotion. His inaugural address, "The Union of Science and Piety," reflected his conviction that education must be suffused with Christian orthodoxy. Green's most notable innovation in this regard was his initiation of weekly Bible studies on Sunday afternoons, attended by students and faculty alike, a routine that would later be duplicated at Princeton Seminary. As might be expected from his upbringing, Hodge adapted readily to the new regimen. He not only attended Green's Bible studies but also reported favorably on those who spoke in chapel, including Green and eventual faculty colleagues Samuel Miller and Archibald Alexander. And Hodge referred to the junior recitation room as "the birth-place of many souls."[6]

The college experienced an outbreak of revival in the winter of 1814–15, Charles's senior year. Hodge succumbed to the swelling influence of the revival and wrote to his brother in deeply emotional terms: "I cannot but think that all who see the present state of the College must also feel that this is indeed the harvest, the accepted time, the day of salvation. O! my brother! Though it is only your little Toby who is writing to you, yet he loves you . . . and shudders at the thought of your wanting the one thing needful." Hodge discounted exaggerated reports that may have circulated about the revival, but conceded that about thirty "are really changed" and that "almost all the college attends the prayer meeting which is held every evening at 8 o'clock." Lectures by Green and Alexander were also well attended. His peers reported Hodge's conversion and subsequent influence leading to other students' conversions. After publicly professing faith in Christ, he joined the Presbyterian church on January 13, 1815. While only 12 of the 105 students before the revival had professed religion, half the remaining 93 made public professions along with Hodge.[7]

How one interprets Hodge's conversion is crucial to understanding his view of religious experience. The sequence of events in Hodge's conversion fits into what became his view of the role of revivals and conversion and illustrates yet again a unique blend of evangelical pietism and Presbyterian confessionalism. His experience was profoundly real. But his conversion's most remarkable characteristic was how it fit into the flow of his life, its continuity with what preceded and what followed it, rather than any dramatic discontinuity between his life before and after the experience. That is, Hodge viewed his conversion not as a spontaneous, stand-alone beginning of his Christian faith but as the culmination of nurture that had begun with his tutelage as a child. His faith was reinforced through instruction, encouragement, and support of his family and church environment. It was more of a capstone event, culminating all that had preceded and a platform for all that would follow, rather than an initiation into a life radically different from his upbringing.

Richard Robert Osmer describes this view of conversion the "Nurture/Development model" because conversion comes at the end of a long development consisting of nurturing elements that we have noted in Hodge's family and church experience. Hodge's youth was suffused with religious experience. His Christian faith did not begin with his conversion at Princeton but was in covenantal gestation that began with his baptism and continued with catechesis, regular church attendance, and instruction from both hearth and pulpit. Such a view is summarized in the Romeyn Report. Presented at the Presbyterian church's General Assembly in 1812, this report considered children part of the covenant community of believers, subject to its instruction and discipline. The role of parents assumed a prominent position in the report: "[Parents] must, moreover, teach them their Catechism. Their relation to the Church, as baptized children ought to be sedulously impressed upon their minds, as also their consequent obligation to walk in newness of life, and their subjection to the spiritual authority which Christ hath established in this Church. From the first dawnings of reason, they ought to be taught to consider themselves as the Lord's children, solemnly dedicated to him, and bound to glorify him in soul and body." One would be hard pressed to find a better description of Hodge's childhood and youth. According to this model, a public profession of faith and participation in the Lord's Supper marked an individual's coming "to years of maturity," or what was also called the age of discretion, when a person could "discern the Lord's body," make a credible profession of faith, and then participate in the Lord's Supper.[8]

Interpreting Hodge's conversion in these terms follows from several considerations. First, Hodge does not directly mention his conversion in the autobiographical portion of *LCH*. While its absence does not mean that he repudiated it or denied its importance, this omission requires an explanation. Instead of discussing his own experience of conversion, he describes the revival's effects on his associates.[9] Hodge noted a change of tone from spiritual indifference and rote performance of religion to "personal religion—the salvation of the soul became the absorbing subject of attention." He likened the effects of hymns on Princetonians to the spiritual influence of Martin Luther's hymns on Germany. He also enumerated those who furthered the revival and those affected by it. Mentioning others but not discussing his own conversion may owe to several considerations, most probably his lifelong reluctance to draw attention to his inmost feelings. At a minimum, it seems reasonable to assume that while Hodge considered evangelical conversion a valid religious experience—thus he readily and happily recounted its occurrence among his fellow students—he was reluctant to narrate his own experience because it was a private matter. The latter factor, if true, would indicate his affinity toward the confessionalist practice of rarely speaking openly about one's private experience.[10]

Second, the content of Mary Hodge's letter to her son Hugh about the revival at Princeton indicated how the Hodge family viewed conversion as a part of one's larger religious experience. Her letter not only affirms a general approval of events on the campus, but also even provides details of several conversions. Students known for gambling and frequenting a tavern were dismissed from the college but subsequently came under the effect of the revival. One of the penitents confessed to Mrs. Hodge, "Religion has complete possession of my mind. After a night of agony, under the deepest convictions of my guilt, the morning brought some ray of comfort . . . To your dear Charles I am indebted for these impressions." But Mary wrote primarily to allay any fears that Hugh might have about the authenticity of Charles's conversion, since "this revival, as it is called will no doubt reach the city with much exaggeration." She continued, "I write, therefore, to give you a plain statement of facts . . . I should be extremely sorry that any one should suppose the step Charles has taken was in consequence of a sudden impulse of feeling." She then framed Charles's conversion not as part of an immediate swirl of enthusiasm at Princeton but in the context of his entire life: "An attention to religious duties, you know, has ever been a leading feature in the character of Charles, which has gradually strengthened with his years. The services of the Sunday previous to the fast determined him to make a public profession of them on the approaching sacrament." Then she added: "You may suppose it has been a period of considerable agitation with me. The important step Charles has taken occasions much solicitude. He was so young, I could have wished it had been deferred at least to the end of his College course. But you know his importunity, and when duty and feeling urged him forward, I could not throw a straw in the way."[11]

Mary Hodge may have severely underestimated her son's abilities and accomplishments, but she knew her Presbyterian heritage and how Charles's conversion should fit into a larger expected norm. The revival at Princeton differed from the majority of revivals associated with the Second Great Awakening, which began in the last years of the eighteenth century and early decades of the nineteenth century. Emotional upheavals emerged as the primary characteristic of camp meetings on Kentucky's frontier, and Arminian theology fueled revivals in western and upstate New York. Princeton's revival, however, and Charles's participation in it resembled what Arthur Thomas called the "reasonable revivalism" among educated Virginians. Although not totally lacking religious feeling, Presbyterians conducted services in Virginia with decorum and reason. Pastors prepared for genteel hearers carefully crafted sermons that, while aimed at producing conversions, explicitly discouraged emotional outbreaks and continued to uphold Reformed doctrine.[12]

Mary Hodge supported the Princeton revival and her son's conversion experience as genuine because she interpreted them as modeling the reasonable Virginia pattern. She viewed them through her New Side heritage, which emphasized a vital subjective element in religious experience, but also as supported by the objective doctrinal content of Presbyterian confessionalism. Charles's conversion formed part of his progression toward an adult profession of faith, a progression that she had fostered since his childhood. His conversion and public profession were the requisite prelude to his participation in the Lord's Supper. Therefore, her evaluation of Charles's experience remained consistent with both the former New Side and the Nurture/Development views of conversion.

4

Following the Plan

In September 1815, Charles Hodge graduated from the college. While he did not achieve first honors as his brother had, he gave the valedictory address and shared second honors with another student. A year later, after taking a year's absence from academics to further his general reading and recover his health, which had suffered from the rigors of his college studies, Hodge enrolled at Princeton Seminary along with twenty-five other students. Although several factors shaped his life appreciably during the next three years, the most dominant influence arose from his association with Archibald Alexander, who left his imprint both on the impressionable Hodge and on the newly established seminary by virtue of being its first professor. To Hodge he served as teacher and surrogate father.[1]

Alexander set the intellectual tone of the school, founded in 1812, in several ways. He collected scholarly works across several academic fields. Although he drew upon many sixteenth- and seventeenth-century Reformed masters from Geneva, Holland, Germany, and France, he favored Francis Turretin, whose massive *Institutes of Elenctic Theology* served as the primary theological text. Alexander also selected philosophical treatises of Enlightenment writers as well as the best apologetic works by Catholics, Lutherans, Dutch Remonstrants, and Socinians. The lack of courses in Hebrew was a deficiency in Princeton's early years; the contributions by such men as Germany's H. F. W. Gesenius and America's Moses Stuart were not yet available. Hodge's preparation for future work suffered from this deficiency.[2]

Hodge rose to the demands of graduate study by adopting a rigorous schedule. Perhaps in response to his mother's low estimation of his work ethic, Hodge opened a letter of January 11, 1817 with the defensive comment "I am not quite so lazy here as I am when at home." He mentioned that he had awakened with the prayer bell and been up an hour before beginning his letter at 8 a.m. This reflected his daily routine, which included waking before sunrise and rarely retiring before midnight. Meetings of various organizations and societies that were primarily theological in character occupied his evenings until 9 p.m. As an indication of his intellectual curiosity, Hodge took Alexander's recommendation of thirty works on a single topic as virtually mandatory reading. He would read all of them before moving to the next topic in his assignments. He eventually came to conclusions that graduate students must make for surviving. First, one cannot master everything. Comparing himself with Hugh, he writes, "I begin to feel as Hugh used to do, at seeing so much more before me than I can accomplish. But it is not in my nature to worry myself much about what I cannot help, and it is surely best to do as much as you can and let the rest go." Second, he came to the realization that a fundamental feature of graduate education is learning where one can find information. Knowing the sources and having the tools of research prepares one for a lifetime of learning. Finally, he became more convinced that he had indeed found his genuine vocation. Hodge comments, "To be constantly occupied is to be happy, provided you are convinced that the occupation is important in itself, and proper for you. Accordingly I never was in better spirits than I have been in all this session." Herein Hodge displays not only his incentive to realize his fullest potential intellectually, but also the positive disposition that characterized his demeanor through the vicissitudes of his life. While Hodge was not exempt from anxiety and periods of depression, optimism permeated his analyses of himself and others, enabling him to weather illnesses and tragedies in his personal life as well as those of the larger American culture.[3]

Despite comments implying lack of time for anything but study, Hodge became a master of forging relationships that would sustain him not only during his three years of academic preparation but for the remainder of his life. The coterie of friends at Princeton became the first of many circles of friends he cultivated first as a student at the seminary, then during his further education in Europe, and eventually within his denomination and the broader spectrum of nineteenth-century evangelicalism. Anything but a recluse, Hodge fed off these friendships. He shared information, engaged in lively dialogue, and drew support and encouragement from others, and returned likewise in kind through face-to-face conversations, written correspondence, and intermittent visits.[4]

The first circle of friends originated during his college and seminary years. Among peers, Hodge forged strongest ties with John Johns, his main competitor for undergraduate and graduate academic honors and later bishop of the Episcopal Church of Virginia; Charles P. McIlvaine, bishop of Ohio; and John Maclean, tenth president of Princeton and author of the two-volume *History of the College of New Jersey*. Once Hodge cemented a relationship, he proved a loyal and warmhearted friend. When others visited him or he reciprocated with friends, his congeniality and openness overcame any stiltedness or reserve that might result from lengthy separation. One could pick up with Hodge after months or even years of no contact as if no hiatus had occurred. He excelled at making people comfortable in his presence and conversing freely over the widest range of subjects.[5]

Foremost among these relationships, however, was his long association with Archibald Alexander as mentor, confidant, correspondent during Hodge's European travels, and then colleague on the faculty. Because Alexander served as Hodge's surrogate father, Charles appropriately named his son after his mentor. Hodge remembered sitting in the balcony as a teenager listening to Alexander's inaugural address on August 12, 1812 as the seminary's first professor. Following Hodge's enrollment in the seminary, their relationship became inextricably bound together. A. A. Hodge recounts that his father "was moulded more by the character and instructions of Dr. Archibald Alexander, than by all other external influences combined." In the fall of 1816, they spent the first extended period of time together during a six-hundred-mile trip via stagecoach and horseback throughout Virginia as Alexander visited the venues of his earlier ministry. Hodge found in Alexander the maturity and counsel that he had lacked in his youth and adolescence because of the early death of his father. In turn, Alexander found in this young protégé an impressionable and pliable spirit that could be readily shaped for service to the seminary and the church. Although Alexander fathered several sons of prodigious ability who also became professors at Princeton, he took special interest in the young Hodge, who responded willingly with filial devotion.[6]

Hodge's religious life, as we have already seen, conformed to a pattern consistent with Alexander's views on confirmation, which affirmed adherence to New Side piety and Presbyterian confessionalism. That Hodge would continue to model both traditions did not happen by accident. Instruction by his mother grounded him in the doctrinal standards of Presbyterianism, which in turn reinforced his own pietistic disposition. Ashbel Green further cemented these elements together in his roles as pastor, college instructor, and advocate of the Princeton revival. Another influential element in establishing Hodge's lifelong practices came through his three years at Princeton Seminary. This influence resulted from the charter of the school, "Plan of the Seminary,"[7] which mandated in detail not only the theological identity of the school, but also how it would in turn mold the lives of its students.[8]

The Plan, a remarkably detailed charter, consisted of eight articles outlining structure and governance,[9] role of faculty, curriculum, and character and piety of students. In addition to the articles, the history of the Plan published in 1838 included figures that indicate the cost of living for seminarians in the early nineteenth century. "The expense of board in the Commons varies from $1.25 to $1.75 per week. Board may be obtained in private families at from $1.50 to $2.50 per week. Expense of fuel from $6 to $10 per year. Washing $8." The seminary did not charge tuition or rent for rooms, but each student paid $10 per year to the "General Expense Fund," which defrayed expenses of the school. "Indigent students" received aid from the Board of Education of the General Assembly or the American Education Society. Due to students' experiencing financial difficulties, *BH* describes the endowment of scholarships at the cost of $2,500.[10]

The Plan itself established a seminary that attempted to balance the features of Presbyterian piety and confessionalism.[11] As for its confessionalist characteristics, professors were to subscribe "solemnly and *ex animo*" to the Westminster Standards and affirm that they would not "inculcate, teach or insinuate any thing which shall appear . . . to contradict or contravene, either directly or impliedly, any thing taught" in them. The Plan ensured that students would become theologically and biblically literate by prescribing specific fields of study and the requirements within those fields. By immersing themselves in "Natural Theology, Didactic, Polemic, and Casuistic Divinity," they would learn to "support the doctrines of the Confession of Faith and Catechisms, by a ready, pertinent, and abundant quotation of Scripture texts." In addition, they would become "well-skilled in the original languages of the Holy Scriptures" so that they could discern between "apparent inconsistencies, real obscurities or objections arising from history, reason, or argument."[12] They would study both "Jewish and Christian history, geography and oriental customs." Apologetically, students would become well versed in the "deistical controversy." In pastoral matters, students would acquaint themselves with the best works on practical religion and compose two lectures and four popular sermons. Finally, students would familiarize themselves with polity as practiced by "Protestant Churches." In sum, each graduate would become a "sound biblical critic . . . defender of the Christian faith . . . able and sound divine and casuist . . . useful preacher, and faithful pastor . . . qualified to exercise discipline, and to take part in the government of the Church in all its judicatories." To accomplish these goals, faculty would submit content and methodology in each course for approval by the board of directors in such detail "so that eventually, the whole course through which the pupils shall be carried, shall be no other than that which the board of directors shall have approved and sanctioned." Any alteration to courses once established had to receive board approval.[13]

Alongside detailed academic requirements, consistent with Presbyterian confessionalism, the charter document also included precise instructions for shaping students' character and spiritual life. Phrases dispersed throughout the document mandate the indispensability of moral living, Christian character, corporate worship, and individual spirituality. But Article V spells out standards of "Devotion, and Improvement in Practical Piety." It begins with the general injunction to achieve "enlightened devotion and fervent piety," without which "all other acquisitions will be comparatively of little worth." While such improvement must first transpire between the individual and God, the Plan delineates an appropriate "path of duty." Students were expected to spend "a portion of time every morning and evening in devout meditation, and self-recollection and examination; in reading the holy Scriptures solely with a view to a personal and practical application of the passage read, to his own heart, character, and circumstances; and in humble fervent prayer, and praise to God in secret." Another paragraph explains at length how to spend the Lord's Day consistent with the Westminster Confession. No activity, intellectual or otherwise, except attention to matters of devotion was permitted. Reading and conversation should focus entirely on the activities of practical religion. In addition, each student should set aside one day each month "for special prayer and self-examination in secret, accompanied with fasting."[14]

Article VI, "Of the Students," reinforces the previous article with additional regulations: professors would stipulate hours for study and recreation; students should exemplify the highest moral standards and exhibit due respect to faculty; students should be "temperate in meat and drink" and display "cleanliness and neatness in . . . dress and habits"; "excessive expense in clothing is strictly prohibited." Just as professors subscribed to the theological position of the seminary, students affirmed the following before enrolling: "Deeply impressed with a sense of the importance of improving in knowledge, prudence, and piety, in my preparation of the Gospel Ministry, I solemnly promise . . . that I will faithfully and diligently attend on all the instruction of this Seminary, and that I will conscientiously and vigilantly observe all the rules and regulations specified in the plan for its instruction and government." The denomination sought to graduate educated, pious pastors whose leadership would leave a permanent impression on its membership and the rest of American life, as evidenced by the "Introduction" of the Plan: "to form men for the Gospel ministry, who shall truly believe and cordially love, and therefore endeavour to propagate and defend . . . that system of religious belief and practice which is set forth in the Confession of Faith, Catechisms, and Plan of the Government and Discipline of the Presbyterian Church; and thus to perpetuate and extend the influence of true evangelical piety, and Gospel order."[15]

The weightiness that faculty attributed to requirements for personal piety appears in Hodge's "Certain Evils in the Seminary," a document cataloguing reports of students' exhibiting "boisterous, hilarity and loud noise" in 1851. Students were also reported importing barrels of cider in the refectory and being intoxicated in town. After researching the reports, Hodge stated that most were "gross exaggerations." Nevertheless, the faculty warned students against unseemly behavior. They should not "allow their reaction against the extreme principles and ungodly spirit of some temperance men" to result in unseemly behavior. Instead, they should "follow after those things which make for peace."[16]

Even a casual perusal of the Plan reveals the seriousness with which Princetonians undertook their mission. The Plan proved consistent with the college and seminary's New Side heritage. Princeton therefore exemplified what David H. Kelsey has called the "Athens" model of theological education. The Athens approach, the oldest ideal of education in Christianity, held *paideia*, instruction, to include not only teaching theological content but also "culturing the soul." "Schooling as character formation" stood foremost in pastoral training. Knowledge of God, said Kelsey, entailed not simply disseminating and internalizing theological content, but also facilitating students' "personal appropriation of wisdom about God and about themselves in relation to God." Knowing God demanded a conversion in which the soul turned from the things of this world to transcendent spiritual realities. The Athens model of theological education required that each professor who taught must possess extraordinary learning and personal gifts, to function as a midwife assisting students in their appropriation of revealed wisdom. Instruction occurred within a communal context. While learning was individual in that each must do it for himself, it did not occur within a solitary context. Education was a community affair, as minutely illustrated by the Princeton Plan.[17]

Although occurring years later, criticism of seminary education questioned the entire Princeton model as a basis for theological education. The Plan's vision for pastor-scholars or a learned ministry came under sharp attack by New York pastor Gardiner Spring in his 1848 book, *The Power of the Pulpit*. Spring lamented a decline in the pastorate. He criticized the seminary model because it produced professors rather than pastors. While conceding parts of the criticism, Hodge viewed Spring's proposal as too sweeping in its conception. It alleged a wholesale deterioration in the ministry, blamed professors training ministers for the outcome, and posited that the remedy lay in returning to the private method of theological education by individual pastors. Hodge denied both charges and their supposed cure. Depreciating contemporary pastors in comparison with distinguished ministers in the past only revealed a generalization made by people who assumed the past superior to the present and therefore criticized every practice in the present. Hodge accused Spring of assuming rather than proving deterioration of pastoral care. In every age, people denigrated not only pastors but also lawyers, doctors, and statesmen because they supposedly did not manifest qualities of their predecessors. Hodge, however, alleged that the nineteenth-century church had already witnessed many gains. He asked rhetorically, "Has not, in short, the whole country been going forward in all the forms of life?" If that be so, "it would be a most startling and unaccountable fact, if the ministry alone, in the midst of this universal progress, were either stationary or degenerated." Hodge then appealed to clear evidences that the church had made progress in numerical growth, piety, and even orthodoxy and that the wider public highly esteemed the clergy and its ministry.[18]

Hodge accused Spring of the fallacy *post hoc, ergo propter hoc.* Even if one admitted a decline in ministry—which Hodge denied—it would be improper to argue that it owed only to one factor (the origin of seminary training) just because seminary training of pastors had preceded the decline. Hodge challenged Spring's assertion that seminary education neglected or suppressed activities associated with the older method of studying under pastors—interaction through questioning and debate, conducting worship, attending religious meetings, and benefiting from social contacts. Hodge refuted every point—students regularly questioned their professors and discussed with their peers; they also led fellow students in devotions, participated in a variety of religious and prayer meetings, and socialized regularly outside seminary environs. Far from being secluded and subjected to "scholasticism," Hodge asserted, "a large part of the student's time in most of our seminaries is spent in the manoeuvring of committees and societies, bearing directly on the great benevolent enterprises of the day." As for the charge of "a continuous imprisonment of three years duration," the academic year contained breaks from studies that totaled three months, during which students engaged in meaningful labor ranging from ministry as missionaries to rather mundane manual tasks.[19]

To the charge that seminaries ought to require practical experience under pastoral supervision, Hodge conceded that such a proposal had merit. Until such a practice was implemented, however, the seminaries should continue to carry out their educational responsibilities, just as law and medical schools should educate law and medical students before they established their practices.[20]

To the charge that theological seminaries were an American novelty, Hodge responded that gathering of students for theological instruction "has always existed in the Reformed churches since the Reformation." The only newness that one could attribute to American seminaries was the different ways in which they had developed as institutions. While contemporary seminaries differed from the modest beginnings of log colleges, suggestions to revert to earlier forms overlooked the obvious advantages that had accrued in seminaries' development. One-on-one training may have suited previously, but the assembly and the church decided that "a thorough education is desirable," that is, carried out by faculty who could teach more efficiently than individual pastors, who had other pressing responsibilities. Hodge then listed the many curricular requirements reflecting Princeton's Plan as evidence that pastors could hardly fulfill all of them individually. In short, Hodge argued, "The proposal to revert to the old method is therefore virtually a proposal to discard all professional education for the ministry." The purpose of seminaries "was not intended to give pastoral experience, but to give learning, to discipline the mind, to cultivate piety and the social affections, to bring a number of young men together to act upon each other, and to become friends prepared to act heart and hand in the service of the Lord."[21]

Finally, Hodge addressed the issue—sensitive to Hodge because it involved him directly—of faculty who possessed no pastoral experience. The only requirement of the Presbyterian church stated that faculty must consist of ordained men. No external requirement, such as Spring's proposal that only pastors should teach, could prevent seminaries from becoming deficient. Pastors were no different from professors. Only as the ministry of the entire church maintained standards of piety and truth could seminaries continue without declining. Decay owed not to the absence of pastors in the professoriat, but to weakness in those who taught, whatever their vocation. While every seminary should include a professor of pastoral theology "to whom the widest experience in the pastoral life would be invaluable," the primary purpose of the seminary remained "to impart the requisite knowledge for the work of the ministry." Experience, on the other hand, was "to be acquired in the field."[22]

Charles Hodge, therefore, was both product and propagator of a Reformed vision of theological education known for both its breadth and its depth. His seminary education occurred under the aegis of a carefully conceived Plan that would train a learned ministry. Instruction would both educate the intellect and encourage the heart. While nineteenth-century America witnessed a wide variety of what qualified a person for ministry, Princeton would gain its reputation for being among the most demanding of its students.[23]

5

Fledgling Ministry

The Princeton Plan originated when the country desperately needed pastors, but Presbyterians were not about to provide merely a makeshift institution to train them. The details of the Plan reflect the theological and experiential vision of the Presbyterian church in the early nineteenth century, a vision wholly consistent with Charles Hodge's combination of New Side / Old Side upbringing. Hodge not only accepted its goals as generally defined but also warmly embraced the detailed means for carrying it out. Thus, when Archibald Alexander asked him to consider joining the faculty to relieve him in the field of biblical languages, Hodge gladly accepted the opportunity to further Presbyterianism as God's calling.[1]

To prepare himself for the post, Hodge agreed to study Hebrew and its pointing with Dr. Joseph Banks, a scholar and pastor in Philadelphia. Hodge believed in their necessity for the ministry: "they are as essential to a student as tools are to workmen of a different kind." He reported his progress with Banks to Alexander: "early in November I commenced attending Dr. Banks, and recite to him five days in the week." He also reported reading in Genesis and Psalms as well as reciting in Greek.[2]

Hodge also utilized the year's hiatus between graduation and teaching at Princeton to engage in missionary activity in the Philadelphia area. Following licensing to preach by the presbytery, Hodge sermonized twice each Sunday for thirty weeks from October 24, 1819 until May 20, 1820 at venues close to his home.[3] During this time, Hodge maintained the only religious diary he ever wrote. It provides a most revealing glimpse of Hodge often alluded to but never seen directly outside his family—his piety.[4] What stands out in these brief paragraphs (each entry contains approximately fifteen lines) is how much they reflect a young pastor's attempt to live up to the spiritual standards set by the Plan of the Seminary. They record Hodge's self-examination not just upon his preaching but upon his attempts to achieve a meaningful realization of piety in the process, and thus of his own fitness for ministry.

Each entry follows a formulaic structure that includes more or less the following: the time and place of his preaching, his text / topic, the audience (size, makeup, alertness, and reaction to the message), and finally an introspective reflection of his own religious experience upon leading the service. His comments on the audience range from their alertness ("the people appeared quite serious and attentive"; "the audience small but serious"; "unusually serious & some deeply affected") to their disinterest ("several persons seemed offended, others seemed disposed [to] turn it rather to ridicule"; "several strangers present who seemed to have little respect for religion"; "I could easily perceive from the manner of the people the effect of the monotony of my manner"). Occasionally he refers to conversations with those who attended. His desire to discern positive results from his preaching took several forms. He longed for his hearers to benefit from the worship service. Mostly, however, he expressed a desire to witness conversions resulting from his preaching. On March 5 he states mournfully, "It is painful to preach Sabbath after Sabbath, and I see no solitary instance of seriousness and conversion. For 5 months have I been a preacher of the Gospel & have yet had no visible fruit resulting from my labours."[5]

The most notable feature of the journal, however, lies not in Hodge's observance of outward responses from his audience, but in what can only be called his obsessive attempts to catalogue and evaluate his own internal experience. The most frequently used words—*feeling[s]*, *piety*, and *pious*— repeat like a metronome throughout the journal.[6] Frequently he exhorts himself to realize some concrete improvement in his spirituality or admonishes himself for failing to do so. Hodge set himself a goal of realizing or feeling some experience from worship or his preaching. If that goal was achieved, his remarks took the form of the following: "I enjoyed the service"; "the Lord granted me more feeling and ease"; "the service was pleasurable"; "my own heart in some measure felt the truth"; "I felt what I said & endeavoured to make the people feel that they must be born again." On one occasion he prefaced his remarks by writing, "Piety is the life of the minister." To lack piety indicated spiritual deficiency. Thus, not only did he want his audience to be "serious" and experience "impressions," he set similar goals for himself as the preacher.[7]

Hodge's words echo similar pietistic laments throughout church history. Such utterances are not limited, however, to classical pietists. Similar accounts of spiritual struggles punctuate diaries of church leaders from Augustine onward. In Hodge's tradition, Puritan divines tracked their introspective pilgrimages with equally intensive analyses of their religious affections. Hodge's comments on his failure to use the Sabbath properly reflect the expectations of the Westminster catechisms and the Plan of the Seminary: "This method of spending the Sabbath I find very unprofitable. I have neither the talent nor the piety to give a spiritual & devout character to conversation & hence other subjects than piety become the matters of discussion."[8]

Remarkably, the tenor of the journal reflects more failure than success in achieving his spiritual goals. He exhorts himself in light of his failure to have the requisite impressions, as evidenced by the following entry for November 28, 1819: "I have experienced very little spiritual enjoyment. My heart has been too far from God & worldly thoughts have too much occupied my mind. This I suspect has arisen from my conduct during the past week. It is impossible to gain and loose [*sic*] at pleasure spirituality of mind, it must be cultivated constantly. Let not my soul this week on which you now have entered find you still at such a distance from God—Oh Holy Spirit return unto thy rest, deign to make my bosom thine abode, & oh attend my feable [*sic*] preaching by thy almighty energy for Jesus sake." Another entry despairs, "I felt almost depressed under the apprehension that I shd [*sic*] never become even a moderately acceptable preacher." In still another he asks, "Have I felt as I ought the truth I declared to? . . . And have I been the means of doing even a little good? Oh that I could with confidence answer these questions in the affirmative. But it is evident that the first requisite for preaching is fervent piety and as mine has been dull I must confess myself to have come short." The entry for April 30, however, illustrates how quickly he could turn from a positive evaluation to a negative: "I have seldom been enabled to preach with greater freedom or with more pleasure than I enjoyed this afternoon. I affectionately reasoned with the people & urged on them a compliance with the divine exhortation. But all the entreaties or arguments God put into my lips seem to have passed away, at the least the good I see not."[9]

A final feature of this diary sheds light on how we view Hodge's pietism and confessionalism. Charles Cashdollar points out that the diary "exposes the limited amount of liturgical consciousness within the denomination—Christmas and Easter pass without mention in Hodge's diary." Entries on December 19 and 26, 1819, the Sundays before and after Christmas, and March 26 and April 2, 1820, the Sunday before Easter and Easter itself, receive no attention in Hodge's diary. Obliquely this may manifest the confessionalist strand in Hodge's heritage. Presbyterians who adhered zealously to the Westminster Standards deemphasized the liturgical calendar as remnants of Romanism. In this tradition, sermons would not be based on lectionary texts and thus would not follow liturgical practices in church history. While congregations might sing Christmas carols and Easter hymns, sermons might focus on whatever sequence of texts the pastor was using at the time. Therefore, Hodge's omitting any reference to Christmas and Easter would not be unusual. The other consideration at work here is that Hodge's diary was so focused on his own personal piety that we might not expect him to comment on something as extraneous as liturgical forms.[10]

Thus Sunday after Sunday, Hodge, a mere twenty-two years old, set himself the weekly task of preaching and evaluating his success entirely by whether or not he and his congregation exhibited characteristics consistent with "piety." And for all the number of times he used that word or synonymous expressions, more often than not by his own admission he fell short of his expectations. This journal was the only spiritual diary Hodge ever wrote. We do not know why he never wrote another. When he recorded his travels and studies in Europe several years later, some remarks reprise themes in this earlier pietistic record. His European journal, however, did not repeat either in frequency or in introspective intensity comments like those during his missionary preaching in Philadelphia. As Hodge matured, he questioned the value of such records as valid indications of genuine spirituality, and he came to see that anguish over the presence or absence of such experiences hindered rather than furthered spiritual growth.[11]

Perhaps the next-to-last entry in the 1819–20 diary demonstrates that Hodge learned that focusing so exclusively on examining his feelings proved more a hindrance than a help in actually realizing spiritual impressions: "I have almost uniformly found that when I have commenced a service under a little depression of spirits it has proved more than usually pleasant." That is, he found that the more a person examined his subjective state, the less apt he was to experience what he was looking for because he sought it as something under his control. When focusing so intently on experience, the cognitive act itself precluded a person's experiencing the alternative subjective activity being sought. Genuine spiritual "experience" would come not as the result of efforts to achieve it but as something given by God. Hodge hereby recognized an irony in spiritual experience. The religious affections were not subject to human manipulation; rather than being under human control, they arise as a gift. Thus, when Hodge was least apt to think positively about his experience because of spiritual depression, taking his thoughts off looking for the beginning of spiritual impressions actually freed his mind so that the affections stirred by God could emerge. Perhaps Hodge came to realize that descriptions of pious experience such as those he narrates in his diary were a disguised form of what he would condemn in other contexts as "works righteousness."[12]

6

Expanding Vistas

While Charles Hodge was engaged in mission preaching over the winter of 1819–20, his primary focus on his future followed from a conversation with Archibald Alexander regarding the possibility of joining the seminary faculty. Specifically, Alexander hoped Hodge might relieve him of teaching the biblical languages. In May 1820, the General Assembly approved Alexander's proposal by appointing Hodge assistant in original languages. Hodge moved back to Princeton, and his first letters disclose immense pleasure with the prospect of teaching, his new environment, and even his creature comforts. He wrote to his brother, "My situation here is as pleasant as even my fondest wishes had desired. I have a pleasant room at the upper end of town, and board with Dr. Alexander's family. This I find a very advantageous arrangement, as the intercourse I enjoy with the Doctor cannot fail of being very profitable. I take a good bit of exercise, think my horse the best in the world, and am very well." Hodge's annual salary was $400. He also updated his mother and brother on the rheumatism that afflicted his leg, a malady that flared up throughout his adult life when he overextended himself.[1]

Before the fall semester began, Hodge embarked on a trip to New England that proved immensely helpful to his future as a professor by enlarging his intellectual and spiritual horizons. He had previously benefited from a similar journey through Virginia with his paternal mentor, Dr. Alexander. The three-week sojourn to New England with a friend, Benjamin Wisner, who preached as a pastoral candidate in Boston in October 1820, introduced Hodge to cultural centers and scholars with whom he would interact during his subsequent academic career. Two letters to his mother reveal the significant impression they made on him. In Boston, Hodge stood at the southeast corner of the Boston Common, viewed its vast green expanse, and looked with awe up Park Street at the dome of the state house at the top of Beacon Street. As he described the scene, "it exceeds anything I have ever seen." While his friend preached at South Church, Hodge preached the morning and evening sermons at the historic Park Street Church, famous for its location on "Brimstone Corner"—so named because gunpowder was stored in the church's basement during the colonial uprising.[2]

More remarkable than scenic vistas were the people he met during his journey. Both on the way to and from Boston, Hodge visited Nathaniel W. Taylor, pastor of the prestigious First Church, New Haven. His description of their first meeting presciently anticipated his later strong differences over salient Calvinist teachings. He described Taylor as "a young minister [he was nine years Hodge's senior], who is the pride of the southern part of Connecticut." Hodge's account reveals the type of stimulating conversation that Hodge relished with friends and associates: "We found this one of the most improving incidents in our journey, as this young man . . . who possesses uncommonly fine talents, differs very considerably in his theoretical opinions from the Princeton gentlemen. He kept us pretty constantly in an animated though temperate discussion of our differences." His summary of Taylor—the person and their meeting—reflects the respect he consistently accorded to anyone, even those with whom he radically disagreed.[3]

Probably the most unexpected occasions in his New England sojourn were when Hodge made the acquaintance of Massachusetts Lieutenant Governor William Phillips and Dr. John Thornton Kirkland, president of Harvard. Hodge expressed surprise at the attention he received from both. After first meeting with Phillips, the lieutenant governor accompanied Hodge and Wisner across the Charles River to Cambridge to introduce them personally to Kirkland; then he remained with them as Kirkland gave all three a tour of the campus.[4]

The crowning events of his trip consisted of two meetings with Moses Stuart, professor at Andover Seminary and America's foremost authority on the Hebrew language in the early nineteenth century. The second session spanned several days as they discussed how Hodge should pursue his vocational plans at Princeton. His letter exudes praise of Stuart as a person: "I think Stuart is the most interesting man I have seen in New England. He is kind, sociable, condescending and communicative; free from all formality, he becomes your friend at once. His talents are of the first order, and no man in the country has made any progress comparable to his in the department of Biblical literature." But Hodge expresses even greater admiration for the assistance Stuart offered in clarifying how Hodge might pursue his calling: "He has done me great good, has marked out my road, and told me the right path, and enlarged my views as to the extent and importance of the study, more than I could have conceived it possible."[5]

Hodge could not have asked for a more profitable trip prior to beginning his teaching. He traveled outside his familiar environs, visited with some of the most influential religious, political, and educational leaders in the oldest part of the country, and, most importantly, garnered counsel regarding his future vocation. Following his custom of writing detailed letters, in addition to his summary estimation of Taylor and Stuart he assessed the character of New Englanders as a whole. When his brother asked whether they were "more intelligent and better informed," Hodge answered in the affirmative: "I do [think them so], most decidedly, and the ladies beyond comparison." He closed his letter to his mother with his highest commendation: "We have been the more struck with the propriety of calling Boston the clergyman's paradise." High praise, indeed, from a future Princeton Seminary professor! His remarks reflect an observant young scholar from the relatively countrified surroundings in New Jersey appraising the intellectual milieu in Brahmin Boston.[6]

7

Fledgling Professor

Fresh off his stimulating journey to New England, Charles Hodge launched into the precarious waters of first-year teaching and found the task more demanding than expected. Within weeks he was lamenting the taxing nature of supervising class recitation. He expressed his weariness in a letter to Hugh on November 21, 1820: "I never knew, until I undertook it, that hearing a class of twenty or thirty students recite is one of the most fatiguing things in the world. The unbroken attention you are obliged to pay for an hour and half together, and the necessity of talking a good deal, withal, is more tiresome than any one that has not felt it would imagine." In addition to the daily pressure of preparation, Hodge also experienced the enormous pressure not to be caught in a classroom mistake, especially in Greek. He found himself teaching those who had studied the language for years and some who had even taught Greek themselves. Yet, consistent with his temperament never to linger too long on the negative side of things, he playfully adds: "but in Hebrew I have more the advantage of them. There is one thing greatly in my favor, that I have not got your modesty to bother me."[1]

As the semester drew to a close, Hodge gave fuller expression to his contentedness in teaching: "I am becoming daily more pleased with present duties and future prospects . . . I do not think I could devise a plan of life more suited to my desires, than the one Providence appears opening before me . . . I hope to be cheerfully resigned to whatever Heaven may determine."[2]

Though General Assembly approved his appointment as professor of original languages in May 1821, Hodge pursued ordination in the Presbyterian church. The Presbytery of New Brunswick had appointed him stated supply in April, and Hodge commenced preaching in Lambertville, New Jersey, for six months and then at Trenton First Church. On November 27, 1821, Hodge and one other candidate were "examined on their experimental acquaintance with religion, on Theology, Natural and Moral Philosophy, on Church Government and the Sacraments, and their examinations on these subjects were sustained." Hodge preached his ordination sermon on 1 Corinthians 1:21, and he was ordained the next day.[3]

His suitability for academics and his penchant for encouraging scholarly research among fellow professors and students surfaced quickly. In 1822, his second year, he organized a society devoted to exploration and discussion of issues in the field of biblical criticism. Although senior professors Archibald Alexander and Samuel Miller attended, Hodge served as the driving force behind the society by organizing meetings and assigning topics for students to research. Hodge inaugurated the society by giving the first lecture, "The Importance of Biblical Literature." He wrote to his brother, "This [lecture] is a duty which [the society's] constitution thrusts upon its President. I am so well convinced of the necessity of this nature that I generally submit cheerfully."[4] His colleague Miller was sufficiently impressed that he suggested that Hodge publish his address to familiarize clergy in the denomination with his ability and thus enhance the possibility of making his position at Princeton permanent. While in his letter to his mother Hodge modestly thought this "unseemly," Alexander seconded Miller's recommendation, saying that "it ought to be done, and . . . it can be done at the request of the Society, without any impropriety or indelicacy." Hodge closed the letter with the comment, "This is a question to be left to my parental Professors. I am willing to follow their advice, even with hesitating steps."[5]

Hodge's fifty-one-page *Dissertation* marked his first formal assessment of biblical literature, the field that occupied his scholarly vocation until his appointment to theology in 1840. This lecture was the first to be published in his academic career. In it he set the tone for Princeton's views on biblical scholarship that would endure throughout the nineteenth century and into the twentieth. He began by distinguishing two fields in biblical literature, "*Criticism, and Interpretation*, or *Hermeneutics*. The object of the former, is *to determine what is the genuine text of sacred scripture*; of the latter, *to discover and exhibit its meaning*" (italics in original): the inspiration and authority of Scripture, the proper tasks of biblical scholarship, and the dangers of such scholarship conducted on the basis of modern views. Study of the Bible should proceed from the recognition that its "books are . . . Scripture." They should be studied "under the deep impression that they are the Word of God" and that "the divine origin of the Scriptures should exert a considerable influence on the principles by which they are interpreted." Thus, "if the doctrine of the plenary Inspiration [that not only the ideas but also the words expressing those ideas were inspired by the Holy Spirit] be true, God is the real author of the Sacred Scriptures."[6] To Hodge, plenary inspiration did not, however, preclude rigorous linguistic demands on those who translated and interpreted the Bible. Scholars were to become familiar with "the circumstances by which the import of words and phrases is regulated in all languages; such as the opinion, laws and customs of the people, the peculiar circumstances . . . which have influenced the language and modes of expression characteristic of the Bible." Before interpreting the Bible, students also "should be convinced of the canonical authority, authenticity, and inspiration of the Sacred Scriptures, that we may be able to take their divine authority as proved." Thus Hodge presupposed biblical study based on an apologetic that supported scholarship as compatible with pious devotion to the text. This comported with Princeton's insistence that theological education should nurture students intellectually and spiritually. Students and faculty would not study the

Bible with a disengaged reason consistent with modern rationalism, that is, by a supposedly dispassionate objectivity by which students suspended belief in texts that they sought to comprehend.[7]

Hodge, therefore, fully supported textual criticism of the Bible with the purpose of determining the genuine texts of the Bible among the variety of manuscripts available. In this regard, Hodge praised efforts of European scholarship, and he believed that pastors ought to be fully cognizant of such scholarly studies. He readily acknowledged that no extant text of Scripture was free from error by admitting that "the number of discrepancies is very great, and indeed at first view appalling." Since no text is "immaculately pure [it is necessary] to inquire into the various sources of the errors found to exist, and to arrange them in their proper classes." Biblical scholars should ascertain the content of the original sources using the modern methods of textual criticism so that "the purity of the text may be restored." Only when biblical criticism has established the text may scholars proceed to interpret Scripture and unearth its doctrinal teaching.[8]

Hodge optimistically affirmed that textual critics could establish the biblical text. He confidently stated that evidence from textual studies would confirm "that the Bible we now have is essentially the Bible, which proceeded from the sacred writers." But he was less sanguine about the future direction of biblical interpretation. While textual or "lower criticism" offered positive benefits to theological students by bolstering their regard for biblical authority, Hodge expressed strong reservations about "higher criticism," which frequently challenged the content, meaning, and authority of biblical texts. Hodge foresaw a potential struggle looming between those who revered the Bible as the Word of God and those whose studies proceeded on principles "fundamentally erroneous," which would prove more destructive than helpful to theological students.[9]

As for the role of pastors in making biblical content accessible to their congregations, Hodge affirmed Presbyterians' confidence that producing an educated clergy in America would make a significant impact on American life. He stated reassuringly that "no class of men have greater influence in society than the clergy." They possessed the unique calling of making Christian truth known. They did so based not on a narrow familiarity with "particular texts" but on a foundation as "broad as the Bible." Professors must teach that Scripture contains a unified, coherent truth. Hodge readily admitted that this view was being challenged by an opposition that was organized, educationally well equipped, and intent on spreading new interpretations exceeding theological innovations already manifest in America. Hodge identified that source as the German universities. The theological situation had radically changed since Martin Luther launched the sixteenth-century Protestant Reformation. Germany had distinguished itself for progress in biblical scholarship, but false doctrines had proliferated in the process. German scholarship approached the Bible not on the basis of the text itself, properly interpreted, but on the basis of false philosophies imposed on the text. While not naming particular individuals or schools, Hodge explained that critics reached radical conclusions not from sound exegesis of biblical texts but by foisting false philosophical speculations on them: "[Practitioners of recent criticism] have regarded the Bible as a mere human production, and treated it as such. Hence, they have felt at liberty to explain the accounts of the Old Testament, as the dreams of philosophers; and the miracles of the New, as mere natural occurrences. They, with many others have adopted the *Philosophical* mode of interpretation, making their expositions, which of course must vary, as their philosophical principles vary . . . The doctrines of the Trinity, Incarnation, and Atonement, fade from the Bibles of those, to whom they are unphilosophical." Departures from traditional confidence in the truthful content of the Bible would inevitably produce an impending conflict—the "most momentous that truth and piety have ever yet endured."[10]

Hodge did not underestimate the challenge confronting his institution. The opponents are "wise and learned," their "plans are well laid and extensive," and Hodge warned that "the battle is not to be with an individual, nor in a day, but constantly and everywhere."[11]

Should seminaries require students to become acquainted with German scholarship, punctuated as it was with "false doctrines, and the most irreverent treatment of the Sacred Scriptures"? Would not students as a result of exposure to false teaching fall prey to its errors? Would it not be safer to protect students by not exposing them to such studies?

Should a confessionalist seminary with a mission such as Princeton's commit its students to such issues? These were indeed difficult questions over which "good men think very decidedly, though very differently." Some strongly opposed teaching biblical criticism altogether. They argued that students who lacked the skill to "separate the poison from the food" could read "able misrepresentations of the truth" and fall prey to skepticism. Because benefits gained from critical studies outweighed the dangers, Hodge disagreed and proposed a bolder stance. "This is a question on which we must all think for ourselves . . . This decision should be made without regard to the opinions or practice of others, because it is peculiarly a personal concern, as a liberty on this subject, which might not be injurious to one, may prove destructive to another." Exposure to current studies in biblical literature offered a mixed blessing: "[German scholars'] abuse of reason and learning, does not prove, that neither are to be used in the exposition of Scripture; nor does the fact, that many, who have possessed great external advantages, for understanding the sacred writings, have shamefully abused them, prove that these advantages are dangerous or worthless." Thus Hodge proposed a course that would distinguish Princeton's reputation for training an educated ministry. This New Side seminary would equip pastors to defend their Calvinistic heritage and also keep them apprised of the cutting edge of scholarship. Thus, years before venturing to Europe to confront German thought firsthand, Hodge recognized the shift of scholarship from premises with which he had long been accustomed to studying the Bible. He did so, confident that the believing scholars could turn the tools of criticism against those who had misused them.[12]

A final objection to engaging in critical scholarship stated that it "[would be] unfriendly to piety." Would not criticism undermine the roots of students' whole upbringing—to say nothing of the pious aims of the Princeton Plan? Hodge answered simply, "This depends on the manner in which it is conducted." He again conceded, "All familiar intercourse with holy things is dangerous. The ministry itself, from its official attention to religious duties and religious truth is perilous." Despite potential hazards, Hodge answered the query with another question: "Is there any thing in the nature of such a course inimical to piety?" He answered, "Surely not." If students approached their studies with the conviction of the Bible's truthfulness and inherent authority, no intellectual study would threaten their piety. He ended his discourse with a rounding affirmation: "Fully persuaded however, that the course of study of which we have been speaking, is not only extensive, and delightful; but in its nature, calculated to enlarge our views of divine truth, and to purify the heart; it is with confidence, I commend to this Society formed for improvement in Biblical Literature, and in the knowledge of the Bible, to the diligence of its members, and to the benediction of the Great Head of the Church." Hodge never wavered in his evaluation of the source of error in biblical and theological scholarship—i.e., German universities—and his conviction of the necessity of a counteroffensive from American seminaries and the pastors they produced.[13]

In his *Dissertation*, Hodge recorded in seed form the direction of his and the seminary's futures. Alexander's and Miller's teaching and writing under the guidelines of the Plan of the Seminary prepared their protégé well. They impressed Hodge with his responsibilities as a biblical scholar. His *Dissertation* indicated the necessity of rigorous scholarship if biblical studies were to continue in an orthodox direction. Little did they or Hodge know that despite his present position as professor of biblical languages, Hodge would make his most prolific contributions in the field of theology, not biblical criticism. Hodge correctly perceived that despite biblical criticism's being in its early stages, it was already veering away from orthodox moorings. That movement resulted not from the actual content of the biblical text, but from interpretations of the text being driven by unorthodox theology. He and the seminary would not evade the controversies that would inevitably follow. In addition, pastoral students would not be sheltered from this scholarship but be fully apprised of its presence and its eventual impact on the church and its ministry. Hodge would not shrug the responsibility for polemically confronting error as he perceived it. Scholarship at Princeton would be scholarship for pastors and thus scholarship that directed the church's ministry. Biblical and theological studies at Princeton would never be an end in themselves but a means of glorifying God by training like-minded pastors whose preaching and ministry would edify God's people.

Having followed the advice of his superiors to have his *Dissertation* published, Hodge found himself mildly anxious as the General Assembly gathered to consider appointing another faculty member. As he pondered how to spend his summer vacation, he clearly hoped to retain his position at Princeton. To that end he sought to improve his attractiveness as a faculty member by learning German so that he could read primary texts of European scholars. Someone went so far as to suggest that Hodge learn German by spending part of his summer vacation in Bethlehem or Nazareth, Pennsylvania, with a German pastor. That never materialized, but Hodge remained convinced that learning German should be a priority in his academic preparation. Only as he cultivated his own skills in the language of those who posed a threat through their writings could he hope to train Presbyterian pastors, who in turn would teach and defend the faith to their congregations.[14]

As events unfolded, Miller's strategy proved successful. Princeton's board of directors approved a new position of professor of Oriental and biblical literature in May 1822 and appointed Hodge in September at a salary of $1,000 per year. His inaugural address, on September 24, carried the following line within its opening sentences: "It is the object of this discourse to illustrate the *importance* of Piety in the Interpretation of Scripture" (emphasis added). Hodge's son commented on the implications of his father's inaugural address: "The first sentences . . . constitute a divinely significant omen for the professional life now opening." Throughout his ensuing career, Hodge remained confident that preparation for Presbyterian ministry would combine exacting scholarship with traditional orthodoxy and piety.[15]

Ironically, within months of his lecture, he urged his brother to enter the publishing world as well, but in the medical profession. He perceived an apologetic need among physicians because he was convinced that the majority of people in the medical profession tended toward a materialist view. He urged his brother to "come out against this doctrine of materialism and its tendency to irreligion and also to bear your testimony to the importance of religion in a physician." He continued, "It may require some courage to do this, but the open avowal of conviction never hurt anybody yet." Humorously he added that "a lawyer is not ashamed sometimes almost to turn to preach. . . . You want a subject novel and important and here is one worthy of you and one you may treat without making a sermon of it."[16]

In the interim between the close of the spring semester and assuming his new duties in the fall of 1822, Hodge married Sarah Bache, great-granddaughter of Benjamin Franklin. The couple first rented and then "went to housekeeping" in a house opposite Nassau Hall in the spring of 1823. Eighteen months later they moved into the home they built on seminary property, where Hodge lived for the rest of his life.[17] All but the oldest of the Hodge children were born in this home. In the first four years of marriage, the Hodges had two children, Archibald Alexander, named after Hodge's mentor, in 1823 and Mary Elizabeth in 1825. Hodge regularly showered his affection upon them and indeed in later correspondence over all his subsequent six children.[18]

In a Christmas Day 1825 letter to his mother, Hodge effused over his recently born daughter, Mary. Archibald Alexander had baptized her earlier that afternoon, and Hodge used the occasion to reflect on his covenant responsibilities as a father: "Our dear little children we have promised to educate for heaven, and as God shall enable us, we mean to perform our vows. To this every thing must be made secondary." In addition, Hodge further connected his daughter's baptism and educating her in the faith as his attempt to imitate how his mother had raised him and his brother: "We feel, therefore, determined, if God shall render us faithful to our purposes, to bring up your dear little grandchildren, as we are sure you would have us do, with the one object supremely in view of fitting them for heaven." His words express not only his mother's successful raising of her sons but what he hoped for his daughter: "I have great confidence in the effect of religious truth upon the infant mind. Children are so susceptible, their associations are so strong and lasting, that it does not seem strange that the effect of early education should so frequently be felt through life. And if we add to this God's peculiar promises to those who endeavor to bring up a child in the way in which he should go, we shall see that there is abundant reason to hope that exertions properly directed will be crowned with success."[19]

Whatever his work ethic may have been previously and however it was perceived by his mother, Hodge worked himself to the bone in his first year teaching. He initially viewed his impending life's work with a great deal of idealism, little realizing the efforts involved in composing lectures, staying ahead of assignments, and maintaining one's stamina in hearing and responding to students' recitations. In addition to the wearying routine of weekly classroom interaction, composing exegetical lectures on Romans, Corinthians, and hermeneutics, and preaching regularly in the village of Princeton and other neighboring churches, he attempted to pursue both ancient and modern languages: Greek, Hebrew, Syriac, Arabic, German, and French. He repeated his concern that his students nipped at his heels. Echoing the sentiments of innumerable fledgling professors, he confessed, "I look forward to a pretty severe term, I must keep before my students or they will find it [i.e., his inadequacies] out."[20]

As 1825 began, Hodge's academic conscientiousness resulted in another burden to his workload—editing a journal. Consistent with Princeton's goal of graduating educated pastors and his previous efforts to establish a theological society among the students, Hodge founded this journal in theological and biblical studies, first named *Biblical Repertory*. It began with modest goals—a quarterly with the sole purpose of publishing reprints and translations of scholarly works, as indicated by its subtitle, *A Collection of Tracts in Biblical Literature*.[21] Only later would the journal take on the role of publishing original pieces and become a prime entry in the heyday of American religious journalism. For the first four years of its existence, Hodge cooperated with the Rev. Robert Patton, professor of Greek at the College of New Jersey, and two sons of Alexander—James W. and Joseph Addison—both gifted in ancient languages. Hodge served as editor and contributed two articles in the 1828 volume, reviews of "History of Theology in the Eighteenth Century" by August Tholuck and "Life of Kant" by Professor Stapher of Paris. Both of these translations reveal aspects of Hodge's future agenda for the seminary—maintaining its theological tradition and its proclivity for making learning and piety prerequisites for pastoral ministry. He would find in Tholuck a kindred spirit during his study abroad and share a favorable estimation of German pietism.

They would become lifelong correspondents. Hodge would also solidify Princeton's version of evangelical doctrine and piety over against its deistic manifestation in the religious life of Immanuel Kant.[22]

Despite letters describing satisfaction and even joy in his labors, in the following year Hodge gradually grew even more distressed at deficiencies in his academic preparation. Given his assignment as professor of Oriental and biblical languages, he came to the solemn realization that only a prolonged period of intense study could remedy his academic shortcomings. In August 1826 he wrote to his brother, "You will perhaps think me beside myself before you are done reading this letter, but I am about to speak the words of soberness and truth." He professed himself at "very serious disadvantage" and "incompetent" in his teaching and elaborated the reasons for his sense of disquiet: "You remember I never opened a Greek Grammar until I came to Princeton in the spring of 1812. In the fall of that year I entered College, joining a class in which all its members had been studying the language from one to two years. The Sophomore year we studied Greek several times a week. During the Junior and Senior years, only once a fortnight. The year subsequent to my leaving College I did nothing at it. During my three years in the Seminary, my time was occupied with other concerns. This has been my Greek course. What a preparation for a Professor!" After assuming his duties at the seminary, he undoubtedly expended all his energies preparing lectures and holding recitations. Thus he spent less time maintaining the academic edge required to carry out his linguistic instruction. He concluded that he desperately needed more training. While Hodge may well have overstated his deficiencies, since he was given to self-deprecation, his exclamation to his brother is surely surprising.[23]

Hodge proposed a drastic measure to remedy his weaknesses. He asked the board of directors for a two-year hiatus from his teaching to free him to go to Europe for concentrated study. He would learn firsthand from the best European scholars the latest trends, methods, and conclusions of biblical, linguistic, and theological disciplines. To bolster his French and German, he planned to spend half the time in Paris and half in Göttingen. In exchange for the seminary's hiring a replacement who could substitute for him in the classroom, he would return much better prepared for carrying out his duties and add to the reputation of Princeton. Difficulties to overcome in this scheme entailed prolonged separation from his family and financial arrangements for his wife and children. As he struggled with his decision, he wrote to his brother of another reason for his hesitation, which reflected yet again on his relation with his mother: "I shall as usual have a great deal to say for myself and satisfy Mother if I can't you."[24]

The two senior professors lent their support when Hodge appealed to the seminary board. They praised the junior faculty member's carrying out his duties "in a manner which reflects equal honor on his attainments, his capacity, his diligence and his fidelity." They also added that other institutions had approved similar ventures to improve their schools. The board concurred with Hodge's request. It granted a two-year leave, continued his salary, and appointed John Williamson Nevin as Hodge's replacement. Hodge assured the board that Nevin would carry out the responsibilities of teaching with eminent ability.[25]

By the time of his departure for Europe, the lines of Hodge's spiritual and intellectual outlook lay firmly in place, imbedded by the training of a diligent mother, reinforced by his pastor, and further refined by the faculties of the College of New Jersey and Princeton Seminary. Both head and heart robustly affirmed a distinctive religious heritage from which he claimed never to have consciously wavered. Steeped in New Side experience and confessionalist discipline in his youth, he then attended a seminary that traced its roots to and required its students to evidence New Side zeal. He manifested a devout spirit and robust confessionalism thanks to his home life and his worship experiences in Philadelphia. His education, however, although formally completed, left gaps that he hoped to fill by intensive study. Furthering his education abroad under the tutelage of French and German scholars might appear a rash, even perilous undertaking for someone so young, pious, and inexperienced because of his relatively sheltered background. Yet 1826–28 proved to be defining years, not in the sense that they marked a radically new course in Hodge's life, but in the sense that events and associations during this period only confirmed the experiences of his formative years.

PART 2

Broadened Abroad

In the next two years, Hodge engaged in an intensive attempt to bolster his academic training in Europe. The decision to further his studies followed an awareness of gaps in his linguistic training in both modern and ancient languages. Furthermore, he became fully cognizant that European scholars in his field displayed expertise beyond what he possessed from his college and seminary training. Not only did Europe exceed America in sheer numbers of scholars and universities, but the old country manifested traditions that were each steeped in a unique heritage. As Hodge quickly learned, the universities at Göttingen, Halle, and Berlin varied greatly in their reputations for rigor of scholarship, curricular innovations, theological orthodoxy, and expressions of piety. In the process of honing his own skills, Hodge's major discovery was not of differences in intensity between European and American studies. Though a disparity existed on that level, his most important finding was of the nature of theological training itself and what it entailed for ministry—how theological education shaped its students and what was required of ministers in their calling. Far from a minor element in Hodge's life, his two-year hiatus abroad played a major role in developing skills for biblical and theological scholarship, forging new friendships, exposing him to perspectives other than his own, and shaping his character.[1]

8

Separation from Family

American ministerial education began with the founding of Harvard College in 1636 to train Congregationalist pastors. Andover was founded in 1808 as the first American seminary. Trinitarian Calvinists started Andover to further theological orthodoxy in reaction to Unitarian Henry Ware's occupying Harvard's Hollis Professorship of Divinity in 1805. Princeton, therefore, was one of only two seminaries at its founding in 1812, but it was the first to use the term *seminary* in its official title.[1] By the 1820s, Presbyterians had made significant progress from their initial efforts in theological education. The denomination traced its emphasis on theological education to William Tennent's modest Log College in 1726 after he became pastor of the Presbyterian church in Neshaminy, Pennsylvania. Tennent built his one-room school as an alternative to students' attending prestigious schools in the Northeast, such as Harvard and Yale, or one of the still older universities in Europe. Though the Log College prepared only about twenty pastors over a period of twenty years, it illustrated American Presbyterians' emphasis on a highly educated clergy.[2] If Princeton were to participate effectively in theological education, its professoriat would have to be conversant with the growing number of subjects offered in seminary curriculums.

Thus, when in the opening decades of the nineteenth century a trend developed for professors to round off theological training they received in America by a sojourn in Europe, the prospect appealed to the young Charles Hodge. Hodge was the first Princeton graduate to consider such a route. He would leave the intellectual and moral environs and the supportive network in which he had lived and labored for over twenty years to pursue intensive study at France's and Germany's elite universities. The two-year interruption in his teaching would shore up his educational deficiencies and expose him to scholars, ideas, movements, and cultures beyond his accustomed vistas. Students would benefit from exposure to the latest in theological and biblical scholarship. It would prepare them for the primary task of pastors—to preach the gospel, teach the content of Scripture, and maintain the doctrines handed down free from modern innovations.[3]

Several factors created an urgency in Hodge to further his studies. In letters he expressed his frustration over weaknesses in his academic preparation as professor of Oriental and biblical literature. First priority, therefore, lay in increasing his facility with the original languages of the Old and New Testaments essential to producing sound biblical exegetes. Hodge was convinced that he needed more comprehensive instruction in Greek, and although his consultations with Moses Stuart in New England had resulted in fledgling efforts to learn Hebrew, he felt constrained to surpass these meager beginnings. He also believed he should be conversant with other ancient Oriental languages, such as Arabic and Syriac, to enhance his understanding of contexts relevant to biblical history and culture. Also, the burgeoning of theological and biblical literature from Continental scholars that would culminate in nineteenth-century liberalism demanded that Hodge attain a working knowledge of French and German so that he could keep abreast of scholarly developments in his field. The prominence of European names in biblical and theological studies both in numbers and in reputation would require his having more than passing acquaintance with their works. Finally, his founding the *PR* illustrates his growing awareness that the duties of a seminary professor—classroom instruction, publishing articles and commentaries, and interacting with scholarly writings by professors from other academic institutions—required greater expertise than he possessed. His earlier visit to New England and conversations with emerging scholars at seminaries and their innovative theological views alerted him to the necessity of fleshing out a distinctively Princetonian perspective of the rapidly growing scholarship in biblical criticism.

Hodge's decision did not come easily. Personal insecurity and family members' reservations about his proposal to marshal his talents into productive labor troubled him. In the end his decision to embark on a prolonged educational mission reveals a resolve that would lead him to the height of his profession in the following decades. His senior colleagues at Princeton supported Hodge's educational enrichment as important to the future of the seminary. Their encouragement, however, came with a significant caveat. They viewed study in the European milieu as potentially dangerous to both his orthodoxy and piety. Archibald Alexander wrote cautionary letters while Hodge was in Germany. He reminded his young charge in his letter of March 24, 1827 that "you breathe a poisoned atmosphere. If you lose the lively and deep impression of divine truth—if you fall into skepticism or even into coldness, you will lose more than you gain from all the German professors and libraries."[4] Samuel Miller voiced similar concerns. In addition, however, he vented impatience with Hodge's confessed inadequacy born of his sensitivity to his mother's criticism and moments of less-than-perfect performance in the classroom. Miller mingled encouragement and rebuke in his letter of July 21, 1827. As Hodge's elder, he began by building up the junior professor: "I do not believe, my dear colleague, that you appreciate as you ought your importance and acceptance in our Institution." He nevertheless chastened Hodge for thinking himself unqualified to teach: "I know that your mind was often much oppressed by a sense of your own want of adequate qualification, and I was willing and even desirous that you should visit Europe if it were for nothing else than to get cured of this inordinate and morbid impression. But pray come back as soon as you can . . . We greatly desire and need your presence." Though written to Hodge near the end of his stay in Europe, these letters indicate both the encouragement and the caution that accompanied him when he set sail in 1826.[5]

Despite his self-deprecating remarks, Hodge did not embark on this endeavor totally unprepared. Fortified by rigorous confessionalist catechesis internalized by pervasive New Side habits, Hodge possessed qualities that would serve him well, however difficult or hostile the foreign environment. His upbringing by his mother and pastor resulted in a disciplined yet sensitive intellectual and moral stamina. While by later standards weaknesses existed in his schooling, he had unquestionably excelled in his undergraduate and seminary educations. The salient principles of Reformed faith permeated his worldview, yet his convictions did not prevent him from familiarizing himself with ideas and perspectives different from his own. He had absorbed the cultural milieu of Philadelphia, itinerated in Virginia with Alexander to observe the state of the Presbyterian churches outside his immediate surroundings, and conversed comfortably among the cognoscenti of New England and even published articles of foreign scholarship.

He also took with him the accumulated wisdom of his previous studies. Hodge consistently paid homage to Alexander as his father in the faith and attributed to his instruction the intricacies of Reformed theology and the principles of Scottish philosophy. But he was also indebted to Samuel Miller. For three years he sat under Miller's tutelage, and for another four years he served as his colleague on the faculty. Miller illustrated Princeton's recurring concern that pastors be informed of the intellectual and cultural landscape beyond the seminary's curricular offerings. Thus Hodge was apprised of the broad trajectory of Western thought primarily by Miller's *Retrospect of the Eighteenth Century* (1803). In this work Miller provided a comprehensive "Princeton-looks-at-the-world" perspective by bringing a vast array of topics under his critical analysis—philosophy, science, medicine, geography, visual arts, literature, biography, journals, and education. In many respects Miller's *Retrospect* would serve as a model for how the young Hodge would also leave no cultural phenomenon unexamined in his editorship of the *PR* after his return from the Continent. The inclusive scope of Miller's work also stimulated Hodge's native curiosity that impelled him to take in as many facets of European life as possible during his two-year visit. Fortified by such various influences, he would exploit every opportunity afforded him while in Europe to further his knowledge of the world.[6]

9

Maintaining Family Connections

Charles Hodge departed for Europe in October 1826. Charles and Sarah had initially considered taking the trip as a family. Financial constraints, however, led to Sarah's remaining behind with their two children, Alexander (A. A.) and Mary, in the care of his mother in Philadelphia. The rent he received for his home during his absence paid Nevin's salary. During the early days of Hodge's absence, the couple discussed in their letters the feasibility of the family's joining Charles when he became settled in his routine. But the difficulty of Sarah and the children's undertaking a voyage unaccompanied and the interruptions that their presence would occasion to Hodge's study led them to abandon such notions.[1]

Charles and Sarah continued the Hodge tradition of extensive correspondence during their two-year separation. In addition to writing to his wife, mother, brother, and faculty colleagues, Charles, the compulsive recordkeeper, kept detailed notes of every phase of the voyage. He noted the longitude and latitude of each day's sailing, the countries they passed, and the prevailing weather and its effects on the passengers. A gale of several days slowed their progress and made navigating the deck next to impossible. Almost all passengers succumbed to seasickness. Although Hodge experienced nausea and headaches, he never lost a meal, but listlessness rendered him incapable of either studying or even conversing with others. He narrated to his wife their passing an upturned boat that showed no signs of surviving crew members, who had either perished in the sea or been "taken to their boats." On the first Sunday in the voyage, he preached to all English-speaking passengers, though he lamented that the majority did not give "the slightest indication that it was the day of God." Shades of his earlier missionary work![2]

The contents of Charles and Sarah's correspondence reveal their ardent affection for each other and the preeminent place of family in their lives. A. A. Hodge refers occasionally in *LCH* to the familial ties that bound all members. A survey of letters not included in that volume abundantly substantiates his claim. The opening and closing words—passages that any husband or wife would savor by reading and rereading while waiting for the next letter—gave full expression to feelings they had for each other. In his first letter, Hodge commented that no women or children were on board to remind him of his wife: "If you were with me my heavy heart would be light." Expressing his affection and piety but forgetting the difference in time zones that would separate them in days ahead, he proposed a means of maintaining connection with each other: "Dearest we can meet at the throne of God—meet me there at 10, at 1 and 9 o'clock if only for a few minutes or only in heart, every day."[3] A few days later he wrote, "My eye is not always dry when it turns westward. Keep yourself occupied and keep your heart my dear Sarah in the work of God and you will be happy. Tho your husband be thousands of miles from you, I hope you remember our appointments."[4] Hodge's love for details led him to urge Sarah to be more specific in her letters to him: "I wish my dear that you would be more particular in telling me your feelings, whether you are happy and contented, you may suppose that this is a subject on which I feel deeply anxious and upon which you may not enter too much into detail . . . A record of every work & look & action I could read & read again & again with ceaseless pleasure."[5]

Both Charles and Sarah devoted extended paragraphs to their children. In his first letter, Hodge commented on the value of keepsakes in his possession: "I have a lock of your hair and one of dear Alexander's but none of sweet Mary. I would be exceedingly gratified to be able to receive one of her little curls."[6] Sarah habitually commented on details of the children's lives that would endear them to their father. On October 12 she penned, "AA is a very good child, as amiable as he can be and today mastered some of the sounds. 'Don't you want me to write now, Mother, to dear Father?'" Two weeks later she wrote, "I wish I could share with you the comfort of our sweet dear children that I could waft to you some of the silver sounds that so constantly salute my ears and some of the cherub kisses that so frequently find their way to my lips. AAH has just sent you a kiss on the spot on which his name is written."[7] A circle on the page marked the spot where Alexander had kissed the paper. The pages of some letters separated at the seams where they were folded because Hodge opened and closed them so many times after he received them. The affection with which Sarah expressed herself and portrayed the children and their home life in his absence led Charles to fulfill his promise to submerge himself in her letters.[8]

Hodge's intense interest in and attention to his children not only emerged in this early correspondence but resurfaced in later sections of *LCH*. His son describes how his father facilitated contacts with his children on an everyday basis in the construction of the study in his home. One door opened to the outside where seminary students could enter. But another interior door to the rest of the home had no latch but only springs. Thus even the smallest members of the family always had easy access to their father. Children remembered hearing their father sing hymns as he paced in his study and family worship in which everyone gathered about their father.[9]

In addition to numerous letters, Hodge kept a journal of his entire trip. Taken together, they reveal the utter devotion to detail that characterized Hodge's life.[10] Attentive to every detail, he committed his observations to writing. The peculiarities of people and the landscape in which they lived and labored, local customs and traditions, cost of goods and services, his daily routines, subjects of conversation, political events, architectural design, historical data—all are duly recorded. The letters bulge with tidbits of information filtered through his American Presbyterian eyes. Since he wrote to so many people, the wonder is that so little is repeated. Recipients would circulate his epistles so that he would not have to reiterate his happenings and observations.[11]

His Parisian sojourn extended to mid-February 1827, during which time he learned French rapidly and took up Arabic and Syriac in a class of eight taught by Sylvestre de Sacy. Long given to daily routine, Hodge wrote to his wife, "I rise about eight, at which hour I have my French teacher to attend on Tuesday, Thursday and Saturday. On other days he comes at two o'clock. I read and study until half past ten, when I go to breakfast. I then return to my room, and remain until half past three, when I go three times in the week to my Arabic teacher. At five I go to dinner. . . . The evening is almost always spent at home reading and studying until twelve, when I go to bed. When I go out it is generally from ten to two." Hodge's diligence in learning French led him to practice by writing large portions of his letters in French to Sarah: "I suspect my love you wish I had some other way of learning French than by worrying you with my rude essays. But I think I deserve credit, considering how lazy I am that I am willing to take so much trouble & it is this or nothing, for I have neither the time nor the patience to write for writings sake."[12]

Among his first impressions of Europe was the thoroughness of religious education among young people that rivaled even his catechetical experience. In Paris he was captivated as he listened to two hundred boys reciting their prayers and other religious lessons to their priests: "I have never in any Sabbath-school, nor in any Protestant church in our own country heard children recite so well. They appeared to have got their tasks perfectly, and repeated them with wonderful volubility. The priest appeared to take a great deal of pains in instructing them, explaining and enforcing what had been recited . . . It is no wonder that the Catholic religion takes so firm a hold of its votaries, since it is so faithfully instilled into the minds of the young. I fear that in this respect Protestants are not as assiduous."[13]

Ever curious about matters lying outside his immediate disciplines, Hodge attended meetings of the Asiatic Society, at which members read and discussed papers of a literary and scientific nature. He immersed himself not only in language studies but also in French culture—the Louvre, the Luxembourg, and the king's library. He attended High Mass in the Tuileries and later at Notre Dame. He regarded many of these instances as pomp of church and state designed to make the Catholic faith imposing to the French people. In general, he found little in these services that was "at all adapted to make any man either wiser or better."[14] Wherever Hodge went, not only in Europe but also at home, he managed to observe and in many instances contact public figures or people in the upper social strata. He witnessed the royal family dining in public—King Charles X and his officers, including Talleyrand. Bearing a letter introducing him to General Lafayette, Hodge attempted unsuccessfully to visit him several times. The general and several of his daughters and granddaughters, however, attended an English church where Hodge preached. As a result, Lafayette entertained Hodge and the German naturalist and explorer Baron Alexander von Humboldt at his home. Humboldt kindly offered to write letters of introduction to prominent German men, a favor that the young American quickly accepted.[15]

While not as momentous as what would follow in Germany, Hodge accomplished much in his Parisian surroundings. He acclimated himself to an alien culture, adapted his predisposition to orderly routines, preached several times with members of Lafayette's family in attendance, and met another American professor who like Hodge was visiting France to study the Oriental languages. What lay ahead in Germany would surpass all that he experienced in Paris.

10

Student, Conversationalist, Cultural and Ecclesiastical Observer

Charles Hodge left Paris on February 15 for Germany. He originally planned to study at Göttingen, but a letter from Edward Robinson of Andover, whom Hodge had met during his visit to New England, noted the loss of Göttingen's best faculty and persuaded Hodge that the University of Halle would prove much more productive for his needs. Uppermost in Hodge's consideration was the presence of August Tholuck—young, gifted, and, perhaps most significant, orthodox in his theology and pious in his manner of life. Robinson's proposal could not have been more propitious. It resulted in countless hours of social contact and lengthy conversation exploring mutual interests and eventually a longtime friendship. Hodge wrote to Sarah on March 11 in glowing terms of his respect for Tholuck: "I walk [with him] three or four times a week for an hour or two. . . . He has been also kind enough to call two or three times and read German with me. Being a young man and a pious one, and being very fond of exercising himself in English, which is one of the fifteen languages he understands, he puts us [others whom he taught] entirely on a level with himself, and is very instructive. I look at him frequently with wonder. Not older than I, he is the author of some of the best Biblical works in Germany, and has a fund of knowledge which few men attain at the end of the longest life."[1]

As Hodge began in Halle, his first order of business was to master German sufficiently to make his study worthwhile. Because learning German proved more difficult than French, Hodge struggled to attain proficiency in the language so that he could attend lectures. His journal entry for March 12 reads: "Spent mostly at home alone pursuing the dull task of learning German." Then he adds, "Heard Wegscheider in the morning and Gesenius in the afternoon." Thus he had made enough progress in a month since his arrival to benefit from lectures. In addition to Tholuck, Hodge met Augustus Neander and Friedrich Schleiermacher, with whom he would have subsequent contact in Berlin. Despite his difficulty with German, he acknowledged that the German method of teaching language was superior to the American. Upon reading Tholuck's *Encyclopedia of Theology*, Hodge reflected on the advantages and disadvantages of the catechetical versus the lecture mode of instruction. The former fully engaged the learner's attention and allowed the teacher to adapt to the student's capacity to learn. It also enabled the teacher to be satisfied that the student has fully understood material by correcting misapprehensions through probing questions. On the other hand, Hodge also admitted that lectures offered the advantage of imparting more information than recitation, and they enabled the teacher to explore first principles and offer students a general view of the subject. Lectures facilitated a habit of reflection when the mind was fully awakened. Upon his return to Princeton, Hodge would continue the Princeton method of teaching by combining both recitation and lecture in the classroom.[2]

His relation with Tholuck bloomed immediately as Hodge attended his lectures and the two engaged in frequent conversation. Tholuck proved not only a congenial teacher, but a unique gateway to the

German scholarly community. He ranked foremost among theologians who mediated between the diminishing number of orthodox theologians and biblical scholars and the burgeoning cadre of liberal scholars. Tholuck's lectures and their extensive conversations proved invaluable to Hodge. Although they largely resonated with Hodge's views, especially on the necessity of piety in the Christian life, they also posed a challenge to Hodge. Tholuck had forged his evangelical views in the crucible of the German intellectual milieu permeated with philosophical and theological perspectives that at points diverged sharply from Hodge's Reformed confessionalism and Common Sense Realism philosophy.[3] Thus, while Hodge felt comfortable as they probed their differences, he gained experience in dialoguing with those whose views were informed by ideas other than his Calvinist tradition. Their almost daily encounters prepared Hodge for his various roles as teacher, author, and denominational leader on the American scene long after he returned from Europe.[4]

Hodge took copious notes on Tholuck's lectures and writings. Whether the subject was modern theology, theological method, church history, or practical religion, Hodge found Tholuck's ideas largely congruent with his own. On the history of theology, Tholuck confirmed Princeton's interpretation of modernity. He criticized modern theology classes in the university as totally devoid of exegesis and deficient in ecclesiastical history. Tholuck characterized German sermons as "uninteresting grammatical remarks upon the text or childish playing on words." Pietists, on the other hand, received high praise for their resistance to clergy who "were ashamed to condescend to the humble duty of catechetical instruction." In his lectures Tholuck heralded Philipp Jacob Spener, author of the manifesto *Pia Desideria*, for launching the pietist reaction against Lutheran scholasticism and inducing the Prussian Elector to require exegetical lectures in universities. In his lecture "Conflict of Faith with Infidelity," Tholuck subjected Enlightenment deism to trenchant critique, especially deists' contention about the origin of natural religion. To their claim that deistic tenets rose de novo from autonomous natural reason, he countered that they blatantly borrowed from the Christian past: "Were it not for what [deism] derives from history it would be nothing. It is ungrateful to Christianity to which it is indebted for all its clearness and stability. Deism presents itself in opposition to revelation. It pretends to be a system which can qualify itself at the bar of truth . . . It will admit only what it can by argument establish. In this light it is a system utterly unsatisfactory." Tholuck also claimed that England's Lord Herbert of Cherbury's five truths of natural religion in *De Veritate* were greatly indebted to Christianity. Such themes clearly appealed to Hodge; they resonated with Princeton's charter to make refutation of deism a primary goal of the seminary curriculum.[5]

In a lecture on the history of theology, Tholuck contrasted pantheism and deism and the emergence of pantheism as the reigning philosophy. Tholuck contended, "In no land has it so thoroughly pervaded every department of society as in some parts of Germany." Whereas in other lands clergy "stood as watchers and guardians against the attacks, despisers of religion in Berlin [as Friedrich Schleiermacher characterized Romantics in his *Speeches on Religion to Its Cultured Despisers*] translated freethinking works from England." Tholuck, however, moderated his criticism by conceding that Schleiermacher's *Speeches on Religion* was "the most profound refutation of deism ever written." It attacked rationalism at its foundation by contending that religion pertains not primarily to the intellect but to the feelings. In later conversation Tholuck also credited Schleiermacher's ideas with producing much good because of the "respect which he manifests for the Bible, and the reverence with which he speaks of Jesus Christ." Tholuck thus attributed much good to Schleiermacher's influence because of his emphasis on "deep religious feeling."[6]

Tholuck thus provided an invaluable service by interpreting the contemporary intellectual landscape of Europe. Hodge hung on every word as they discussed which systems prevailed and whose ideas most influenced philosophy and theology. In two journal entries Hodge attempted to digest Tholuck's report. Not only did Hodge delight in hearing that Kantianism had been universally abandoned, but he also learned that Immanuel Kant's successors—Johann Gottlieb Fichte and Friedrich Wilhelm Joseph Schelling—had faded, to be replaced by two versions of pantheism: the philosophical system of G. W. F. Hegel and the theological system of Schleiermacher, both of the University of Berlin. He wrote the following as a summary of their views in his journal: "The present systems are all Pantheistic. Hegel and Schleiermacher both deny the personality of the Deity and the individuality of the soul of man. The universal principle with them is God, and, according to Hegel, the world itself is the Realitat of the Deity, and all it contains, the different races of men and the animals in their various orders, are all modes of existence of this one universal principle." On the other hand, Tholuck reminded Hodge that Schleiermacher "would not admit the appellation of Pantheist," which he reserved for "the materialistic Pantheists." Not only did Tholuck profess himself deeply affected by Schleiermacher, so did Neander. Hodge, however, expressed utter frustration in comprehending their systems: "This, at least, is the idea I got from Tholuck's description. For I do not pretend to understand a system which its author says is comprehended only by two theologians in Germany." On another occasion Tholuck read a passage from Schleiermacher's *Dogmatik* that only further confused Hodge. He lamented that the speculative spirit exercised considerable influence over biblical theologians so that "it seems impossible they should be restrained within the bounds of sober and important truth, except by the influence of religion on their hearts."[7]

Of all the subjects Hodge discussed in his European journal, pantheism stands out as the one that he had most difficulty in comprehending and the one broached most repeatedly in conversations with his hosts. He did so because while his closest associates criticized it for its deleterious effects on German religion and philosophy, he also noted that Neander and Tholuck themselves admitted to its impinging on their own ideas. In a long conversation on April 6, Neander denounced the speculation of German philosophers' "making themselves God, or reducing God to an idea." Hodge immediately asked about similar notions passing into evangelical writings, specifically the idea that "alles Seyn ist das Seyn Gottes [all being is a being in God]." Neander retorted, "By no means—all that was meant by that phrase is that God is the only real independent substance, and that all other existences are grounded in a mysterious way in Him. This . . . was contained in the idea of the omnipotence of God, and in the declaration of Paul that 'in Him we live, and move, and have our being.' "[8]

Tholuck's comments about the demise of Kantianism and the subsequent ascendancy of pantheism may explain why Hodge never explored Kant's theology in greater detail in his later writings. Only seven references, for example, mention Kant's thought in the index to Hodge's *ST*, and none mention his definitive work on religion, *RWLRA* (1791). Hodge thereby missed an opportunity to contrast his view of religion (evangelical piety combined with confessionalism) with Kant's primary contribution to German deism, which reduced Christianity to a rationalistic moralism. Hodge, following the Princeton model, placed a premium on Reformed theology's doctrines of grace (original sin, Christ's atoning sacrifice on the cross, and justification by faith) and the means of grace in living out the Christian life (communal and individual worship/devotion, prayer, Scripture reading, and the sacraments). In sharpest possible contrast, Kant dismissed the fall as unhistorical, repudiated substitutionary atonement as grossly immoral, and labeled justification by faith as being harmful to religion. According to Kant, these doctrines relieved people of the responsibility of living moral lives for themselves. Kant also dismissed traditional means of grace as utterly alien to rational religion, which consisted of moral activity. Not only were acts of traditional piety not genuinely religious (he labeled them "pseudo service," "superstitious illusions," and "fetishism"), he claimed that traditional religions of worship were nothing short of magical attempts to manipulate God by substituting acts that were not genuinely religious (devotional acts) for what is (moral behavior, which alone makes a person good). Hodge's omission of a detailed analysis of Kantianism represents a missed opportunity in his mature writings to identify the primary thinker in the modern period whose philosophy powerfully influenced the modern cast of Western thought.[9]

While in Halle, Hodge worshiped in various churches, and as in his earlier diary on his preaching in Philadelphia, he focused on the content of the service and its effects on other participants or himself personally. Upon hearing "a real evangelical sermon" by a Rev. B. Kurtz on April 1, he exulted, "My heart overflowed with joy. . . . It has been long since I have enjoyed so much pleasure in hearing a sermon. For here there are few who appear to feel the Spirit of the gospel." On the following Sunday, he attended a Lutheran service in the afternoon during which fifty to a hundred children were confirmed. Worship included half an hour of catechetical exercise, a sermon expounding the principal doctrines of the Bible, a reading of the Apostles' Creed, and a blessing by a Superintendent Tiemann on the children. Hodge's comments on the service replicated his remarks about the catechesis he had witnessed in Paris and reflected again his advocacy of religious instruction: "The impression which this whole service made upon my mind was very pleasant. And I could not help feeling that however little authority there may be for confirmation, as of divine appointment, that some service of the kind might properly be introduced into our churches. It would have at least this good effect, that baptized persons would then be brought more under the discipline of the church, and the nature of their connection with it would be rendered more definite."[10]

On several occasions he complained of not hearing "what we in America call a good doctrinal sermon." Most sermons he described as "hortatory," although he noted his approval when he heard sermons that were "pious and animated." At the opposite extreme, he lamented that a party of Reformed German believers carried their belief in predestination into practical antinomianism: "These people feel themselves above the gospel and all its ordinances, and when they condescend to enter a church it is easy to see from their listless, careless, assured manner, that they think the doctrines which they hear are only fit for babes." Upon attending a Lutheran celebration of the Lord's Supper, Hodge noted how clergy chanting the consecration service, placing wafers, and offering wine without recipients' touching the elements resembled Catholic liturgical practice. Hodge lamented, "I felt like a stranger here, and longed for the time when again, in the simple Scriptural manner of our church, I could partake of the memorials of our dying Saviour's love."[11]

He expressed general appreciation for what he observed in Halle: "From all I could see and hear, I should judge that the spirit of pure and simple piety is preserved in a high degree among these people, and the superior comfort and intelligence of the inhabitants was very striking." Throughout the journal Hodge interjected his New Side interest in the prevalence of religion or piety among the various places he visited, churches where he worshiped, or groups that he encountered.

He narrated whenever possible how individuals he met—especially scholars—had been converted from the reigning rationalism or pantheism. Reference to conversion or radical change in philosophical or theological perspective became the primary means by which Hodge expressed his positive assessment of an individual. Reflecting his interest in conversions, Hodge expressed special pleasure in detailing how academic acquaintances such as Tholuck, Neander, and Hengstenberg had come to evangelical faith.[12]

Hodge trusted Tholuck as his interpreter of the German intellectual and theological milieu. He dutifully recorded his mentor's assessment of the history of theology, the principal strengths and weaknesses of old and new systems, and their many conversations covering a wide range of topics in theology, philosophy, and culture. That did not mean, however, that the two agreed on all matters. When he read Tholuck's views on Romans 5:12ff.—Hodge's litmus test on the fall in Genesis 3 and its effects on the human race—he wrote, "Sorry to see that his view of 5:12 did not coincide with my own." He expressed his most blunt negative judgment of Tholuck's epistemology by writing, "One very important principle of Tholuck's whole system seems to be entirely false. He appears to make what the Germans call *Anschaaung*, the test of all truth respecting invisible things, that is the ability of forming a distinct image of the subject before the mind. This they call intuition, and when they cannot have such an *Anschaaung* of any subject they cannot feel its truth. But as I said to Tholuck, it is utterly impossible to form such a *bild*, or image of the soul, or of God, or of any spiritual subject. But he maintained that all clear ideas of these subjects assume this form, and that this is the test of the correctness of these ideas." Their exchange of ideas reflects significant differences between their respective epistemological premises. Hodge and the vast majority of other Americans in the early nineteenth century judged all knowledge using Scottish Common Sense Realism and Baconian induction, which prized the reliability of reason and empirical induction over intuition as sources of knowledge.[13] While not divulging his own ontological and epistemological premises, Hodge reported an extended argument in which Tholuck and a colleague held that "everything in nature had *Bewusstseyn*, a consciousness, a sense of life—trees, stones, everything that exists." Hodge recorded his explanation for Tholuck's holding such a view: "The arguments for this opinion were mostly drawn from general pantheistic principles. For although these gentlemen abhor Pantheism, they have, as far as their philosophy is concerned, many principles in common with it." Tholuck even admitted to Hodge specific ways in which Schleiermacher had influenced his thinking.[14]

During his stay in Halle, Hodge also confronted, as he had expected, scholarship that departed from traditional orthodoxy. The clear division that existed in Germany between those who retained orthodox views and proponents of new ideas manifested itself in hostile attitudes on both sides. Traditionalists expressed disdain for theological novelty, and in return innovators viewed all orthodoxy with contempt. Tholuck related the animus that he experienced from the "enemies of piety." Opponents spread false reports about him, which reflected what the Germans called *Kleinstadtigkeit*, "little-cityism." Such pettiness led to Tholuck's being disparaged because he continued to hold views that critics considered outmoded in light of Enlightenment thinking. Of course, Hodge evaluated what he read and heard according to whether it conformed to Reformed theology. Of the theological lecturers he heard, he found Gesenius "by far the ablest," yet also "doing the most harm."[15] Gesenius did so by going beyond examining and exegeting the text. He remained indifferent to doctrinal implications of the text: "He says a book is genuine or not, without caring in the least whether it pleases one party or the other [liberals or conservatives]. And this increases his influence as it gives him the appearance of impartiality." Hodge and his Princeton colleagues addressed lower critical matters, but they suspected higher critics of imposing an alien worldview when they interpreted the text. Whereas Gesenius viewed criticism as an end in itself, Hodge believed that biblical criticism served a higher end of providing the content for theological formulation. Princetonians mined biblical texts for their orthodox doctrinal content.

Gesenius attracted over three hundred students to his lectures on Job, which he delivered in a clear, animated manner. Hodge also attended lectures on the Acts of the Apostles given by Julius Wegscheider, professor of theology at the University of Halle. He particularly noted Wegscheider's dismissive statement that Paul's holding to the

Calvinist doctrine of predestination is "proof of the little dependence we can place on that Apostle." Incidents such as these reminded Hodge of his mentors' warnings that exposure to hostile scholarly opinion posed a danger to his orthodoxy. But he did not experience the full thrust of that assault until his studies at the University of Berlin.[16]

Hodge also made several cultural excursions to neighboring cities while he studied at Halle. After visiting a gallery of paintings in Dresden, he commented on several artists. *The Holy Night* by Antonio da Correggio made only a negative impression on him: "I can conceive that an artist can take pleasure in discovering the beauties of the proper distribution of light, which proceeds from the infant Saviour, but this is all little adapted to the untutored eye, as the intricate harmony of sound to the untutored ear. The figures in this piece have no individual beauty." Of Peter Paul Rubens's works he commented, "The coloring is indeed surprising, but the effect, for me, seldom either strong or pleasing." On the other hand, Hodge extolled the Christ child in Raphael's Madonna as "wonderful." He thought Raphael's depiction of the Virgin reflected "what the human frame may be when this corruption has put on incorruption, and this mortal is clothed with immortality." While he admitted that he viewed the paintings with an untrained eye, he found that repeated visits to the gallery changed his views. He added, "But on every visit I was attracted and held bound by Raphael's Madonna."[17]

Halle, therefore, served as Hodge's entryway into German culture. Considering his age, it was no mean accomplishment to launch into a foreign culture and intellectual environment at the highest level and succeed in extracting benefits. As was his habit throughout life, Hodge made the most of his opportunities. The very antithesis of an intellectual recluse, he learned a foreign language on the run. He possessed the enormous advantage of an extraordinary native curiosity and of finding almost immediately a like-minded and affable individual in Tholuck, who shared a stout intellect and willingness to initiate a friendship that would continue not only as Hodge moved to Berlin but for decades to come.

11

Berlin—The Reigning Center of Nineteenth-Century German Culture

After seven months, Charles Hodge left Halle in October 1827 to complete his studies in Berlin. On his way through Wittenberg, he visited a seminary and attended the church where Martin Luther had preached and where the Reformer and his associate Philipp Melanchthon were buried. Hodge arrived in Berlin on October 12 and began an intense period of study under some of the most productive minds in Germany's nationalistic resurgence after the setbacks of the Napoleonic era. He listened in the lecture halls and conversed outside with scholars from a wide range of academic disciplines. He heard Franz Bopp, specialist in Indo-European languages, Karl Lachmann on Hebrew, Karl Ritter on ancient geography, and Alexander von Humboldt on physical geography. Humboldt's lectures were so popular that students had to apply a month before the lectures began in order to attend them.[1]

Again he benefited from the company of August Tholuck, who was visiting there and introduced him to still another community of like-minded Christians with whom Hodge would associate for the next six months. This circle included legal officials, military officers, theologians, preachers, and various political figures. The younger Hodge would use Johann Friedrich Bachmann's biography of Ernst Wilhelm Hengstenberg to characterize his father's association with this group. They illustrated a remarkable evangelical catholicity that prevailed in various parts of Europe beginning in 1823 when small "circles" met for times of fellowship. Tholuck summarized the motivating force of these evangelical groups as one in which "consciousness of that which unites the Church of Christ far out-weighed the consciousness of that which divides it." The younger Hodge explained this pietism as one in which "confessional differences constituted no barrier to the communion in love and work for the kingdom of God; in the joy and custom of what is common, the ideas of a union of believers out of all churches could arise." Bachmann called this phenomenon "the new pietism." Its members represented Lutheran, Reformed, and Catholic churches. The "old pietism" of Philipp Jacob Spener and August Hermann Francke stood against the lifeless Lutheran state church. It manifested a sectarian tendency by separating from traditional public worship services into smaller circles of fellowship. The new pietism, on the other hand, opposed rationalistic distortions of doctrine within the church itself as being carried out by the rising German liberalism but fully supported traditional public worship. In addition to their appointed hours of corporate worship, these groups met for fellowship on Sundays and weekdays. Hodge cites Bachmann's summary: "The pietism of the revival times had not, like the old, orthodoxy as its opposite, but it carried orthodoxy in its bosom."[2]

Thus, when Hodge settled into a new routine of study in Berlin, he did so in the company of newfound friends who shared his evangelical piety, if not the details of Reformed doctrine. Their bond of unity consisted primarily in affirming evangelical religious experience and their opposition to the corruption of doctrine due to rationalist influences.

His closest friends in addition to Tholuck were Ludwig von Gerlach, conservative judge and politician, and his brother Otto, pastor of the Church of St. Elizabeth, and Augustus Neander, a converted Jew, student of Friedrich Schleiermacher, prominent church historian, and like Tholuck among those called mediating theologians between orthodox and liberal views.[3]

Hodge's journal also contains detailed observations on the state of religion in Germany. Wherever he visited, he commented on the presence or absence of evangelical piety among the people. Virtually every Lord's Day entry recorded where he worshiped, who preached, and the content of the sermon. Invariably he commented on the form of worship or whether the sermon was evangelical or not. After hearing fellow American Rev. B. Kurtz in Halle, for example, Hodge warmly pronounced his message "a real evangelical sermon on Eph. iii.19." His most negative comments describe his visit to Jena, where Napoleon defeated the Prussian army in 1806: "I heard two miserably cold antichristian sermons: the one delivered in the University Church, was by a young man without a trace of *Christian* character in his discourse, and was intended for the students, of whom I saw only one present. I have nowhere else been so strongly impressed with the total absence of religion. I am told that the students boast of the fact that they have nothing of fanaticism among them. Fighting duels seems to be as common here as ever."[4]

Several journal entries describe revivals that occurred during his visit. Because of his New Side proclivities, Hodge reported such events with unabated enthusiasm because they contrasted with the predominant religious practice in Germany. On December 27, while having tea with a Lieutenant von Senfft, he learned of a revival of religion in a village in Silesia in which about "thirty persons of all ages . . . were converted to the Lord, and were living in the faith and love of the gospel. From this village the fire spread to others in the neighborhood." Later entries on a revival in Pomerania not only include more details but draw a comparison between "great revivals which have occurred in Germany of late" and those circulating "in the south and west of our country" (the outbreaks of the Second Great Awakening in Kentucky in 1801). Most interesting are the spiritual and physical manifestations he reported and changes that his son made when recording them in *LCH*. The entry for Sunday, December 30 included the following (wording of the account in *LCH* appears in brackets):

> In Pomerania, cases of what were called demoniacal possession occurred. A young woman was often thrown into the greatest bodily agitation, rolling over and over, and her mind subsequently thrown into a state resembling the heathen ecstasy, in which she would prophesy (in what sense of that word I know not). These [were] appeared to be as it were only transient seasons; for the rest she appeared to be a true, humble Christian. There extraordinary appearances soon ceased. It is certainly remarkable that on both sides of the Atlantic, seasons of religious excitement should be attended by such similar outward appearances [disturbances]—whether the people under such influences in our country said that they saw visions or not I do not know—it was the case here. Is it any thing like that of the N.T.? [*LCH* ends with "disturbances."][5]

Hodge's recounting of the Pomeranian revivals—to say nothing of his son's alteration of the journal!—reflects his struggle to comprehend the reality and validity of phenomena associated with New Side religious categories. A. A. Hodge's substitution of "were" for "appeared to be as it were" and "disturbances" for "appearances," and omission of his father's query whether they were of the same nature as events recorded in the Gospels and Acts, speak volumes of how Princetonians would evaluate similar reports in American revivalism. Whatever might be the case when he returned to America and wrote about the theology and experiential nature of the First and Second Great Awakenings, Hodge's journal expresses a favorable view of the revivals because they stood in stark contrast to the prevailing German religious milieu. However much he would later cast such phenomena in negative terms, as indicated by the way in which his son changed the record in *LCH* lest readers get the wrong impression of his father's estimation of bizarre experiences, while in Europe Hodge demonstrated at least a willingness to consider the validity of the reports.[6]

The same ambiguity about revival phenomena surfaces in the March 12 entry when Hodge learned that the Pomeranian revival had continued with similar reports of extraordinary experiences among participants: "[Revival] has broken out anew. Eight hundred often assemble. . . . Much that is disorderly and much that is very remarkable has occurred—visions, prophetic powers, possessions, etc.—as might have been expected among a people so little cultivated, and in a state of so much excitement. With these two gentlemen [those who reported the revival] I was exceedingly pleased. They had the same fervent freshness of feeling which men active in revivals most commonly have among us. Before the evening was over they proposed singing and prayer." As evidence of how revivals were being received in Germany, Hodge reported instances in which ecclesiastical and civil authorities opposed such outbreaks of revivalism. In his entry for December 6, 1827, he reports that Pomeranian officials under the influence of "rationalists" issued an order to disperse assemblies gathered for revival. Only after appealing to higher authority was persecution avoided. "This is not the first instance I have been informed of, in which the king and members of his family have shielded true Christians from the oppressions of the civil and ecclesiastical authorities." On January 18, 1828, he states that a "Mr. Ancillon, one of the Councillors of State spoke very severely against devotional meetings, and thought that all religious meetings out of the Church should be forbidden. His reason was that those assembled could talk of politics." Hodge and his colleagues who shared pietist sympathies found such reports of revivals an encouraging breath of fresh air in the midst of the new perspectives on Christianity emerging in Germany. As important as these reports of the variety of religious manifestations in Germany were, the most significant of Hodge's experiences in Europe was of a new perspective in theological education. To that we turn in the next chapter.[7]

12

A New Model in Theological Education

In Berlin, Charles Hodge found himself in the midst of a crucible. On the one hand, letters from Princeton colleagues reminded him of his obligation to maintain his religious heritage. Echoing the letter referred to earlier in chapter 8, Archibald Alexander used almost identical language in cautioning Hodge in the latter stages of his European sojourn of the dangers of imbibing too much German thinking. On July 27 he wrote, "The air which you breathe in Germany will either have a deleterious effect on your moral constitution, or else by the strength of faith required to resist its effects your spiritual health will be confirmed. I pray God to keep you from the poison of *Neology*! I wish you to come home enriched with Biblical learning, but abhorring German philosophy and theology. I have been paying some attention to Kant's philosophy, but it confounds and astonishes me." By this and similar warnings, Alexander reminded Hodge of his theological roots and the traditions that Princetonians wished to uphold in the Athens model of seminary education.[1]

Despite instances to the contrary, Hodge found much in Germany that reinforced his worldview. Intellectually the camaraderie developed through extended conversations with August Tholuck and Augustus Neander proved stimulating and stretched him as he occasionally stood by himself as they debated points of theology and church polity. New Year's Eve 1827 found Hodge and his friends discussing a wide range of topics—high-church principles and religious freedom, the influence of Catholicism on the Continent, and inspiration of the Scripture. The ultimate debate, however, erupted over predestination. Hodge found himself alone among all participants when he defended Calvinist views. Neander contended that predestination entailed a "dangerous tendency" to make God the author of sin. He admitted that "it is entirely of grace, that men are brought to faith and salvation. But it lies with every man, either to accept or reject this grace." Tholuck added, and they all agreed, that a mean was needed between Pelagian freedom of will and making God the author of sin. Neander further insisted that one can infer from the full contents of the Bible that those who have no exposure to the gospel in this life will receive an offer in the world to come. Both Tholuck and Neander also opined that since only the sin against the Holy Ghost is unforgivable, this implied that "sinners might be brought to faith in Christ after death." Although he did not record how he defended Calvinism, Hodge believed he won the respect of both men; he wrote in his journal that Neander affectionately took his hand and said to Tholuck, "Tell our friend Hodge, that though we dispute with him, we belong to the same Lord, and are one in heart."[2]

Although Hodge enjoyed intellectual and theological rapport with Tholuck and Neander, the scholar with whom he shared most in common theologically was Ernst Wilhelm Hengstenberg, Lutheran churchman and theologian. Overshadowed by his more famous colleagues Friedrich Schleiermacher and G. W. F. Hegel at the University of Berlin, Hengstenberg took defiant stances against his colleagues by defending the infallibility of the Bible and espousing traditional biblical themes. Converted from rationalism by Moravian pietists, Hengstenberg advocated the orthodoxy of the Augsburg Confession and championed a return to Lutheran confessionalism. Utilizing his expertise in the Old Testament, he defended traditional doctrines that liberals reinterpreted based on their radical biblical criticism. Like Hodge, he was young—about twenty-five at the time—and he founded a theological journal, *Evangelische Kirchenzeitung*, which became a venue for defending conservative views. He also authored monographs on theological and biblical topics. As evidence of his bold orthodoxy, he stated in one of his opening lectures at Berlin, "It matters not whether we make a god out of stone, or out of our own understanding, it is still a false god; there is but one living God, the God of the Bible." Hodge illustrated the contemporary strife between theological parties by adding, "This declaration was received with hissing and scraping [of feet] by a large part of the students, by which he was little intimidated." On a daily basis Hengstenberg faced a far more hostile audience than Hodge ever did at Princeton.[3]

Hengstenberg's rude reception highlighted the tension that conservatives faced in the European milieu and the differences between previous theological education and what emerged at Berlin. As evidence of a radical shift in content and goal of pastoral training, Hengstenberg surprised Hodge with his assertion that German clergy under the tutelage of liberalism received vastly different training at Berlin. The majority of pastors, Hengstenberg claimed, could not read the Greek Testament. This deficiency stood in sharp contrast with former practice, when "almost every preacher was in the habit of taking the original Scriptures in the pulpit and commenting on them more or less in every discourse." Such a defect in pastoral training added to what Hodge witnessed and heard about theological students and their education in Germany. He evaluated every report of theological learning in the light of the goals of Princeton's charter that espoused Reformed orthodoxy and evangelical piety as being of equal importance in pastoral education.[4]

As Hodge observed the diversity of theological opinions in Germany, he confronted the fundamental change in the goal of theological education. He ventured to Europe to engage with the best minds in his discipline. Hodge's astonishment at the preparation and practice of German pastors brings into focus perhaps the most significant impact of his European sojourn. He witnessed firsthand the radical differences between Princeton as an exemplar of the traditional Athens model of theological education in America and the new German model that emerged in the early nineteenth century. As mentioned in chapter 4, the Athens model stressed *paideia*, in which excellence in theological education entailed rigorous study of texts, which in turn resulted in students' knowing God and transforming their character by inculcating Christian virtues. Theological orthodoxy and evangelical piety went hand in hand. Conversion stood at the heart of ministerial training as appropriation of revealed wisdom resulted in holiness of living. Such a model conformed well with evangelical revivalism that not only fueled American religion as a whole but also shaped Hodge's New Side Presbyterianism. Hodge was a product of rigorous academic training in Reformed theology combined with pious religious experience. The most significant challenge under the *paideia* model entailed achieving a balance between maintaining a high level of intellectual rigor and a corresponding stress on piety. If the former dominated, education degenerated into merely imparting information; if the latter prevailed, theological education morphed into sentimentality.[5]

Over against *paideia* a radically new model of theological education appeared in the founding of the University of Berlin in 1810. Considerable dispute arose among its founders not only about how theology should be taught but whether theology ought to exist in the university curriculum at all. Such questions emerged because those who founded the university did so in a conscious effort to reform education utilizing the secular principles of the Enlightenment. Because of the radical shift in worldviews between premodern and modern perspectives, some academics believed that theology no longer belonged in the university curriculum. Training of ministers, therefore, would proceed within a radically new intellectual context and with a different goal in view. Berlin replaced Athens' *paideia* with two distinct and potentially disparate functions: "*Wissenschaft* or orderly, disciplined critical research" on the one hand and "professional" education for the ministry on the other. Such a paradigm shift signaled the emergence of scholarly research as virtually an end in itself instead of a means to shape the spiritual life of the student. The only degree that Berlin offered, for example, was the doctorate. Instead of studying texts that exemplified a received and authoritative body of truth, the new curriculum treated all knowledge not as something fixed and established but as in the process of being developed. The operative term describing *Wissenschaft* was *critical*. Authority as something absolute and unchanging gave way to authority as the product of continuing research. Scholars questioned or extended previously accepted norms or findings. Only what could be demonstrated using rigorous critical methods of Enlightenment thinking and then situated within the largest possible context of other similarly established relationships counted as knowledge. One of the authors of the charter of Berlin said that research universities "always treat knowledge as an as yet unresolved problem, and thus always stay at research."[6]

Such a method proved problematic for theology as "queen of the sciences." No longer could theology claim hegemony among the other disciplines; it had to establish its credentials even to remain at the table with other disciplines. Theology's very existence within the new paradigm of the research university was jeopardized. In Reformed theology, biblical and theological studies rested on revelation and were not subject to the strictures of the new scholarly methods. The modern intellectual milieu demanded academic freedom for the professoriat. Whereas pastors were morally bound to teach and defend their respective confessional standards, teachers in the university were not so bound. In fact, professors operating within totally different moral parameters were obligated to subject religion to rational criticism and follow their research wherever it led them regardless of its orthodoxy.[7]

Ironically, Schleiermacher played a major role in affirming theology's place in this new educational context.[8] As a founder of the University of Berlin, Schleiermacher had to defend theology's inclusion in the curriculum, for it was not immediately apparent that theology could be taught within such a radical paradigm shift. He did so by adding a second pole to theological training—it had to be "professional." While the *Wissenschaft* pole focused on rigorous academic research—biblical texts, worship practices, moral standards—the reason for studying them entailed not the goal of shaping the religious life but of preparing pastors as professionals, to be leaders of Christian communities. In this regard theological education should contribute sociologically by providing the cognitive foundation to meet the larger needs of German society. While theology did not technically meet the standards of "science" as conceived by the Enlightenment, it nevertheless offered in its intuitive experience a unique topic for examination using the disciplined method of *Wissenschaft*.[9]

Significant consequences followed from this paradigmatic shift in theological education. The Berlin model assigned a different role to theological faculty. Instead of being steeped in firmly established fields of theological and biblical tradition and modeling Christian virtues to their students, faculty must demonstrate facility in scholarly research. Kelsey summarizes the role of faculty: "[It] is not simply great learning in already established knowledge, but demonstrated capacity to engage in scholarly research; and it is not so much personal capacities to be midwife of others' coming to an understanding of God and of themselves in relation to God as it is the ability to cultivate capacities for scholarly research in others." The change from shaping pastors' lives by biblical and theological content to a research-oriented professionalization of the ministry represented a sharp departure that would significantly alter the Christian ministry as traditionally understood. The Athens model espoused by Hodge and his fellow Princetonians remained every bit as rigorous in scholarly demands as demanded by *Wissenschaft*. Theological education, however, must remain true to received biblical content. Princeton, therefore, differed radically when it came to the purpose of theological training. For Berlin, the goal was more sociological in nature. At Princeton, pastors were not trained for a sociological task but to preach, teach, and communicate the truths of the Bible so that parishioners might benefit from its teaching in the same way the pastors had in their theological training.[10]

Hodge witnessed firsthand and at its earliest stages the development of the Berlin model of theological education (the university had been founded a brief decade and a half before he arrived). He had left America with the goal of furthering his skills in languages and gaining an acquaintance with developments in biblical and theological disciplines. While he expected to confront ideas radically different from his own in biblical and theological content and method of study, Hodge probably did not expect a paradigm shift in the very nature of theological education. He anticipated hearing and reading views differing from traditional Calvinism, but Hodge's interminable journal references to the presence or absence of piety, divergences from orthodox theology, the "religious state" of areas he visited, and the effect of all these factors on student attitudes reveal his stark realization that what he experienced during his visit represented nothing less than a striking departure from the model he prized in Princeton.[11]

Apropos of Berlin's emphasis on the professionalization of the ministry, Hodge clearly differed in his view of the task of the pastorate. Whereas the new model focused on the minister's sociological mission, Hodge and his fellow Princetonians maintained the traditional view of the ministry as a spiritual calling and not a profession.[12] Though written subsequent to his European studies, Hodge penned a manuscript, "Call to the Ministry," that outlined the pastor's task. The minister is charged with communicating the gospel—a spiritual calling. Ministry, says Hodge, is "impossible without it." Hodge lays out the conditions by which one may obey the calling and how others may recognize it. A minister's calling is "an inward operation on the heart to seek the office from right motives." He continues, "To preach the gospel from spiritual motives comes from the Holy Spirit." He adds, "God uses a man in turning many unto righteousness." From these requirements, Hodge viewed the pastor's task to be of a spiritual nature; he is primarily a broker of the truth—hence Hodge's earlier comment about not hearing a "good doctrinal sermon." These duties arise not from professional training but from learning how to minister the Word of God to people through pastoral ministry. He repeats, "What is essential is the call of God."[13]

Outside of his concern about theological education, entries in Hodge's journal relate to his perception of the ferment roiling German culture at large and in the more narrow confines of theological education. Hodge leaned heavily on Tholuck to interpret the complexities of the religious situation as it was evolving in Germany. While "neology" as well as Kantianism lay largely in the past, the introduction of pantheism and critical attitudes toward Scripture lingered much longer. Tholuck took great pains to acquaint Hodge with Hegel's and Schleiermacher's systems. In the case of the latter, Tholuck did not hesitate to enumerate both positive and negative influences stemming from his peculiar views. Even some among the mediating school credited the Berlin pastor and professor with bringing them to faith. Others saw in his ideas a clear diversion from genuine belief.

Hodge expressed consternation upon hearing Schleiermacher preach at Trinity Church on October 14. He called the sermon "peculiar": "The words were Biblical, but the whole tenor so general, the ideas so vague and indefinite, that it was impossible for me to understand exactly what he meant." Speaking on Jesus' interpretation of the Great Commandment, Schleiermacher said that ultimate love of God could come only through Jesus Christ, "whom he called the source of all truth, and the truth itself. The difference between this law as presented in the Old Testament and as it stands in the New, is this, that in the Old Testament it was part of a law, a coercive, external command, while in the New it is the spontaneous result of a renovated nature. It is no longer a law, but the voluntary bent of the heart; and to bring about this spontaneous tendency of the soul to God is the great work of Christ." Hodge immediately adds, "This is what I took to be the drift of his discourse."[14]

Hodge's confessed difficulty in comprehending Schleiermacher's message may owe to his hearing the sermon in his recently acquired second language. Hodge, however, professed no such problem in understanding Tholuck, Neander, and others in their many discussions ranging from complex issues of doctrine, philosophy, and history to contemporary European politics and other cultural phenomena. The glaring exception to this was Hodge's frank admission that he found Germany's newest philosophical trends—the pantheisms of Hegel and Schleiermacher—virtually impossible to comprehend. To the extent that pantheistic premises infiltrated Schleiermacher's preaching, this could explain Hodge's difficulty in understanding the sermon. Hodge was again confronting a shift in mode of thinking from his accustomed Reformed worldview buttressed by Scottish Common Sense Realism. After all, Hodge gloried in the straightforward clarity that characterized his Reformed heritage in the Westminster Standards. And while the complexities of Francis Turretin's Reformed scholasticism could tax the cognitive powers of even gifted students, the profound differences between Hodge's Reformed worldview and the emerging German mind only heightened his confusion. The language and the difference in philosophical perspective presented a massive project for the young Hodge to comprehend.

Hodge's European experience was not the first time he confronted a perspective differing from his own. His dialogues with leading New England thinkers had stretched his intellectual horizons and alerted him to alternative interpretations of Reformed faith. Such conversations, however, at least had as their premises a common medium of understanding in Scottish philosophy. Such was decidedly not the case in Europe. For the first time Hodge was forced to think of material that had shaped his entire life in clear, structured patterns as being reconfigured in ways alien to his preconceptions. For the remainder of his career, he would conceive of the emerging German liberalism as a position requiring a worthy effort to discern its premises and interpretive method, but an opposing perspective nonetheless. He would witness Schleiermacher's views not only garnering broad support in Europe in the nineteenth century but also eventually making inroads in America. Just as he came to terms with his friends' views as they differed in minor matters, so he would face the more daunting task of making Schleiermacher's understandable. He would struggle to be fair in that effort, but would nevertheless view Schleiermacher's theology with suspicion as inconsistent with the content of the Bible and his Reformed heritage.[15]

Yet not all was confusion. Despite the vagueness of the sermon, Hodge deduced Schleiermacher's high estimation of Christ as both the source of the truth and truth itself. Schleiermacher's high Christology struck a chord with Hodge that lasted a lifetime of trying to make sense of the German theologian. Decades later in the Christology section of his *ST*, Hodge would refer remarkably of Schleiermacher's place in heaven.[16]

When the time came for Hodge to leave Berlin, his circle of friends gathered to bid him farewell. They expressed their gratitude for the half-year spent with their American visitor by presenting a "German Stamm-Buch," a book in which friends wrote their names under their dates of birth together with inscriptions expressing their warm relationship with the recipient or stating some truth to be remembered. Hodge was especially taken by Neander's entry, written in Greek. Translated, it read, "Let us stand fast in the liberty in which Christ has made us free; whom alone to serve is a glory and a joy; and let us not become slaves of men or of any other creature, To rejoice in the Lord, to be nothing in one's self; in the Lord all things." Several days later, Hodge summarized his own sentiments upon his leaving his friends: "I did not expect to have my heart so interested by a stay of six months in any place. The kindness, the Christian love, the warmhearted conduct of those with whom I have passed this winter so happily, will remain deeply impressed on my heart as long as I live. When I bid my friends farewell I cried like a child. Neander's farewell I shall never forget."[17]

13

Assessing the Sojourn in Europe

Charles Hodge's two-year hiatus in Europe gave him much to ponder. He arrived armed with his mentors' admonition to reap as much as possible from his immersion in ancient languages and exposure to new perspectives in biblical and theological studies. But he also undertook his work mindful of their equally strong warning against falling prey to "neology," the prevailing ideas that carried theology and biblical studies away from traditional formulations.[1]

Hodge would have been hard pressed to take more advantage of his visit than he in fact did. To say that he left hardly a stoned unturned may be an overstatement. Rather than avoid or retreat from what might challenge his worldview, however, he seized the occasion to advance his comprehension in virtually every field of intellectual and cultural activity. A notable exception was his refusal to attend the theater in Paris, which he reported to be less offensive to his sensitivity than American counterparts. Despite his pious upbringing, he even learned to drink German beer. Time and again he took advantage of opportunities across the academic and cultural spectrum and did not shelter himself either by avoiding lectures that would challenge his Reformed perspective or by remaining passively silent when conversation turned toward viewpoints differing sharply from his own.[2]

Hodge worshiped in a wide variety of contexts. He clearly preferred to hear evangelical preaching, and while often dissatisfied with the content or manner in which services were conducted, including the sacraments, he sought various places of worship. His fastidious journaling and letter-writing reveal a mind constantly engaged in all circumstances.

In light of these matters, how did Hodge himself evaluate his two years in Europe? Two letters, one to Archibald Alexander and another to his mother, written but one day apart (April 5 and 6, 1828), poignantly reflect his estimate of what he learned over against his expectations. To his colleague he wrote:

> Having nearly reached the end of my study period in Europe it is natural for me to ask myself what has been gained? A question which I am bound to consider as a very serious one, as I am here in the service of the Church and its master. That I should gain but little is what you foretold and I myself expected, but that it would be *so* little I *did not* expect, and I confess my conscience upbraids me for under all the disadvantages of ignorance of languages, etc., I might and ought to have gained more. With regard to real solid acquisitions I am now conscious of very little progress. Of that kind of information which comes through the eyes and ears without any effort of my own I have gained something. I have seen German professors and German universities, observed the manner of instruction, become convinced that learning is not obtained by magic even in Germany [and] my mind is more satisfied. The magic lent by distance to everything this side of the ocean has in great measure vanished on a near approach. The superiority in point of learning which unquestionably belongs to the professional men in this part of the world may be explained on very material grounds arising from circumstances which will probably never be all combined among us. You may be disposed to ask whether upon the review I regret having come abroad. By no means! It has been a great satisfaction to me and great advantage for which I am

> sincerely thankful although the advantage does not consist in positive acquisitions. A more important question perhaps which you have a right to ask is whether my faith has been shaken in the doctrines of the church? No, the reverse. This answer is perfectly candid and sincere and although I make it with gratitude I do it without any feeling of self-satisfaction (unless self-deceived) because as I have mentioned in my previous letter I have had nothing to try but everything to confirm my faith. My intercourse with those of opposite opinions has been casual and distant, with those who hold the same hope and the same faith with us it has been intimate and affectionate.[3]

To his mother he wrote:

> It will give you great pleasure to hear that I have never regretted coming abroad—that the advantage has been proved a full compensation for the sacrifice attending so long a separation from all who have been dear to me. I shall not return wiser but more satisfied having seen for myself what the great institutions of men in this part of the world really are. It is a satisfaction which will last as long as I live for had I not come there would always have been a great indefinite something before me which others had seen and had the advantage of, and consequently a feeling of inferiority which would have been a constant source of dissatisfaction and pain. It is this negative advantage which I feel to be one of the most important. There are indeed others of a more positive character and although I have learned far less than I expected, the result on the whole is that I greatly rejoice that I came.[4]

How closely Hodge's words resemble the August 16, 1827 letter that Hodge received from Alexander: "You must come home loaded with riches. Much will be expected of you. But I know how little can be acquired by man in the course of a lifetime—and when I think that you have the disadvantage of having the language to acquire and the multiplicity of objects to which your attention must be turned, I confess that my hope of any great success is not sanguine. But it will be worth while to have gone to Germany to know that there is but little worth going for. It will at any rate place you on a level with the other *traveled* literati of this country."[5]

Hodge's words beg for some critical reflection because of their mixed message and the fact that historians have underplayed the two years he spent abroad. Taking into account the two different responses may help in understanding why his son devoted such an extended chapter in the biography of his father.

At first glance Hodge's assessment of the European sojourn seems unduly negative. On the one hand, he professes how little he gained from his trip. He upbraids himself for not benefiting more from the experience. He also concedes that his mentor's pessimistic prediction has proved correct. Obviously, in this regard he needed to convey that his prolonged exposure to German thinking had not dissuaded him from his previous convictions. By these words he also unburdened himself of his previous assumption that European scholarship bore inherently superior value in comparison with American studies. Gone was the aura of "magic" that he had previously associated with Continental academics. Thus Hodge needed to express clearly to his family and colleagues that he had in fact confronted the "great indefinite something" of modern thought and found it wanting.

On the other hand, Hodge returned to Princeton with a positive spin as well. In both letters he stated that he did not regret the trip. His further education only solidified his conviction that Princeton's seminary training could and should stay the course outlined by its charter. One need only consider the sheer volume of notes taken during lectures he attended across a broad range of disciplines, his extensive journal detailing conversations and visits to places of cultural and historical significance, and the friendships begun and solidified through correspondence in the following decades to temper the negative words. The most significant conviction that he brought back was a robust confidence that his intellectual and spiritual heritage could stand on its own as the nineteenth century advanced. Hodge was undoubtedly bolstered in this opinion by his experience with his Continental colleagues. Though they did not hold identical theological views, and though Hodge's proved consistently more conservative, Hodge returned assured of several things. His intellectual and spiritual moorings remained intact and were shared by competent scholars who labored where liberalism was already making great inroads. He maintained the respect of intellectual peers as their conversations probed everything from the narrow intricacies of theological education to broad social, political, and cultural topics. Hodge would not teach or write in the future having never been exposed to ideas and worldviews differing from his own. He and his Princeton colleagues would labor knowing that they had respected supporters on the Continent. While differing theological winds would eventually blow in America, the Princetonians would also know that even where modern ideas gained greater prominence, pockets of continued orthodoxy and piety remained.

Thus, as a result of his European experience, Hodge retained the conviction that Princeton should continue the complementarity of truth and piety as equally indispensable in the *paideia* tradition of theological education. Upon his return, he would further Princeton's pursuit of educational excellence more committed to academic excellence. He shared Presbyterians' belief that theological education demanded curricular requirements in original languages, facility in biblical criticism, and intensive instruction in Reformed theology and biblical content. He left Europe with the conviction that Princeton need never renege on its charter. Having seen both the strengths and weaknesses of European theological education at the University of Berlin and having subjected himself to the rigors of modern scholarship resulting from the Enlightenment only further confirmed Hodge's belief that Princeton should preserve its stringent academic program. If August Tholuck, Augustus Neander, Ernst Wilhelm Hengstenberg, and others could stay the course in an extremely hostile environment, so could Princeton. The seminary should continue to avail itself of the latest in modern scholarship as it evolved, but should also equip its students with tools necessary to combat the incursion of new ideas that would subvert Reformed orthodoxy. Princeton would therefore continue its young tradition of producing pastor-scholars. The role of Presbyterian ministers need not develop in the direction of the new Berlin professional model.[6]

Of no less importance, Hodge's experience in Europe also convinced him that Presbyterian ministry should continue with its twin goals of conveying the truths of the gospel to its congregations and modeling a piety commensurate with its theological orthodoxy. Presbyterians should preserve piety as an indispensable prerequisite to ministerial education and service in the pastorate. Pastors should be genuinely converted men who manifested a vital spiritual life as evidence of the state of their hearts. Hodge's almost obsessive preoccupation with piety in his journal, both as he observed it in others and as he labored over its presence in his own life, reflects his insistence that intellectual training leading to confessional adherence alone does not qualify a person for ministry. In addition to subscribing to the Westminster Standards, Hodge believed that a pastor must exhibit a heart for the gospel as manifested in his manner of life and private devotional practices. This would be the pattern he would defend and model for the remainder of his teaching career.

Thus the European sojourn was no minor element in Hodge's life. While one might be tempted to dismiss it as possessing little significance because it occurred so early in his young career, his son appropriately gave it extensive coverage. It reconfirmed a foundation from which Hodge never wavered. Convinced of his calling, committed to the agenda of his seminary and its model of theological education, equipped to educate pastor-scholars who would in turn minister to congregations steeped in Presbyterian heritage, Hodge would take advantage of European scholarship without its Enlightenment trappings.

Hodge would solidify distinctives inherent to Princeton's founding. Fortified with additional tools, he would impel his seminary forward in the future from its rather humble beginnings in William Tennent's Log College. By the 1820s European schools in the main had diverged from their original orthodox moorings of the sixteenth-century Reformation. They differed widely in their reputations for academic rigor, theological orthodoxy, and expressions of religious experience. The same would not happen to Princeton. Hodge would help his seminary to stay the course established less than two decades previously. In turn, he would also aid his denomination to resist efforts to diminish its traditional Calvinism. We turn to that development in the remaining chapters.

PART 3

Moderate Old School Presbyterian

By the summer of 1829, almost one year after Charles Hodge returned from Europe, approximately 500 students had attended classes at Princeton, and 132 had graduated. Second in size only to Harvard as a school of theological education, the seminary was on its way to becoming a leading institution in American education.[1] The school accomplished this feat in the midst of controversy between rival theological institutions, a resurgence of revivalism distinguished by new debates over their theological basis and methods by which to conduct them and extended ecclesiastical struggle to define and control the Presbyterian denomination. Charles Hodge would weigh in on all these scenarios. He had honed his linguistic and critical skills not only for his performance in the seminary classroom but for interaction with the best minds that probed and contested biblical and theological issues that would define Presbyterianism in the first half of the nineteenth century. In doing so, his name would become one of several that would be synonymous with Old School Presbyterianism in their opposition to New Schoolers, who favored innovations in Calvinist thought and practice. Hodge and his colleagues, however, would distinguish themselves by their moderation from other Old Schoolers in disputes that arose within the denomination over doctrine and polity. Although he was a part of the conservative party that claimed to be legitimate heirs of historic Presbyterianism, Hodge would not advocate some of the actions that led to one of the major schisms that roiled the denomination. His son stated the contrast between his father's rather low stature in the denomination in 1828 and his eventual reputation by midcentury: "He returned from Europe comparatively an unknown young man, and he entered his new professorship of Didactic theology in 1840, with very much the same general reputation he enjoyed to the end of his life."[2]

14

Newfound Confidence

Upon his return to Princeton, Charles Hodge made immediate use of his experience abroad. He opened the 1828–29 academic year with the introductory lecture in which he drew on his recent trip to encapsulate his vision for religious education not just in seminaries but also in American religion as a whole. In considering both the method and content of religious education, he believed that both American and German institutions made distinctive contributions. First, expressing his deep-seated patriotism, he praised American religious and civil liberty. Separation of church and state and freedom of religion offered the unique possibility of "elevating the intelligence and character of all classes of the people, and setting religion and the church free from the trammels of the State." Hodge expressed his gratitude for cultural advances in American life. He especially prized liberties that he believed derived from the gospel proclamation of freedom from sin.[1]

Despite America's advantage in permitting free dissemination of religion, Hodge thought German schools were superior in training young children in "knowledge and religion." He outlined the German method throughout all grades in which religion was "as systematically taught as any other subject." Each class of schools used appropriate texts that set forth scriptural history, doctrines, and morals. The quality of instruction depended on the individual character of the teacher, and while often of a summary nature, it successfully inculcated a foundation for Christian faith in students. He continued, "So thoroughly is this system carried through in Prussia, that I never met a boy selling matches in the street (and I made several experiments of the kind) who could not answer any common question on the historical parts of the Old and New Testaments." While Hodge's limited sampling could easily be challenged, his estimation of the German method is reminiscent of his childhood catechizing that he prized so highly. Just as the German system provided for education of Protestants, Catholics, and Jews, so Hodge hoped that various sects in America might unite to prepare texts in which "historical facts and essential doctrines, in which all evangelical denominations agree, may be taught and inculcated." His proposal indicates his optimism that principles at work in the European context could be easily transplanted to this country. It also reflects the assumption that evangelical principles exercised widespread influence in American culture in the early decades of the nineteenth century.[2]

Less positively and more in keeping with our analysis in part 2, Hodge used his experience in Germany to alert students of the negative influence of the new speculative theology on practical faith in theological institutions. Expressing a theme that would recur throughout his more than fifty years of teaching at Princeton, he warned of the dire effects of innovations in theology on moral character. Without mentioning Berlin by name, he stated that Germany's distinctive religious parties offered concrete evidence of the negative consequences that false ideas have on practical religion. He repeated what he had heard many times from conversations with German colleagues that the leading factions were the orthodox (evangelicals such as August Tholuck and Ernst Wilhelm Hengstenberg), the rationalists (those still influenced by the Enlightenment philosophers such as Immanuel Kant), and the pantheists (followers of Friedrich Schleiermacher and G. W. F. Hegel). Each in turn held principles that either supported or corrupted Christian orthodoxy and piety. "Wherever you find vital piety—that is penitence and a devotional spirit—there you find the doctrines of the fall, of depravity, of regeneration, of atonement, and of the deity of Jesus Christ. I neither saw [nor] heard of a single individual who exhibited a spirit of piety who rejected any one of these doctrines. Holiness is essential to the correct knowledge of divine things and the great security from error." Thus, at the outset of his reentry into theological education, Hodge reiterated Princeton's insistence on the distinctive views of Reformed theological education—the classical *paideia* model with its emphasis on orthodox theology complemented with piety—and the weakness of the new speculative Berlin model.[3]

Though Hodge does not further elaborate, Kant's moralistic *RWLRA* explicitly reinterpreted the traditional Christian doctrines that Hodge mentioned. Friedrich Schleiermacher also reinterpreted the same doctrines in *The Christian Faith*. Schleiermacher's and Hegel's pantheistic thought lacked the personal God that Hodge believed essential to genuine pious devotion. The safeguard from theological error was to "beware of any course of study which has a tendency to harden your hearts and deaden the delicate sensibility of the soul to moral truth and beauty." Perhaps here as in no other utterance, Hodge expressed his adherence to the Athens view of theological education over against the Berlin model. Though Hodge and the Princetonians would endeavor to maintain the highest level of academic preparation for the ministry, piety and orthodoxy would forever trump speculation in the training of ministers. Since Hodge witnessed theological students and faculty who manifested deficiency in theological orthodoxy and spiritual life, as controversies erupted over the ensuing decades he would critique similar tendencies in American religion and within the denomination he served. As he began his teaching anew in 1829, he made piety a focal point, but he also asserted that piety did not stand alone. He linked it with evangelical doctrine. Thus he stated, "Religious truth, viewed in the general, produces devotion; metaphysically analyzed it destroys it." He advocated that Princeton students should adhere to the former and reject the latter. While a person might espouse theological orthodoxy yet fail to manifest a fully pious life, he contended that he never observed a pious Christian who did not hold the great truths of evangelical doctrine.[4]

Hodge also maintained contact with German friends through sporadic but warm correspondence. He shared and invited news about topics they had discussed over the previous months—primarily developments in theological scholarship and the religious state of the German and American churches. In a letter of October 12, 1828, Hodge writes that "our seminary is prospering, and is furnished with its ordinary number of students. The piety has not declined among them, and perhaps more of a disposition to embark in foreign missions was manifested during the last term than usual." After sharing other news, he concludes, "Tell me whatever of interest occurs in your section of the kingdom of God. Let me know of important theological works which you think I ought to send for." On February 28, 1829, he writes: "Let me know how things look in Halle. What progress the cause of truth is making there and elsewhere in Germany?" He comments that on his side of the Atlantic religious liberty offers definite advantages to the church. Hodge was ambivalent, however, about the state of religion in America. On the one hand, he noted "the general prevalence of truth and piety in most sections of our country." While revivals of religion prospered in America, however, secular leaders, unlike their counterparts in Germany, paid little attention to religious matters. He complained that "our worldly men are more worldly even than yours." Whereas in Germany public figures, in both church and state, paid a "formal regard" to religion "as a part of one general secular establishment," the same was not true in America. "Everything depends with us on public opinion, and this will, in the main, be right as long as vital piety be prevalent to the extent that it is at present."[5]

Following up on the primary reason for his trip—to buttress his academic credentials—Hodge determined not to fall behind in his field. He solicited his friends' assistance in staying abreast of developments in European theological scholarship. He instructed Tholuck: "I am very desirous to be kept informed of the progress of theological literature in Germany, and for this purpose have ordered several of your periodicals—the Tubingen *Zeit-Schrift* . . . [Hengstenberg's] *Evangelische Kirchen-Zeitung*, and several others . . . July, 1928, is the last number that I have received of the Berlin journal. Please speak to Mr. Funke . . . and beg him to forward the periodicals as rapidly and as regularly as possible. Please order for us, from time to time, any book which you may think important for us to have, to the amount of from 50–100 Prussian dollars annually. You know the kind of books I want, *valuable* [emphasis in original] works on the language, literature and exegesis of the Old and New Testaments." Later he wrote, "I wish to receive the most important of your theological works, that I may be kept going, so to speak, with the German mind." In a subsequent letter he covered all areas of interest by requesting of his friend Tholuck whatever he deemed important to Hodge's intellectual pursuits. Hodge believed such acquisitions essential not only to his continued research as a scholar but also for the instruction of his students. Although Hodge would never acquiesce that *Wissenschaft*, the scientific study of theology, meant that theological truth had no absolutes or norms, that did not preclude diligent theological study. Princeton would avail itself of the benefits of scholarly research, no matter how different the theological orientation might be.[6]

The Princetonians, however, would never agree that theological research be subjected to any Enlightenment paradigm of knowledge. Hodge and his colleagues maintained the seminary's firm commitment to the unique combination of the Athens model consistent with Reformed confessionalism. Standing as the lone Presbyterian seminary for several years, Princeton took the lead in defining American Presbyterian belief and practice. By its curriculum, its firm advocacy of the Westminster Standards, and the requirement that its faculty remain faithful to both, the school developed a theological perspective that would profoundly shape the ethos of the denomination throughout the nineteenth century. As America expanded, all denominations struggled to keep pace with the demands of a growing population and developing frontier. As a result of their commitment to producing an educated ministry, Presbyterians would establish no fewer than seven additional seminaries before midcentury. Each emerged in a new geographical area and developed its own distinctive theological and ministerial perspective.[7] Eventually, therefore, Princeton found itself surrounded by competitors more than willing to engage in rigorous and even heated interaction over theological positions, biblical interpretation, revivals, ecclesiastical maneuverings, and cultural strategies.

As Princeton progressed in this educational milieu, Hodge attacked his duties with newfound enthusiasm. Absent was any trace of earlier doubts about his calling resulting from duress in class or the burden of preparing lectures incumbent on neophyte professors. He revealed both his state of mind and his earthly welfare in his first letter to Tholuck after his homecoming: "You can hardly think how happy I am. My lovely children (for they are *very* lovely), are hanging on my knees all the time, and my dear wife—I will not talk about—you must come and see her! Our seminary is prospering, and is furnished with its ordinary number of students." Each day before noon he taught Hebrew language, literature, and exegesis, and in the afternoon he taught New Testament literature and exegesis. In addition, he prepared courses on biblical criticism, hermeneutics, sacred geography, and exegesis of books in both Old and New Testaments.[8]

His positive state of mind at this time reflected a disposition that remained uniformly cheerful throughout his academic career. Though he struggled occasionally with deep sadness over theological divisions within Presbyterianism and eventually with the enormity of America's political upheaval resulting in the Civil War, Hodge maintained a remarkably optimistic demeanor.[9] This despite the one physical ailment that plagued him for years—a chronic pain in his right thigh. Countless letters to his family plaintively refer to the vicissitudes of "my limb." The condition emerged first before he went to Europe, but while his ailment flared up occasionally, it did not significantly curtail his activity. His discomfort intensified greatly in 1833 as a result of his canvassing in New York City for funds for a new seminary chapel. Though the problem was never definitively diagnosed, he suffered a wide range of debilitating treatments, including leeches, blistering, and a "galvanism" applied to his hip, knee, and thigh. Lack of an effective remedy left him for long periods in splints, on crutches, and eventually on a cane for the rest of his life. He lay confined to his study for months at a time but continued teaching his students and writing "without serious interruption." Relief came only in October 1838 after the application of cold and hot douches. By 1842 he had sufficiently recovered to begin preaching again in local churches.[10]

In addition to Hodge's physical ailment, another discouraging element following his return from Europe surfaced in 1829, and it again entailed his relationship with his mother. In July Hodge wrote to his brother of her despondency. While he attributed her unhappiness in part to her frequent bouts with bad health, he also stated that their relation had been severely strained after his homecoming: "I tax myself to be kind and attentive to her which my feelings of affection and respect as well as sense of duty would of themselves lead me to do. But I cannot get near her. She appeared to have lost a good deal of her feeling for me. I do not speak this as complaint but as a misfortune for us both. Sarah says she has always noticed it and never more than in my return from Europe. Her gratification at my return seemed hardly to last an hour. If I knew what to do I would gladly do it. But I almost despair of seeing Mother happy." Thus while Hodge spoke well of her and continued including her in his correspondence, A. A.'s comment about Charles's never receiving due respect during his college and seminary career and to the remainder of his life may well have been an understatement.[11]

In the midst of physical trials and concern for his mother, Hodge gained recognition as Princeton's most visible professor and articulate advocate of Reformed theology. While he could have arguably fulfilled this role without his European travels, the two years abroad in frequently hostile intellectual and spiritual environments benefited him immensely. His previously shaken confidence appeared remarkably transformed. Hodge profited from exposure to two worlds—to the best minds in German lecture halls and to intense stimulation from an intimate circle of friends who shared his orthodoxy and, perhaps more importantly, his pious proclivity. Hundreds of hours' listening to lectures was balanced with a like amount of time assessing that content within his coterie of friends in Halle and Berlin. Hodge retained his poise and forged his self-assurance without the camaraderie he enjoyed at Princeton. True, his German friends shared pietist inclinations. But while Tholuck, Augustus Neander, and Ludwig and Otto von Gerlach held relatively orthodox theological views, Hodge found himself the sole defender of classical Reformed doctrine. His persistent advocacy of the truth of the system he believed most faithful to biblical teaching, and his conviction that it was capable of cogent defense against rival theological systems, would serve him well as the controversies of the 1830s played out.

15

A Prodigious Journalistic Venture

Charles Hodge's stature in American Presbyterianism grew as the decades unfolded. He occupied his professorship at a time when theological and ecclesiastical matters were not marginalized from broader cultural concerns. Religion in general and theological discussions in particular were not relegated to the private dimension of individual experience, isolated from public life. The opening decades of the nineteenth century found religious and theological issues integral to public discourse. This is most evident in the role that evangelical activism played in attempting to improve the quality of American culture. The 1820s and following decades were the heyday of voluntary societies, groups consisting of like-minded individuals—primarily laymen—whose common beliefs united them in accomplishing specific social objectives. Denominational cooperation frequently stood at the forefront of civic discourse and shaped opinions both social and private. Not only did pastors enjoy respect as public figures, but their preaching gained wide recognition as publishers printed sermon collections, and theological journals experienced a wide readership. Hodge benefited greatly from these circumstances and emerged as a leader in the confluence of theological, ecclesiastical, and cultural discussions.[1]

Hodge's emergence as a leader owed to his high profile in the proliferation of theological journalism that characterized the early nineteenth century. All denominations contributed in the heyday of weighty quarterlies that littered the religious landscape. Presbyterians took the lead among major denominations by publishing several journals to reach their various constituencies. Princeton's *PR* was the primary organ for Old School views in the North, while the *American Presbyterian and Theological Review* and the *Presbyterian Quarterly Review* trumpeted New School interests and the *Southern Presbyterian Review* and the *Cumberland Presbyterian* served Southern Presbyterians.[2]

Originally intended merely to reprint and translate works by foreign scholars, the *PR* stated its goal as being to "assist ministers and laymen in the criticism and interpretation of the Bible." Although the journal advertised itself as edited by an "Association of Gentlemen," Hodge was its moving force, and he originated the journal out of the same concern that had prompted him to found the theological society in his student years.

When he returned from Europe, he resumed editorship and carried out his duties of soliciting and evaluating contributions until 1871. In January 1829, when the journal was renamed, the change brought with it a greatly expanded mission beyond reprinting or translating works by foreign scholars. The new mission encompassed no fewer than eight goals: (1) to provide readers with "facilities for a right understanding of the divine oracles"; (2) to review philosophies and literature of the era and "correct and expose the error of founding religious doctrines on isolated passages, and partial views of Bible truth, or forcing the Scriptures to a meaning which shall accord with philosophical theories"; (3) to delineate "the dangers of the particular form of error prevailing in the period"; (4) to review the history of doctrine and opinion with special attention to "the revival of exploded doctrines and their effects on vital religion"; (5) to "consider the influence of different principles of ecclesiastical polity on piety, morals, literature and civil institutions";

(6) to examine and encourage various "Christian benevolences, especially the vast and growing interest of Sabbath-schools"; (7) to focus attention on "important interests of general knowledge, and select literary information"; and (8) not to carry out each of these goals in the spirit of controversy but to exhibit biblical truth "temperately and mildly, yet firmly and fearlessly." To say the least, the agenda was ambitious and comprehensive! One might summarize its mission under the appellation "Princeton looks at the world."[3]

With such large-scale aims, it is no wonder that the *PR* achieved the reputation over the decades of being the most prominent mouthpiece for nineteenth-century Calvinism. In summarizing the influence of the journal, Glenn T. Miller stated that to read it was "to have a panoramic view of the intellectual life of the nineteenth century."[4] To achieve such a goal, Hodge needed help. William Hutchison has pointed out that as editor, Hodge drew on colleagues and friends from the larger intellectual community. He called on "a stable of reviewers of very marked theological and literary ability, chiefly from outside the seminary." The journal would tax its readers by the depth and breadth of its scholarship. Hodge's ability to shepherd the journal while maintaining Princeton's high standards owed to his and his coworkers' facility in selecting writers who shared Princeton's perspective, whatever the issue being discussed—theology, biblical studies, history, philosophy, literature, the political scene, or even world affairs. Thus the *PR*, typical of religious journals of the day, propounded a uniform message reflecting the prevailing views of the seminary as a whole.[5]

When Hodge wrote his "Retrospect," he reiterated that the theological and ecclesiastical aims guiding its contents were rooted in the belief that "the Westminster Confession of Faith, the system of the Reformed Church and of Augustinians in all ages is the truth of God revealed for His glory and salvation of men." In addition, contributors held that "the organization of the Presbyterian Church, its form of government and discipline, was more conformed than any other to the Scriptural model, and the best adapted for preserving the purity and developing the life of the Church." Echoing a claim that became a trademark of Princeton, he continued, "They have advanced no new theories, and have never aimed at originality. Whether it be a ground of reproach or of approbation, it is believed to be true that an original idea in theology is not to be found in the pages of the *Biblical Repertory and Princeton Review* from the beginning until now. The phrase 'Princeton Theology,' therefore is without distinctive meaning." As Hodge expected, his claim received both accolades and heaps of abuse. Princeton's supporters hailed the remark as its unique contribution to preserving Calvinism in the modern era; detractors viewed Hodge's statement as quixotic in light of modern advances in knowledge and the necessity of theology and biblical studies to adapt to cultural changes.[6]

Despite his detractors' criticism of the static nature of the *PR*, Hodge's experience in Germany and the rising Berlin model of theological education forever remained in his mind as motivation for his Calvinistic conservatism. He wrote, "As the modern German philosophy and theology have exerted great influence in America as well as Europe, no Review in this country, devoted to theological literature, could fail of being called upon to discuss the principles which these new theories involved so far as they affected the integrity of Christian doctrine." German "speculation" based on the idea that all truth—including theological doctrines—is never absolute lay behind modern innovations in theology that Hodge opposed so strenuously. He noted that James W. Alexander "presented a general view of the recent German philosophy." Hodge also referred to his sharp exchange with John Williamson Nevin over the latter's monograph on the Lord's Supper, *The Mystical Presence*, in 1848. Hodge labeled Nevin's doctrine "the application of the modern German philosophy to the explanation and subversion of Christian doctrine." The *PR* review of Philip Schaff's view of the church in 1854 "is a discussion of the doctrine of 'historical development,' involving another phase of the German philosophy." The last illustration of problems posed by German methodology in theological matters involved the review of the article "What Is Christianity?" (1860). German thinkers had posed that Christianity was only a life and not a doctrine and a life. Although Hodge did not identify figures holding this position, he undoubtedly had in mind not only Friedrich Schleiermacher and Mercersburg theologians Nevin and Schaff but also his friend Augustus Neander. Neander articulated his theanthropic principle—that "the purely human life of Christ, developed by a natural process in the church, as the life of Adam was developed in his race," with the result that "redemption, (atonement and justification, as well as sanctification,) is purely subjective." Thus in his "Retrospect" (1870) Hodge divulged what lay behind his often-quoted claim that a "new idea" never arose either at Princeton or in his theological journal. He had witnessed firsthand German theological innovation in its earliest form. While he also mentioned American theological disputes as occasioning the *PR*'s entry into controversy, his experience in Germany provided him with initial sufficient cause for maintaining Princeton's adherence to firmly stated doctrinal and polity positions in the Westminster Standards. Such doggedness proved essential to Princeton's remaining faithful to its original vision throughout the remainder of the century.[7]

Undergirding the journal's mission was the comprehensive worldview that Hodge and his associates embraced as their intellectual and spiritual legacy. Its historical sweep encompassed the seventeenth-century Westminster divines, sixteenth-century Geneva, fifth-century Augustinianism, and ultimately first-century Pauline theology. No major issue was exempt from the *PR*'s purview. While the majority of its articles probed biblical, theological, and ecclesiastical questions, its editor did not hesitate to solicit pieces on all manner of topics.[8] Its coverage reflected the confidence that Hodge had brought back from his European studies; he and his associates acknowledged no bounds as they turned their attention to the marketplace of intellectual discourse. Just as Hodge and his German friends in numerous conversations had broached topics from theology, biblical interpretation, philosophy, literature, politics, and science, so Hodge envisioned a journal that would do likewise. He and his Princeton colleagues would take on the entire world of ideas and subject them to rigorous analysis and Reformed critique. The journal would demonstrate that theological and biblical reflection pertained not simply to the training of pastors for the ministry, but to everyone—indeed, to all of life. Everyone could digest its pages—from scholars in major academic disciplines to pastors and laymen seeking to keep abreast of the church and its relation with the world. Over the next forty-six years Hodge would be its primary contributor by writing 142 articles totaling some five thousand pages. Given the variety and extensiveness of labors involved in achieving the *PR*'s success, he could jokingly characterize the journal as his "ball and chain."[9]

16

Old School–New School Rivalry

From the 1800s to the 1830s, Presbyterians experienced significant growth, which should have augured well for the denomination. General Assembly minutes recount major advances in membership. Robert Ellis Thompson estimated that "not less than two hundred thousand" were added to evangelical churches between 1826 and 1832; more particularly, E. H. Gillett reported that Presbyterians gained "not less than fifty thousand" between 1816 and 1828. Yet while membership grew in the denomination, so did differences between the parties, which became known as Old and New Schools in their sympathies. The greatness of Presbyterian gains was matched by an equally vigorous rivalry within the denomination over its defining doctrines and practices. Each side claimed legitimacy as espousing authentic Presbyterianism.[1]

As the *PR* became a leading voice of nineteenth-century Calvinism, the journal also launched Charles Hodge as the primary Old School interpreter of developments within the Presbyterian church and its impact on American life. He established this reputation not only through the sheer number of articles he wrote on various biblical, theological, and cultural topics but also through lengthy summaries of the annual meetings of the General Assembly. From 1835 to 1867, Hodge wrote extensive accounts of the conduct of the assembly—reports of General Assembly committees, resolutions submitted, the primary participants in debates over the resolutions, and the extended arguments they used to support their points. Claiming no neutrality on the discussion, and sometimes a major contributor in the debates, Hodge intended nevertheless to present a fair report of the proceedings while clearly supporting Old School positions. As the years unfolded, distinctive positions on a wide variety of issues developed to such an extent that the denomination found itself divided into factions that rivaled the Old Side–New Side division of the previous century. The primary areas of disagreement and Hodge's role in shaping the debate deserve careful attention.[2]

Old School Polity vs. Voluntary Societies

Of all the achievements of the *PR*, its advocacy of Old School Presbyterianism in the North proved to be its most notable. The Old School and New School factions within Presbyterianism emerged as the denomination experienced another internal convulsion in the early 1800s. Just as the New Side–Old Side schism had resulted from disputes over the revivalism of the First Great Awakening from 1741 to 1758, Presbyterians suffered a similar division over a wider set of issues from 1837 to 1869. The split took years to materialize, and Princetonians played a central role as the rupture grew imminent, burst apart, and eventually healed. Hodge and his colleagues claimed that the Old School preserved traditional Presbyterianism over against innovations advanced by New Schoolers. Hodge's defense and promotion of Old School principles entailed labors on many fronts: maintaining Presbyterian polity in opposition to evangelical ecumenism; defending traditional Reformed theology in the midst of growing theological diversity; opposing the theological basis and techniques of the Second Great Awakening; limiting the role of voluntary societies as agents in furthering ministries in the church; rebutting the theology and techniques of revivalism of the Second Great Awakening; and adjudicating the various controversies over the institution of slavery.[3]

Ecclesiastically, Old Schoolers believed polity indispensable to carrying out the church's mission. The Presbyterian system of government, consisting of church judicatories or courts from local church sessions to presbyteries, synods, and the General Assembly, was not a peripheral matter to church life but the proscribed system of government by which the denomination maintained its order and discipline. Thus they opposed the 1801 Plan of Union, which facilitated cooperation between Presbyterians and Congregationalists in planting churches in expanding western territories. To Old Schoolers, cooperating with Congregationalists undermined the means by which the church governed its members, educated its ministers, carried out missionary activity, and in other ways directed the life of the church.[4]

Hodge and other Old Schoolers believed that Presbyterian polity rendered their participation in voluntary societies a complex matter when carrying out the denomination's mission. Voluntary societies combined with the Second Great Awakening became major components of American religious life in the first quarter of the nineteenth century. Evangelical Christians mounted major campaigns to convert sinners and combat moral evils. Taken together, the two movements constituted an evangelical activism that would convert not only individuals but society as a whole from their sinful ways. The voluntary societies, roughly comparable to today's parachurch organizations, were nondenominational in character and existed outside of ecclesiastical governance. Lay leaders—primarily Presbyterian and Congregational church members—did not represent their respective churches as they directed their agencies. Instead, they mounted nationwide ecumenical crusades to make America a more moral country.[5]

Drawing on broad support from the various evangelical denominations, groups attempted to transform America into a benevolent empire by ridding the country of its social ills.[6] Bible and tract societies combatted biblical illiteracy, temperance groups staved off drunkenness, Sunday school unions promoted Christian education, and missions societies recruited, trained, and commissioned domestic and foreign missionaries. Other groups worked to reform prisons, oppose prostitution, enact Sabbatarian laws, and perform other minor functions. While Methodists, Baptists, and Episcopalians participated in such efforts to create a more moral society, Presbyterians were divided over the advisability of cooperative efforts. New School Presbyterians wholeheartedly supported revivalism and all voluntary societies as the means of Christianizing America. The Old School presented a decidedly more cautionary view.[7]

Hodge used the *PR* as the primary vehicle for articulating Princeton's nuanced Old School response to such groups. He did not oppose their existence and their various missions carte blanche. He insisted, however, that Presbyterian polity mandated that some ministries can function only under ecclesiastical boards. In a review of New Schooler John S. Taylor's "A Plea for Voluntary Societies and Defense of the Decisions of the General Assembly of 1836 against the Strictures of the Princeton Reviewers and Others," Hodge stated criteria for legitimate formation of voluntary societies. At the broadest level of ministry, Hodge believed Christ had commissioned the church to evangelize the world. Some activities to that end might most effectively be carried out through voluntary societies, and Presbyterians could participate in their efforts: "Wherever the field of operation is common to different denominations, and the proper means of its cultivation are also the same for all, there is an obvious reason why all should unite." He cited Bible and tract societies and their distribution of literature to convert and edify readers and Sunday school unions' efforts to promote knowledge of the Bible as primary examples.[8]

He also conceded that causes such as temperance to oppose drunkenness and abuse of alcohol may exist that permitted shared ministries. Hodge did not write any of the articles on temperance that appeared in the *PR*. He did, however, devote several pages to intemperance in his "Retrospect." He condemned drunkenness as a "soul-destroying sin, and one of the most prolific sources of misery and crime." Even though he considered drunkenness a potential scourge on society, he opposed temperance societies' tendency to insist on abstinence as a biblical mandate. In Hodge's view, while any "use of a thing, lawful in itself, may become wrong," moderate use of alcohol was not sinful.

Hodge himself did not drink, and he strongly encouraged his children not to imbibe.[9]

Temperance, however, became a matter of serious concern at the 1843 General Assembly after a synod report recommended that the "retailing of intoxicating drinks" be made "a test of piety and a term of membership in the Presbyterian church." Hodge used the occasion to expound on Christian ethics. "It makes all the difference in the world, whether a thing is wrong in itself, or for reasons extraneous to its own nature." Temperance advocates contended that selling and consuming alcohol were inherently sinful. They seriously erred, however, according to Hodge, because "it is a fact, just as clear as any other fact in the scripture, that God and Christ did not prohibit, but allowed the use of such drinks." Therefore, the synod recommendation was "infidel in its spirit and tendency, however many good men may have been cajoled or driven into the sin of giving it their sanction." Hodge used the examples of Paul's circumcision of Timothy and refusal to circumcise Titus and the question of liberty in eating meat in stating that "any rule of duty founded on expediency must be variable." He used Jesus' refusal to comply with the scruples of his generation "but consented to be called a sabbath-breaker and wine-bibber, because he saw their good and the cause of truth required it." He continued, "It was in the same spirit of enlightened Christian ethics that Luther urged his followers to observe certain religious days, adding however, if any man says you must do it, then go to your ordinary work as hard as you can." From these examples Hodge reached a radical conclusion: "Thus . . . in our day, it is a duty in many parts of the country to practice on the principles of total absence [if it offends a brother]; in others no such obligation may exist; and we suspect in others it is an imperative duty openly to refuse to do it [i.e., one should partake of alcohol if someone makes it a religious obligation to abstain]." In the debate over temperance, "it follows from the very nature of expediency, that every man must be allowed to decide and act for himself. He is not to subject his conscience or conduct to the judgment of others in such cases." Thus Hodge opposed abstinence positions as a new form of piety, not supported by the Bible and inconsistent with a correct interpretation of expediency in Christian ethics.[10]

While Old Schoolers readily acknowledged the value of voluntary societies in mobilizing Christians of all denominations to foster certain goods and combat other evils, Hodge strongly opposed voluntary societies as appropriate means of educating ministers and supervising missionaries. As unstinting advocates of interdenominational cooperation in making America a more Christian nation, New Schoolers supported nonecclesiastical agencies as the primary means of churches' avoiding competing among themselves and duplicating efforts to train pastors and missionaries. Hodge insisted that more was at stake than efficiency. Training pastors and commissioning missionaries fell outside the boundaries quoted above—their "field of operation is common to different denominations and the proper means of its cultivation are also the same for all." While some churches might dismiss differences in polity as inconsequential to carrying out the church's mission, Presbyterians did not have that liberty. Their polity insisted that only ecclesiastical boards were authorized to carry out such tasks.[11]

Hodge believed that since each denomination had its own theological system and form of government, each should perpetuate its ministry in conformity with those standards. He stated that denominations devised various means by which they extended the gospel, and he emphasized that "of these means beyond all comparison the most important are the education of ministers, and the organization and support of churches." Groups that engaged in carrying out these tasks held nothing less than the "destiny of the church in their hands." To relegate these activities to voluntary agencies existing outside the church and thus having no vested interest in what the denomination believed and how it was governed transferred the authority that Scripture consigned the church to a group that was not a duly constituted church. When these groups assumed the direction of ministerial candidates, assigned where they were to receive training, required them to report on their activities, and then verified their fitness for service, they were thereby "assum[ing] the rights and privileges of an ecclesiastical court; they usurp an authority and power which do not belong to them, and which they have no right to exercise. People may cry out against all this as high churchism. It is Presbyterianism." Hodge summarized his case by saying that the "power possessed by these societies is inordinate and dangerous" because it threatened the integrity of Presbyterian belief and governance.[12]

Thus, for Hodge and other Old Schoolers, Presbyterian polity prescribed its own unique means to extend the gospel. Within the Presbyterian system, licentiates and pastors prepared for and carried out their ministry under the direction of presbyteries and church boards that alone have the responsibility and authority to do so. If agencies such as the Home Missionary Society, as well-meaning as they may have been in fulfilling such roles, ignored Presbyterian doctrine or polity in educating pastors and directing missionaries, they nevertheless subverted Presbyterianism. Hodge alleged that the Home Missionary Society, unfortunately, "under the management of its Secretary, has become a great party engine, operating most unfavourably for the peace, union, and purity of the church."[13]

Hodge issued this harsh judgment because New Schoolers in their enthusiasm for cooperative efforts of voluntary societies supported the Home Missionary Society at the expense of the denomination's boards. His objections involved both principle and action. As for principle, Hodge viewed the society as ill-equipped to supervise Presbyterian missions because Congregationalists dominated the leadership. Under such circumstances, the society was "hostile on principle to our polity, if not to our doctrines." He reiterated the "great party engine" metaphor when he added, "[The society] sent out men educated in New England holding sentiments condemned . . . by Old-school Presbyterians." Thus New Schoolers, whose very name suggested innovation in many areas of ministry, contravened established Presbyterian principle and practice. As in the case of the Plan of Union of 1801, voluntary societies' disadvantages significantly outweighed whatever minor advantages might be gained through cooperative ventures to reduce duplication of ministries.[14]

In his previous year's review of the General Assembly in the *PR*, Hodge had urged the establishment of a Presbyterian Board of Foreign Missions. New School opponents such as Taylor contended that forming a Presbyterian board would be sectarian—that its effect would be to advance Presbyterianism instead of simply advancing the gospel. Hodge refuted the charge of sectarianism as an "amiable chimera . . .

the mere illusion of an ardent mind." Hodge reasoned, "No such thing exists on the face of the earth as Christianity in the abstract; and no such thing ever has been or ever can be propagated." Every Christian, Hodge contended, is of some denomination, and "no one is a Christian in the general." When missionaries evangelized and planted churches, therefore, they did so in the faith in which they had been trained. In the same manner they taught converts, administered the sacraments, ordained new leaders, and applied a polity as Presbyterians. Hodge concluded, "Under these circumstances, it would seem wise to send [the faith] in that form which you conscientiously believe to be the best." In his view, Presbyterians thereby held no animus against other denominations for their specific beliefs and practices. They merely followed a different polity. He considered other churches to be united in the body of Christ. Unlike New Schoolers such as Taylor, however, Hodge insisted that Presbyterians maintain the integrity of their faith by entrusting the education of their ministers and supervision of their missionary activity to boards specifically designed for that purpose and not relinquish these important tasks to other groups.[15]

Old School Theology vs. New School Innovations

Closely related to Presbyterian polity and of even greater importance to Hodge and his colleagues, New School ideas threatened Presbyterianism's theological moorings. When Hodge reviewed the *PR*'s four-decade advocacy of Old School concerns in his 1870 "Retrospect," he devoted more attention to "doctrines" than to any other topic. What Old Schoolers faced within Presbyterianism reflected trends that affected other evangelical denominations in that era. In the aftermath of the American Revolution, a process of democratization spilled over from the political realm and began to infiltrate intellectual and religious life. As old structures, visions, and authorities gave way to new, Presbyterians confronted the question of what form Reformed theology would take. Would Calvinists continue to maintain their unique identity by adhering to theological formulations of the earlier European confessions? Would they stress God's sovereignty, human depravity, and the doctrines of grace? Or would they modify these beliefs by softening the edges if not the core of these doctrines in keeping with the newly emerging evangelicalism? Such questions lay behind Hodge's staunch defense of Old School views.[16]

Hodge supported his claim of lack of new ideas in Princeton's journal by rehearsing key articles in the *PR*'s history harking back to Archibald Alexander's "The Early History of Pelagianism" in 1830. This article foreshadowed a series of rigorous, closely argued pieces that would follow, all devoted to defending the traditional doctrines of the Reformed faith. Of those articles, most would focus on the nature of sin and its ramifications. Hodge enumerated their topics: "the nature of Adam's sin; the effect of that sin on his posterity; the relation between him and his descendants; the nature of the hereditary depravity (or original sin); the inability of sinners; the work of the Holy Spirit in regeneration and sanctification of the soul." Not only did Hodge leave his distinctive mark on all these themes, they became signature elements in his theological career. Reflecting his negative comments on August Tholuck's views on Romans 5, Hodge believed that in explaining biblical redemption, only by beginning with original sin rooted in the imputation of Adam's sin to his posterity could one properly flesh out the remainder of Calvinistic orthodoxy on human passivity in regeneration, the imputation of Christ's vicarious sacrifice, and the nature of the Christian life. In six compact pages Hodge listed almost forty articles on these themes by title or subject matter, date, and contributor. He prefaced one paragraph by saying, "It is unnecessary, and would be tedious, to refer particularly to these articles. Few only need be specified." He then proceeded to illustrate his questionable definition of *few* by listing over fifteen articles![17]

Hodge forged his views in the theological controversies of the 1830s by engaging recently published works by prominent authors and subjecting their texts to trenchant review. He began with Andover Seminary professor Moses Stuart's commentary on Romans in 1833. Stuart was a Congregationalist and therefore not technically a New Schooler. His reputation at Andover Seminary as a biblical scholar with substantial linguistic skills resulted in his commentary on the book of Romans receiving high critical acclaim. His divergent interpretation of Romans, the key New Testament book for theological debate on the issues of human nature, attracted Hodge's attention. The critical review in the *PR* contributed to Hodge's assuming the front ranks as defender of Old School theology. He expressed admiration for Stuart's being "the great American reformer of biblical study" by training ministers in exegetical study of the Bible. But he lamented that Stuart, rather than interpreting Paul using philological skills honed by "the modern German school of expositors," had instead been captivated by variant theological views. At crucial points Stuart allowed theological views to take precedence over careful exegesis.[18]

Interpretation of Romans 5:12–19 would consistently be Hodge's litmus test of Westminster orthodoxy. Paul's exposition of Adam and Christ became the classical text for the doctrine of the imputation. A clear parallel existed between verse 12, in which the sin of Adam was the cause of the condemnation of the human race, and verse 19, in which the obedience of Christ was the basis for justification of believers. He sharply criticized Stuart for holding that the connection between Adam's sin and condemnation of all men was not expressly stated. For Stuart, "sin began with Adam, and as he died for his sin, so all men die for theirs." In Stuart's view of Romans 5:12, "The connexion between Adam's offence and the sin and condemnation of all men, is not *expressed*: it is merely *hinted at*" (Hodge's emphasis). For Hodge, on the other hand, a clear forensic unity existed between Adam's sin and the sinfulness of mankind and Christ's obedience and its effect on Christian believers. What held them together was the idea of imputation: Adam's sin and its consequence, death, was imputed to his posterity, and Christ's obedience and righteousness resulting in life was likewise imputed to believers, as explicitly stated in the doctrine of justification by faith. Hodge then succinctly framed the doctrine of imputation of Adam's sin: "The sin of Adam is so put to his posterity, that they are condemned on account of it, antecedent to any act of their own." Only on the basis of imputation can the parallel exist between Adam's sin and the condemnation of the human race and the righteousness of Christ and the justification of all believers. Hodge used this depiction of Adam and Christ as federal or representative heads, each legally representing a community—Adam representing the sum of mankind on the one hand and Christ representing believers on the other—as the central motif for understanding the cardinal doctrines of original sin and redemption. Each doctrine rested on the idea of imputation. Romans 5 held the two together as inseparable as a basis for understanding the human race as being lost and redemption of believers as its cure.[19]

The criticism of Stuart's commentary served as the first of many that Hodge lodged against other views of Romans 5. A year later, in 1834, Albert Barnes, pastor of First Presbyterian Church in Philadelphia, published a commentary on Romans, *Notes, Explanatory and Practical, on the Epistle to the Romans, Designed for Bible-Classes and Sunday Schools*. Although a graduate of Princeton, Barnes had already come under suspicion of holding unorthodox views in 1829.[20] His sermon "Way of Salvation" was accused of advocating views similar to those of New England Congregationalist Nathaniel W. Taylor, whom Hodge had met years earlier. In his famous sermon "*Concio ad Clerum*" (1828), Taylor advocated diverging from classical Calvinism's doctrines of original sin and Christ's atoning work because in his judgment they inhibited revivalism. Among Taylor's serious faults was his denial of the imputation of Adam's sin, asserting that man retains the power to obey the law and claiming that Christ's atoning work was for all.[21]

Barnes's book on Romans followed closely on the heels of his similarly popular treatment on the Gospels, which Hodge reviewed favorably in the first article of the 1835 *PR*. How quickly Hodge's opinion changed on Barnes's ability as a commentator is evident from the fact that the eighth article in the same issue subjected the Romans commentary to more searching criticism. Barnes's statement in the preface of the Romans commentary did not augur well for the rest of the book. Barnes wrote, "The design [of the book] has been to state what appeared to the author the real meaning of the epistle, without any regard to any existing theological system." While Barnes's statement conformed well to the emerging German critical method, for Hodge it could only stand in stark contrast with Barnes's ordination vows with regard to the Westminster Confession as a Presbyterian minister: "[Barnes] publically [*sic*] and solemnly assented to the truth of an existing 'system of doctrine.' It must therefore be to many an offensive declaration, that he does not care whether what he teaches falls within or without the pale of that system." Barnes's statement agreed more with Immanuel Kant's modern distinction between the responsibility of pastors and scholars than with Presbyterianism's confessionalist demand on its clergy regarding subscription to the Westminster Confession. In the context of the Enlightenment, Kant insisted on distinguishing between the moral obligation of scholars to present the result of a free investigation of mistaken views in church confessions versus the moral obligation of pastors to adhere to the church's creed in catechizing, teaching, and preaching. For Hodge, such a dualism was impossible, and Barnes would do well to accept the moral obligation of his ordination vows to write as a scholar within the boundaries of his confession.[22]

Hodge charged Barnes's work with a "want of maturity." Using a colorful phrase, he wrote that Barnes had "plucked his pear before it was ripe." Hodge's review read like a professor's marginal remarks after grading a student's paper: "There is a neglect of precision, accuracy and consistency in conducting his exposition, which evidently results from a lack of familiarity with the language of the Scriptures, or of disregard to the minutiae on which the correctness and certainty of interpretation depend . . . These and other similar evidences of want of accuracy, or strict attention to the original text, are very frequent." Hodge traced the deficiencies of Barnes's commentary to lack of proper regard of the original languages as required by Princeton's charter.[23]

Hodge proceeded to justify this judgment in the remainder of his review. On Barnes's treatment of Abraham's faith in Romans 4, he claims that Barnes had paid little attention to the text itself: "He takes it up as he would a sponge (wet with the dew of heaven) and squeezes every drop of moisture from it which he can express, and throws it to the reader as dry as he can make it." Hodge found Barnes's analysis of Romans 5:12–21 remarkably consistent with that of Stuart. Not surprisingly, he repeated his earlier criticisms—that Barnes rejected the imputation of Adam's sin and that the exegesis displayed "the same want of accuracy and philological correctness." In addition, when discussing Romans 8, Barnes remarked, "Sin has its seat in the fleshly appetites." Hodge retorted, "This is a common doctrine in Germany, and is the grossest form in which the doctrine of physical depravity has ever appeared," but it is "most assuredly" not Paul's view. In the final section of the review, Hodge moved from exegetical to doctrinal matters. He found the same "defects" as previously: "On the subjects of ability, depravity, imputation, and justification, we find the same inaccuracy and inconsistency which can only be accounted for from the immaturity of the author's views."[24]

One of Barnes's most glaring inconsistencies was his equivocation on original sin. In one passage he expressly denied the idea of depravity. Yet in commenting on Adam's sin he stated, "In like manner, although men are indubitably affected by the sin of Adam; as, e.g., by being born with a corrupt disposition; with loss of righteousness; with subjection to pain and woe; yet there is no reason to believe that they participate in the direct effect of sin, in eternal death, without being personal transgressors." Hodge was astonished at Barnes's inconsistency: "What more could anyone desire? This [the early part of the sentence] is nearly the definition of original sin given in the confessions of the Reformation." In discussing Barnes's treatment of imputation, he calls it "the great bugbear."[25]

Hodge concluded by denying any aggressive motive on his part in criticizing the commentary. Despite the sharp tone of the review, Hodge claimed merely to be defending traditional Reformed teaching. The hostility lay in Barnes's court—in his "violent . . . and gratuitous attack upon some of the most important doctrines of the church." Like Stuart before him, Barnes advanced innovative ideas that gave the New Schoolers their reputation for theological innovation. Rather than affirm doctrines that Presbyterians had long received as basic to the gospel—and that Barnes had confessed in his ordination vow—he chose to propagate new teaching. Hodge called him "an advocate for the progressive improvement of Theology." While progressivism may well fulfill the model for European theological education, given the proposed audience of Barnes's *Notes*—"Bible classes and Sunday schools"—within the Presbyterian church, Hodge believed it inappropriate to publish views before they could be corrected: "It would appear natural that he should allow room for his own growth instead of submitting to the process of petrifaction in his present state." In

Hodge's judgment, despite Barnes's original claim not to have written with any system in mind, given the content of the commentary, "the system of doctrines contained in the standards of the Presbyterian church seems to have been constantly before his mind. Instead of stating and defending his own views, he frequently and at length attacks those of the Confession of Faith."[26] Hodge was not alone in his criticism that Barnes's book put him at odds with his ordination vows. The General Assembly in 1831 had criticized his sermon "The Way of Salvation" for "unguarded and objectionable passages."[27]

In 1835, the Synod of Philadelphia suspended Barnes over content in *Notes on Romans*. The Barnes trial, combined with sharp disagreement over voluntary societies discussed above, illustrated the growing tension between Old and New School factions at the 1836 General Assembly. Not only did Hodge address at length differences over voluntary societies, but he sharply criticized the assembly's handling of Barnes's case when Barnes appealed his 1835 suspension.[28]

The appeal resulted in Barnes's acquittal, and Hodge's criticism of the assembly's handling of the affair appeared in his annual report in the *PR*. The New School manipulated the acquittal by demanding a simple "yes" or "no" vote on Barnes's suspension without distinguishing Barnes from his views. Supporters of Barnes contended that his orthodoxy in his subsequent explanations of sections in his book—the doctrine of original sin, the federal headship of Adam, and justification on the basis of imputation of Christ's righteousness—trumped the original objectionable content. Therefore, the assembly acquitted Barnes. Hodge found inexcusable that by its simple vote the assembly had exonerated both the man and the book. He argued that Barnes should have admitted his errors, thus separating himself from false views so that the assembly could exonerate him of the charges. According to Hodge, the view prevailed that Barnes's book taught "the New Haven doctrines" and "the New Haven men openly and constantly claim him as belonging to their side." By dismissing the book "without reproach," therefore, the assembly left itself open to future convulsions over what was acceptable teaching in the church.[29]

In his concluding remarks, Hodge expressed fear that a schism might eventually split the church, which, while beneficial to the portion that withdrew, would nevertheless "bring irreparable evils on others." Separation of a church was a most extreme action, and showing himself moderate in his views, Hodge doubted that the Presbyterian church in the majority had become unsound. He cited the closeness of votes on issues dividing the two factions to demonstrate that while differences existed, the "orthodoxy of the Presbyterian denomination" could be confidently asserted. Hodge trusted the denomination's polity to weather the storm of controversy: "To give up now would be to turn back when we have the goal in sight. All that we need is Presbyterianism—let our system have its way—it is able to stand worse times than these." Then he stated what would in fact become his line in the sand for dividing the church: "We cannot see, therefore, how any set of men can with a good conscience, desire to effect the division of the church until they are called upon to profess what they do not believe, or required to do what they cannot approve." This would become the moderate Old Schooler's mantra.[30]

When Stuart's and Barnes's books appeared, they, along with the commentary that Hodge's friend August Tholuck had published in 1824, became prominent texts on New Testament studies. Ironically, during this very period Hodge was preparing his own commentary on Romans, which appeared in 1835. Thus, in just over a decade, several major works on Paul's magisterial epistle became the point of contention between Old and New School theologies. Hodge produced his while enduring extreme discomfort in his leg and was confined to writing at his couch. He exchanged notes with his senior mentor over the method and content of the work, consulted several scores of other scholars, and quoted orthodox figures from the early church to Jonathan Edwards as colleagues in support of Calvinistic Old School theology.[31]

The Princeton Tradition

In the changing theological climate, as evidenced by the differing views of Stuart and Barnes, Hodge carried out his professorial responsibilities under the twin obligations of a biblical scholar and a Calvinistic confessionalist. Biblical studies at Princeton were not autonomous disciplines as they were in Europe. Whereas Barnes clearly viewed strict adherence to theological systems as too confining, demanding a priori what an exegete could find in a passage, Hodge labored under a more positive view of the relation between biblical studies and theology. He believed that the Westminster Confession conformed better than any other theological system to the entire content of Scripture. Therefore, as a Reformed biblical scholar, he carried out his exegetical research confident that the meaning extracted from the text would not contradict confessional content.

Hodge's son expressed Princeton's view of biblical scholarship succinctly by enumerating the two qualities that distinguished a good commentary. First, it must "show evidence of scholarship and exegetical tact and skill in the interpretation in detail of the words and sentences constituting the original text." Second, it must "discover a comprehension of the subject discussed, and of the design of the writer and the scope of ideas which constitute the subject-matter of the treatise commented on." Hodge was enabled to perform the former by his European sojourn; he was prepared to produce the latter by his entire education from his youth to his seminary training. And the son adds further, "It is self-evident that in Dr. Hodge's Commentary the latter of the two characteristics predominates. He has done his best honestly to get at what the words and sentences mean."[32]

These matters bring to the fore Hodge's abilities as an exegete both in classroom lectures and as an author and reviewer of biblical commentaries. Evaluations of Hodge's scholarship vary considerably.[33] Without exception, his critics, both positive and negative, agree that whatever the text, he excelled at mining its *doctrinal* content. Benjamin B. Warfield, who succeeded the Hodges as professor of theology at Princeton, analyzed and critiqued Hodge's classroom instruction.[34] Warfield claimed that Hodge's commentaries mirrored his lectures in their clarity and insightfulness: "Dr. Hodge's sense of the general meaning of a passage was unsurpassed. He had all of Calvin's sense of the flow and connection of thought. Consequently the analysis of the passages was superb. Nothing could surpass the clearness with which he set forth the general argument and the main connections of thought. Neither could anything surpass the analytical subtlety with which he extracted the doctrinal contents of the passages."[35]

Fellow Old Schoolers repeated on many occasions glowing assessments of Hodge's theological grasp of the text. Francis L. Patton, who served first at McCormick Seminary in Chicago and joined the Princeton faculty in 1881, labeled Hodge "a dogmatic exegete." He excelled at explaining the primary ideas of a passage, especially those relating to Reformed theology. But Adolphe Monod, who translated the commentary into French, stated the matter even more pointedly: "Dr. Hodge belongs to the religious opinion known in America by the name of the 'Old School.' His doctrine is precisely that of our own churches, and it is exhibited in the Commentary with remarkable distinctness and vigor. If we may venture the inquiry, we would ask as to this point whether the matter is not rather more precise and formal in Dr. Hodge's exposition, than in the Bible itself. We have learned from this Holy Book to have some dread of formulas that are too straitened, and of what Felix Neff, with his usual originality calls 'squared doctrines.' Happy are the authors who know how to preserve the proportions and balance which the Holy Spirit has observed in the development of the various topics of divine revelation." Neither Monod nor A. A. Hodge elaborated on "squared doctrines," but the term implies Charles Hodge's intention and success in stating clearly and forcefully what he construed as the meaning of the text and that the interpretation "squared" with the confession.[36]

Even Hodge's staunchest defenders, however, noted weaknesses. While Warfield's analysis of Hodge's theological expertise fairly sparkled with praise, his assessment of Hodge as an exegete was far less glowing: "He had, however, no taste for the technicalities of exegesis. He did not shrink from them in his lectures, indeed; but on such points he was seldom wholly satisfactory. His discussion of disputed grammatical or lexical points had a flavor of second-handedness about them. He appeared not to care to have a personal opinion upon such matters, but was content to accept another's without having made it his own. He would state, in such cases, several views from various critical commentators, and then make a choice between them; but I could not always feel that his choice was determined by sound linguistic principles. He sometimes seemed to be quite as apt to choose an indefensible as a plausible one—guided, apparently, sometimes by weight of name, sometimes by dislike to what seemed to him over-subtlety, and sometimes, it seemed, by theological predilection." Lest one remember only Hodge's weakness as an exegete, Warfield quickly added that he considered Hodge to be the best teacher he ever had: "He was in fact my ideal of a teacher. Best of all men I have ever known, he knew how to make a young man think."[37]

As he completed chapters on his Romans commentary, Hodge solicited comments and suggestions from his mentor, who willingly obliged. Alexander proved to be Hodge's most encouraging critic, and he did so by proposing a difficult goal—that Hodge address his commentary to a dual audience. Foremost would be the academic community. Hodge's work would join Moses Stuart's as another major exposition of the apostle Paul's letter. Hodge's book would be the Old School's contribution to the growing field of biblical commentaries, utilizing tools he had honed while in Europe. Very much aware of the inroads made by the "new anthropology of the New England school," Hodge would refute the notion that its proposed changes were "improvements"—rather, labeling them as divergences from Reformed theology. Hodge's work would feature a Reformed analysis of passages crucial to a Calvinistic interpretation of Paul's teaching—those passages regarding the fall and its effects on human nature, necessitating God's sovereign grace in Christ's saving work.[38]

In addition, Alexander proposed that Hodge's work reach beyond the scholarly world to a much broader community: the lay audience. The church as well as the academy needed the Reformed faith. To this end he urged Hodge to address comments on the original Greek in notes at the bottom of the page: "Let the text of your Commentary be pure English. By this means it will be studied by all intelligent Presbyterians, and will become a *hand-book* for teachers of Sunday Schools and Bible classes." In another note commenting on Romans 8, Alexander contended that Hodge's work would possess "an incalculable advantage over Stuart's and other learned works, as it can be read by the plain, intelligent Christian who knows nothing of the original [languages]." Alexander wished for his pupil's book to have the same impact that John Calvin's first edition of the *Institutes* had had in the sixteenth century when it made Reformed views of the Bible accessible to the widest possible audience. Barnes's earlier commentary on the Gospels had had the same influence on the American church. Alexander rendered his favorable opinion on the chapters and expressed the hope that the book would figure largely in the rising conflict between Old and New Schools within the denomination. In the exchange of notes between the two, Hodge stated several times that he valued his mentor's opinions and that he clearly wanted to be warned lest he publish anything "incorrect." Alexander also offered the assistance of his two sons, James and Addison, prolific writers in their own right. The spirit of camaraderie that almost universally characterized the Princetonians emerges from this correspondence.[39]

Hodge's Romans commentary proved a success. Not only was it translated into French, but Alexander's suggestion resulted in an abridged edition that appeared in 1836, which appealed to a lay readership in both America and England. It established Hodge as a leading interpreter of Old School theology over against those who wanted to improve theology by importing ideas from New England. Decades later, in 1864, a revised edition was published in which Hodge included German works published in the interim.[40]

Hodge's use of the *PR* illustrated the confidence with which he took up his duties following his European studies. Through his efforts, the journal became a major arm of Old Schoolers as they differentiated their views from those of New Schoolers. Not only did Hodge articulate a nuanced assessment of voluntary societies, but he also carefully distinguished Old School doctrinal views from those of other prominent biblical scholars. The vision of his original *Dissertation* of the necessity for proliferation of orthodox views in the rising climate of theological change was becoming fulfilled under his editorship of the *PR*. His reviews reflect a readiness, even boldness, to take on all comers. Lack of self-assurance lay in the past. He would also ensure that the orthodoxy of the past would not be forgotten.

17

Old School Nurture vs. New School Revivalism

A third issue that Charles Hodge debated with New Schoolers was the Second Great Awakening—its legitimacy, leadership, and theological principles, as well as the means by which it spread. Charles Grandison Finney, who rose from obscurity in upper New York state, published sermons and theological works that earned him a national reputation for his role in revival campaigns and advocacy of Arminian and—even more radically—Pelagian views. Finney compounded the matter by implementing highly pragmatic "new measures" as the means of carrying out revivals throughout the Northeast. Hodge's opposition to Finney and New School revivalism knew almost no bounds. His assessment of the history of American revivalism not only illustrates the solidification of previous views of Presbyterian piety but also represents a shift from his earlier opinions of revivals, which strained his relationship with his mentor, Archibald Alexander.[1]

Hodge entered the controversy over the revivalism of the Second Great Awakening by broaching the nature of the Christian life. We noted in chapter 3 Richard Robert Osmer's distinction between the nurture and crisis models of conversion that developed among Presbyterians during the First Great Awakening. These differences resulted in the Old School–New School schism that divided Presbyterians from 1741 to 1758. Initially, Presbyterians supporting the awakening understood conversion not as an independent, freestanding event in a person's life but rather as an event that culminated in an extended nurturing process of catechizing covenant children in the Westminster doctrines. Mary Hodge had followed this paradigm in raising Charles and his brother. Not only did she "drill" them in the Westminster Catechism, but the family also attended church each Lord's Day. They participated in corporate worship, witnessed the sacraments of baptism and the Lord's Supper, received instruction, and observed church discipline as such cases arose. The family minister, Ashbel Green, reinforced this spiritual regimen through pastoral visits to the home, where he questioned Charles and Hugh on the catechism. Hodge's conversion during the revival at Princeton therefore marked a continuity with the past as well as a culmination of the means of grace practiced individually and corporately. Nurture served as the foundation for all of Hodge's religious experience. In fact, it provided the context that gave meaning to all stages in Hodge's life—his infancy, early childhood, adolescence, and adulthood. Nurture functioned as the epistemological grid through which Hodge interpreted all his experience.

The purpose of catechism in the "crisis/nurture" model changed significantly, however, with the arrival of the Second Great Awakening early in the following century. As emphasis shifted to the necessity of conversion as the basis for church membership, catechizing declined in importance. Conversion in this new model did not follow on the heels of careful instruction so that it occurred in continuity with individuals' entire upbringing. Instead, conversion began to stand alone. Osmer states, "The importance of theological or scriptural knowledge gained through a lengthy period of education and discipline in the church was giving way to an instantaneous view of Christian conversion." Osmer continues: "Revivalism now threatened to turn [prominent New Side Presbyterian supporter of the First Great Awakening Gilbert] Tennent's portrayal of catechetical instruction and admission as a time of spiritual awakening into a freestanding, full-scale conversion, independent of the nurture of the church."[2] Dramatic conversions gave the Second Great Awakening its salient reputation—converts testified to extravagant life-changing experiences. Old Schoolers, though they did not disparage conversion per se, believed that separating it from the context of Christian nurture placed undue emphasis on a one-time experience at the expense of a previous lifetime of training and worship in the home and church.[3]

A further transformation of piety took place with the emergence of Finney's New School revivalism. Whereas Jonathan Edwards in the First Great Awakening had called revivals surprising works of God's providence, Finney claimed that revivals were not special providences but rather man-made works in which people used perfectly natural means to produce conversions, much as a farmer used long-recognized agricultural methods to guarantee a harvest. His "new measures" transformed the very nature of revivals. They consisted of protracted meetings (campaigns of several days or a week in a geographical area designed to generate interest in revival), addressing people directly and mentioning well-known sinners by name from local areas, employing women in the pulpit, and perhaps the most famous measure: the anxious bench—an area at the front of the church or meeting place where persons could respond to an altar call. No longer were revivals miraculous, God's mysterious and providential gifts from heaven; they were merely the result of utilizing ordinary means. Finney famously stated that a revival is not a miracle but is "a purely philosophical result of the right use of the constituted means." Finney vacillated in his view of human capacity to produce revivals. Portions of his *Lectures on Revivals of Religion* led people to condemn Finney's view as espousing the idea that man can manipulate revivals simply by utilizing the new measures. Charged with a rather blatant pragmatism, Finney at other times softened his view of the new measures.[4]

Baptism of Infants

Hodge is frequently remembered for his charges in the *PR* that Finney's revivalism intruded Pelagian doctrine into the denomination.[5] Not so well known is Hodge's lament that revivalism, rather than furthering traditional piety, severely undermined nurturing piety. Mary Hodge's understated comments about her son's conversion at the Princeton revival reflect a similar concern. The logic of Finney's New School revivalism led to still another radical change in piety that rankled Hodge—the decline of infant baptism. Hodge used a notice of George D. Armstrong's work on baptism as a pretext for an extended article in 1857 on the "neglect of household baptism" in the Presbyterian church. Hodge explored the neglect of baptism by examining the denomination's view of children and their position in the church, the sharp decline of paedobaptism in practice, the causes for this neglect, and how the trend could be reversed.[6]

Hodge began by asserting that children of professing Christians were members of the visible church. This view contrasted with traditional Baptist belief that only adults were members of the church. Baptists' children were regarded as merely existing under the foster care of the church until they experienced conversion, confessed Christ publicly, and then submitted to baptism of immersion. Only then did they become members of the church. Hodge protested vehemently against such exclusion of children from church membership. He contended that the "old common doctrine" declared children church members upon their baptism as infants. It rested on the minor premise in the following syllogism: "Members of the Church are the proper subjects of discipline: All baptized persons are members of the Church: Therefore, all baptized persons are the proper subjects of discipline."[7]

Since children were members of the church, the confession and the Scriptures affirmed that they were "within the covenant and therefore ought to be baptized," following Jesus' command to baptize in the Great Commission of Matthew 28:18–20. Thus, Hodge concluded, parental and congregational neglect of baptizing children constituted a "great sin . . . against God, and serious injustice . . . to . . . children." It was "a breach of covenant, and a rejection of the grace presented in the ordinance." Forgoing baptism cut children off from the benefits of "church oversight and care." Baptizing children also fulfilled Christ's command to feed the sheep. Depriving children of the seal of the covenant deprived them of edification that came through the church's ministry. Thus, under the influence of growing sympathy with Baptist views of the church, Hodge uncovered a serious flaw emerging in Presbyterian practice.[8]

Perhaps most interesting in the article is Hodge's meticulous documentation of the neglect of infant baptism that prompted his article. He constructed two tables to summarize statistical reports of baptisms submitted by church sessions. The tables displayed the proportion between the number of members and children baptized from 1807 to 1857. He emphasized the following stunning statistics: "Fifty years ago, there were about 200 children baptized for every thousand communicants; now [1857] but 50—only one-fourth as many. Fifty years ago, there was one child baptized for every five members; now but one for 20! . . . In 1811 there were only 23,639 communicants, and yet there were 4,677 baptisms. And yet in 1856, with ten times as many members, we have only twice as many baptisms of children; showing . . . 34,328 children excluded from this holy ordinance within the past year, being almost three-fourths of the infant members of the Church!" He hypothesized that no child had been left unbaptized in 1811. Based on the figures submitted over the fifty-year period, "there should have been . . . 1,249,776 children baptized, whereas there were but 424,470, only one-third of that number, leaving 825,306 children . . . 'cut off from their church' by their parents' act . . . a number nearly equal to three times the whole number of members at present in the Church!" After fully summarizing the data, Hodge concluded that "*more than half* [emphasis in original] of the offspring of the Church are deprived of this ordinance." Some proposed that the decrease in number of baptisms might be due to factors other than willful neglect, such as inaccurate reporting and decrease in size of Presbyterian families. Hodge retorted, however, that more attention was currently paid to recordkeeping than formerly and that decrease in family size—if it actually existed—was out of proportion to the remarkable decline in baptisms.[9]

All this number-crunching provided fodder for Hodge's complaint against the New School. The decline from 198 baptisms per thousand communicants to 51 per thousand occurred when New School and Congregational elements were most dominant in American Christianity. After the 1837 schism resulting in the loss of New School families, the number of infant baptisms slightly increased in Old School congregations. Using another table, Hodge showed that the New School church, after the denominational split, exhibited greater neglect of infant baptism than was true of the united church. "This increasing difference continued until in 1847 the New-school reported only 19 for each thousand members, the Old-school, at the same time, reporting 52, being nearly three times as many to the thousand amongst the Old-school as amongst the New." Hodge then demonstrated that if as a norm there ought to be one baptism a year for every six members (the figure that he used in his previous analysis), "there should have been amongst the New-school 400,413 baptisms instead of 62,250, the number reported; that is, six children out of seven, or six-sevenths of their children, being 338,163, are unbaptized! All of them of 18 years old and under." The full implication of this neglect was that since these children were not baptized, they were also not considered members of the church and thus did not receive the benefits of its nurture and discipline.[10]

New School Presbyterians were not the only denomination to register a decline in infant baptisms. Congregational churches in New England showed an even more precipitous drop. Vermont reported but 7 baptisms for every thousand members; New Hampshire registered 14 and Maine 16 per thousand. Having analyzed the stark statistics, Hodge posed the startling question with tongue firmly in cheek, "Can it be their intention to place it [baptism] amongst the five rejected sacraments of Rome?"[11]

Hodge focused special attention on widespread refusal among Presbyterians to recognize children as members of the church and churches' failure to instruct young people after their baptism.[12] He cited the lack of doctrinal instruction on baptism and particularly the absence of sermons on the subject. While sacramental seasons always witnessed sermons on the responsibilities of believers' participating in the Lord's Supper, sermons on baptism were remarkable by their absence. Hodge noted that if pastors neglected baptism in their public teaching, people would fail to discharge their duties regarding their children. When he queried confirmands during his European visit, he was happily surprised with their ready answers to topics covered by the catechism. In stark contrast, few Presbyterian young people understood their relation to the church. He wrote, "We have asked scores of them, and in a very few instances only have we received an intelligent reply." Unlike the custom of his own childhood, Hodge claimed that pastors did not gather children for instruction in doctrine and the sacraments, despite directives from several General Assemblies. Hodge also accused the Second Great Awakening of being a cause of this neglect. In 1830 the annual number of adult baptisms was three thousand and the number of infants was twelve thousand. Nine thousand were received by profession of faith. But in 1832 (in the midst of great revivals), the number of members received and the number of adults baptized tripled, while the number of infants baptized was only one-twelfth of the previous number. This routine continued "during the excitements in our churches from 1831–36, which were of New England and Congregational origin. 'New measures' were popular, and the old doctrine of infant baptism shamefully neglected."[13]

As revivalists in the Second Great Awakening doubled their efforts to make conversion a freestanding event and the decisive precondition for church membership, Hodge refined his view to the contrary. Fully aware of Baptist views of the gathered church—the ideal of a fully converted membership—infiltrating his denomination through revivalism, Hodge reminded his audience of the Presbyterian doctrine of the church in a lengthy article, "The Church Membership of Infants." While he admitted that the vast majority of Christians taught that the church consists of the true people of God, the distinction between the visible and invisible church necessitated an inclusive but not indiscriminate membership. By this he meant not to dilute the qualifications for church membership, but simply to acknowledge that Christ did not establish the criteria of a gathered church. Since only God knows the heart, no one was permitted to demand evidence of regeneration as a prerequisite for membership. To be sure, Christ never commanded "the impossible task of making a church . . . consist exclusively of the regenerate." Instead he required that we "recognize as Christians all those who, having competent knowledge, profess their faith in him, and are free from scandal." Since only Christ could discern between wheat and chaff, the church could not detect the true state of another person's heart. The only possible answer to the question of what should be required for church membership was a "credible profession of the true religion, or the filial relation to a parent who professes the true religion." Therefore, following Jesus' clear teaching, the church must treat as Christians "multitudes who are unrenewed in heart."[14]

Hodge explored the importance of infants' being included in the church as members and not simply as potential converts. In the political realm, for example, children were considered citizens by virtue of their relation with their parents, and parents acted on their behalf until they became old enough to make decisions on their own. Similarly, under biblical covenants, parents professed faith for their offspring. What did membership of infants in the church entail for Hodge? "We do not assert their regeneration, or that they are true members of Christ's body; we only assert that they belong to the class of persons whom we are bound to regard and treat as members of Christ's Church. This is the only sense in which even adults are members of the Church, so far as men are concerned."[15]

Hodge proceeded to outline the biblical view that had formed not only his life but the relations of all believers. Those relations cohered within a vast inclusive covenantal framework—a covenant of grace originating with Abraham. By covenantal injunction, children were treated as being within the covenant because not only did all adults "who make a credible confession" accept the covenant for themselves, but they also "lay hold of the same covenant in [their children's] behalf." The covenant relationship was then sealed by the sign of circumcision, which "marked those who were visibly included in the covenant of grace." Since the existence of the church was the New Testament fulfillment of the Abrahamic covenant and baptism succeeded circumcision as the sign of covenant membership, "the argument for the Church membership of infants is conclusive."[16]

Hodge demonstrated the connection between the two covenantal signs by analyzing circumcision as the "token" or seal of the covenant because the physical act signified the spiritual "circumcision of the heart." To support his view, Hodge cited Deuteronomy 10:15–16; 30:6; Jeremiah 4:4; 9:26; and Acts 7:51. He concluded, "As baptism with water is the symbol of the baptism of the Spirit, so circumcision of the flesh was the symbol of circumcision of the heart. If infants cannot be baptized, because the symbol of regeneration can be applied to those only who give evidence of regeneration, neither could circumcision." All those who received the token were "*foederati*," participants in the covenant. Hodge confidently asserted that the church the world over, excluding Baptists, considered children within its bounds and thus the recipients of its promises and benefits. Thus Hodge returned to his original intent in the essay by asserting, "The neglect of infant baptism is therefore the rejection of those promises and privileges."[17]

To solidify his point, Hodge asked a series of questions to stress the importance of putting children in a position to benefit from their inclusion in the church: "Is it nothing to be within that covenant in which God promises to be our God? Is it nothing to belong to that class in which almost without exception the blessings of redemption flow? Do we wish to exclude our children from all interest in the special promises made to the baptized, that is, to those who bear the seal of the covenant?" To refuse to baptize one's child, like refusing to circumcise one's child in the Old Testament, put the child's salvation in jeopardy. Including children within the covenant people did not remove their responsibility to affirm their faith upon reaching adulthood. Just as a Jewish child had to come to the point of submitting to God's covenant, so baptized children when they came to a "suitable age, and have the requisite knowledge . . . should be required to assume for themselves their baptismal vows, and should, as other church members, be disciplined for any neglect or violation of their covenanted obligations."[18]

Hodge then summarized an argument that logically he had begun in the 1857 article on the neglect of infant baptism. He did so by quoting chapter 9 of the *Directory* in the Westminster Standards: "Children born within the pale of the visible Church, and dedicated to God in baptism, are under the inspection and government of the Church; and are to be taught to read, and to repeat the catechism, the apostles' creed, and the Lord's prayer. They are to be taught to pray, to abhor sin, to fear God, and to obey the Lord Jesus Christ. And when they come to the years of discretion, if they be free from scandal, appear sober and steady, and to have sufficient knowledge to discern the Lord's body, they ought to be informed that it is their duty, and their privilege, to come to the Lord's supper."[19]

The article ends abruptly. The *Directory*'s entry needed no further comment. It served as the model for Hodge's family and thus his own Christian experience. It was in danger of being superseded by New School piety. The quotation summarized his case that he had begun with his statistical lament of the decline of baptismal practice of his denomination a year earlier. New School revivalism had diverged from traditional piety based on Presbyterian practice. It did so by making conversion a freestanding event separated from the time-tested means of grace, which included nurture within the Christian home, learning under the preaching of the Word, and observation of the virtues of the Christian life practiced within the covenant community. New School practice also made conversion the overriding prerequisite of church membership. Anyone who could not identify a crisis conversion was made to feel that his or her religious experience was inferior and perhaps even invalid. It also presumed that people could inspect the hearts of those applying for church membership, make a judgment of their spiritual state, and either accept or reject their membership in the church, rather than presume that people were among the elect as manifested by their credible profession and life free from scandal.

Christian Nurture

The most obvious way in which the seminary fulfilled its obligation to nurture students consistent with its Plan occurred weekly in the Oratory. Wednesday evenings were devoted to prayer. Sunday afternoons, on the other hand, were set aside for a more extended time when students and faculty gathered for prayer and discussion of themes relating to the affective elements of the Christian life. A. A. Hodge described the purpose of the Sabbath conferences: "Here the venerable professors appeared rather as friends and pastors than as instructors. The dry and cold attributes of scientific theology, moving in the sphere of the intellect gave place to the warmth of personal religious experience, and to the spiritual light of divinely illuminated intuition" and thereby "exerted by far, their most widely extended and permanent influence."[20] The text or topic, announced beforehand, was addressed by the professors, with the most senior speaking last. In the early years, Hodge preceded Miller and Alexander; as time progressed, Hodge spoke in the place of honor. That the intellect was not eliminated, however, is clear from the practice of some students' taking notes![21]

While Hodge spoke movingly on the topics, he fell short of his mentor, who had the greater reputation for eliciting deep emotional responses from his hearers.[22] Hodge addressed the conference without notes, interspersing his exposition with illustrations. While his remarks had the appearance of spontaneity, his son found Hodge's desk drawer filled with detailed preparations for each occasion—a "careful analysis or skeleton of every Conference discourse." Though some topics repeated over the years, Hodge never used the same outline twice but always penned a new outline.[23]

Hodge's attention to detail becomes evident when one examines the discourses. In compiling the volume, his son grouped the 249 outlines under ten headings, among which were "God and His Attributes," "Christ, His Person and Offices," and "Death, and the Consummation of Redemption." Apropos of the purpose of the Sabbath conferences is the fact that most addresses appeared under topics directly related to the spiritual life, such as "Conversion—Entrance upon the Christian Life" and "The Means of Grace—The Scriptures, Ministry, Sacraments, etc." While many sections of the collection contained only about fifteen sermons, the largest section, "Christian Experiences, Characteristics and Privileges," contained over a hundred messages. Like the sermons he preached in the various pulpits of the Princeton area, Hodge never omitted addressing the spiritual implications of the Scripture text or the topic.[24]

Hodge, and Old Princeton in general, frequently came under criticism by historians for never effectively combining the cognitive and affective elements of Christian religious experience. Whether that lay within the limits of possibility remained an open question because of the frail and fractured nature of the human condition.[25] Hodge and his fellow Princetonians, however, should not be faulted for lack of effort. Hodge's most detailed exposition of the problem of integrating a theology of the intellect and theology of the feelings appeared in an extended debate over eighteen months through three articles in the *PR* with Edwards Amasa Park. Hodge primarily contended that truth in intellect and truth in feelings in Christian experience must never contradict each other.[26]

In addition to his direct contribution to the nurture of seminarians through sermons and conference addresses, Hodge addressed the issue of nurture as a topic in his review of Horace Bushnell's *Discourses on Christian Nurture* in 1847. Bushnell, minister of Hartford's North Congregational Church, also opposed revivalism by his thesis that the ideal Christian conversion is gradual. The child should grow up never knowing himself to be other than a Christian as a result of faithful parental training and pastoral instruction. In the opening line of his review, Hodge praised the book for its "organic" influence—its emphasis on family and corporate church life. He paid Bushnell's book a high compliment by saying that it had "very much of an 'Old School' cast." Hodge applauded Bushnell for emphasizing that strong familial ties were "the great means for the salvation of the children of the church." As a result of parents and the congregation fulfilling their covenantal responsibilities, when the child "comes to maturity" and professes faith, "it is obvious that in such cases it must be difficult both for the person himself and for those around him, to fix on the precise period when he passed from death to life." Hodge even went so far as to say that "this is the appointed, the natural, the normal and ordinary means by which the children of believers are made truly the children of God." While a danger existed that such childhood training might degenerate into "mere formality and hypocrisy," resulting in a life "destitute of religion," a worse mistake would be to go to the opposite extreme and ignore Christian nurture. Thus revivalists, by making a conversion experience the only way of coming to faith, counterintuitively seemed to presume it better to leave their children to grow up unconverted. In their view, conversion could "only be effected in a sudden and sensible manner, a work necessarily distinct to the consciousness of its subject and apparent to those around him." Hodge contended pointedly, "We see [this mistake] in the disproportionate reliance placed on the proclamation of the gospel from the pulpit, as almost the only means of conversion; and in the disposition to look upon revivals as the only hope of the church."[27]

Hodge immediately paused to affirm his belief that revivals involving Jonathan Edwards, George Whitefield, Gilbert Tennent, and Samuel Davies had brought great blessing to the church. He rejected, however, the "hurtful error" that "these extraordinary seasons [were] the only means of promoting religion." In light of his earlier critique of the Great Awakening, he could not resist adding that the gospel did not advance by "sudden and violent paroxysms of exertion"! Unfortunately, revival excitements offered potentially dramatic and spectacular experiences, which rendered "the ordinary means of grace . . . insipid or distasteful." Even ministers fell prey to relying on revivals "so that all other means are lost sight of." Hodge insisted that the less spectacular and unremarkable means of grace from an external point of view produced far more reliable and lasting work in people's inner spiritual lives.[28]

Hodge could hardly have come upon a book whose thesis comported better with his own views. Thus he fairly gushed with enthusiasm as he unfolded Bushnell's argument. Most obviously, *Christian Nurture* mirrored Hodge's own life. Bushnell's account of familial and corporate nurture captured in virtually every detail how his mother and pastor had contributed to Charles's spiritual trajectory from early childhood to profession of faith at Princeton. While Hodge may not have called his conversion "gradual," clearly his advancement from early experiences to mature faith reflected Bushnell's developmental model. Bushnell also explicitly stated that his case for nurture depended on traditional doctrines that Hodge so fondly expounded—above all that a natural depravity inhibited the will so that when it "would struggle up towards it own ideals, it cannot reach them, cannot apart from God, even lift itself towards them."[29]

After praising *Christian Nurture* for its affinity to traditional piety in some matters, Hodge proceeded to point out its most serious defect—that despite Bushnell's claim to be a supernaturalist, the book exhibited naturalistic undertones in its depiction of nurture. While Bushnell was a naturalist neither "in the sense of the French school" nor in advocating a merely mechanistic operation of the universe, Hodge said that in Bushnell's treatment "there is no distinction between God's providential agency and the operations of his grace." Thus Bushnell viewed regeneration as merely a providential event analogous to acts of nature: "It is the privilege of the Christian . . . that by the grace of God dwelling in him [the parent] and the child, fashioning his own character as an organic mould provided, he may set forth the child into life as a seed after him—one that is prepared unto a godly life by causes prior to his own will; that is by causes metaphysically organic." Despite grateful appreciation for Bushnell's use of "nurture," Hodge made the strongest possible distinction between the agency used by God in the ordinary operations of nature and the agency of God's Spirit in conversion. Bushnell made no such distinction.[30]

Hodge's contribution to piety as an Old Schooler reiterated his family's long-standing model of Christian experience. Nurture constituted the driving force of his own intensely personal religious life. At every stage of his life he benefited from experiences that taken together shaped his character and spiritual life. By his own admission, God used nurture to establish a spiritual sensitivity that gradually matured into a fully formed adult spirituality. Hodge considered this the normal pattern of sanctification. Because he made the closest connection between Christianity as a doctrine (set of propositions) and a way of life, the two were inextricably woven together. He realized that more was at stake in the nineteenth century than simply the content of Reformed theology. Since he viewed Calvinism holistically, any changes to theology inevitably infringed on piety. Hodge therefore recognized the benefits that accrued to his denomination from God's providential control of the revivals of both the First and the Second Great Awakenings. He even acknowledged with gratitude the conversions reported in the "burned-over district" of western New York. But the awakening had its downsides as well. It often spawned enthusiastic excesses; its model of conversion threatened to replace nurture; and it even put infant baptism, one of the Reformed church's undisputed sacraments, in jeopardy.

Orthodoxy in theology must, if it is genuine, manifest itself in an equally orthodox piety. Mark Noll has commented that Hodge "could wax lyrical at the end of the driest theological demonstration."[31] Thus his impassioned plea for a reinstatement of infant baptism followed his rather dry statistical charts. We are not surprised that nurture also figured most prominently in his critique of revivalist religious experience. He issued carefully measured responses to what he considered the advantages and disadvantages of revivalism. He exploited another opportunity to champion the Old School perspective because nurture in all its practical ramifications made the most rewarding connection between Christianity as a doctrine and a life.

18

Abolitionism vs. Gradual Elimination of Slavery

A final issue separating Old and New School extended beyond the topics of biblical, theological, and ecclesiastical matters and indicates how Princeton and Charles Hodge as its most representative voice contributed to the national political scene. Hodge advanced beyond his elder colleagues in the level of his involvement in political debate. Samuel Miller's two-volume *Brief Retrospect of the Eighteenth Century* explored a broad range of cultural topics, and in the political arena Miller was noted for his disdain for Jeffersonian democracy. Archibald Alexander, on the other hand, shunned political matters, rarely even voted, and never used the pulpit to express political views. In sharp contrast, Hodge, following the tradition of earlier Reformed thinkers, believed political affairs worthy of careful attention by Christian thinkers. Politics affected everyone's life to a greater or lesser degree and clearly manifested God's providence in the wide spectrum of public life. Thus Hodge engaged in extensive and perceptive comment on issues and events that roiled mid-nineteenth-century American culture.[1]

The most volatile political topic was the notorious issue of slavery. An intellectual battle over slavery broke out in American churches before actual hostilities erupted in the Civil War. Debates over the morality of slavery and whether or how it should be abolished easily became the most contested issue among the various social crusades and the voluntary societies they spawned to reform antebellum America. Presbyterians were no exception. They went on record at the General Assembly of 1818 declaring that slavery was "a gross violation of the most precious and sacred rights of nature . . . utterly inconsistent with the law of God . . . totally irreconcilable with the spirit and principles of the Gospel of Christ" and that it was "manifestly the duty of all Christians to efface this blot on our holy religion, and to obtain the complete abolition of slavery throughout Christendom, and if possible throughout the world."[2]

After that initial straightforward declaration and challenge, however, the denomination became more passive on the matter because of strong disagreements among its membership. Presbyterians feared that more pronouncements would only foment irreconcilable differences among the church's members. These disparities lay along Old School–New School lines. New Schoolers favored abolitionists' insistence that slaveholding was inherently sinful, that it should be abolished immediately, and that slaveholders should be subject to church discipline. Old Schoolers, on the other hand, ranged widely between avid, proslavery Southerners and Northerners who favored gradual elimination. Southerners such as James Henley Thornwell, Old School theologian who taught at Columbia Theological Seminary, believed that the Bible not only permitted slavery but taught that it ought to be perpetuated as foremost among various means that God established to regulate relations between whites and blacks. Southern Old Schoolers also believed that the spirituality of the church militated against the denomination's active involvement in the slavery question. As Hodge entered the discussion over these issues, he found himself advocating a mediating position, caught in the crossfire between ardent New School abolitionists and equally zealous proslavery Southerners.[3]

Hodge established his case in three definitive articles in the *PR*: "Slavery" (1836), "Abolitionism" (1844), and "Emancipation" (1849).[4] Hodge fashioned his social, ethical, and political views to carve out a centrist position between ideological extremists on both flanks. Foremost among his concerns, as Mark Noll has pointed out, he wanted to ground his views in biblical teaching. He used the grammatical-historical method of exegesis rather than a strict literalism to articulate a nuanced biblical perspective. His hermeneutical maxim was to allow Scripture to interpret itself: "our object is not to discuss the subject of slavery upon abstract principles, but to ascertain the scriptural rule of judgement and conduct in relation to it."[5]

Opponents at both ends of the spectrum, in Hodge's opinion, failed to follow this method. Responding to New School lobbying at the General Assembly of 1836, Hodge argued that the "grand mistake" of abolitionists was that "they do not discriminate between slaveholding in itself considered, and its accessories at any particular time or place." Abolitionism differed fundamentally from the antislavery position. Whereas antislavery advocates wanted abuses within slaveholding addressed and slaveholding removed gradually, abolitionists demanded the immediate end of slavery because they falsely assumed that slavery was universally based in manstealing, piracy, and murder, and that wherever slavery was practiced in America, marital and parental rights were violated, whips and chains harassed slaves, and vice and degradation predominated. Hodge compared abolitionists to extremists in the temperance movement who, rather than preach temperance, denounced all alcoholic consumption. Abolitionists would be on sounder ground, said Hodge, if they cited New Testament writers who condemned the injustices associated with various Roman institutions but not the institutions themselves.[6] Their fault was their extremism: "They have upheld the most extreme publications and made common cause with the most reckless declaimers. The wildest ravings of the *Liberator* [William Lloyd Garrison's abolitionist Boston paper] have been constantly lauded. . . . We do not doubt their sincerity; but we marvel at their delusion." Hodge believed abolitionists demanded an immediate end of slavery not from mandates of biblical text but from abuses within the system of slavery, which they then used to read into the text their concept of *malum in se* slavery (slavery as evil in itself). In their treatment of Scripture, New School abolitionists exemplified "willful and violent perversions of the sacred text" by forcing the Bible to support their views rather than submitting their views to biblical teaching.[7] Hodge therefore opposed New Schoolers' version of abolitionism. Their three main demands—acceptance of slaveholding as a sin, advocacy of excommunicating slaveholders from the church, and abolishing slavery immediately—not only were not justified by the Bible but if acted on would wreak havoc within the church and on the country.[8]

For Hodge, the biblical view exemplified by Christ and the apostles differed radically from that of the abolitionists. He asked, "How did they [Christ and the apostles] treat it? Not by denunciation of slaveholding as necessarily and universally sinful. Not by declaring that all slaveholders were men-stealers and robbers, and consequently to be excluded from the church and the kingdom of heaven. Not by insisting on immediate emancipation." Instead they laid down moral principles obligating specific treatment of slaves. They taught "the true nature, dignity, equality and destiny of men; [and by] inculcating the principles of justice and love; and by leaving these principles to produce their legitimate effects in ameliorating the condition of all classes of society." Therefore, the Bible addressed the morality of slavery by concentrating on abuses and injustices that accompanied not only slavery but all other human institutions existing under the infection of human sin. Because the abolitionists' solution differed from that of Christ and the apostles, the former "must be wrong and ought to be modified or abandoned."[9]

Following that lead, Hodge considered the Southern slave laws fair game for vigorous criticism based on clear biblical teaching. Southerners' failure to engage in this criticism was foundational to his opposition to proslavery advocates. He enumerated abuses involving marital and familial relations and property, educational, and spiritual rights of slaves. In each instance Hodge applied what he considered appropriate biblical passages that offered unambiguous instruction. He condemned slaveowners' failure to recognize marriages of slaves. He used marital passages from the Pauline corpus to condemn as sin the failure of Southerners to protect the marriages of slaves.[10] The humanity of the Negro entailed by the unity of the blood of all nations meant that slaves should receive all of God's provisions for mankind, including the institution of marriage.[11] Familial rights derived naturally from slaves' humanity. Southern laws permitting owners to sell children needed revision because they violated the biblical injunction for parents to raise their children in the nurture and admonition of the Lord.[12] Their humanity and the sixth commandment's prohibition against stealing meant that slaves had the right to own and possess property. Slaves should be able to work and earn wages apart from their owner's property. In addition, slaveowners who confiscated slaves' property should be subject to legal consequences.[13] Slaveholders not only had the duty to prohibit such practices, but should be proactive in ameliorating the miserable conditions of slaves. Slaveholders bore responsibility for elevating slaves' physical, moral, and spiritual needs. Not only should they feed and house their slaves as any father would his children, they should educate them, despite the fear that slaves would, in the aftermath, use their education to gain freedom.[14] Finally, Hodge believed that owners should attend to their slaves' spiritual welfare. They should evangelize their slaves and encourage them to advance in the Christian faith.[15] He summed up his concern by offering this warning: "The South, therefore, has to choose between emancipation by the silent and holy influence of the gospel, securing the elevation of the slave to the stature and character of freemen, or abide the issue of a long continued conflict against the law of God."[16]

Despite his defense of slavery as morally permissible, Hodge considered the institution a lower form of civilization. Slavery, he argued, should not be perpetuated because by "its nature [it is] a transition state. It supposes a low form of civilization, and must disappear as society advances and the slaves rise in intelligence and power." His frequent analogy depicted slavery as a lower form of despotism—despotism on an individual scale. On the larger political stage of the Roman Empire in the first century, Paul addressed how Christians should live under a pagan government. He admonished readers to subject themselves to Nero's despotic rule. He did not authorize believers to overthrow Roman government but to submit to authorities as their Christian duty. If Christians should submit to Nero's policies, which could result in the commandeering of their possessions and property, one could not demand the dismantling of slavery. To his credit, Hodge also admitted that despotism ought eventually to be eliminated in favor of other forms of government: "It is one thing to say that a despotic form of government is in a low state of civilization at best, and another that a low state of civilization should be perpetuated for the sake of despotism." Thus, ironically Hodge ended up using the argument of improving from a lower form of government to a higher in support of emancipating slaves.[17]

If Hodge was not at his most consistent when he argued against abolitionism, he was even weaker when addressing what should be done to correct injustices associated with American slavery. He believed Southern slavery entailed evils that needed solving, but he wanted them to be resolved without unduly disrupting public order. Constructing concrete solutions to repair social injustice played a significant role in the unfolding of the Reformed tradition. John Calvin and his heirs labored to advance beyond Martin Luther's passive resistance to political oppression in the sixteenth century. Luther contended that believers should pray that God relieve social injustice but must never take direct action against political authorities. They must await God's providence for relief. Calvinists, on the other hand, believed that Christians should work to end injustice, but not through rebellious disorder. Rather, minor officials—those already holding political office—were obligated to wield their powers to effect change. In light of that tradition, Hodge believed slavery was a problem for the state to handle, not the church. The church's contribution consisted only in encouraging slaveowners to obey commands in Scripture alluded to above. Hodge naively believed that Southern Christians and pastors would not allow flagrant disobedience to the gospel to remain unchallenged: "Of course those who do not comply with the rules, laid down in the word of God, as to their conduct, either as men, or parents, or masters, are justly exposed to the censure of the church, and the church is bound to inflict such censure." By the same token, the church should "abstain from denouncing as a crime what God has not pronounced; withhold our hands from the laws of the land, for which, as a church, we have no responsibility; and confine ourselves to teaching all classes of our members their duties . . . We should commend ourselves to every man's conscience in the sight of God."[18]

Hodge repeatedly affirmed a gradualist approach to the end of slavery. Just as despotic governments should introduce free institutions to ameliorate the effects of cruel and unjust rule, so people should work for the gradual improvement of slaves through education and other concrete benevolent acts: "We hold it to be the grand principle of the gospel, that every man is bound to promote the moral, intellectual, and physical improvement of his fellow men." Repeated gradual improvement over time would eventually bring an end to the institution. If people acted according to biblical principles, slaves could be elevated and become free citizens. Hodge remained committed to gradualism by drawing the analogy for reform. Genuine and lasting change "resembled the work not of a western farmer hacking down great forests to make room for corn, but that of a humble mason working on a great cathedral, 'placing a single brick or stone into the glorious edifice.' " As slavery lingered largely unchanged, some voiced the view that gradualism of a "brick at a time" in light of the immense task really meant indefinite postponement of slavery's elimination. Princetonians, however, including Hodge, refused to be moved to abolitionist immediatism. Committed to an orderly social order, they feared that immediacy would only introduce such horrors as the radicalism of the recent French Revolution.[19]

Hodge's hesitancy did not mean total lack of activity at all levels of responsibility. That activity should spring not from the strict limits of the mission of the church itself, but from believers' exercising their calling as Christian citizens. By advocating a gradual elimination of slavery, Hodge diverged from initial agreement with Thornwell that slavery could not be condemned because the Bible did not denounce it as sinful. Hodge and Thornwell, however, drew different conclusions from the Bible's silence on the issue. Hodge stressed that the Bible allowed for slavery to exist as an institution; Thornwell, however, viewed the Bible as sanctioning slavery. As a result, their views conflicted most significantly in their interpretation whether the churches should play any role in the continuation or elimination of slavery. In their attempts to explain their views, both affirmed what has been called the doctrine of "the spirituality of the church."

Hodge defended the spirituality of the church many times in the *PR* and carefully distinguished between the Northern and Southern versions of the doctrine. In the 1865 article "The Princeton Review on the State of the Country and of the Church," Hodge addressed the topic in detail under the heading "The power of the Church and the Proper Sphere of Its Action." The spirituality of the church meant that the powers assigned to the church were those determined "directly or indirectly by the word of God." Church courts must limit themselves to matters of the church and must not intrude into secular affairs under the jurisdiction of civil government, such as "matters of commerce, agriculture, or the fine arts, nor with the affairs of state." In performing their duties, churches could "only expound and apply the word of God to matters of truth and duty." Churches must teach, instruct, and propagate divine truth; they could not engage in those activities by direct action in behalf of secular concerns. The church, however, did have a public moral duty. It was not only authorized but obligated "to press upon the consciences of men whatever the law of God pronounces to be morally right, and to warn them against whatever the same authority declares to be morally wrong." Since the Bible did not prescribe any particular form of civil government or economic policy, the church could testify against only those actions and policies that conflicted with divine law.[20]

Thornwell went further in limiting the church's role by insisting on what Hodge dubbed "a new theory" of the spirituality of the church. Thornwell so restricted the term *spiritual* that it confined the church "to what pertains exclusively to the religious element of our nature, to what concerns the method of salvation as distinct from the law of God." Hodge pronounced this view "obviously false." Thornwell understood the term *spiritual* in a way "so limited as to deny to the church the right to protest against the slave trade, or unjust slave laws, as well as against rebellion and disloyalty."[21]

Worse still, Hodge accused the Southerners of hypocrisy without actually using the term. Hodge's argument deserves to be quoted in full:

> We find Dr. Thornwell preaching from the sacred desk elaborate sermons on slavery and writing articles in religious journals on the state of the country. The pulpits of the South rang perpetually (as we have been credibly informed), with political harangues . . . designed to "fire the Southern heart" in the struggle . . . We do not blame those brethren for violating a false principle [an incorrect interpretation of the spirituality of the church] and disregarding their own erroneous theory, but we protest against their condemning in others what they justify in themselves. If they may preach and write to prove slavery is "a Divine institution," we may endeavour to prove that it is a "low state of civilization," from which the slaves should be elevated and delivered as soon as possible. If they may, heart and soul, embrace the Southern cause and advocate Southern principles in the pulpit, in church courts, and in the religious journals, we may do the same for the national cause and national principles. There is, however, no room for debate on this subject. This new theory of the church is as practically dead . . . as is the theory of secession, and both, as Siamese twins, may be allowed to pass into oblivion together.[22]

The church, therefore, had its clear duty—to expound scriptural teaching relative to improving the condition of all men, including slaves. Likewise, citizens had a moral and legal responsibility to repeal unjust slave laws:

> Christians who are members of communities in which such laws are in force, have their share of responsibility with regard to them, as citizens—But it is no part of the vocation of the church, as such, to interfere with civil laws. The apostles did not call a synod at Jerusalem, to denounce the Roman laws, but they laid the foundation of a spiritual society, and let the world make its own laws. We would not brook the legislatures of our States passing denunciatory resolutions against our rules of church discipline; and we should not call upon the church to meddle with the laws of the land. As citizens we have the right and duty to demand just and equal laws; but as a church, we have other and higher duties.[23]

To achieve the goal of producing freedom for blacks gradually, Hodge proposed means by which they could achieve that freedom within a generation. He endorsed the emancipation of all those born in slavery when they reached their twenty-fifth birthday. He urged adoption of educational practices that would elevate slaves. The solution that attracted most criticism, however, was to expatriate freed slaves. Colonization enjoyed a history at Princeton extending back several decades. The organizing meeting of the American Colonization Society, one of the voluntary societies that Princeton supported, was attended by faculty and students on the campus in 1816. Archibald Alexander believed in colonization so firmly that he authored the society's history, *A History of Colonization on the Western Coast of Africa*.[24] Hodge followed Alexander's lead, by calling colonization "an essential feature of any wise plan of emancipation." Populating the republic of Liberia would offer the opportunity for freed slaves not only to live out their freedom productively but to engage in an evangelistic mission—to "carry with them the seeds of religion, civilization and of liberty to an entire continent." Such an enterprise would imitate America's forefathers, who had done the same thing generations ago when they came to America. Fearing that whites and blacks could not live together, he pronounced colonization "the great hope of Africa." He continued, "Let us, however remember it is not simply men that Africa needs, but enlightened and Christian men, who shall carry with them religion and knowledge, the minister and the schoolmaster." Objections rose against colonization, and the project ultimately failed to arouse broad financial, political, and social support necessary for its implementation. Though it attracted attention to the plight of freed blacks, it really deflected the attention and energy of those who could have dealt more appropriately with the real issue, which was how to ensure the effective and peaceful end of slavery.[25]

Hodge continued to develop his views on slavery and emancipation as the Civil War unfolded. His vote for Abraham Lincoln and his subsequent support for the Emancipation Proclamation signaled his move from gradualism to the immediate end of slavery. His advocacy of the rightness of Lincoln's emancipation, however, stemmed from political pragmatism, not from obedience to a biblical injunction or from the view that slavery was inherently evil. The South by its secession from and rebellion against the Union established an intransigent position that mandated the immediacy of Lincoln's declaration: "The South not only refused to enter on any course tending to the abolition of slavery, but became more and more enamoured with the system; more than ever devoted to perpetuate and extend it, and at last, to accomplish this end rose in rebellion for the overthrow of the constitution and violent disruption of the Union. This altered the whole case. Slavery then became not a matter for the South only, but assumed the posture of an avowed enemy of the nation." Southerners had also signally failed to do their Christian duty to revise slave laws and to alleviate slaves' degraded position. Therefore, seizure of Southern property and immediate emancipation emerged as the North's only recourse.[26]

The frequency and sense of urgency with which Hodge addressed slavery and commented in the *PR* on the state of the nation during the Civil War testify to Hodge's almost overwhelming pathos regarding internal divisions that racked both the church and the country. As a centrist, he felt the ire of Old School Southerners who fiercely resented challenges to their peculiar institution, and he experienced the rage of abolitionists who could not abide any more foot-dragging on such a supremely important cultural matter.[27] While by today's standards his contributions appear timid, overly cautious, and lacking in courage to speak out more forcefully on the evils of slavery, Hodge espoused ideas that by his own admission were conservative. His and others' support of colonization demonstrated a reluctance to confront colonization's inherent patronizing attitude toward the blacks. He did, however, attempt to frame his views not with abstract speculation but with due attention to biblical texts. After all, he was addressing an important cultural issue as a theologian and biblical scholar. To move beyond biblical mandates in opposing either extreme party on his flanks would have invited even by his own lights appropriate censure.[28]

19

Schism of 1837

As sentiments hardened into settled convictions on both sides of these debates between Old and New Schoolers, individuals and groups coalesced into the factions that would be identified as Old and New School Presbyterians. The Princeton faculty remained united in their support of the Old School, which they viewed as the true heir of Scotch and Scotch-Irish Presbyterianism. At the early stages of the conflict, Charles Hodge, as a young professor with little prior expertise in ecclesiastical affairs, possessed little influence in denominational matters. That changed dramatically as a result of what we have just surveyed—his prolific pen as editor of the *PR*. While Hodge did not serve as a General Assembly delegate in the decisive votes that brought about the 1837 schism, he and his faculty colleagues remained supporters of Old School efforts. A. A. Hodge in his description in *LCH* chapter 8, "The Disruption of the Presbyterian Church (1834–1838)," stated how Princeton identified itself throughout the turbulence leading up to the schism. Princetonians saw themselves as "the Middle party," which "was wholly Old

School, adhering in principle and affection to the original normal type of doctrine and polity."[1]

As the General Assembly convened each year, resolutions made and actions taken depended largely on the makeup of delegates. When New School delegates predominated, decisions and actions reflected New School positions. Similarly, when Old School delegates were in the majority, votes sustained Old School views. To gain an advantage in this growing conflict, Old Schoolers began to convene meetings before the assemblies to strategize how best to achieve their goals. Before the General Assembly of 1834, potential members of the Old School drew up a document, the "Old-School Testimony and Memorial," that would precipitate several immediate actions in pursuit of their purposes, but because of the New School majority, the assembly rejected its proposals. In 1835 a similar effort managed to gain some headway. In 1836, however, New Schoolers benefited when a narrow majority of delegates voted to acquit New School Philadelphia pastor Albert Barnes in the dispute over his commentary on Romans.[2]

Old Schoolers regrouped before the 1837 Assembly, convinced that only immediate and concerted action could ensure the continuation of their denomination's theological and ecclesiastical standards. Old Schoolers wanted the Plan of Union abrogated and the churches formed under its provisions to be either reorganized according to Presbyterian principles or eliminated.[3]

While most historical sources separate the denomination into two parties—Old and New School—the Princetonians, including Hodge, distinguished four groups. A. A. Hodge enumerated them as follows:

> (1) Those congregations and groups of congregations which were imperfectly organized, and those ministers and people who maintained the extreme type of error they styled "Taylorism."[4] These occasioned all the trouble. Without them all the other parties could have coalesced together in a sufficiently homogeneous Presbyterian church. (2) The New School party as a body. These were in themselves sound Presbyterians, although somewhat tinged with the Hopkinsian quality of theology.[5] Their peculiarity arose from the fact that from their position, antecedents and associations they were disposed to prevent the discipline of any whose opinions departed further from the type

> of normal Presbyterianism division than their own, and to oppose the abrogation of the "Plan of Union," and the reorganization, by force of ecclesiastical authority, of the churches formed upon it; and to keep the church open to the operation of the voluntary Societies, the exclusion of those under ecclesiastical control. (3) The "Princeton Party" or "Middle Men." (4) The Old School party in Pennsylvania and part of the South, who, under the leadership of Drs. Green, R. J. Breckinridge, George Junkin and others, were convinced that the crisis was imminent, that the evils were so great as to be intolerable, and who, therefore pressed urgently the prosecution of heresy, and demanded peremptorily either the speedy abatement of these evils or the division of the church.[6]

The strategy of the Middle Men was to abrogate the Plan of Union, galvanize support of like-minded pastors to exclude from office those who held the most egregious errors of Taylorism, strongly discourage the pragmatic revivalist methods, and establish church boards to replace voluntary societies to carry out education and missions. Most importantly, they sought to prevent the church from being rent asunder either by Old School extremists' voluntarily separating from the denomination or by the forcible exclusion of the New School. Hodge and his colleagues wished the church to remain united but on orthodox terms. In his "Retrospect" Hodge enumerated those issues on which he and his colleagues were in "entire sympathy with the Old School party": (1) the church's duty to carry out the work of education and missions "by ecclesiastical boards, instead of voluntary, independent societies"; and (2) the "obligation to enforce conformity to our Confession of Faith on the part of ministers and teachers of theology under our jurisdiction." They did not object to the fact that the "Act and Testimony," a document drawn up before the 1835 General Assembly and signed by sixty-four Old School ministers and elders, was a "testimony against false doctrine, nor as a means for arousing the attention of the church; nor as designed to concentrate the energies of its sounder members for the reform of existing evils." They disagreed, however, over "the wisdom of the measures adopted for securing a common object"—the object being to anchor Presbyterianism in the sound basis of the Westminster Confession.[7]

Hodge and his Princeton colleagues distanced themselves from extreme positions taken by those whom they called the "ultra" men, sometimes referred to as the "Philadelphia party." The ultras reciprocated with their own nicknames for the Princetonians. Epithets ranged from "moderates," "trembling brethren," and "compromisers" to "secluded professors," implying their ivory-tower isolation from the front lines of pulpit and pew.[8]

Hodge articulated three points over which the two parties disagreed. The first related to the Act and Testimony. The document drew a strict doctrinal line in the sand and proposed staunch measures to discipline offenders. In Hodge's opinion, the document overreached prudent bounds in its attempt to deal with the New School presence in the church. He did not believe the situation to be as dire as the document alleged, and he judged the disciplinary measures to resolve the situation too extreme. The document, he said, "operated as a new, unauthorized, and invidious test of orthodoxy and fidelity." In addition, it functioned totally out of character with past precedents. Unlike historic creeds and confessions of the church, whose purpose was to unite believers, Hodge argued that the Act and Testimony's "obvious tendency, and . . . its actual effect, was to divide . . . the friends of orthodoxy and order. The document was never signed by a moiety [majority] of the Old-school body." In essence, Hodge labeled the document schismatic: "it seemed schism was the natural consequence, if not the intention" of the document. In addition to its divisive purpose, the Act and Testimony established a new test of orthodoxy. Hodge called it "an extra-constitutional and revolutionary measure, which many good and true men could not approve."[9]

Rather than adopt extreme measures against the New School, Hodge argued for restraint using means provided by the Westminster Standards: "redress should be sought in the regular exercise of the constitution and laws, unless the evils be such as justify revolution." In accord with these moderate proposals, the Princeton men abstained from signing the Act and Testimony, which earned them the scorn of the ultras. Princetonians remained aloof and did not press for further action at the upcoming General Assembly. Hodge restated his rationale for their failure to close ranks with extremism: "so long as the standards of the church were unaltered, and its ministers were not called upon to profess what they did not believe, or prevented preaching what they believed to be true, or required to do what their conscience condemned, to withdraw from the church was the crime of schism, which the Scriptures so expressly forbid." Taking the long view of things rather than being limited to present circumstances, Hodge warned that acting precipitously would set a rash precedent that by the nature of the growing controversy would only resurface and eventually splinter the church into ever smaller fragments. To leave the church whenever "adverse majority gained ascendancy for a time" would inevitably invite innumerable divisions.[10]

A second point dividing Hodge's moderate party from radical Old Schoolers entailed the proper grounds of ecclesiastical discipline. While unequivocally committed to the Westminster Standards, Hodge showed his moderation by flatly denying that heresy saturated the denomination. He contended that insufficient evidence existed that great errors permeated the church. He wrote in 1837 that "the majority of the church is sound, and sound as Presbyterians."[11]

Instead of assuming that doctrinal error ran rampant within the denomination, he articulated the presuppositions that should guide cases of discipline: "no doctrine . . . consistent with the integrity of that system is the proper ground of discipline. It is not enough that a doctrine be erroneous, or that it be dangerous in its tendency; if it be not subversive of one or more of the constituent elements of the Reformed faith, it is not incompatible with the honest adoption of our Confession." He acknowledged that Presbyterians had tolerated differing viewpoints in the past and continued to do so in the present. Such differences even existed within the Old School party. Subsidiary issues, such as immediate or mediate imputation of Adam's sin or a realistic theory of original sin, should not drive the disciplinary process. On the other hand, those who denied that all men are born in sin and that after the fall people possessed plenary ability to fulfill the law would be subject to discipline. Hodge thereby distinguished between minor differences in doctrine that remained within the boundaries of the confession and major divergences that did not.[12]

A third point of disagreement between the Old and New School parties also involved the Act and Testimony. The Princeton men opposed how the dissolution of the Plan of Union should be implemented. Because of the Princetonians' firm belief in Presbyterian polity, Hodge stated that Presbyterian participation in the Plan had been unconstitutional from the time of the Plan's inception because the standing rules had never been submitted to the presbyteries. Hodge summarized the Princeton consensus by saying, "All that the Assembly has the right to do was to require that such union should forthwith and thenceforth cease." Thus, when Archibald Alexander, Princeton's representative at the assembly, joined the majority vote of 143–110 to dissolve the Plan, Hodge and his associates concurred. The mere abrogation of the union, however, left unanswered the practicality of terminating relations with synods and their respective presbyteries and churches formed since 1801. Hodge wrote, "This was the ground taken by Dr. Alexander and the majority of the conductors of this *Review*." Rather than adopt this measure, however, the majority pressed for heavy-handed immediacy by passing "Abscinding Acts," which excised four synods formed under the Plan of Union. By this action the assembly excluded twenty-eight presbyteries, over five hundred ministers, and almost sixty thousand members. Hodge and his associates agreed only on the excision of the Synod of Western Reserve because it alone was largely Congregational. The three synods of New York—Utica, Geneva, and Genesee—had mostly Presbyterian churches. The Princeton men were divided about the necessity of eliminating them. Although he favored action to safeguard orthodoxy within the denomination, Hodge, reflecting his moderate temperament, favored a gradualist proposal that would require judicatories containing Congregational churches to conform to Presbyterian polity utilizing the courts of the church.[13]

In July 1837, Hodge penned a lengthy letter to his brother, summarizing the events of the assembly and the Princetonians' consensus about its outcome. First he summarized their agreement: "The fact is that we are all agreed as to all the principles involved in the questions before the Assembly, and agreed also as to their application [except the case of the three New York synods]." He believed, however, that the *PR*, as the journal representing Princeton as an institution, should not imply a total agreement on the excision of the three synods: "I therefore insisted on stating in a note that some of the conductors . . . felt that we had not as yet a sufficient knowledge of the facts in the case to enable us to see the propriety [of the excision]." Hodge hoped that evidence would eventually emerge that would justify the harsh action of the assembly. He stated his conflicted state of mind over whether to publish in the *PR* that the Princeton faction was not totally united: "I never had such a time in my life. On the one hand my own views of duty and propriety and even expediency were clear and unwavering. On the other hand was the opinion of almost all my friends, and the vehement expostulations, appeals, and forebodings of a good many of them. Dr. Alexander did just what he ought to have done. He said he could not see the grounds of my scruples, and thought the thing inexpedient, but gave his cheerful assent to my saying in the note just what I pleased. You may depend upon it is very hard for a man to act upon his own opinion, when opposed not only to the opinion of those he has been accustomed to reverence, but to the ardent expostulations and dreadful forebodings of others. I believe, to be sure, it was all nonsense; that no such terrible consequences would follow. However, I feel thankful the thing is arranged without producing a breach, and that I have still a good conscience." Throughout the controversy, Hodge labored over the danger of being schismatic and of fostering to any degree a lack of unity within Old School ranks. The ongoing prosperity of the Presbyterian church depended, humanly speaking, on Old School members' maintaining their cohesiveness as the dispute unfolded. Hodge emphasized, however, that to achieve that end, "the *Repertory* will not be made a party concern. I am persuaded that the conductors would rather see it die." Little did he know that he and Alexander would disagree again in the near future.[14]

Finally, Hodge could not resist the temptation to set the whole controversy in context in his "Retrospect." To demonstrate how radically opinion about Princeton as a rigid Old School institution had sharpened in the interim between 1837 and 1870 when he wrote his "Retrospect," he added ruefully: "What, however, was regarded as very lukewarm Old-schoolism in 1837, has now come to be looked upon as obsolete and narrow-minded."[15]

When he faced his annual task of reporting the proceedings of the General Assembly in the *PR*, Hodge opened a letter to his brother with a stark assessment: "I have at once to prepare a history of the doings of this momentous Assembly, in which the New School have experienced a Waterloo Defeat. Their only recourse is now the law, which I suspect will give them small consolation. I think substantial justice has been done, though there may have been some informality in the mode of doing it. I have little doubt that public sentiment of the church & of men of other denominations will sustain the proceedings of the Assembly, as soon as they are fairly understood." He believed that the New School, after initial "foaming & complaint," would form themselves into a separate church, resulting in two Presbyterian denominations.[16]

Subdued in his 1838 General Assembly article, Hodge wrote, "The General Assembly of 1837 will probably form an epoch in the history of the American Presbyterian church. We enter on the task of giving its history with very serious feelings. This is not an occasion either for exultation or crimination." Though he did not mention the cause for his extreme dismay at the impending case in civil court, Hodge undoubtedly had in mind Paul's condemnation of divisions in the church as nothing short of scandalous. In 1 Corinthians 6:1–11 Paul berated Corinthian Christians for taking each other to court; and he particularly upbraided them for putting their dispute into the hands of unbelievers: "When one of you has a grievance against another, does he dare go to law before the unrighteous instead of the saints? . . . If you have such cases, why do you lay them before those who have no standing in the church? I say this to your shame." As in the case of what to do with presbyteries formed under the Plan of Union, Hodge believed that church judicatories should resolve such issues. In this case, however, the issue had already reached the status of being irresolvable at the highest level of Presbyterian polity.[17]

Although the assembly was clearly divided over the excision of the synods, the actual division of the church did not occur until the following year. In convening the 1838 Assembly at Seventh Church in Philadelphia, the moderator refused to recognize New School delegates from the excised synods until after the assembly was duly constituted.

A tumult resulted, with New School members' organizing separately and electing their own moderator and clerk.[18]

While he disagreed with the severity of the exscinding act, Hodge set the blame for the schism squarely on the New School. He believed that the two parties could have resolved the issue of property and funds without a schism. The New School, however, chose to retaliate for the 1837 excisions by proclaiming itself the true General Assembly of the Presbyterian church. Hodge said that New Schoolers could have proposed "an amicable division upon the terms proposed at the last Assembly, to which both parties had assented." Instead they chose to follow "some young legal gentlemen" who alleged that they could secure not only "their own portion of the property, but get the whole [including the two Old School seminaries, Pittsburgh and Princeton]; and in an evil hour, they determined to make the attempt." They attempted, he wrote, "to claim the whole; to involve the church in protracted law suits, and to apply for a decision of the civil courts which they knew, would, if given in their favor, be attacked with greatest practical injustice. We have little doubt that the Christian community will pronounce this course of conduct to be wrong." Rather than having both parties within the same denomination, the New School "chose . . . to claim the whole," thus plunging the church into "protracted law suits."[19]

Though Hodge had not sided with the ultras before 1837, after the schism his charges against the New School exhibited a new sharpness. He accused the New School of being "a Congregational party" because it "advocates the amalgamation of all sects [by adhering to the Plan of Union]," yet it ironically and thus falsely "claims to be the TRUE Presbyterian church" and would thus "deprive the majority, nine-tenths of whom are Presbyterian by birth and education, of all right or standing in their church." In addition and even more serious, the New School party "advocates a more or less latitudinarian construction of [the doctrinal standards]." In the aftermath of the 1837 Assembly, the overriding issues were theological and polity differences and their implications for which faction could claim to be the legitimate Presbyterian denomination.[20]

As the dispute over the schism unfolded toward a legal conclusion, Hodge wrote to Dr. Henry Boardman, Hodge's close friend and chairman of the Presbyterian Board of Publication, of his plans for a book on Presbyterian history, to be published as a means of holding the Old School together. Hodge expressed great confidence in the power of historical evidence supporting the Old School's claims to be the genuine Presbyterian church: "My own impression is that evidence of the strictly Presbyterian character of our church from the beginning is so clear, and the proof arising from the facts in the case so conclusive against the principles adopted by our New School brethren that it is important that this evidence should be published as soon as possible. Our presbyteries will meet early in April. . . . Many who have hitherto wavered must then decide, when they come to choose commissioners to the Assembly. If this history is to do any good, it ought to be out soon enough to let the facts which it contains operate before every man has taken his stand."[21]

Despite his confidence in the potential influence of his historical record on Old School delegates to the General Assembly, Hodge feared that the ecclesiastical complexities of the case might not augur well for the outcome of the trial in the civil court. As early as 1838, Hodge expressed extreme apprehension about settling the dispute between and Old and New School claims of the church in the hands of a randomly selected jury. He wrote to Boardman, "How are the preparations for our lawsuits going on? Who are to be our lawyers? What a deplorable thing it is that a question involving as many interests is to be submitted to a dozen grocers, butchers or dairymen as the case may happen." While his comments may be interpreted as an elitist view of the church, Hodge feared that placing the final decision outside a church court where he could be more confident that those deciding the case would be knowledgeable of church polity could result in terrible harm to the denomination. He wrote, "The funds and institutions, though matters not to be slighted, are but a portion of the great interests at stake, and to have these interests committed to twelve men, taken up at random, is a very serious matter. It seems to be one of God's purposes in this dispensation to make us feel that we are completely in His hands. The decision of a jury in such matters is very little different from the casting of the lot; and I should feel nearly as I feel now if the great question at issue were to be decided on Monday by the throwing of the dice."

Strange words for a Presbyterian theologian! Hodge concluded his thoughts, however, by saying appropriately that "should the cause be decided in our favor, I trust there will not be one word of exultation uttered from any quarter."[22]

Hodge did not witness the trial personally but followed its proceedings through correspondence with Boardman. On March 10, he wrote to Hodge, "I anticipate a drawn battle." Probably in response to Hodge's concern about the jury, he described in detail the selection of the jury. He even recorded the occupations of the respective jurors and how they might vote. On March 11, he wrote of the cross-examination of the two clerks of the Old and New School, with the following comment: "[The cross-examination] was very minute and rigid and very humiliating to the Christian ministry. Nearly all ministers have manifested the same reluctance to tell the *whole* truth and resorted to the same acts of evasion and concealment which usually characterizes witnesses testifying in cases in which they have a *personal* interest" (emphases in original). He adds, "I fear that even if we gain the cause it will be at such sacrifice of ministerial reputation, such a letting down of the clerical character in the community, as we shall not recover from in many years." The hapless spectacle of two parties within the denomination was only magnified by what Boardman viewed as prevarications in testimony offered by clergy. The reasons for the apostle Paul's disapproval of schismatic rancor as a public spectacle were being exemplified.[23]

Hodge in turn expressed utter dismay when the court's ruling supported the New School, giving it control of all aspects of the denomination, including the seminaries. He conveyed his severe disappointment to his brother: "As you may well suppose, the decision of the protracted law-suit against us has taken us altogether by surprise. No one here considered such a result as more than possible." Boardman's calculation that the jury might be against them, however, was exceeded by the trial judge's pronouncements, which Hodge said went beyond all good sense: "that the Judge should be against us, and that with bitterness, never appeared as even possible. All our friends, legal and clerical, had perfect confidence in our ultimate success up to the moment when the Judge pronounced his opinion." Hodge pronounced Judge Rogers's decision "preposterous . . . a very great calamity" and a "severe judgment of God." Yet he remained hopeful that God would bring good out of evil. In the meantime, cognizant of the differences between the ultras and the Princeton Old Schoolers that had contributed to exscinding of New School presbyteries in the 1837 Assembly, he feared that the Old School would not hold together: "there are so many geographical and sectional causes of disunion that I am very much afraid that if once deprived of the bond of a common and venerated name, and of common property, we shall be split into insignificant fragments." He stated the matter bluntly: "We are in the eye of the law, a secession from our own church; the New England men have succeeded in getting that church to themselves."[24]

Foremost he fretted over the seminary's future. Princeton and what it stood for in theological education clearly hung in the balance. He, his fellow professors, and supporters of the school had long labored to make it the American model of faithfulness to the Reformed tradition. The thought of coming under New School control through the denomination pained him deeply. He wrote to his brother, "I trust our leaders in Philadelphia [the ultras] will be preserved from rashness and imprudence and all evil speaking. A dark cloud is hanging over us, and our ways seem to be hedged up. It is very painful to think of Princeton Seminary going to ruin; for it must go to ruin in the hands of New School men. They have a seminary in New York [Union], and cannot possibly supply both with students. Still, the Lord reigns, and He will do all things well." Thus Hodge hoped that the seminary would not be destroyed by either its enemies or its friends.[25]

As expected, the Old School appealed the initial ruling to the Supreme Court of Pennsylvania. As the succeeding year developed, Hodge wrote to Boardman of various options lying before the church. The outcome depended largely on the manner in which the Old School proceeded. Above all, he believed that continued unity on the part of Old Schoolers was paramount. In light of the diversity among Old Schoolers, he insisted that no one person or small group could act in behalf of the whole. While some favored reunion with the New School, Hodge rejected that idea as unachievable in light of differences separating the two groups. On the other hand, choosing to remain "aloof" and claiming to be the true church would render them "seceders in the eye of the law" and even more importantly would open up protracted legal proceedings in various parts of the country that would result in "the great scandal of the church and injury to religion." Hodge deemed neither of these solutions acceptable. A third option would entail compromise. Amazingly, Hodge went so far as to consider altering the charter of the seminary: "Why may not the charter be so altered as to [confer the right to appoint members to the board and to control the expenditure of funds] on the two Assemblies? Let each have nine trustees in the board, and each be authorized to direct the application of the funds, which according to mutual agreement, shall be recognized as belonging to each . . . Neither party would then be in the position of seceders, and all litigation would be prevented throughout the country." This was a truly radical alternative, given the almost sacred status of the charter to the Princetonians.[26]

Hodge's proposal never saw the light of day because in the appeal process the court decided in favor of the Old School. Princeton remained under its control. For Hodge even to contemplate such an alternative, however, indicates how dim the prospects appeared in 1839 for both his church and seminary. Hodge's letter to Boardman also revealed the range of alternatives he would dare contemplate to end the spectacle of Christian rancor and to preclude public scandal.

When Hodge learned of the Old School's successful appeal, he read the trial papers with interest. "Somebody was good enough to send a printed copy of the decision so that I have the *ipsissima verba*. I hope and believe the Old School will behave properly. They have been severely tried, & should learn wisdom. The New School papers are assiduous in pouring poison in the wounds of the church. You can have no idea of the character of those papers."[27]

Ironically, as the Old School–New School disruption evolved, Hodge was compiling data that he hoped would bolster the Old School claim that it rather than the New School represented historic American Presbyterianism and would thereby represent Hodge's contribution to the Old School's maintaining its unity. The book, however, would not only distance him from his previous New Side roots but also create a breach with his mentor, Archibald Alexander.[28]

20

Revisionist Historian

As evidenced by their arguments in favor of Old School positions, Princetonians loved history. They did so for good reasons. They believed history favored their perspective on many fronts. Historical acts of redemption in the Old and New Testaments firmly anchored the Christian faith in history. The historicity of key events—the fall, the exodus, the incarnation (birth, death, and resurrection of Christ)—undergirded Reformed orthodoxy in the biblical and theological controversies that Charles Hodge waged with New Schoolers who either challenged the veracity of the biblical record or strayed from traditional interpretations. Also, steeped in Scottish Common Sense Realism, Hodge believed that historical events' being accessible to careful study served as powerful apologetic points. Harboring none of the modern, let alone postmodern, suspicions regarding historians' ability to recover and correctly interpret past events, Hodge believed historical study essential to defending Reformed dogmas and correctly understanding current controversies.

These beliefs lay well embedded within the Plan of the Seminary. Article V, "Of Study and Attainments," listed the subjects that students preparing for the Presbyterian ministry must master—facility in original languages, careful biblical exegesis, and faithful adherence to the Westminster Confession. Sometimes overlooked were references to historical study. Pastors would be "versed in Jewish and Christian antiquities, which serve to explain and illustrate Scripture"; they would be acquainted with "ancient geography"; they must have "read and digested" literature relative to the "deistical controversy"; and they "must have a considerable acquaintance with General History and Chronology, and a particular acquaintance with the history of the Christian Church." Historical events and their correct interpretation assured believers of the ontological truthfulness of the gospel. Thus, history was no mere vestigial appendage to theological study; it played no marginal role in the Princeton curriculum. History not only provided a source of general revelation, but stood as an integral component of special revelation as well. As such, it served as a significant tool in the scholar's hands, especially apologetically, which is the nature of Hodge's only historical publication. Though many of his articles would display his affinity for historical argument, his *CHPC* would be his only monograph of that genre, and the controversy it created would test his relationship with colleagues.[1]

Apropos of supporting the Old School during the 1837 schism and its aftermath, Hodge wrote to Henry Boardman several times that he wanted to get the *CHPC* manuscript into print as expeditiously as possible. It would encourage cohesiveness among Old Schoolers. In March 1839, written after the first court decision favored the New School, he wrote, "Perhaps it is now more important than ever that the work [*CHPC*] should be done, if, as I hope may be the case, it will tend to increase the respect and affection of Presbyterians for the church of their fathers. We shall need now every bond to keep us together."[2]

The book, however, would not be without its controversial features. Hodge had outlined the contents of the book to Boardman in a previous letter. He warned that the book should not be published by the assembly because only he, Hodge, should bear responsibility for its contents. He specifically mentioned that his views of "the parties of 1741, the great revival and schism" would evoke criticism. While he hoped that the book would unite his brethren, he warned that it might result in a "storm" coming down upon Boardman and himself.[3]

A. A. Hodge called his father's book "the least natural, and most laborious work he ever undertook." Charles disclosed in his letter of October 12, 1838, to his brother, "I am not the man for such business." Physical discomfort from his lameness only added to the difficulty of his research. Immediate concerns, however, about which faction—the Old or New School—represented authentic American Presbyterianism demanded marshaling the evidence in favor of the Old School. In light of current crises, the task needed to be done. After considering the options, Hodge realized that the original plan for a pamphlet-sized piece would not do. As he conversed with colleagues, a consensus emerged that enlarged the vision to produce a general review of the history of the Presbyterian church. Hodge stated in his preface that "the design of this work is to exhibit the true character of our Church; to show on what principles it was founded and governed; in other words, to exhibit historically its constitution, both as to doctrine and order." He would provide "a distinct account of the present controversies in our Church" that reviewed the formation of the denomination and key subsequent events in the eighteenth century: a "documentary history" of the formation and development of American Presbyterianism—its roots, the Adopting Act of 1729, the Old Side–New Side schism, and other events. Only in this larger context could the recent division be understood.[4]

What is interesting in retrospect is how Hodge identified the various parties in his constitutional history. He began chapter 1 by talking about the 1837 schism: "The controversies which have so long agitated the Presbyterian Church, have, at length, resulted in its separation. It would not be easy to state, in a manner satisfactory to both parties the points of difference between them." But he did not use terms that we would expect—*Old / New Side* and *Old / New School*—to identify the parties, presbyteries, or synods as they were formed or key proponents of positions that distinguished the parties (e.g., Jonathan Dickinson, John Thompson, Gilbert Tennent). He named presbyteries and synods and identified protagonists, but he utilized no labels commonly used to identify the factions. Instead, he referred to "Puritan" and "Scotch-Irish" parties and New Brunswick and Philadelphia presbyteries to probe the positions that each side took. Hodge's intent in this method was to focus the history on the very points of debate—polity positions, doctrinal subscription, and views that fueled events such as the Adopting Act of 1729, the Great Awakening of the 1730s and 1740s, and the schism of 1741. The labels that we would expect to find do not appear. Yet Hodge did not thereby take a neutral position on the controversies. Far from it. He did not prejudice his case by applying terms familiar to all his readers. Instead, he believed that as he unpacked the historical record, the facts would speak for themselves.[5]

Hodge began with the controversy at hand—the dispute in which "one party is in favour of a stricter adherence to the standards of the church, as to doctrine and order, than the other." Regarding Presbyterianism at its founding in America, Hodge insisted that in doctrine and form of government, the church "was every where, in all its distinctive and essential features the same." Its unique feature was to vest the government "of individual congregations . . . in the pastor and elders, and not in the brotherhood." It also gathered particular churches into presbyteries composed of ministers and elders and grouped presbyteries into synods.[6] In defending the Scottish system, Hodge particularly countered the idea that the Scots were significantly more strict than the other European forms of church government. Hodge defended this view to oppose New Schoolers who argued that because other European churches were more lax in order and doctrine, the American church should likewise allow more diversity. Hodge asserted in his thesis sentence of the book that this matter could be settled by showing that the Presbyterian church "has always demanded adherence to the system of doctrines contained in the Westminster Confession of Faith and Catechisms, as the condition of ministerial communion; and that it has ever claimed and exercised all the distinguishing powers of Presbyterian government." Hodge thereby affirmed that from the church's inception, though it did not establish de jure a constitutional basis for doctrine and form of government until the Adopting Act of 1729, it was Presbyterian de facto.[7]

These views contrasted with the views of those who contended that Presbyterians owed their ecclesiastical existence to Congregationalism and that ministers had only to assent to essential doctrines of the gospel. The two matters were inextricably related. Regarding the former, Hodge devoted his first chapter to an examination of various groups that had brought Presbyterianism to America—English Puritans, the Dutch, the Germans, the French, the Scotch, and the Irish. He rehearsed the details of each group—their numbers, dates and geographical areas where they settled, key leaders, and controversies in their early life in America. In every instance he showed how each group exhibited a distinctive Presbyterian heritage. Hodge concluded pointedly that "nothing but sectional vanity little less than insane could lead to the assertion that Congregationalism was the basis of Presbyterianism in this country." Herein we find Hodge's support against the 1801 Plan of Union, which facilitated cooperation between Presbyterians and Congregationalists.[8]

Next Hodge probed two issues that had emerged in the 1720s—the synod's authority in governing the conduct and life of the denomination and creedal subscription as the basis for ministerial ordination. To stave off any consideration of a revised Calvinism such as that of Taylor's New Divinity, Hodge contended that from earliest records, the Presbyterian church had been thoroughly Calvinistic. In the early decades after the founding of the first presbytery in 1706, the church did not have a constitutional basis for ministerial communion. What should be the basis for acceptance into the ministry and for approving ministers transferring from one presbytery to another? Were these processes accomplished by demanding adherence to a number of evangelical doctrines? Hodge characterized this view as bringing "their demands down to the low standard of absolutely essential doctrines." Or were these processes accomplished by requiring belief "in that system of doctrines, which for convenience' sake, has obtained the name of Calvinism"? The strongest evidence for the latter was that during the era preceding the Adopting Act, no one had opposed the use of the Westminster Confession and "there was not a single member of the Synod who objected to any one article in the Confession of Faith, except that which related to the power of the civil magistrates in matters of religion." Hodge concluded as he set the stage for adoption of the confession by saying, "The church did not become Calvinistic by adopting that Confession; but adopted it because it already was so, and always had been."[9]

His next chapter, which occupied almost a third of volume 1, deals with subscription to the Westminster Confession as prerequisite to Presbyterian ministry. Hodge's initial tone appears defensive. He wondered why after a century the confession "should be held up to reprobation . . . by members of our own communion. As every other church has a creed, why should not the Presbyterians have one?" Detractors claimed that the adoption of the confession resulted from "sectarian bigotry and heartless orthodoxy." Hodge conceded that a measure of truth exists in the belief that "it was the Scotch and Irish members who were in favour of the measure, and the English members who opposed it." His admission points up that two parties existed. Both affirmed the Westminster Confession. But the Scotch-Irish group wanted to make subscription to the confession the sole basis for ministerial communion. The New England Puritan party, on the other hand, sought to make profession of spiritual experience more primary as a qualification for ministry. The former party, led by John Thompson, took the initiative by proposing that subscription to the confession become prerequisite for acceptance into ministry. Since the church lacked a system of doctrine, Thompson argued that it needed a confession to confront "pernicious and dangerous corruptions" from "Arminianism, Socinianism, Deism, Freethinking, &c.," which threatened orthodoxy. The confession would also embolden and encourage those who were timid and dispirited.[10]

What emerges as truly remarkable in light of our previous characterization of Hodge as a New Side Presbyterian is his favorable comments of John Thompson, who Hodge admitted had a "notorious" reputation for opposing New Side piety and revivalism. Hodge seized the opportunity to correct previous vilification of Thompson and the prevalent impression that Old Siders disparaged practical religion by citing six lengthy passages from Thompson reminiscent of Hodge's own experientially focused diary and journal entries from his mission preaching in Philadelphia and his European sojourn. In one passage, Thompson said of pastors that "every one [should be convinced] . . . how far we have come short of that exemplary piety, circumspection, and tenderness of walk, and spiritualness of converse with others, which as ministers of the gospel of Christ we should have studied; as also, how far we have failed in degree of love, care, zeal, and tender concern for the souls of men." In another Thompson exhorted, "Let us earnestly labour to get our affections weaned from the world and all sublunary things, and to set them on things above." In still another he challenged ministers to press people for conversion: "For this purpose we should not only assert and maintain the necessity of regeneration and converting grace, and of a righteous and godly walk, and of increase and advancement therein, but also endeavour to press the same home upon their consciences with all earnestness." Thompson, therefore, in the context of the Adopting Act of 1729, possessed a zeal for godly living in addition to his overture that subscription to the Westminster Confession should be the primary basis for ministerial ordination. Extensive defense of Thompson is the first indication that Hodge was reassessing his views of seventeenth-century revivalism—that Old Siders like Thompson were not the disreputable adversaries of experiential religion as they were often portrayed.[11]

Jonathan Dickinson, Congregationalist-turned-Presbyterian, led the other party, the New England Puritans, in opposing Thompson's overture. While Scotch-Irish members were accustomed to stress the primacy of confessional subscription, Dickinson demurred. The reason for doing so, however, owed not to the confession's Calvinist content. Dickinson's reluctance originated from an aversion to demanding subscription to any document other than the Bible. He argued that requiring subscription to any human composition was tantamount to placing it above Scripture or making it a substitute for Scripture. Hodge cited Dickinson as saying that acknowledging Jesus Christ "for our common head, of the sacred Scriptures for our common standard both in faith and practice, with a joint agreement in the same essential and necessary articles of Christianity, and the same methods of worship and disciple, are a sufficient bond of union for the being or wellbeing of any church under heaven." Since Presbyterians already had such bonds, no additional means of ensuring orthodoxy were necessary. More to the point, said Dickinson, "a subscription to any human composure as the test of our orthodoxy is to make it the standard of our faith, and thereby to give it the honour due only to the word of God." Far from producing union in the church, Dickinson charged, "the requiring and enjoining [of] any unscriptural terms of union or communion is a direct and natural means to procure rents and divisions in the church."[12]

As strong as Dickinson's words were, however, Hodge downplayed his position by contending that Dickinson belonged "to that small class of persons who are opposed to all creeds of human composition." Hodge pointedly dismissed Dickinson's remarks: "How many of the members of the Synod agreed with him in these opinions, cannot now be ascertained. It is evident that his objections had not a very firm hold even of his own mind; for he joined in the adoption and imposition of the Westminster Confession, the very year these remarks were published." Thus, in the final analysis for Hodge, Dickinson believed firmly in the confession after all.[13]

The two parties reached an agreement in the Adopting Act of 1729, which some twenty-three years after the formation of the first presbytery in 1706 established the basis for ministerial communion in the Presbyterian church. The key segment stated: "all the ministers of this Synod, or that shall hereafter be admitted into this Synod, shall declare their agreement in and approbation of the Confession of Faith, with the Larger and Shorter Catechisms of the Assembly of Divines at Westminster, as being, in all the essential and necessary articles, good forms of sound words and systems of Christian doctrine; and so also adopt the said Confession and Catechisms as the Confession of our faith." The only scruple with the confession mentioned specifically concerned the article about the civil magistrate's authority in the church. Historians have endlessly debated the meaning and implications of the act—especially the insertion of the phrase "essential and necessary articles" and its implications for the act as a whole. As a result, subscription still vexes portions of Presbyterianism today. By probing various explicit ways in which it was used in subsequent formation of presbyteries, Hodge showed that it consistently formed the basis of ministerial communion. He concurred that the act was a compromise, but one in which both parties were satisfied. He summarized what it meant for the church to have adopted the confession: "If then the Westminster Confession is a part of our constitution, we are bound to abide by it, or rightfully to get it altered. Ever since the solemn enactment . . . every new member or candidate for the ministry has been required to give his assent to this confession, as containing the system of doctrine taught in the word of God. He assents not merely to absolutely essential and necessary articles of the gospel, but to the whole concatenated statement of doctrines contained in the confession. This, whether right or wrong, liberal or illiberal, is the constitutional and fundamental principle of our ecclesiastical compact." Thus Hodge substantiated his claim that the church was firmly established on the basis of the Westminster Confession. Even those initially reserved about a confessional basis for the church acquiesced that such a basis was necessary for good order.[14]

Hodge then set the stage for the main topic of his second volume by saying of the aftermath of the Adopting Act (the 1730s), "There is scarcely any period in the history of our Church more prolific in acts and overtures than the one now under consideration. These acts proceeded in nearly equal proportions from each of the two parties into which the Synod now began to be divided."[15]

Hodge portrayed the initial skirmishes of what evolved into the full-blown Old Side–New Side controversy, which pitted the pro-revivalist New Side Presbytery of New Brunswick against the anti-revivalist Old Side Presbytery of Philadelphia. In the 1730s Gilbert Tennent continually broached matters of practical religion, charging the denomination with lack of concern about ministers' religious experience. The synod rejected Tennent's charge that Old Side members had "more zeal for outward order than for the main points of practical religion." In rebuttal of Tennent, Hodge cited the synod's injunction in 1733 that presbyteries "examine into the manner of each minister's preaching," and that ministers preach "in the most solemn and affecting manner" and to "convince . . . hearers of their lost and perishing state whilst unconverted, and put them in the diligent use of those means necessary, in order to obtain the sanctifying influences of the Spirit of God." Of Tennent's remonstrances that the denomination lacked evangelical zeal, Hodge argued, "It is obvious that neither the knowledge nor power of evangelical religion could be dead in a church which was willing and able to issue such admonitions as the above."[16]

In the last pages of the chapter, Hodge divulged the growing rift between the two parties. He viewed them as "intimately connected to the schism of 1741." Disputes arose from cases involving false doctrine, ministerial misbehavior, itinerant preaching, and ministerial attention to practical religion. In response, the synod in 1735 exhorted the presbyteries to "take special care not to admit into the sacred office, loose, careless, and irreligious persons, but that they particularly inquire into the conversation, conduct, and behaviour of such as offer themselves to the ministry; and that they diligently examine all the candidates for the ministry in their experience of a work of sanctifying grace in their hearts; and that they admit none to the sacred trust that are not, in the eye of charity, serious Christians." In treating these matters, whenever possible Hodge mentioned John Thompson as championing appropriately moderate positions and criticized Gilbert Tennent for unbecoming stridency. His narration of these events set the stage for his estimation of the 1741 schism.[17]

By the end of his first volume, Hodge's task had been partially accomplished. The Adopting Act succeeded in joining the two parties that comprised early Presbyterianism in America and demonstrated Presbyterianism's consistent adherence to historic Reformed theology. The union, however, turned out to be temporary. Instead of peace, purity, and productivity in the denomination, a general decline in religion infiltrated not just Presbyterians but other American churches as well. By all accounts, a spiritual lethargy had settled over the American Colonies that effectively deadened their religious vitality. Presbyterians and other American churches, however, witnessed a renewal. But the denomination eventually divided over the very issue that revitalized it—the Great Awakening. Presbyterians fragmented into factions over the primacy of religious experience in the Christian faith and what constituted legitimate experience.[18]

Hodge unequivocally admitted the necessity of the revival. Since Princeton Seminary had originated from the same tradition as Princeton College, which in turn had arisen out of Tennent's Log College, a New Side institution, one might expect Hodge to favor New Side tradition as he traced the era in which New Siders had made their most significant impact. Given his conversion during a Princeton revival and his obsession with reporting European revivals, it is ironic that Hodge instead expressed his sympathy for the Old Siders as intrinsic to his defense of the Old School. Indeed, Hodge stated clearly on a matter in which he definitely changed his mind: "The writer has faithfully given the results of careful examination of these contemporaneous publications [mentioned in the preceding paragraph]. The conclusions to which he has arrived, as to the merits of the controversy, differ in some measure from his own previous impressions; and may differ still more from the accounts preserved by tradition in various parts of the church." His transfer of loyalty was foreshadowed by the reserve with which his family greeted news of Charles's conversion during Princeton's revival. Hodge and others distinguished between genuine revivals and illegitimate revivals or, at a minimum, those containing a mixture of great good and serious defects. Thus he subjected the eighteenth-century phenomena to careful scrutiny regarding their authenticity.[19]

The section on revivals proved to be pivotal to Hodge's defense and also the most controversial. Hodge began by claiming that all revivals manifested both purity and impurity, as evidenced by their leadership: "some of the best and some of the worst men in the church, were to be found on either side." The epoch-making events of the mid-1700s involved the titanic figures of Jonathan Edwards and George Whitefield but also figures such as James Davenport. Though in other denominations divergence from orthodox doctrine accounted in part for disputes over the genuineness of the revivals, Presbyterians on both sides of the revival held Calvinist principles. Therefore, the matter came down to distinguishing genuine from false religious experience and whether one could distinguish the genuineness of another person's conversion. The revival was most pure in several locales. Hodge gave expansive coverage to authentic movements of the Spirit in New Jersey (virtually town by town), Pennsylvania, New York, Virginia, and Massachusetts. He cited Archibald Alexander's glowing testimony of Presbyterian minister and revivalist Samuel Davies, who conducted himself "with so much dignity, affability, and prudence that he gained the high respect of all the distinguished laymen in that part of the State [Virginia]." He also cited examples from the arduous labors of Edwards, Whitefield, and Tennent that demonstrated genuine conviction of sin, desire to be delivered from the dominion and penalty of sin, and acceptance of God's forgiving mercy through the work of Christ. He could even say that "[the revival] was in the main a work of God."[20]

Rapid decline in religion and emergence of errors of all kinds in the wake of the awakening, however, cast strong doubts on its genuineness: "This low state of religion, and extensive departure from the truth, in that part of the country where the revival had been most extensive, is certainly *prima facie* proof that there must have been something very wrong in the revival itself." Hodge bluntly attributed the emotional outbursts associated with dramatic conversions not to the work of the Spirit but to mental disorders: "a very large portion of the emotions so strongly felt, and so openly expressed . . . arose not from spiritual apprehensions of divine truth, but from mere imaginations or mental images [produced by the oratory of the evangelists]." While emotional excitement might attend genuine religion, it was not necessarily a genuine sign of it.[21] Hodge faulted Edwards's and Whitefield's failure to discern that bodily agitations accompanying emotional outbursts often stemmed from a contagion that spread through crowds under the influence of powerful speakers: "That a large part of these results was to be attributed to natural causes, can hardly be doubted; yet who could discriminate between what was the work of the orator, and what was the work of the Spirit of God?" The final blow militating against their genuineness was that "there is nothing in the Bible to lead us to regard these bodily affections as the legitimate effects of religious feeling."[22]

Hodge focused extensive criticism on his own denomination and the revival's most outspoken advocate, Gilbert Tennent. Tennent's name appeared repeatedly in Hodge's accounts of education of ministers, the synod's role in examining candidates, itinerant preaching, and the spiritual state of the clergy. Tennent censored anti-revivalist ministers and accused them of being unbelievers. His penchant for attacking fellow clergy reached its peak in his sermon "On the Danger of an Unconverted Ministry" (1741), preached in Nottingham, Pennsylvania, outside his own presbytery. Among other inflammatory epithets in the sermon, he accused fellow clergy of being unregenerate, pharisees, and hypocrites. Hodge labeled it "one of the most terrible pieces of denunciation in the English language."[23] At one point Hodge said of his leadership, "Mr. Tennent was so completely the soul of the party to which he belonged, that without him it never would have existed. He is often, therefore, addressed as the party itself, and his writings and declarations are referred to as speaking the language of his associates."[24]

Hodge recapitulated his case against New Side revivalism as "a formidable array of evils": "There was too little discrimination between true and false religious feeling. There was too much encouragement given to outcries, faintings, and bodily agitations . . . There was in many, too much reliance on impulses, visions, and the pretended power of discerning spirits. There was a great deal of censoriousness, and of a sinful disregard of ecclesiastical order." Throughout his treatment, although Hodge rarely used the terms *New Light / Old Light* or even *New Side / Old Side* to identify the parties and their views, he nevertheless laid the foundation for blaming the schism of 1741 on those who came to be known as New Siders.[25]

The two parties disagreed strongly over the educational qualifications of ministers and itinerant preaching. Tennent in behalf of the New Side Presbytery of New Brunswick objected to the synod rule that those not receiving their training at either a European university or a New England school (Harvard or Yale) be examined by the synod as to their qualification for ministry. Tennent strenuously objected to this because he "believed the rule was designed to operate against his father's school [the Log College]." By this rule, the synod thereby encroached on what was the sole right of presbyteries—to judge the qualifications of pastors. Hodge sided with the Old Side majority by pointing out that not only was the synod the highest court of the church, "but it [also] included all presbyteries. Its determination or acts, therefore, were of the same nature with our constitutional rules when adopted by the majority of presbyteries. They were the expression of the will of the whole church." Therefore, the synod "laid claim to no power either unreasonable in itself, or inconsistent with uniform practice and acknowledged constitution of the church, as it then existed."[26]

Although admitting that both sides had valid concerns, Hodge clearly sided with the majority vote against the New Brunswick men: "Whatever unworthy motive may, on either side, have mingled with better feelings, there is no doubt that the majority, which included almost the whole Synod, were influenced in the adoption of the rule in question, by a sincere desire to secure an adequately educated ministry, and the minority by an equally conscientious belief, that the operation of the rule would be inimical to the progress of religion in the church." Translated, this meant that the synod believed Log Colleges, such as that of William Tennent, functioned more like internships in which pastors served as tutors, and the education they provided lacked the advantages of more established colleges—a more substantial curriculum, faculty experienced in teaching those subjects, and well-equipped libraries. The New Brunswick party, on the other hand, feared that university studies unduly diminished piety. Because they believed that as a result of this rule the synod had approved spiritually unqualified ministers, the New Brunswick party sanctioned the practice of itinerant preaching in which New Side pastors ventured uninvited into Old Side territories and encouraged parishioners to abandon churches led by unconverted men.[27]

Finally, Tennent and his New Side colleagues pressed repeatedly for more rigorous inspection of ministers' spiritual experience. At synod in 1740, Tennent unleashed an attack on some of his colleagues' spiritual qualifications. He claimed that as a result of their "powerless and unsavoury preaching" and being "soft and flattering . . . afraid to use the terrors of the Lord," he was inclined "to suspect their [spiritual] state." Though he admitted that "there is no infallible knowledge" of a person's spiritual state, "yet there is a satisfactory knowledge to be attained." Appalled, Hodge argued that "the whole proceeding, though doubtless well intended, was in every point of view exceptionable." Tennent's charges were "so vague, that they could neither be proved or disproved; they rested on hearsay evidence." After exploring the most colorful parts of Tennent's sermon on unconverted ministry, Hodge summarized his case against the New Siders: "The truth is, Mr. Tennent, like other vehement men, often said more than he meant. He acted more from feeling than from principle . . . It may easily be conceived what a state of things would be produced by some half-dozen ministers assuming the prerogative of judging of the hearts of their brethren, denouncing them as unconverted, entering their congregations, exhorting their people to leave them, and every where erecting new congregations. This the New Brunswick brethren did very extensively; and this, more than any thing else, was the cause of schism."[28]

Nevertheless, Hodge took great comfort in pointing out Tennent's change of mind regarding these matters, as illustrated by his contrite retractions after the schism ended. In his *Irenicum Ecclesiasticarum* (1749), Tennent apologized for his earlier censoriousness. Hodge cited extended portions of various documents in which Tennent repudiated his former stances. Hodge confirmed this claim by showing substantial concurrence by Tennent and Thompson on matters that supposedly separated the two opponents: the nature of conviction, the call to the gospel ministry, and the doctrine of assurance. When Hodge finally encapsulated the rupture, he stated, "It was not diversity of opinion as to doctrine or discipline, but loss of confidence and alienation of feeling arising from the different views entertained of the revival which then prevailed." In the main, Hodge was convinced that the Tennent party, "the New Brunswick brethren," were "the aggressors." Unfortunately, the "opposite party" responded in kind by adopting "violent measures for redress, which removed none of the evils under which they suffered."[29]

21

To Publish or Not to Publish

Several matters beg for comment as we consider Charles Hodge's *CHPC*. Most obviously, he wrote outside his discipline, and he admitted as much.[1] Nevertheless, his willingness to do so illustrates Princetonians' insistence that all disciplines in the seminary curriculum needed to be utilized in defending their Old School Presbyterian heritage. He deviated slightly from the explicit purpose of the book by including so much extraneous material on matters other than Presbyterian, that is, to revivals associated with Congregationalists in New England and the work of George Whitefield. In the process, he generally ignored the fact that Jonathan Edwards took great pains to distinguish between genuine and false revivals in *The Distinguishing Marks of the Work of the Spirit*. Edwards also acknowledged abuses by James Davenport and subjected them to the same trenchant criticism as Hodge.

We also note that Hodge's view of religious experience had matured from his earlier views. Whereas his youth had been characterized by confession of religious experience and fascination with revivals as nonnegotiable indications of spiritual life, in his treatment of Gilbert Tennent Hodge questioned whether any observer could ultimately judge another person's spiritual condition. Thus, as apparent in his treatment of infant baptism, Hodge insisted that when people applied for church membership, what was required was a credible testimony and a life free from scandal. New Siders' tendency to overstate what examiners could obtain through testimony and questioning must be subject to restraint. Though Hodge never intruded his own experience into the document, one cannot help but infer that he learned much from his earlier immature religious experiences. His painful attempts to discern his own heart and his rather naive acceptance of reports of excitements in the Pomeranian revivals had given way to more mature discrimination. His son's editing portions of the European journal also become understandable. While to the end of his days Hodge exhibited an emotional, subjective strain to his faith, it was tempered with what we can identify as Old School piety—appreciation for subjective features in religious faith coupled with an equally strong adherence to the indispensability of faith's cognitive dimensions.

Of equal importance for the ongoing camaraderie of the Princetonians, Hodge's attempt to defend Old School Presbyterianism historically also offended Archibald Alexander. It produced one of the few fissures in their otherwise warm, lifelong relationship. Alexander objected to Hodge's view of synodical power regarding investigating ministerial candidates. He flatly stated, "The examination of candidates, with a view to ordination, is properly a Presbyterial and not a Synodical act." Thus Hodge's extended defense of the synod's prerogative fell on deaf ears and unnecessarily cast aspersions on Tennent's Log College education. The synod, for Alexander, had no right to require students under William Tennent's tutelage to submit to synodical examination. The Old Siders' rule created an unnecessary embarrassment of New Side education that led to invalidating their ordination.[2]

Even more objectionable to Alexander was Hodge's extended criticism of New Side enthusiasm and his favorable portrayal of the Old Side. After all, the seminary itself traced its roots back to Tennent's Log College, which had produced ministers who became leaders of the awakening, and humanly speaking, Alexander owed his own conversion to the revivalism upon which Hodge now cast a shadow. Although he had learned the Shorter Catechism and portions of the Larger, Alexander had expressed little interest in spiritual matters until after a series of events he professed faith at a revival in Lexington, Virginia, in 1789, which marked the opening phase of the Second Great Awakening. Alexander thus entertained a more positive view of the eighteenth-century phenomena.[3]

Hodge described Alexander's strongly negative reaction to Hodge's interpretation of the revival and subsequent schism in a lengthy letter to Henry Boardman. He began by admitting that the history might well offend a good many of their Old School friends—"the kind of offence which men feel when they see a different view of any subject than their own represented." He mentioned specifically his representation of Whitefield and the 1741 schism. Hodge confessed of his earlier view of the eighteenth century, "I had received the impression that all the old side were irreligious, unworthy men, and that all the new side were excellent and fervently pious. This impression among the older ministers who received the traditionary accounts of that period, is so strong as to take something of the character of the original party feeling." Hodge thereby revealed that his opinion about revivalism and their manifestations had significantly changed from his opinions of the Pomeranian revivals he heard about while he was in Germany.[4]

He rehearsed his differences of opinion with Alexander on the book. He wrote to Boardman, "Dr. Alexander, after reading the manuscript, wrote me a long letter telling me what he had heard about the character of the two parties when he was a young man, and how strong his feelings still were upon the subject, and his conviction that the Old side were a great deal worse and New side a great deal better than I had represented them. This letter gave me, in one view, a great deal of uneasiness."[5]

Despite the embarrassment of disagreeing with his colleague and in contrast to his previously favorable views of the New Side, Hodge felt constrained to stand by his historical research. In doing so, he revealed perhaps more clearly than in all his other writings that historical evidences do not simply speak for themselves but must be carefully weighed. Hodge had written to Boardman in 1838 that he was finding a vast amount of material as he researched his subject.[6] Now his findings inclined him to revise his previous views. Hodge found that interpreting such a tumultuous time entailed making historical judgments about what facts to include and how to evaluate them. Describing the events of the eighteenth century simply in terms of black and white had to give way to a more nuanced treatment. Distanced by decades from the dramatically charged revivals and being exposed to writings that did not conform to his and his friends' opinions led Hodge to arrive at views that, although differing from many accounts that he had perhaps blindly accepted in the past, could still be seen as consistent with genuine Old School principles. These matters profoundly influenced his overall characterization of the eighteenth century. The meaning of facts he took for granted was not as apparent as he and fellow Princetonians frequently understood them. His preconceptions had to give way to his carefully researched study.

Whether to express the results of his examination weighed heavily on Hodge: "I know that documents and books retain and transmit a very imperfect view of the spirit of any age, and therefore felt that my representation might be very far from the truth. But at the same time, I must go by those documents, and to take the traditionary representations of those who had conversed with the actors in those scenes, and who had all the feelings of the conflict, would make a perfectly one-sided story." Hodge's telling remark reflects his desire to represent the history of Presbyterianism accurately. That entailed presenting the awakening in such a way that both sides of the titanic struggle were fairly represented.[7]

Hodge responded to Alexander's letter, and his mentor replied, according to Hodge, that "he would not have me alter anything out of deference to any body; that he had no responsibility, but that mine was very great." Then, apropos of Hodge's confliction about who should publish the book, he wrote, "I do not mean to give you the idea that the Doctor thought the history very wicked, or that he would object my publishing it, or of sanctioning such a representation as I have given of the violence & disorders of the zealous men of that day." Nevertheless,

Hodge summarized his convictions to Boardman: "I must feel perfectly free to write as my judgment and conscience dictate."[8]

Alexander's reaction and Hodge's close relation with Boardman made Hodge consider carefully who should publish the book. Hodge confessed in a letter to Boardman that "all my friends here whom I have had the opportunity of consulting agree with me that your Board ought not undertake the publication." As a result of this mini-crisis, Hodge's *CHPC* was published by Wm. S. Martien in 1839 (vol. 1) and 1840 (vol. 2). The Presbyterian Board of Publication did not publish it until 1851. While not claiming infallibility in his findings, Hodge believed that the generally accepted favorable interpretation of the revivals and of individuals on both sides of the issues needed correction. Given his position at the seminary and its historical legacy, his history marked a revisioning of the Old Side–New Side controversy. While Alexander thoroughly concurred with Hodge's historical apologetic that the Old School could lay legitimate claim to being historic Presbyterianism, that need not entail casting aspersions on the Old Side, which contended with the very faction that had spawned the seminary.[9]

Hodge faithfully advanced Old School views on biblical and theological interpretation, revivalism, Presbyterian polity, voluntary societies, slavery, and piety. As he progressed in his career from the 1820s through the 1830s, he clearly emerged as the champion of Old School Presbyterianism in the North. Later in the century, that term was often construed as unduly narrow, dogmatic, and hidebound. Hodge's positions, while always conservative, were often carefully measured and nuanced. He fashioned his reputation by fulfilling a number of roles: seminary professor, journal editor, book reviewer, biblical scholar, historian, and, in general, commentator on all things Presbyterian. In each of the areas, he contributed voluminous amounts of material. While his opinions display great erudition and breadth of vision, his writing is frequently verbose and repetitive. The summaries of General Assemblies could often delve into details that seem picayune to the casual reader, but as many acknowledged, they were the first pages that informed Presbyterians read when the summer issue of the *PR* arrived in the mail. The reader is never in the dark about where Hodge stood on an issue. While he might claim that a new idea never arose in the seminary, Hodge was capable of changing his mind, as in his views on how quickly slavery ought to be eliminated and his estimation of the New Side tradition. One interpretation might be that Hodge discarded his New Side heritage in his *CHPC*. More likely, he demonstrated a willingness to reassess matters in light of careful reconsideration of all the evidence at his disposal. Above all, Hodge was able in this period to claim that Princeton stood as a mediating party in the various controversies of the Presbyterian church. That claim will be explored further in part 4.

PART 4

Old School Controversialist and Churchman

Princeton Seminary and American Presbyterianism thrived on controversy. Controversy in the nineteenth century reflected the vitality of Presbyterian faith. The frequency, sharpness, and popularity of debates illustrate how much religious issues permeated American life. From the Adopting Act (1729) in which parties disputed the terms of ministerial communion through the Old Side–New Side disruption and into Old School–New School schism of the nineteenth century, Presbyterians debated their convictions straightforwardly. The openness and intensity of the disputes reflected their continuity with Protestant tradition as various churches distinguished themselves through confessional documents. Charles Hodge participated in controversies on several fronts—within the scholarly community, in dialogue with various expressions of Reformed theology, in the annual General Assemblies, and in the broader religious and cultural contexts. Though not polemical in personal relationships, Hodge excelled as a defender of Old School principles against New

School innovations, in internecine debates over polity and the church's mission with Southern counterparts, and in pointed altercation with Mercersburg theology. With great frequency Hodge won support in crucial battles for and against resolutions in the General Assembly. He exhibited the fervor with which Presbyterians held fundamental convictions as debate swirled on the floor of the denomination's annual meetings. Old Schoolers were justly famous for the ardor with which they espoused their views. Passion for principles both small and great characterized the Old School. Yet even in the midst of controversy, Hodge showed himself a man of the center, particularly in his views on Roman Catholicism. Given his attention to detail, no topic was too minor and no principle so seemingly insignificant for Hodge not to have an opinion. He argued them fully. Hodge's capacious intellect and facility in marshaling facts in support of his arguments made him a formidable opponent whenever he attended General Assembly. And he used the *PR* to great effect to advance what he favored and forestall views and practices he opposed. The journal may well have been his "ball and chain" for over forty years, yet without it, he may never have received recognition as a formidable controversialist and churchman.[1]

22

Changes

The 1840s witnessed several life-changing events in Charles Hodge's personal and family life. His family, having grown to eight children, began to disperse. A. A. and his wife Elizabeth went to China as missionaries in 1847. Hodge struggled with his son's plans to go to the mission field. While an avid supporter of missions and having served on the Board of Foreign Missions since 1846, he believed his son's gifts lay in intellectual pursuits. As Charles wrote to Hugh, "his real strength is his intellect—clear, logical discriminating mind which is much superior . . . to any of the other of our children and inferior to very few if any in the seminary."[1] Eight months later, just before A. A. left for the Far East, his father reiterated his assessment: "He has a philosophical head and is a good writer. He was decidedly the best theologian and the best theological writer of his class." Despite his reservations, Hodge acceded to his son's calling: "It is a great comfort to have a son preaching the gospel even if thousands of miles away." Signs of weakness in A. A.'s chest and palpitations in his heart surfaced before he and his wife left, but they followed through on their commitment to the mission field. His health issues did not subside, with the result that they returned from India in 1850.[2]

Hodge's daughter Mary married William Scott, also a graduate of Princeton Seminary, and they left for Danville, Kentucky, where he taught ancient languages at Center College. Both his son's and daughter's departures were bittersweet. Hodge expressed thanks for his son's commitment to spreading the gospel, yet his leaving and the distance separating them elicited concern for health and safety in lands more distant than Hodge had traveled himself. As for his daughter's marriage, Hodge wrote to his brother, "To marry a daughter I find to be a very different thing from marrying a son." Expressing his conflicted feelings, he continued, "Still we had M__, for two and twenty years, and that is a good deal, and though she is not, and never again can be to us what she once was, she is still our precious child. I trust we shall be happy in her happiness."[3]

Of these events A. A. wrote, appropriately as it turned out, "Our family was never completely regathered on earth again, for before the son returned home from India, the Mother was making the beginnings of the home in heaven."[4]

Hodge's involvement outside the seminary increased in the 1840s and 1850s as he assumed responsibilities within the denomination. His influence as a churchman extended beyond his annual reviews of the General Assembly. Consistent with his strong advocacy of boards in the church, in 1846 he became a member of the Board of Foreign Missions, and twenty-two years later he assumed the presidency of that board, an office he held until 1870. A colleague on the board described Hodge as "one of the ablest and most earnest supporters of the cause of Foreign Missions we ever had in the Presbyterian Church." He also served on the boards of Domestic Missions and Education.[5]

When Samuel Miller died in 1850, Hodge succeeded him as a trustee of the College of New Jersey (renamed Princeton University in 1896). Hodge's concern for the college reflected those qualities of education that he had sought at the seminary upon his return from Europe. Faculty vacancies received his special attention. Whereas in the college's earlier years tensions had mounted over whether preparation of ministers should take precedence over preparation for government service, during Hodge's years on the board competition arose between the classics and science. According to a fellow trustee, not only did Hodge urge the filling of positions expeditiously, but also at every opportunity he sought to maintain "the importance of the languages and the humanities in competition with the pressure of the physical sciences." Much later, in the 1870s, he would warn against the deformations that positivism would introduce into American scientific study. While fascinated with and always supportive of science—its methods and accomplishments—he believed that science should operate from a base consistent with its long compatibility with Christian truth.[6]

In his twenty-seven-year tenure as a college trustee, Hodge also insisted on maintaining the religious tradition of the college associated with its Presbyterian founding. Paul Kemeny reports that when James McCosh assumed the presidency in 1868, speaking as the senior member of the trustees, Hodge charged McCosh with preserving the "true religion" that had characterized the college since its founding. Students "should be made to feel that the eternal is infinitely more important than the temporal, the heavenly than the earthly." He believed the college's religious heritage should directly influence administration policies. Of equal importance, Hodge wanted the school to preserve the highest standards of scholarship. The trustee wrote, "[Hodge] had a dread of a *little* as well as of an unsanctified learning. The completion of his own education in Germany furnished him with the standard of the higher culture attained in the European universities. Hence he was anxious to advance prudently, but as rapidly as possible the standard of learning in our colleges as a preparation for all the diversified enterprises of American life." Hodge also cautioned against allowing enthusiasm for scientific advancement to eclipse study of the classics. The full goal of education was to "develop mental power." "[The] best mental development is attained," he argued, "by the study of the classics and mathematics." He used the term "balance" as the metaphor that would produce "the kind of development and culture in which grace, strength and efficiency are conjoined." Thus Hodge exploited every opportunity in both college and seminary contexts to press the case for religious orthodoxy married to academic excellence. In both instances he had in mind the standards for excellence established by German scholarship while avoiding its errors in perspective.[7]

Hodge's activity continued within the denomination. The Old School–New School separation that began with the 1837 General Assembly surpassed in duration the earlier Old Side–New Side schism of the eighteenth century by a decade and a half. The schism over the Great Awakening extended from 1741 to 1758, while the nineteenth-century rupture lasted until 1869, well after the conclusion of the Civil War. Hodge's stature at the beginning of the dispute was relatively minor. In his early forties and the junior member of the faculty, he was overshadowed by his senior colleagues Archibald Alexander and Samuel Miller. As the needs of the seminary grew, Alexander's age became a concern. At a proposal initiated by Alexander and forwarded by Princeton's board of directors, the 1840 General Assembly made changes in the appointments of professors. Alexander remained professor of pastoral and polemic theology, the position he held until his death, but Hodge took over the duties of professor of exegetical and didactic theology. Alexander's son J. A. Alexander assumed Hodge's former chair as professor of Oriental and biblical literature.[8]

The change in Hodge's duties suited him perfectly. As evidenced by his participation in denominational and academic debates on doctrine and polity and spirited defense of Old School Presbyterianism, Hodge's facility in theology emerged as his greatest strength. From the beginning of his teaching, he recognized deficiencies in his grasp of the ancient languages—deficiencies that he attempted to offset by his studies in Europe. Those efforts never went unrewarded. As Benjamin B. Warfield's assessment of his linguistic skills in the classroom clearly illustrates, however, Hodge did not realize the potential in Oriental and biblical literature that by all accounts he eventually achieved in theology.[9] Given the goals of Princeton's theological perspective to ground theology in biblical content, a great advantage that Hodge brought to his new appointment, in addition to his native intellectual abilities, was his linguistic training. As A. A. Hodge stated in his biography, while biblical exegesis was not his father's forte, his "twenty years in a department of theological study to which his natural tastes did not dispose him" in the long run proved to be the very foundation for his facility in systematic theology. More to the point, Hodge's teaching biblical languages supplied him with the one qualification in which "the vast majority of speculative theologians [were] more or less deficient." Whatever his father's limitations might have been in his previous duties as professor of biblical languages he more than made up with his careful precision in theological discourse.[10]

Among other changes in Hodge's personal life during this period, the loss of colleagues affected him most profoundly. The first was the premature death at the age of forty-one of Albert B. Dod, professor of mathematics at the college, member of the "Association of Gentlemen" responsible for the *PR* and a contributor of several articles to the journal. Hodge and Dod spent several days each week playing competitive games of chess or engaged in animated conversation reminiscent of Hodge's associations in Europe. Hodge's study provided the venue for their extended meetings. As in Europe, nothing fell outside their interests—theology, mental and moral science, metaphysics, politics, literature, and the fine arts. With J. W. Alexander, Dod wrote a scathing critique of New England transcendentalism for the January 1839 *PR*, and Hodge followed suit in 1840 with a similar critique, "The Latest Form of Infidelity," which we will examine in chapter 30. Thus, when Dod fell ill, Hodge comforted his friend in the last week of his life. Hodge wrote of their final conversation in November 1845: "I had often known of men's dying in peace or in triumph, but to see a man dying cheerfully in the full possession of his intellect in calm, unexcited confidence in Christ as his God and Saviour, was to me a perfectly novel sight. His death is the greatest loss I have ever sustained in the death of friends." As in all instances when Hodge gave full vent to pious remarks, he displayed strong emotional feeling.[11]

The deaths of his wife and Princeton's first two professors followed. His wife fell ill in September 1849, and despite the doctor's optimism that she would recover, she grew worse. Hodge kept his brother apprised of Sarah's condition almost daily via letters. Hugh visited several times from Philadelphia but could do little but comfort Charles and the family. Hodge recorded conversations that he and Sarah had during his bedside vigil as she prepared to die. Those accounts resemble earlier letters in which they exchanged thoughts of the God they served together. At her request he repeated the words of favorite hymns, and he elicited her final words of faith. She succumbed early Christmas morning with the family by her side, and Hodge wrote to his brother, "She was full of peace, humility, faith and has left us a rich treasure of blessings."[12]

Deeply affected by Sarah's death, Hodge expressed his grief by visiting her grave at least weekly. He remembered her in his "Memoranda," a daily account of weather conditions and other miscellaneous notes, sayings, and records, by numbering the Sundays following her death ("first Sunday after," "second Sunday after," etc., for 132 weeks) and he placed a thick black line beside each December 25 entry from her death until 1854. He never, however, let his sorrow degenerate into melancholy. In a consoling letter to his brother almost a year later when Hugh lost a son, he wrote, "Pious sorrow, that is sorrow mingled with pious feeling, with resignation, confidence in God, hope in his mercy and love, is [in] every way healthful to the soul; while melancholy is irreligious, and is a cancer to true peace and spiritual health. The great means of having our sorrow kept pure is to keep near to God, to feel assured of his love, that he orders all things well, and will make even our afflictions work out for us a far more exceeding and an eternal weight of glory."[13]

On July 8, 1852, Hodge married a second time, to Mary Hunter Stockton, a friend almost from childhood and a confidant to Sarah. She was immediately accepted into the household and successfully assumed the duties of completing the training of the remaining children. She would survive Hodge by a mere twenty months.

Additional deaths intruded sadness into Hodge's life—those of the two senior faculty members. Samuel Miller died in 1850 and Archibald Alexander in 1851. Hodge spoke effusively of the contributions that both had made to the seminary. Because the faculty members were so few, their mutual commitment to Reformed theology, the mission of the school, and their frequent verbal exchanges added to their camaraderie. The ties with Alexander, however, were even stronger. They extended back to 1812 as Hodge had leaned on the balcony railing of First Presbyterian Church and listened with rapt attention as Alexander delivered his inaugural address. In one of their last conversations,

Alexander transferred the account book of seminary scholarships into Hodge's care. Then he solemnly passed the torch to his protégé in the form of a carved white-bone walking stick that he had received from a chief of the Sandwich Islands, the historical name for the Hawaiian Islands. Expressing his affection for both the tradition of Princeton up to that date and the promise of Hodge's career in the present and into the future, he said, "You must hand this to your successor in office, that it may be handed down as a kind of symbol of orthodoxy." Hodge paid tribute to his mentor by writing, "To no man have I ever owed a thousandth part what I owe to him and while he lived I always felt I had a visible refuge—now there is none but God."[14] A. A. Hodge wrote that his father walked with Alexander's sons in the funeral procession, thereby "claiming to be a true son also."[15]

23

An Evangelical Theology

Shortly after the change in his teaching duties, Charles Hodge received an opportunity to display his theology to a wider audience than the Reformed community. In 1841 the American Sunday-School Union, in recognition of Hodge's growing prominence outside the limits of Presbyterianism, solicited what amounted to a popular or layman's theological book. The Union was one of the select few voluntary societies that Hodge heartily approved as appropriate for meeting common needs of evangelical denominations (including Old School Presbyterians!). The book would speak to all evangelical Christians who wanted a practical summary of Christian theology regardless of their denominational background. The Union had originated in Philadelphia in 1824 to promote Sunday schools, distribute literature for teachers and students, and encourage biblical literacy among children and adults. Given Princeton's reputation as a Calvinist institution and the Union's mission to minister to a broad spectrum of denominations, his colleagues expressed surprise that the Union approved Hodge's volume. Mark Noll notes that the only point of debate regarding its content was its title—Hodge preferred *The Nar-*

row Way, which the Union rejected. After several passes, both parties agreed on *The Way of Life*. While intended for youth, the work clearly demands more intellectually of the reader than average young people can muster. The book immediately found a wide audience, however, as a nontechnical theological explanation of the way of salvation.[1]

What immediately strikes the reader in light of Hodge's expertise as a theologian is the simplicity of his method in drawing the reader into a theological way of thinking. He begins by substantiating the Scriptures as the Word of God. He does so by appealing to the "internal evidences" of the Bible's divine origin. That is, he appeals not to rational arguments or external evidences, such as fulfilled prophecy, the attesting value of miracles, and the content of the Bible—its reporting of historical, geographical, and cultural data—which the reader might expect from Hodge's fondness for Common Sense philosophy. In fact, he states unequivocally, "No amount of mere external evidence can produce genuine faith." Instead, Hodge claims that the condition of the heart and its openness to receive internal evidence carries far more influence in correctly appropriating biblical faith: "Goodness carries with it its own evidence. To appreciate evidence of this kind requires no great degree of knowledge of refinement. It requires merely right moral feelings. Where these exist, the evidence that goodness is goodness is immediate and irresistible." Thus the moral and spiritual content of the Bible—the character of God it describes, the voice that utters "He that believeth on the Son hath everlasting life," the holiness of life that the Bible demands—all provides indisputable and convincing evidences of its divine origin and authority. Hodge believed that Christian truth—the God it proclaims, the salvation it offers, and the way of life it demands—makes an immediate and powerful impression on the reader or hearer of the gospel.[2]

Having established the intrinsic reliability and authority of the Bible, in the remainder of the book Hodge builds on that authoritative Scripture. In successive order he treats the doctrines of sin (its universal nature, people's willful indifference to and suppression of sin, and personal conviction of its power), justification (described in biblical terms as Christ's righteousness being both its ground or basis for salvation and its practical effects), faith (the condition and nature of saving faith and its relation to justification), repentance and profession of religion (the necessity of public profession, baptism, and the Lord's Supper), and holy living (the nature of a genuine religious life and the means of sanctification).

As chapter topics illustrate, Hodge probes not only the content of Christian teaching but also the practical application of those doctrines. Didactic content does not remain merely abstract propositions, a system of truth disconnected from daily life. Thus the title of the book. Biblical content does not preclude but rather represents practical living as a necessary by-product. Hodge draws his audience in so that they do not merely examine Christian teaching cognitively, but are also invited to share in its life-changing message. Hodge functions at his best when, instead of speaking in the third-person singular or plural, he includes his reader by using the first-person plural. He treats his message not simply as an abstract system of truth but also as something to be appropriated and expressed experientially. When talking about sin, for example, he reminds his readers, "[In our sinful state] we look upon sin in a very different light from that in which it is presented in the word of God." He continues on the subject of repentance: "Our repentance needs to be repented of, unless it leads us to confession and restitution in cases of private injury; unless it causes us to forsake not merely outward sins, which attract the notice of others, but those which lie concealed in the heart; unless it makes us choose the service of God, as that which is right and congenial, and causes us to live not for ourselves but for him who loved us and gave himself for us."[3] Typical of virtually all his sermons and talks addressing practical issues, Hodge presses home practical claims that make an immediate impression on the hearts of his hearers or readers.

A distinguishing feature of every chapter is the use of footnotes at the bottom of the pages, citing biblical texts supporting statements in the text. The pages vary in the number of passages listed. Most pages have at least one citation and some have up to a dozen or more per page to indicate that the way of life is biblically grounded. Hodge thus leads the reader to think as a Christian and to recognize that, practically speaking, Christianity has its roots in the Bible. Christian truth and Christian living—the way of life—have a single premise: the Word of God. What Christians believe and how they live rest not on what speculative reason can conjure up but on the true content of Scripture, which makes its own distinctive claim on the heart.

Hodge completes his description of the way of life with extended treatment of the sacraments and the process of sanctification resulting in holy living, or what he calls "true religion." While never using the term *nurture*, his depiction of each reflects that the sacraments, union with Christ, and the work of the Holy Spirit comprise the means by which believers progress in their faith. Interestingly, Hodge's depiction of the sacraments unfolds in such a way as not to offend other evangelical views. He defines the sacraments as "efficacious means of grace, not merely exhibiting to, but actually conferring upon those who worthily receive them, the benefits which they represent." Steering away from potential controversy with Baptists, he does not broach the subject of infant baptism. He views the Lord's Supper as primarily a "memorial of the death of Christ" and "the appointed means for making a public profession of religion" and a "seal of the covenant of grace." While those comments might offend those who view baptism and the Lord's Supper as mere ordinances, not sacraments, they are clearly not polemic in intent.[4]

Apropos of his earlier diary and other reflections on his own religious life, Hodge states that true religion does not consist of "external service; nor is it a mere excitement of fear and sorrow succeeded by peace and joy; nor is it a fitful alteration of such exercises." Instead, "it is a permanent principle of action, spontaneous in its exercises and progressive in its nature." This succinct comment about the nature of true religion—what it is not and what it is—constitutes a more mature assessment of religion than was represented in his own earlier wide fluctuations during his mission preaching in Philadelphia. Hodge thereby establishes a more stable attitude of what represents a model religious life. Religious devotion also consists not of outward duties or rote participation in rituals. Nor should it be characterized by radical oscillations of introspective states. Genuine religion consists of a settled progression toward spiritual maturity.[5]

In one respect *WOL* differs from Hodge's usual presentation of theology. It is not overtly a book of Calvinist theology. He wrote it to appeal to the widest possible evangelical audience, consistent with the mission of the Sunday-School Union. Someone might accuse Hodge that in so doing he advances a more or less generic evangelical Christianity, a violation of his own principle in the debate over educational societies that a person cannot advocate a "Christianity in general." In the *PR* he called generic Christianity "an admirable chimera." His goal here, however, was not the training of Presbyterian ministers, but the propagation of the gospel to an unspecified audience, using a broad evangelical net. The difference lay in the purpose of the writing. Hodge apparently believed ecumenical cooperation in the presentation of the gospel not only appropriate, but advantageous.

In this regard, Hodge's book elicited a warm response from a wide variety of sources. One came from his German friend Ludwig von Gerlach, who called it an expression of "the great fundamental truths of religion." Gerlach, in harmony with the goal of Hodge's book to cooperate across denominational lines, lamented in a letter the continued deterioration of religion in Germany since Hodge's departure. He said that hostile circumstances caused Christians in Germany to "long for catholicity." He continued, "Being surrounded by Atheists and Pantheists we strive to establish a consciousness of the essential unity of all Christians, Romanists not excepted; and the great fact of the *whole* Church being the body of Christ is foremost in our minds." Obviously, the cause of orthodoxy in Germany had not improved since Hodge's visit. Thus, just as Gerlach had appreciated the many instances during Hodge's visit when the circle of friends exchanged their respective views in an irenic context, he praised Hodge's book as an effort in ecumenicity.[6]

Despite fond approval of the work as a whole, however, Gerlach could not resist adding a footnote critical of Hodge's treatment of the sacraments. He complained that the book "does not quite do justice to the 'objective content and import' of these ordinances, but subjects them too much to the state of mind of the recipient." Then he added tellingly: "It is not clear to me, how, according to your doctrine, you can avoid rejecting pedobaptism." Ironically, Gerlach's critique succinctly states what in other polemical contexts Hodge would have said about non-Presbyterian views of the sacraments! Later in his career

Hodge would confront similar issues—the presence of Christ in the Lord's Supper and the extent to which Presbyterians ought to participate in evangelical unions despite their differences over minor points of doctrine.[7]

WOL represents Hodge at his evangelical best. By using the term *way of life* for his layman's exposition of Christian theology, he sets the stage for the correlation between what the mind receives as true (doctrine or propositions) and what the heart feels or experiences (life). By combining the intellect's apprehension of the doctrinal truths of the faith with the heart's affective response to truth, Hodge effectively demonstrates the correlation between Christians' cognitive and emotive experiences. Genuine faith consists of intellectual assent to Christian truths as well as affective or intuitive feeling. Without either an objective content or an appropriate emotive response, Christian faith would not be genuine. Christian faith could therefore be correctly characterized as both propositional in nature and—as in the title of his book—a way of life. If either the objective or subjective element were eliminated, faith would not be genuinely Christian in nature. For Hodge, the cognitive and affective elements of the Christian faith are necessary, complementary, and never in contradiction.

Almost ten years later, Hodge articulated these evangelical views of intellect and feelings under far different circumstances—a polemical exchange with Edwards Amasa Park, professor at Andover Seminary. In 1850 Park, who represented a conservative influence among New England evangelicals, preached a sermon, "The Theology of the Intellect and That of the Feelings," that captured Hodge's attention because it received overwhelming positive response not only from its original audience of Congregational ministers but also from its wide distribution in published form. The heated dialogue between Hodge and Park filled scores of pages in *BS* and the *PR* over the next year and a half.[8] Influenced by the New England theology of Nathaniel W. Taylor, which sought to revise Calvinism by eliminating some of its harsh doctrines, Park questioned the imputation of Adam's original sin and propitiatory views of the atonement. In his sermon Park stated that because intellect and feelings are two different modes of apprehending truth, the two may indeed stand in contradiction.

More to the point, Hodge quoted Park as saying that while theology of the intellect may change (as in the revision of Calvinist doctrines due to changes in theological opinion), "the theology of the heart, letting the minor inaccuracies go for the sake of holding strongly to the substance of doctrine, need not always accommodate itself to scientific changes, but may often use its old statements, even if, when literally understood, they be incorrect, and it thus abides permanent as are the main impressions of truth." Whereas in *WOL* Hodge explicated evangelical belief and practice in terms that laypeople could understand, in the controversy with Park Hodge assumed a polemical role on behalf of the unity of intellect and piety at a higher level of discourse. He defended the integrity of Christianity's appealing to intellect in the form of theological content and to the heart as the wellspring of the way of life. He repudiated what he perceived as Park's attempt to diminish the intellect by proposing that intellect and feelings could contradict each other.[9]

Both intellect and feelings are expressed in language. Hodge conceded that they differed in what they addressed—doctrinal content to the intellect and figurative illustrations to the feelings. One appeals to the mind, the other to the emotions. He refused, however, to allow that either could be discounted and insisted that, counter to Park's proposal, they could never contradict each other. While doctrinal language may appear more "precise and exact" and the language of feelings "vague and inaccurate," he stated that "figurative language is just as definite in its meaning and just as intelligible as the most literal." The expression that God is angry, for example, communicates something as definite as any abstract doctrinal statement about God's holy attitude toward sin. Hodge cited Park's assertion that the seeming contradiction of the two biblical statements "God repented" and "God cannot repent" does not mean that they cannot be reconciled because one is true and the other false. Both statements communicate something definite—that God hates sin and that God is immutable. Not only are intellect and feelings compatible, but Hodge asserted that intellect takes precedence over feelings and also manifests the truth in that it "enlarges and improves that of the feelings, and is also enlarged and improved by it." He illustrated his point by the colorful phrase that "the heart is famished by an idle intellect." He continued, "When fed by an enquiring mind, it is enlivened, and reaches out of an expanded faith."[10]

Hodge viewed the unique correlation between intellect and feelings undergirding all Christian truth to be at stake. Park's views threatened that relationship. Park highlighted his view by focusing on two Calvinist doctrines that he claimed the intellect could no longer accept but that move the feelings—the imputation of Adam's sin and Christ's propitiatory death on the cross. He proposed that while both move people's feelings, they can no longer be accepted as literally true by the intellect. Thus the conflict between the intellect and the feelings. By making theology of the intellect changeable and theology of the feelings permanent and more determinative of Christian belief, Park's views, in Hodge's opinion, resembled more the subjective theology of Friedrich Schleiermacher than the Calvinism that Park professed. If the Christian faith lost or altered the theology of the intellect, Christianity would forfeit its objective truth. Therefore, Hodge insisted that the integrity of mind and heart must be maintained. Intellect and feelings, properly understood, could never conflict.

In Hodge's view, while propositional statements play an essential role in establishing Christian truth, passages that appeal to human emotion or imagination play a no less essential role. The unitary nature of biblical truth necessitates that the two agree. Hodge used the biblical image of God as shepherd as an illustration. "Such language, when interpreted according to established usage, and made to mean what it was intended to express, is not only definite in its import, but it never expresses what is false to the intellect. The feelings demand truth in their object; and no utterance is as natural or effective as the language of the emotion; which does not satisfy the understanding." Passages that represent God as repenting or as having wings under which his people find comfort are just as true, although in a different sense to the understanding. If they were not, they could not be true to the feelings. "It is because calling God our shepherd presents the idea of a person exercising a kind care over us, that it has power to move the affections. If it presented any conception inconsistent with the truth it would grate on the feelings as much as it would offend the intellect."[11]

Hodge attributed Park's incorrect positing of a contradiction between intellect and feelings to an invalid psychology that assumes "two percipient principles in the soul. The one sees a proposition to be true, the other sees it to be false." While Park would undoubtedly deny a dualism in the soul that this view entails, he failed to emphasize that the soul is a unit, that its activity encompasses one life. The soul apprehends, feels, and chooses. It is not divided into three faculties: one that apprehends, another that feels, and another that determines. Hodge contended that moral cognition differs from speculative in that while speculative cognition may be purely intellectual, moral cognition is necessarily complex, involving the feelings.[12]

Hodge also cited the history of the church, its confessions, and its hymns as supporting the idea that intellect and feelings must coincide. Since hymns express Christian sentiment, he challenged Park to identify a hymn used by Presbyterians in worship that contains "a single phrase" inconsistent with the Westminster Confession. Indeed, all hymns about Christ exhibit the same consistency. They express "precisely the same doctrine concerning his person that is found in the Athanasian creed."[13] The same remarks may be made in reference to all theological formulas, whether they express human nature and its relation to Adam, redemption accomplished by Christ's work on the cross, or the work of God's Spirit—"in every case it is the truth as understood that is felt."[14]

In both *WOL* and his polemic with Park, Hodge spelled out the essential elements of his and Princeton's evangelical theology and apologetic. While the former addressed an evangelical audience beyond his immediate Reformed heritage, Hodge demonstrated an ability to state succinctly and accurately beliefs that united evangelical Christians across denominational boundaries. It not only attracted widespread acceptance during his lifetime but has been widely recognized as one of his most influential writings as a winsome summation of Christian beliefs balanced with an equally clear exposition of Christianity as a way of life. It displayed Hodge's ability to express Christianity's principal doctrines in understandable language and to communicate the life that flows naturally from such truth in a warm and engaging manner.

His exchange with Park likewise exhibited Hodge's similar concern in apologetic form. The Christian religion consists of two elements: intellectual cognition and emotive expression. Whereas *WOL* offered readers a clear articulation of evangelical religion that results from the unity of the soul, likewise "The Theology of the Intellect and That of the Feelings" repudiated a faculty psychology that would implicitly divide the soul, which in its various functions—cognition, moral inclination, and feelings—must remain united. Worse yet, those who posited an antipathy between the two would move Christianity off its theological foundation. His exchange with Park illustrated Hodge at his polemical best. He defended both intellect and feelings in a context in which even professing Calvinists such as Park questioned the validity of traditional Reformed beliefs. The Hodge–Park debate set before the American people a fissure within Calvinist proponents. Their sharp differences constituted one among many instances that not only illustrated a split developing within American Calvinism but also foreshadowed its eventual demise.

24

Christian Education

Charles Hodge's editorship of the *PR* and especially his annual reports of Presbyterian assemblies enabled him to keep his finger on the pulse of all aspects of his denomination. As was well known by those familiar with theological journals in the first half of the nineteenth century, potential contributors to the *PR* readily admitted that submitting an article for the July issue of the journal meant that their article would not be the first one read by its recipients. When the third of the quarterly issues of the *PR* arrived in the mail, readers turned immediately to Hodge's report on the General Assembly to get the Princeton perspective on all things Presbyterian. Hodge's yearly summaries were labeled unpretentiously "The General Assembly of [year]." His reports were thorough—many times, articles spanned fifty to sixty pages. Some reports merely related statistics and imparted information regarding the denomination's boards. When circumstances dictated, resolutions relating to the boards' actions and recommendations received Hodge's attention. The more expansive entries recounted protracted discussions on the floor of the assemblies, including names and views of primary participants in the debate. When discussion touched subjects about which Hodge held deep convictions, readers never remained in doubt as to his perspective. His occasional participation in debates and his carefully recorded and persuasively argued assessments established him as one of the most formidable Old School churchmen. As a result, his peers selected him as moderator of the General Assembly of 1846.

Invariably Hodge began his reports by stating the specifics of date, place, and church where the assembly convened, the election of the moderator, and other matters relating to opening the business of the church. Reports of the Board of Foreign Missions, the Board of Domestic Missions, the Board of Education, the Board of Church Extension, and the Board of Publication followed. Hodge's depiction of the Board of Education reports not only sheds light on his vocation as seminary professor but reflects how seriously Presbyterians as a whole emphasized theological preparation for ministry and the role of education in the local church. The manner in which the denomination handled educational matters reveals a kinship with Princeton's Plan of the Seminary. Recurring themes illustrate a principled persistence to make education a priority in the church's ministry.

Ministerial Training and Educational Funding

The Presbyterian church committed itself to establishing schools at all levels from academies to colleges and seminaries, to provide financial assistance for theological candidates, and to tackle the narrower issue of whether or not to engage in parochial education. Throughout the 1840s and 1850s, the denomination repeatedly addressed these issues. The denomination faced fluctuations in enrollment, budgetary constraints and the responsibility of churches to support theological education, the difficulty of academic requirements, the piety expected of candidates, and the role of the state versus role of the church in education. Hodge weighed in on all these issues.

At the seminary level, Hodge's assessments reflected his assumption that Princeton would stay the course mandated by its charter. It would continue its curricular offerings and emphasize intellectual rigor and moral and spiritual integrity while staying within the bounds of

Reformed orthodoxy. Foremost in Hodge's estimation, Presbyterian theological education should rival its European counterparts in scholarship while not succumbing to radical views that departed from classical Reformed theology. Unlike much of the results of professionalization of the American ministry that occurred long after Hodge's demise, Princetonians produced pastors equipped primarily to preach the truths of the faith. In order to accomplish this task, they would have to be acquainted with biblical content, theological systems, and experimental religion—the affective elements of Christian experience. Without all three elements, Presbyterian ministry would not live up to its heritage. Continuing that legacy entailed a well-educated clergy. What enabled Princeton to live up to its reputation as a seminary that maintained, in Paul Miller's words, "a consistent theological system for more than two generations" was its teachers who were "avid—almost fanatical—advocates of scholarship." That would be the heart of ministerial education. What follows are representative samples from the General Assemblies of the 1840s and 1850s that illustrate Hodge's estimation of his church's contribution to American education.[1]

Presbyterians kept accurate records of their schools at all levels of instruction. While not all board reports revealed enrollment figures, when they did, Hodge reported them. In 1843, for example, the Board of Education reported "another year of remarkable prosperity" in which the number of candidates exceeded the preceding year by 16 percent, and the board financially aided 1,330 students in colleges, academies, private schools, and seminaries. As for the moral and spiritual state of students, the board reported that "there was no call for discipline, on moral grounds, or defective piety, for the last three years." Almost all reports contained a resolution requesting prayer for an increase in the number and quality of candidates. Significantly, indicating the frailty of life in the nineteenth century, many reports note deaths of candidates. The only negative feature of the 1843 report that drew a lengthy response from Hodge involved a resolution to devise "a systematic plan of benevolence" to secure sufficient funds to maintain the board's work. Consistent with his aversion to change, Hodge counseled strongly against any drastic revision in the means of raising benevolences. The issue would resurface in future meetings, especially the necessity of urging more churches to contribute financially to the board.[2]

In the following year, 1844, financial contributions increased to $33,419, but the board reported that over half the churches in the denomination had failed to contribute moneys to theological education. Churches' lack of financial participation in the denomination's educational ministry appears more frequently than any other matter of concern. The assembly resolved to pray for an increase in candidates but at the same time expressed "their unhesitating belief that men of a high order of talents, character and training, are now more needed than mere numbers of inferior men." Therefore, the board proposed that all presbyteries "resist kindly but firmly, the recommendation to the Board of unsuitable candidates" and to "discourage the propensity to hasten [candidates] into the ministry without a full course of preparatory study." Hodge added that in the denomination's earlier history a greater temptation had existed "to lower the standard of ministerial education." Stoutly opposing attempts to shorten the period of theological education to two years, he added, "All experience teaches us that ignorance, next to sin, is the most fruitful source of error, and that a few able, well furnished and faithful ministers, are far more efficient for good, than a multitude of uneducated though zealous men."[3]

In 1845 Hodge noted the twenty-fifth anniversary of the Board of Education and that Presbyterians had raised $400,000 and educated fifteen hundred students during its existence. Having stressed academic rigor and financial support for students in previous years, Hodge noted that in this year funds had been withdrawn from thirteen ministerial students not because of lack of piety or talents but because they fell short academically. Prolonged discussion focused on the wisdom of funding needy students. Some questioned the wisdom of any kind of monetary assistance by arguing whether it "would . . . not be better to let them struggle on by themselves." Others contended that "it is derogatory and injurious to the character of young men to receive such assistance." Hodge strongly demurred at the latter view. Whenever the topic arose, Hodge opined that just as churches provided a salary for pastors, they ought also to support pastoral candidates while studying for the ministry. He argued that the church in all ages had supported such a practice and that "every enlightened civil government acts on the same principle." Parallels existed in financial assistance given to students in military academies, whether in Berlin or America's West Point. Finally, against those who argued that funding students inevitably brought into the ministry men from a lower social class who were "deficient in cultivation and good manners," Hodge retorted that refinement in social behavior depends not so much on birth but "on education and subsequent intercourse with society." The very process of educating men for the ministry not only increased their moral and spiritual character but also raised their social standing. Such improvement in all areas of life rebutted opponents' objections to helping those from lower economic and social strata. Hodge substantiated this conclusion from his personal experience at Princeton. Not only had he come from a home without a father and been raised by a mother who labored under difficult economic conditions, but he also observed students at the seminary who received aid from the church and rose in refinement of life and status in society. He stated categorically, "As to piety, as to talents, scholarship, and manners [those who receive economic help because of limited resources and deprived backgrounds] have been quite equal to those who have needed no assistance." Hodge attributed the advancement of such individuals to "the refining influence of piety, knowledge and social intercourse," which placed them "on a par with their fellows." Whereas other denominations might not put such a premium on an educated ministry, Presbyterians would always be known for their belief that while education could not save the soul, it proved indispensable for ministerial training.[4]

Hodge's 1846 report focused entirely on parochial schools. A committee chaired by James W. Alexander, son of Hodge's mentor, recommended the founding of church schools. Debate arose over "the great questions"—whether Presbyterians should join with other denominations in support of "the common schools of the state" or whether they should instead "as far as possible establish Parochial Schools under their own exclusive control." Both opinions had their supporters. Discussion eventually narrowed down to whether, due to "the whole spirit of the age and of our country," the Presbyterian church should join with the majority of evangelical denominations and "throw its influence" to "give the common schools of the country as Christian a character as possible." Some argued that Presbyterians, because of their disproportionate influence relative to their number, should be the last denomination to "withdraw from this partnership." Hodge's remark indicated that Presbyterians remained very conscious of the clout their denomination had in shaping the cultural milieu.[5]

As much as he agreed with this consensus, however, Hodge argued from the Reformed view of the church and his experience in Europe that Presbyterians had a greater responsibility to impart distinctive teachings of Christianity in what was a growing secular environment. The church could not relinquish the task of education to the state, "for it is the very work God has given her to do, and she might as well look to the state to preach the gospel, as to make disciples of the nations by *teaching them*" (emphasis in original). The church could not simply rely on families, Sunday schools, and pastoral instruction to teach the rising generation. Each of these, while important, had severe limitations in light of the daunting task of educating children in all facets of life. Hodge alluded to political programs in Prussia that mandated pastoral instruction, examination, and issuing certificates. Such a practice would never be accepted in America because Christianity was not established as a state religion. Also, Britain's practice of uniting Protestants and Catholics "has proved in a great measure a failure" and would be "inappropriate for this country" because of the vast proliferation of denominations that must be satisfied, including "Socinians, Universalists, and even Infidels."[6] Thus some models from Europe were clearly unsuitable for adoption in America.

Hodge then moved the argument on to different grounds—the advancing secularism in American culture. He stated that "it is already difficult, in many places, to retain even the reading of the scriptures in the public schools. The whole system, in the hands of men of the world, in many of our states, is avowedly secular." Hodge noted that a popular theory in this country was to limit instruction to "secular branches [subjects] exclusively" and to leave to parents and pastors the religious education of children. This scheme, which left education in the hands of "men of the world," was explicitly secular and represented "a novel and fearful experiment." Having experienced religious education in public schools in Europe, Hodge adds, "The idea of giving an education to the children of a country from which religion is to be excluded, we believe to be peculiar to the nineteenth century. Again, it is obvious that education without religion, is irreligious. It cannot be neutral, and in fact is not neutral. The effort to keep out religion from all the books and all the instructions, gives them of necessity an irreligious and infidel character." Hodge viewed this effect as especially harmful to the country as a whole because the common school remained the only venue where a large segment of society received any education. He noted that such views were beginning to make inroads into colleges. He inveighed against proposals that the state could dictate against the teaching of religion in common schools. He asked, "If a people of a particular district choose to have a school in which the Westminster or the Heidelberg catechism is taught, we cannot see on what principle of religious liberty, the state has a right to interfere and say it shall not be done; if you teach your religion, you shall not draw your own money from the public fund?" He believed that prohibiting religious instruction, "enforced by the penalty of exclusion from the public funds and state patronage," was nothing less than "unjust and tyrannical, as well as infidel in its whole tendency." Hodge continued that Christians viewed the evolving educational system as adopting "not a mere negative, but a positively anti-christian character" and that the only self-defense was to establish a system of parochial schools.[7]

Hodge also probed the secularization of American education—"to see what will be the result of bringing up the body of the people in ignorance of God and his word." He pursued this not as an abstract idea but by referring to a noteworthy educational institution in nearby Philadelphia: "[Pursuit of education in a secular manner] is an attempt to apply to the whole country, what Girard has prescribed for his college." Hodge was referring to financier Stephen Girard, the wealthiest man in America at his death in 1831, who had made his wealth as a sea captain turned shipowner, merchant, and eventually sole owner of Girard Bank in Philadelphia. Girard's will provided the massive sum at the time of $5 million for the establishment of Girard College to educate poor white orphan boys. While Girard College became one of a plethora of philanthropic enterprises to benefit from Girard's estate,

Hodge had in mind Girard's provision in the will that expressly prohibited any clergy, missionary, or other ecclesiastical figure from holding a position at the school and even stipulated that such individuals not be allowed on campus. Girard explained that his purpose in these restrictions was to prevent the boys from being distracted by many confusing doctrines. Instead of being instructed in religion, they were to be educated in a diverse curriculum that included reading, writing, mathematics, languages, and various sciences.

The exclusion of religious instruction so that the boys could be free to make their own decisions when they reached adulthood represented to Hodge not only the very opposite of what Presbyterians would desire in education but the antithesis of his own life extending back to his childhood. His entire educational experience and piety in the home, church, and various levels, including college and seminary, presupposed a nurturing continuum. It encompassed the whole of life extending from infancy through youth and adolescence to adulthood. At the heart of that education was the religious dimension. To Hodge it was inconceivable to eliminate the most important factor that shaped a person's character and worldview—indeed, his entire being—from the early formative years of childhood and youth. To postpone religion to adult life would render impossible the chief end for which all, including children, were created—to glorify God and enjoy him forever. Such a plan as Girard's applied to American education as a whole would only foster an areligious life, which should be avoided no matter in what stage of life a person might be. While Girard represented an extreme perspective of education for the early nineteenth century, Hodge viewed emerging signs of secularism as a phenomenon to be countered by a traditional educational system that included religious instruction.[8]

As for appropriate models for Presbyterians to follow, Hodge shifted his attention back to Europe and cited the Free Church of Scotland and its parochial schools. So committed to Christian education was the Scottish church that "with equal strength of conviction and purpose, [it] set about establishing a school in connexion with every parish." The Scottish system of parochial schools "is as much a part of their system as having ministers or elders." He added that American Catholics had surprisingly adopted a similar modus operandi. They had organized their own schools, which already attracted Protestant children because of the reputation of their teachers. Thus Hodge conceded that American Catholics had an edge over Protestants in educating their children in the Catholic faith. Hodge ended his panegyric on behalf of Presbyterian parochial schools with a clarion call to action: "Let the session of the church look out for a competent teacher; let them prescribe the course of instruction, making the Bible and the Catechism a regular part of every day's studies, and we doubt not the plan will meet the concurrence of the people and blessing of God."[9]

The next two assemblies also focused on Presbyterians' establishing parochial schools. Hodge opened his 1847 report with the remark: "It is a subject of gratulation that we are at last fairly embarked in this great work, and in a way that promises the best attainable efficiency." A resolution encouraged "immediate and strenuous exertions" for individual churches to establish "one or more primary schools, under the care of the session of the church, in which, together with the usual branches of secular learning, the truths and duties of our holy religion shall be assiduously inculcated." Another resolution called for presbytery committees consisting of a minister and elder to collect statistics on such matters as the number of schools within presbytery bounds and the number of children who might be educated and to ascertain the prevailing opinion within their bounds about the necessity of additional schools. The Board of Education would receive reports of these matters in order to establish parochial schools.[10]

As matters unfolded in subsequent years, the resolutions of 1847 and 1848 represent a high-water mark of Presbyterian interest in parochial education. An indication that the proposals had peaked becomes evident by the fact that Hodge did not even report on the subject in 1849. Furthermore, at the 1850 General Assembly, opposition to the very idea of parochial schools gained traction. A dispute arose over the denomination's responsibility for educating all Presbyterian children. Dr. R. J. Breckinridge of Kentucky posed the daunting nature of embarking on establishing a "universal [parochial] education." Such an undertaking, he argued, would entail overwhelming resources of "money, time and labor. Millions and millions of money, and efforts no man can calculate will be necessary." In addition, said

Breckinridge, the burden of such a task would fall to a board originally established merely to superintend the education of men for the ministry. As a result of extended debate, the assembly referred the issue of funding education back to the board and turned its attention to funding ministerial candidates.[11]

Sticking to "the Plan"

Underlying all preoccupation with theological education lay the goal of producing pastor-scholars. Funding that effort was but one of many concerns. Should the denomination require students at the undergraduate level to pledge that they would enter the ministry as a prerequisite for receiving funds? Hodge opposed the policy of bestowing scholarships on the basis of merit. He resisted such a practice because of the difficulty of maintaining consistency in awarding them. Standards would vary from place to place among those entrusted with awarding scholarships. But above all was the almost impossible task of estimating the relative importance of academic potential, piety, temperament, and energy for the ministerial calling. The inevitable consequence of these factors, in Hodge's opinion, was that "everything on this plan would be apt to turn on literary proficiency"—that is, awards would rest on who could present himself in the most compelling fashion orally and in writing. While literary proficiency ought to be a factor in the judging process, Hodge argued, it ought not to be the ultimate arbiter. Finally, Hodge added that the very idea of "emulation among theological students"—pursuing grades rather than seeking what prepared one for ministry—should caution Presbyterians against any form of meritocracy emerging as a basis of disbursing funds to ministerial candidates.[12]

Although the assembly did not cease discussing the viability of parochial schools, the denomination, including Hodge, shifted the focus toward encouraging Presbyterians to support the common schools and particularly continued use of the Bible in instruction. The educational policy of the Presbyterian church was summarized in 1853 under four points: "1. To sustain common schools, where it can be consistently done with the Bible in them. 2. To resist the Papal invasion of the State system for the propagation of Romanism. 3. To encourage religious schools and academies under private teachers, where circumstances favour it. 4. To sustain cordially and efficiently institutions of learning under the Church's own care."[13]

Support grew within the denomination for restricting financial assistance to college students to those who pledged to enter the ministry. Hodge held that such a practice, while well-meaning, was manifestly premature. Perhaps reflecting his own vocational vacillation as a youth while preaching in the Philadelphia area, Hodge believed that at an early age a young man could not "know his own mind intelligently" and thus decide whether he was called of God or not. Pledges to enter the ministry in the early stages of education would commit an individual to a vocation that he might not be qualified to fulfill. Not only would the practice bind the candidate prematurely, it would also commit the church to funding his education before the man proved his talents, disposition, and piety. Such a decision should be deferred until the individual commenced seminary studies. Hodge's reflections took into consideration both the individual and the church, for only then could the individual "know himself, and be known to the church."[14]

The final matter bearing on financial assistance focused on whether or not to provide financial assistance to pursue a calling outside the church. Following up his support of eliminating a pledge as a condition for receiving moneys, Hodge stated that this policy opened up the possibility of enabling students following other callings as committed Christians. As a result, "many . . . who have been educated by the church, will enter her service as teachers, physicians, lawyers, merchants, and agriculturists. The church will gain much by this addition to her educated children." Hodge thus articulated the value to both the church and the wider culture of church members who were trained in their respected fields as Christians. Such a policy change would enable the Board of Education "to receive promising youth of good moral character, and give them the advantages of a liberal education." Recognizing that many conversions occur during one's collegiate studies and undoubtedly drawing on his own conversion while a college student, Hodge said that helping those other than simply ministerial candidates to obtain a liberal education would "greatly multiply the resources of the church, increase her strength in educated men, and enlarge her field of choice for ministers and teachers." Hodge concluded his summary with the comment, "It is by expansive schemes alone that we can keep up with the spirit of the times, and as our Scotish [*sic*] brethren would say, can overtake the work God has given us to do." Hodge's expansive understanding of education—its value in preparing people for a wide variety of occupations in addition to pastors—reflects a worldview keen to propagate the Protestant view of all vocations' contributing to the kingdom of God as well as the greater good of society.[15]

The 1851 General Assembly devoted significant attention to Princeton Seminary and its model for theological education. A series of resolutions dealt with appointments of seminary professors and their curricular responsibilities. Of particular interest was the resolution that "each of the Professors . . . give instruction in some portion of the sacred Scriptures." Such a provision ensured that all of Princeton's theological education would remain grounded in the Bible, not simply in the courses in the Old and New Testaments. Beyond commitment to biblical scholarship, the assembly required professors in other disciplines also to teach the Bible as appropriate to their disciplines. Such a policy would prevent the isolation of the various disciplines from one another. Biblical content would drive all seminary courses.[16]

Another General Assembly resolution transferred the "Composition and Delivery of Sermons" and "Church Government" from the professor of church history to the professor of pastoral theology. The change was justified by the remark "the proper arrangement of the departments in a theological faculty has been the subject of much consideration in every country where such faculties exist." The assembly, by resolving that all professors would instruct in some part of the Bible and by rearranging curricular assignments, ensured that Princeton would remain true to its charter's demands to remain faithful to Scripture. Such a resolution would also keep Princeton abreast of contemporary educational practice. As for the latter, Princeton followed the European model of dividing seminaries into four departments: biblical, dogmatic, historical, and practical. Princeton did not rush into restructuring. Hodge stated that the seminary had considered these changes "for years" and that there had been "a gradual approximation in the organization of [Princeton]" as well as in "other similar institutions." By adding this explanation, Hodge reassured the assembly that the changes were not being made precipitously but mirrored practices in other American schools. A chronological account of the hiring of the seminary's first professors followed, along with their respective teaching responsibilities. Changes that were due to resignations and retirements completed the report. Hodge expressed the sentiment that "friends of the Seminary cannot fail to feel gratitude to God for the degree of unanimity by which these important measures were carried."[17]

Hodge added a lengthy explanation of these measures to reassure readers of what would distinguish Princeton's adaptation of the European model. In the Princeton model, the departments would not be kept "entirely distinct." The requirement that each professor teach biblical material illustrated that point. The fact that departments at Princeton would "overlap each other" would ensure that while professors would teach subjects differently, each professor would add what was distinctive from his field to the topic. Thus, for example, "the biblical professor, if he interprets Scripture . . . must teach theology, and that in the most effectual way. How can he expound the word of God without bringing out the great doctrines which it teaches? The sacred historian must trespass on the same field. In giving the history of the Church, he must give the history of doctrines; he must unfold the various systems of error which have come in conflict with the truth; he must show the philosophical and historical origin of those errors, and in so doing, he is teaching theology in a most effective manner." Continuing through all the departments, Hodge illustrated how Princeton had accommodated itself to the newer model of departmental structure without leaving the various departments as freestanding, autonomous disciplines, as in European universities. If professors utilized Scripture in a manner appropriate to their discipline while subscribing to the Westminster Standards as mandated by the charter, the seminary would maintain both its Reformed roots and a unified vision as to the nature and content of theological education. All departments would overlap to a greater or lesser extent. Theologians would act as exegetes and exegetes as theologians. Hodge added, "There is not, therefore, in practice such an entire separation between the several departments in a theological curriculum, as these separate designations might lead us to expect."[18]

Hodge focused on the historical department because the Princeton model would prevent the grievous errors that infiltrated theological education in European seminaries. He explicitly referred to the situation emerging out of Berlin: "Every one knows that the attacks of the modern infidels of Germany have been mainly directed against the Old Testament history and the history of Christ." He cited Friedrich Strauss's *Life of Jesus* as evidence of what happens when New Testament studies stand independent of the other theological disciplines—biblical, historical, and practical. All disciplines must maintain their individual integrity by means of "direct study, vindication, and exposition of the word of God." Hodge pressed the argument that Princeton's "arrangement . . . [is] the very method to secure, with God's blessing, the preparation of precisely that class of works for which there is at present the most pressing need"—texts in all fields of theological study that illustrated the unity and coherence of Christian truth.[19]

Hodge thus foresaw Princeton's curriculum, faculty, and departmental structure as maintaining the highest standard of scholarship as prerequisite for ministerial training. The seminary would remain faithful to its charter and by so doing would forestall what became the norm of nineteenth-century Protestant liberalism in Europe. Because of its commitment to Reformed confessionalism and its vision of theological unity as opposed to theological diversity and its innate aversion to innovation, Princeton would serve as an obstacle to ideas incompatible with its historic orthodoxy. Hodge stated that because of this intimate relation between the different departments of theology, "it is difficult to decide to which of them some subjects ought to be referred." That put Princeton in the enviable position of hiring and assigning professors so adept in their theological schooling that they could feel at home teaching virtually any course in the curriculum. He cited as an example the recent hiring of W. H. Green as the successor to Addison Alexander. He had been appointed tutor of Greek and Latin at the age of fifteen at La Fayette College. At eighteen he had assumed the position of assistant professor of mathematics, and as a seminary student he had distinguished himself in every subject, especially languages. For several years he had pastored churches and contributed articles to the *PR*. With his background in various disciplines plus his pastoral experience, Green illustrated Hodge's point of the variety of courses that a Princeton professor might be asked to teach.[20]

Hodge's thorough reporting on education at the General Assemblies illustrates his command of the issues and his influence in shaping the Presbyterian mind in the first half of the nineteenth century. His view was that the highest quality should characterize all stages of education, whether it be in specific theological disciplines or in secular subjects. Presbyterians should excel in all fields. Pastors were to be trained in accordance with the Princeton Plan. Not only did theological education follow the Athens model, the curriculum and method of instruction combined with Sunday afternoon conferences on matters of practical religion ensured that Reformed confessionalism as well as evangelical piety received equal emphasis. While never citing the Plan explicitly, Hodge assumed its content throughout his reportage of education at the General Assemblies. Thus, during Hodge's tenure, that model never received significant criticism, let alone a frontal attack from its various constituencies. By his teaching and journal articles, Hodge upheld the standards set by his predecessors as Princeton remained committed to high academic standards, Reformed piety, and supporting students with financial assistance. Hodge's successors, however, faced a barrage of proposals that would drastically change theological education.[21]

25

Relations with Roman Catholicism

As an Old School controversialist, Charles Hodge also contributed to discussions regarding Presbyterian relations with Roman Catholicism. In most contexts, Hodge stood with other Old Schoolers in their staunch affirmation of classical Protestantism over against traditional Catholicism. Their confessional heritage—its theology, sacraments, and polity—was nonnegotiable, consisting of matters not to be compromised. Princeton affirmed the magisterial Reformers in their separation from Rome. By avowing key doctrines such as God's sovereign grace in salvation over against cooperative grace, the sole authority of Scripture versus Scripture and tradition, and the priesthood of believers over a priestly hierarchy led by the pope, and limiting the sacraments to two versus Rome's seven, Princeton defended the legitimacy of the Protestant break with Roman Catholicism and its claim to be the sole representative of Christ's church on earth. During the middle decades of the nineteenth century, Catholic–Protestant relations came to the fore as waves of immigration brought thousands of Catholics to American shores, and Catholic leaders objected to Protestant bias in the public schools. The influx of Catholics also brought a nativist and anti-Catholic reaction as evangelicals sought to defend America as a Protestant nation.

Hodge became involved on several occasions in this highly charged situation. On the one hand, he expressed a fear common to many evangelicals, that the influx of foreigners threatened Protestant hegemony in the early nineteenth century. He conveyed his apprehension to his brother in 1844 when he commented on a letter by Bishop John Hughes of New York, a leader of Catholic opposition to nativism. Hughes had written to the mayor of New York, promising reprisal if nativist riots in Philadelphia were ever duplicated in New York City. Hughes interpreted the insurrections as blatantly anti-Catholic. Hodge, on the other hand, argued that the underlying issue was not anti-Catholicism: "[Hughes] confounds two very different things: opposition to foreigners, as foreigners, governing the country, and opposition to Papists as Papists. It is true that most of these objectionable foreigners are Papists, but the opposition to them is as foreigners." Hodge admitted the legitimacy of Hughes's primary concern that nativists would "infringe on the rights of a particular class of citizens." But then, exposing his own sympathies, he added, "But what right have the paupers of Europe to be citizens of America? We must take care of ourselves, or we shall have all our affairs under the control of the mob of foreigners who swarm our cities." Hodge thereby expressed a fear prominent among evangelical Christians that lasted well into the next century. While Hodge's reaction represented an underlying prejudice and was only put to rest by the election of John F. Kennedy in the mid-twentieth century, he had no sympathy for outsiders' potentially wreaking havoc on American soil.[1]

An issue involving Roman Catholicism surfaced again the following year. An overture opposing the validity of Romish baptism passed overwhelmingly 169–68 at the 1845 General Assembly. On this occasion Hodge broke with Old School sentiments when he surprisingly spoke up on behalf of Catholicism. He expressed dismay in his annual *PR* summary that by their action Presbyterians pronounced that "Calvin, Luther, and all other men of that generation, as well as thousands [of others] . . . lived and died unbaptized" because they did not renounce their baptism as infants and become rebaptized. He began his defense of the validity of Catholic baptism by citing the early church's refusal to pronounce baptism by heretics invalid: "It is, therefore, the doctrine of the universal church, that baptism administered in the name of the Trinity, by one professing faith in that doctrine, is not void on account of heresy." Hodge believed that the legitimacy of baptism depended not on the faith or character of the administrator but on God's appointment of the sacrament as the rite of initiation into the church. As long as "the matter [washing with water], the form [invoking the Trinity] and intention [sealing the benefits of Christ's work]" were present, a valid baptism was performed. On the matter, form, and intention of baptism Rome and Presbyterians agreed. What separated Protestants from Catholics on the sacraments was not their design but "the mode and certainty with which that design is accomplished and the conditions attached to it [i.e., according to Catholic teaching, baptism regenerates the infant]."[2]

As for the objection that baptism was invalid because it was administered by priests ordained within the Roman Catholic Church, which was apostate, Hodge reached outside the Westminster Standards for his answer. He cited the twenty-third article of the Church of England as expressing what all churches of the Reformation believed regarding the validity of ordained clergy: "Those ought to be judged lawfully called and sent, who are chosen and called to this work by men who have public authority given unto them, in the congregation, to call and send ministers into the Lord's vineyard." Thus, Roman baptism was valid both in its basis in orthodoxy and by its performance by duly ordained clergy.[3]

Then Hodge addressed the thorniest issue behind the censure of Catholic baptism—that the Roman church is not a true church. Since many had concluded in the negative, Hodge raised the simple question, "Does the church of Rome retain truth enough to save the soul?" He answered by saying, "We do not understand how it is possible for any Christian man to answer this in the negative." He supported this judgment by reminding readers that Catholics affirm the early creeds and councils of the church. He enumerated Catholicism's central tenets: the incarnation, the Trinity, the atonement, forgiveness of sins, the resurrection of the body, eternal life, and final judgment. While he admitted that they may have "perverted and overlaid" these teachings, "still as general propositions they are affirmed. And it must be remembered, that it is truth presented in general propositions, and not with subtle distinctions, that saves the soul." Professing the simple statements of the Apostles' Creed satisfied that criterion. Hodge ventured so far as to propose that "there were more of evangelical doctrine and true religion in [the Roman Catholic Church], than were to be found in the church of England, or in some of the Protestant churches of the continent of Europe, notwithstanding their orthodox creeds." With tongue firmly in cheek, Hodge added that in his disputes with pro-temperance and abolitionist New Schoolers, he had the "misfortune [of being grouped with] the friends of drunkenness, and the advocates of slavery, because we could not believe that alcohol is sin, and every slaveholder a thief; and we fear that even good men may now regard us as the apologists of Popery." Hodge thereby made the point that just as the causes of temperance and anti-slavery suffered from extravagance of their advocates, so Protestantism itself suffered when extremists launched unwarranted attacks against Rome by denying the validity of its baptisms.[4]

Hodge noted that at least the opponents of baptism acknowledged that the Roman Catholic Church contains genuine believers. In light of this concession, he proposed in what sense the church can and cannot be a true church. It is a church insofar as it contains true believers. Following the Reformers, Hodge denounced in strongest terms the papal system and its corruption of doctrine and worship. Though awkward and requiring careful explanation, he said that the Reformers "in the same breath" added that "viewed from a different light, the church is still a church just as the apostate Israelites were still the covenant people of God." Hodge's carefully worded explanation followed: "If the Israelites were denominated from the character of their rulers, or of the mass of the people . . . they were apostates and idolaters. If denominated from the relation which they still sustained to God, from the truth which they continued to profess, or from the real saints who were to be found among them, they were still the church and were so addressed by the prophets, and their circumcision regarded as the seal of God's covenant." Thus Israel was and was not the covenant people of God. Hodge did not thus violate the law of noncontradiction because he did not mean that they were and were not the covenant people of God at the same time and in the same relation. By analogy, on the one hand Old Testament Israel and the Roman Catholic Church were apostate—and in their apostate condition could not require obedience to them as obligatory of all Old Testament Jews or contemporary Christians outside the Roman church. As long as they remained in the state of apostasy, they must be considered apostate. Thus Protestants correctly refused to submit to papal supremacy, clerical hierarchy, transubstantiation, the Mass as a sacrifice, and other beliefs and practices. Hodge concluded that Rome was a true but impure church by virtue of its creedal profession of truths held by all genuine churches.[5]

How then did Hodge square the validity of Romish baptism and the Roman church as a valid visible church with the Westminster Confession's statement that the church of Rome was "antichrist, a synagogue of Satan"? He answered that the terms "refer not to the mass of the people, nor to the presbyters of that communion, or the word of God nor the saving truths which they profess, but to the Popish hierarchy and its corruptions." The hierarchy and its magisterial claims as supreme in the church warranted the accusation of being antichrist. The confession correctly denounced the Romish system but did not condemn the church as a visible church.[6]

Decades later Hodge received another opportunity to state his convictions on the relation between the Presbyterian and Roman churches. Both the Old and New School General Assemblies asked him to respond to the invitation of Pope Pius IX to send delegates to the Vatican Council of 1869–70. Hodge's response, consisting of affirmations and denials, summarized in a short span themes we have witnessed so far. The letter illustrated that while he had previously defended Catholic baptism as valid and the Roman church as a visible church, he had strongest objections to joining with Rome in ecumenical cooperation. He began by affirming Christ's will that the church be united and that all Christians have the duty "to promote Christian charity and fellowship." Despite that obligation, he respectfully stated that Presbyterians could not participate in the council. The reason for that refusal was not that Presbyterians "renounced any article of the catholic faith." He flatly stated, "We are not heretics." Hodge cited arguments he had previously used regarding creedal beliefs, only here he applied them to affirm the orthodoxy of his own denomination. Presbyterians were not heretics, as evidenced by the creeds and conciliar decisions that they affirmed. Hodge summarized their affirmations of the Trinity, the incarnation, and Christ's person and work, including his atoning death. More precisely, and in common with Catholic tradition, Presbyterians "receive all those doctrines concerning sin, grace and predestination, known as Augustinian" approved by synods and ultimately by the Ecumenical Council of Ephesus in 431. Thus Hodge summarized his views of what makes any group or denomination a part of the visible church.[7]

Not only were Presbyterians not heretics, Hodge also denied that they were schismatics[8] by repeating other refrains from his writings: "We cordially recognize as members of Christ's visible Church on earth, all those who profess the true religion together with their children." They had communion with other churches so long as "they do not require, as conditions of such communion, that we profess doctrines which the Word of God condemns, or that we should do what that Word forbids." More specifically, Presbyterians could not participate in the Vatican Council because of "those principles [for which] our fathers were excommunicated and pronounced accursed by the Council of Trent." Hodge listed four beliefs: (1) the view that the "Scriptures of the Old and New Testaments [are] the only infallible rule of faith and practice" over against the view that tradition was to be affirmed as equal in authority with the Bible; (2) "the right of private judgment" over against Catholics' requiring submission to the authority of the magisterium; (3) the "universal priesthood of believers" over against the continuation of a mediatorial clerical priesthood; and (4) denial of "the perpetuity of apostleship" by which "prelates . . . demand the same confidence in their teaching, and the same submission to their authority, as that which is due to the inspired messengers of Christ" and recognition of "the Bishop of Rome entailing as the vicar of Christ on earth, clothed with authority over the Church and world." Because the canons of Trent condemning those who did not hold to these principles remained in force, Presbyterians' declining the invitation to attend was "a matter of necessity."[9]

Several ironies become evident from Hodge's letter. Pius IX was as conservative and anti-modern in the Roman church as Hodge was in his Presbyterian denomination. Pius issued several historic bulls in his pontificate that cemented his status as advocate of traditional dogmas. Though long a matter of discussion since Justin Martyr and Irenaeus called Mary the "Second Eve" in the second century, Pius affirmed Mary as being immune from the stain of original sin. Not all Catholic theologians concurred with the high view of Mary, among them Bernard of Clairvaux, Bonaventura, and Thomas Aquinas. Pius's statement further stimulated Marian devotion. He also confirmed his conservative stance in 1864 when he published the encyclical *Syllabus of Errors*, which listed some eighty items that conservatives repudiated, such as pantheism, extreme rationalism, latitudinarianism, autonomous natural ethics, and the priority of civil authority over religious. The encyclical declared as erroneous the idea that the pope should reconcile himself to modern liberalism and modern civilization. Hodge, of course, disagreed with Mary's immaculate conception, which only added to the number of corruptions in Catholic teaching. He would, however, have applauded Catholicism's repudiation of ideas being trumpeted by liberal German Protestants.[10]

A second irony is that Hodge included in his letter to the pope material identical to that in his *PR* articles. Only here he used the argument for what makes a church valid not to convince fellow Presbyterians that the Roman Catholic Church is a true church but to validate his Presbyterian denomination to the head of the Roman church. One can only conjecture that the pope and Southern Presbyterians such as James Henley Thornwell were not convinced, but for totally different reasons! The third and perhaps the most striking irony of all is that one of the very reasons Hodge cited for not participating in the council—papal authority—emerged as the most memorable canon produced by the council when it overwhelmingly affirmed the dogma of papal infallibility by a vote of 533–2! Although papal authority had long functioned as a fundamental principle in the history of papal pronouncements, the official declaration of that dogma did not occur until Vatican I.

Hodge's journal articles and his letter to Pius IX indicate the breadth and diversity of his views on the Roman Catholic Church. Hodge's unexpected defense of Catholic baptism took many Presbyterians off guard. He rather self-consciously admitted that, as reflected by the vote in the General Assembly, his defense did not meet with "the approbation of a large portion of our brethren."[11] That was rather an understatement, since Thornwell responded with a series of articles that topped out at over 125 pages! As David Calhoun has remarked, Hodge expressed a more moderate view than many of his contemporary Protestants. Yet to call him an advocate of ecumenism, as often construed, clearly overstates the case. He not only rejected the invitation to participate in the Vatican council, but remained a staunch opponent of Catholic errors, consistent with his confessional and evangelical roots. Yet unlike many Old School colleagues, Hodge proved unwilling to reject the validity of Catholic baptism and its status as a part of the visible church. Like all other churches, the Roman church lacked purity, and in keeping with the confession he affirmed its hierarchy as apostate. He deemed it better to affirm all these principles and the resultant ambiguity that it might generate than to denounce the church wholesale.

26

Internecine Controversy: Mercersburg

Sandwiched between his defense of Catholic baptism and his response to the pope's invitation to Vatican I in 1869, Charles Hodge engaged in one of his most intense controversies. It involved Philip Schaff and John Williamson Nevin, propounders of the Mercersburg theology of the comparatively small German Reformed Church headquartered in south central Pennsylvania. Mercersburg never achieved the recognition of the larger seminaries such as Princeton, but it briefly attracted Presbyterians' attention as the result of Schaff's and Nevin's insistence that neither the Old nor the New School faction represented a genuine continuation of Calvinism but rather an Americanized departure from the Reformed theology of the sixteenth century. Such a claim was like raw meat to such Old Schoolers as Hodge in the North and Thornwell in the South, who considered themselves the true heirs of John Calvin and therefore his Old School gatekeepers. As in Hodge's dispute with Edwards Amasa Park, the relationship between the two parties, both of which espoused a conservative Calvinism, produced greater friction than agreement. It is yet another instance in Hodge's controversial writing in which the closer the two positions were on the theological spectrum, the greater the heat in the controversy.[1]

The encounter between Hodge and Mercersburg in the *PR* began with Hodge's review of Schaff's 1844 inaugural address at Mercersburg, *The Principle of Protestantism as Related to the Present State of the Church*. Schaff was a brilliant Swiss who, like Hodge, had enjoyed the company of August Tholuck and Ernst Wilhelm Hengstenberg while Schaff completed his education in Germany. Unlike Hodge, however, Schaff found much that he liked in Friedrich Schleiermacher's and Augustus Neander's views of theology and history. In light of his final paragraph in the review, Hodge's criticism of Schaff's book as "thoroughly German" reflected not only Schaff, but also Hodge's lifelong antipathy with European thought. No epithet, however, could better capture Hodge's opinion of views when they did not accord with his own. As in his frequent puzzlement over German idealism, Hodge expressed his difficulty in evaluating the book: "The mode of thinking, and the forms of expression are so unenglish [what could be more "unenglish" than this term!], that it is not easy for an American to enter into the views of the authors." (Nevin was listed as the translator of Schaff's book.) Perhaps the most satisfactory way to describe Hodge's reaction is to say that he was mystified.[2]

Hodge could not gainsay Schaff's affiliation with Reformed thinking. At Mercersburg, Schaff championed the views of Reformed Christianity through the lens of the German Reformed Church, which had originated in the Palatinate region of Germany, the source of the Heidelberg Catechism. Schaff, famous for his multivolume *History of the Christian Church*, distinguished himself in his attempts to utilize German idealism to augment Calvinist views of the church and worship. Schaff agreed with other Protestants that the deficiencies of the medieval church necessitated reform. In fact, Hodge granted that Schaff upheld the "distinguishing principles of Protestants." Hodge enumerated a litany of evangelical doctrines affirmed by Schaff: justification by faith, ultimate authority of Scripture, imputation of Christ's righteousness to believers, and the priesthood of all believers. But Hodge could not fathom why Schaff should make the church rather than the individual faith of believers so determinative in his view of salvation. Schaff had in mind a broad continuum of religious traditions. The twin threats to Protestantism, according to Schaff, at either end of the spectrum, were the rationalism of modern Germany and the sectarianism associated with American Puritanism. Hodge could accept the former, but he denied the latter. According to Schaff, American denominations, including Presbyterianism, had deviated from Reformed thinking and practice by espousing a sectarian view of the church, embracing a symbolic interpretation of the Lord's Supper, and minimizing the role of the visible church. Hodge denied all three tendencies and charged Schaff with placing too much emphasis on the church as the means of salvation rather than the individual's faith in the gospel.[3]

As for what manifested genuine Christian unity, Hodge contested Schaff's proposal of visible, outward unity as evident in the churches of Europe and even in Roman Catholicism. Hodge denied that American denominations represented sectarianism. He contended that the primary unity of Christians is not visible but spiritual, the indwelling of the Holy Spirit manifested in "unity of faith, of love and of communion." He continued, "There is . . . more of real unity, more real brotherhood existing between the evangelical denominations of America, than is to be found in the church of Rome, the church of England, or in the Reformed or Lutheran church of Germany." Schaff, on the other hand, described a more visible unity across denominations that would preclude divisions that existed in American denominationalism. Hodge quoted Schaff as saying that if the sixteenth century Reformers "had been permitted to preach the pure word of God with freedom, and to administer the sacraments according to Christ's appointment, [they] would have remained in their original communion." Because of this assumption, Schaff censured the Reformers' successors in England for separating from the established Church of England and the Free Church of Scotland for seceding from the national church. Hodge adamantly defended these separations, not as sectarian divisions but as breaks essential to maintaining the integrity of the gospel. Therefore, he held that rather than condemn them as sectarian, "such separations [should be viewed as] a duty, which we owe to God and to the real unity of the church, whenever unscriptural terms of communion are enjoined." Defending the legitimacy of the denominational status quo in America, Hodge asked why Baptists and Congregationalists in Schaff's scheme should be considered any more sects than Schaff's German Reformed Church, or for that matter Episcopalianism.[4]

Hodge suspected that what lay behind Schaff's praise for the progress of the church over time was "German philosophy and German theology." He granted that the "German mind is in some of its attributes favourably distinguished from the English and American [minds]." In keeping with his high opinion of German *Wissenschaft*, Hodge applauded what "can be attained by research and concentrated labour." But the German mind, as he insisted on many other occasions, displayed profound faults in its epistemological premises. "The Germans have never been celebrated for their ability to distinguish between the unknown and the unknowable, they cannot discern the limits of human knowledge; and by passing those limits they lose all criteria of knowledge, and are unable to distinguish between truth and the phantoms of their creative imaginations." Yet again, Hodge affirmed the advantages of Common Sense over German speculation as the preferred philosophical handmaiden to theology. He expressed his confidence that the mind that "rest[s] content within the sphere which God has assigned it . . . , submit[s] to the laws of its nature . . . [and] confide[s] in the principles of belief impressed upon our constitution" is to be preferred as a means of arriving at truth over the high speculation of German thinking. Despite Schaff's adherence to Reformed theology, he manifested an inconsistency by espousing elements in German thinking that Hodge believed incompatible with Calvinism.[5]

As proof for his critique, Hodge contrasted the clarity of the original Reformers with the vague pronouncements of G. W. F. Hegel, Schleiermacher, and their disciples. Hodge and his cohorts were not alone in affirming a stark difference between the two ways of thinking. The very disciples of modern thinking renounced with similar zeal traditional Reformed ideas. "We confess that [moderns' explicit rejection of traditional formulations], more than any thing else, far more than any confidence in our own limited knowledge of these systems and writers, makes us fear their influence." Hodge was thereby willing to confess his inadequacy in probing German thinking. The fact that advocates of the new, innovative philosophy and theology held the old truths with such disdain illustrated the incompatibility of the old and the new. New German theological formulations and biblical interpretations that admired the progression in seventeenth- and eighteenth-century thinking did not constitute progress in Christianity but rather a deviation from its original form.[6]

Thus, again, Hodge found disagreement rooted in the differences he had first encountered years earlier in Halle and Berlin. Never a wilting flower when confronting thinking that did not conform with Old School Presbyterianism, he did not hesitate to challenge this latest invasion of ideas alien to Westminster orthodoxy. The reason for the sharpness in his critique lay in the fact that he expected those such as Schaff and Edwards Amasa Park, who professed to be advocates of Reformed ideas, to hold views more closely conforming to the Westminster Confession's expressions. Schaff's charges that Princeton's and other Old School views represented a departure from Reformed tradition rankled Hodge even more. Typical of his controversial style, however, Hodge gave credit where credit was due. Despite his profound dissatisfaction with parts of Schaff's history, Hodge ended his brief analysis by praising the work. He stated, "The evangelical character of the leading doctrines of his book, the seriousness and warmth of feeling which pervade it, and the high order of ability which it displays, give ground to hope that Dr. Schaf [*sic*] will prove a blessing to the church and country of his adoption [America]."[7]

Hodge's response to Schaff's *History* pales in relation to his reaction to John Williamson Nevin. Hodge's rapport with Nevin began well but deteriorated as Princeton and Mercersburg clashed over distinctives of Reformed theology and practice. Years earlier, in planning his European trip, Hodge had sought a replacement for classroom instruction at Princeton. Nevin had excelled under Hodge's tutelage. Recognizing Nevin as one of his best students led him to recommend rather warmly that he teach in Hodge's absence. We have also witnessed that Nevin in retrospect viewed his experience as a student at Princeton with mixed feelings. On the one hand, he wrote in his autobiography that his days at Princeton were "the most pleasant part of my life." Yet, as mentioned in chapter 5, while a student he had found a disparity between the piety expected of students and the staunch theological instruction in the classroom. He discerned a conflict between the pieties of New England Puritanism and the "old proper Presbyterian theory of the seventeenth century."[8]

Nevin had already unleashed an assault on American Presbyterianism by assailing New School revivalism in *The Anxious Bench* (1843)—a scathing critique of the "new measures" adopted by evangelists such as Charles Grandison Finney in the upper New York state revivals. Given Hodge's advocacy of traditional measures of Old School piety and his critique of New Side extremism in his *CHPC*, Hodge concurred wholeheartedly with Nevin's analysis of revivalist practices as manipulative in nature. Hodge also concurred with Nevin on the neglect of infant baptism among Presbyterians because of revivalism.[9]

Nevin's publishing of *The Mystical Presence: A Vindication of the Reformed or Calvinistic Doctrine of the Holy Eucharist* in 1846, however, elicited a far different response from Princeton. The very title would have been enough to raise Hodge's ire. Years later in his *ST* he would use the term *mysticism* to describe theological systems at one extreme of the theological spectrum, with Schleiermacher as its most prominent advocate. Hodge not only characterized Schleiermacher's system as a whole as mystical in nature, but also faulted the German theologian's adoption of the term to describe Christ's atonement over against traditional "magical" views of vicarious satisfaction. Schleiermacher, as one of his twentieth-century defenders has said, presented "a highly emotional soteriology based on communion with the Redeemer, rather than an 'objective' transactional theory of atonement."[10] In addition to shades of German thinking, Nevin's work claimed to represent Calvin's doctrine of the Lord's Supper. He also contended that contemporary nineteenth-century views—Lutheran and Presbyterian in particular—had departed from the true Reformation teaching and practice. Hodge let the book rest on his table for two years before finally responding to it in an article for the *PR*, "Doctrine of the Reformed Church on the Lord's Supper" in 1848. What finally prompted him to respond was Nevin's concurrence with Schaff on the sectarian nature of American Protestantism. Now that Mercersburg had issued a further challenge in its view of the Lord's Supper, who was he not to rise to the occasion?[11]

After a somewhat perfunctory affirmation—"we gratefully acknowledge the assistance derived from it"—Hodge stated bluntly, "We differ from him indeed, essentially, as to the whole subject, not only as to the historical question, but as to what is the true doctrine." Many studies have probed the debate between Hodge and Nevin in great detail. Confident that he would prevail, Hodge, surprisingly, readily admitted that he did not strictly hold to Calvin's view of the sacrament. Instead, Hodge claimed that European confessions such as the *Consensus Tigurinus*, the Heidelberg Catechism, and the Second Helvetic Confession[12] better represented the Reformed view of the Lord's Supper than did Calvin himself, and certainly those confessions did so better than Nevin. The controversy focused on the presence of Christ in the Lord's Supper. Hodge held that "there is . . . a presence of Christ's body in the Lord's supper; not local, but spiritual; not for the senses but for the mind and to faith; not of nearness but of efficacy." He equated feeding upon the body and blood with the act of faith. As for Nevin, Hodge accused him of simply rehashing the doctrine of Schleiermacher and conflicting with traditional Reformed theology. Even more serious, Hodge alleged that Nevin's views verged on falling into the serious errors of Eutychianism and Monothelitism (heresies stating that after the union of his divine and human nature, Christ had but one nature), Socinianism (denial of the Trinity), and Sabellianism (denial of the personal distinctiveness of the Son and Holy Spirit from the Father). Thus, in brief, Hodge held that, far from remaining within the Reformed camp on this matter, Nevin departed from the Reformed confessions, adopted the Romantic views of Schleiermacher, and flirted with views long considered heretical.[13]

In attacking Nevin, though he did not anticipate it, Hodge sowed the wind and reaped the whirlwind.[14] Mercersburg was not about to let Princeton, despite its reputation for defending classical Reformed thinking, have the last word on such an important issue. B. A. Gerrish points out that Nevin began with rebuttals in the German Reformed Church's *Weekly Messenger*. When readers tired of Nevin's persistence in pressing the issue time and again, Nevin and others at Mercersburg birthed their own journal, the *Mercersburg Review*, in 1849.[15] Finally, in 1850 Nevin published a greatly detailed 128-page refutation of Hodge's original 50-page review. He examined each of the areas in Hodge's analysis and outlined where he and Hodge disagreed. Then he demonstrated that, far from the Reformed confessions' not espousing Calvin's ideas, Calvin's doctrines had found their way into the sixteenth-century confessions. As for Christ's presence in the sacrament, it was not merely mental. Instead, Nevin insisted that Reformed doctrine "asserted always a real presence, not simply as an object of thought or intelligence on the part of men, but in the way of actual communication on the part of Christ—a presence not conditioned by the relations of space, but transcending these altogether in a higher sphere of life; a presence, not material, but dynamic, like that of the root in its branches, and only the more intimate and deep by its distance from all that belongs to the experience of sense." Whereas Hodge called the Lord's Supper "mysterious," in the final analysis he proved unwilling to follow the implication of that term.[16] The mysterious nature of the sacrament, for Nevin, was reflected by the believer's participation in Christ, not just as a metaphor but in reality. Whereas Princeton made the connection between the elements in the Supper to be only outward signs, present only in the mind of the participant, Nevin believed in a true union between the sign and the grace bestowed inwardly. Thus, he alleged, moderns—Princetonians included—eviscerated the sacrament of the Lord's Supper of its full meaning and power.[17]

Charles Hodge was accustomed to overcoming his opponents or at least acquitting himself acceptably in controversy. But the almost universal judgment of historians holds that Nevin thoroughly bested his former teacher. The minimum that can be said is that Nevin clearly won the historical debate over whether Calvin's view faded in Reformation history or appeared prominently in the Reformed confessions. That Calvin's view continued as integral to Reformed faith served as a crucial hinge in Nevin's argument. He subjected the Reformed confessions that Hodge highlighted in his review essay to trenchant analysis to support his contention. Hodge may have admitted that in his memorial view he did not hold to Calvin's position, but Nevin exposed the weaknesses of Hodge's historical analysis of the Reformed tradition.

Calvin and the confessions presented a uniform view consistent with Nevin's. The best evidence that Hodge realized his defeat lay in the fact that he did not extend the controversy by responding as he did in other instances, such as his protracted dispute with Park on theology of the intellect and feelings.[18]

The exchange over the Lord's Supper did not end the differences between the two stalwart theologians. Hodge took up the cudgels against Nevin again in the second volume of his *ST*, further inflaming the relationship. Hodge introduced Nevin's thought in the context of discussing justification, the incarnation, anthropology, soteriology, and the Lord's Supper. Hodge criticized Nevin in each instance primarily because he sensed too much similarity with the German views that he consistently judged alien to Reformed theology. In method, he found Nevin's "three scientific principles" that he offered as modern corrections to the Reformers' view of justification too similar to Schleiermacher's pantheistic tendency. On the incarnation, Nevin favored utilizing Schleiermacher's "Urbild or archetypal man" in his description of human nature. Hodge stated, "It is everywhere assumed that God and man are one; that divinity is the completed development of humanity . . . There is nothing in Christ which does not belong to humanity." In anthropology Hodge stated unguardedly that Nevin's views, while "set forth in different terms," were yet "substantially" the same as Schleiermacher's. In soteriology, Hodge identified Nevin's views with those of "speculative theologians"; and after citing Nevin's *Mystical Presence* for several pages, he stated, "This is the modern view of Christianity introduced by Schleiermacher, modified more or less by his disciples, and which has passed over into England and into this country." In virtually every instance Hodge associated Nevin with Schleiermacher and by extension with pantheism.[19]

Hodge's citations and criticism of Nevin struck a nerve. Given their long friendship extending back to the 1820s, now almost fifty years later Hodge's portrayal of Nevin's Christology as pantheistic and the sharp exchanges between Princeton and Mercersburg wounded Nevin so profoundly that he wrote a lengthy, indignant letter to his former teacher expressing his exasperation over Hodge's portrayal. George Shriver published Nevin's letter in "Passages in Friendship:

John W. Nevin to Charles Hodge" and cast a very negative light on Hodge in the process. In part the letter reads as follows:[20]

Feb 24, 1872
Rev. Charles Hodge D.D.
My Dear Sir:

[In the first paragraph of the letter, Nevin accuses Hodge of misquoting him and of charging him with pantheism.]

Another point. In a late letter a clergyman writes me: "I lately saw in Dr. Hodge's System of Theology some extraordinary statements as to what *you* hold in reference to the *Person of Christ*—virtually charging you with holding that the Son of God is nothing more than the human nature of Christ perfected. It is wonderful that good men can allow themselves to publish to the world, and that in permanent form, such slanderous statements." This and more which I need not quote—what the writer refers to, I presume, is the light in which you place me on p. 446 of your Vol. II, where you charge me with being abundant in asserting "the simple humanity of Christ," in a way which *does* logically imply that I deny His proper divinity. You refer here to the Myst. Pres. p. 169; and yet in immediate conjunction with what you quote, I there again am careful to say that the Life of Christ was also a divine life—"the divinity joined in personal union with our humanity." Whether you hold the qualification to be tenable or not from *your* Christological standpoint, I should at least have been allowed to utter my whole view in my own way, instead of having the one half of it so given as to exclude the other half. It could hardly fail to be known to you moreover, that even if there had been any ambiguity in the utterances of the Myst. Pres. a quarter of a century ago (which there was not) my uniform public teaching and preaching has been more than enough to put to shame any such charges as you here bring against me. No one probably in our American Church has more loudly or constantly than myself proclaimed the Incarnation of the Son of God in the sense of the Apostles' Creed.—On page 449 is another offensive passage in which I am charged with making the "universal life principle" of this world to be God in full pantheistic sense without any proof.

You will excuse me for this frank expostulation. It is due to you, my honored friend and dutifully remembered teacher, and due also to myself. Our mere difference in theology is no offense to me of course,

> [no] more than you say it is to yourself. But the difficulty here is not that. For twenty-five years, I suppose you have been setting forth this difference to your classes (now ministers in the Presb. Church) in a sense and in terms that I solemly [*sic*] disown; and now in our old age, and in my old age too [Nevin was sixty-nine and Hodge seventy-five at the time], the long traditional misrepresentation is committed to your book to fulfill its errand as it best can to my wrong, after we are both dead.
>
> I shrink from no criticism of my theological views. I have courted it in every fair and honorable way, asking only to be heard in my own name and in my own words. This simple right has been denied me very much on all sides. I am either not worth noticing at all, or else I deserve to be noticed otherwise than through the wrong vision merely of others. Take an example of what I mean. Passing over all my own self-representation studiously offered to its view for years, the Princeton Repertory sometimes since prostituted its pages to the use of a morally broken down clergyman of our Church, Mr. Voringham, to belch forth two whole articles of most unliterary nonsense simply as it was generally taken to be because it was at *my expense*. The man has on one hand still two volumes of like insane stuff waiting for publication.[21] But enough, I have thought it best to make a clean breast of my dissatisfaction, while in conclusion I reciprocate your assurance of continued Christian regards on into the heavenly world, and subscribe myself.
>
> Yours affectionately, J. W. Nevin.[22]

Nevin's letter must have moved Hodge profoundly in return. His penchant for controversial writing had led him to cross the bounds of legitimate criticism. Nevin's point-by-point refutation of what Hodge attributed to Nevin prompted a belated response. He did so in the third volume of his *ST* in a lengthy footnote in the section on the Lord's Supper.[23] Taken aback by Nevin's rebuke, yet believing his critique correct in large measure, Hodge attempted a delicate balance. He sought both to mollify his friend's anger but also to justify his previous criticism. He began, "The writer was grieved to learn that his friend of more than forty years standing, Dr. John W. Nevin, considers himself to be unjustly charged by us with holding doctrines which he earnestly repudiates." Hodge then attempted to set the record straight. In comparing Nevin's thoughts with those of Hegel, he did not intend to affirm that Nevin was "a thorough Hegelian." He insisted to the contrary: "nothing was further from the writer's mind than the intention of making such an imputation." He continued, "Neither did we intend to intimate that Dr. Nevin adopted Hegel's philosophy as a system, which we know, from his own authority, he abhors." Hodge thereby acknowledged that notwithstanding rather sharp differences, both he and Nevin labored within the same Reformed camp. Commenting further on Martin Luther's and Schleiermacher's views of the divinity of Christ, Hodge stated, "We doubt not, and have never intimated anything to the contrary, that Dr. Nevin, although he makes Christ the ideal or perfect man [an expression reminiscent of Schleiermacher's views in *The Christian Faith*], attributes to Him in his theory and in his heart, all the perfections with which the most devout believer in his divinity invests the adorable Redeemer. How he reconciles this with his representing Him as the Ideal man; and with the assertion that He has but one life and that life in the fullest sense human, it is not for us to say. The same thing, however, is done by many others besides Dr. Nevin." Having clarified his previous remarks, Hodge did not thereby let Nevin totally off the hook. He stood by his former assessment that Nevin showed a proclivity to identify with German thought, which Hodge found unsatisfactory as a philosophical handmaid of the Christian faith.[24]

Controversialists are not known for being apologetic; they propose to refute, not concede, debating points. Hodge's footnote, therefore, almost certainly represents an unusual olive branch in the context of religious controversy. Admitting being somewhat chastened, Hodge felt it necessary to respond to Nevin's unvarnished reprimand. The exchange between the two men, however, needs to be contextualized. Hodge's original treatments of Nevin appeared in his review of *The Mystical Presence* and the section on Christology of volume 2. Nevin wrote the letter in February 1872, years after sharp journalistic exchanges over the Lord's Supper but only shortly after the appearance of *ST*. And the latter, after all, was Nevin's immediate concern. Hodge's son notes in *LCH* that his father submitted the manuscript for volume 3 to the publisher on October 8,

1872—a full seven months after receiving Nevin's complaint. Hodge clearly intended his footnote, while falling short of a full-blown apology, to mitigate his former criticism and mend some fences with his friend of long standing. Since he could not undo the past, and lest he remain on permanent record as unfairly portraying Nevin, Hodge offered this addendum in a subsequent volume. Interestingly, Hodge's son makes no reference to the unfortunate exchange. In fact, Nevin's name appears but twice in *LCH*—regarding his appointment as Hodge's replacement and the *British Quarterly Review*'s reference to Nevin as one of the controversialists whom Hodge engaged in spirited debate. As in other instances in *LCH* when he changed Charles's account of events, A. A. probably did not record the dispute because, typical of biographies in that era to present its figures favorably, it did not cast a good light on his father.[25]

27

Old School North vs. Old School South

Though appearing mundane to most outsiders, of all the General Assembly disputes that Charles Hodge reported in the *PR*, few were as animated as those involving his differences with fellow Old Schoolers over Presbyterian polity. Because of the intensely polemical nature of the confrontations, an outside observer viewing the proceedings could have been excused for thinking that the two factions were mortal enemies! While Hodge engaged in rigorous debate on the floor of the General Assembly with various Southern delegates, the most memorable disputations involved James Henley Thornwell. Thornwell had been educated at South Carolina College, studied briefly at Harvard, and became the most prominent Old School theologian in the South as professor at Columbia Theological Seminary in South Carolina. He served as moderator of the denomination, wrote prolifically—his *Collected Writings* fill four volumes—and, like Hodge, actively participated in the ecclesiastical debates at the General Assembly.[1]

Despite appearances resulting from their General Assembly skirmishes, the two men were more alike than unlike. Like Hodge, Thornwell founded a theological journal, the *Southern Presbyterian Review*, and exercised strong leadership in the Southern church before and during the turbulence of the Civil War. His vision for the Presbyterian church resembled Hodge's by virtue of his firm confessionalism. He believed the church's Reformed heritage was better served by retaining traditions of sister churches in Europe and resisting changes that would make Presbyterianism resemble other evangelical denominations in America. While neither Hodge nor Thornwell was totally successful in preventing the Americanization of Presbyterianism by the influences of the Puritan revivals in the eighteenth century and evangelical piety in the nineteenth, they did not always agree how Presbyterianism should maintain its uniqueness. This disagreement arose out of their differing views of Presbyterian ecclesiology.

We have already examined their similarities and differences over slavery. They agreed that slavery could not be condemned as sinful and that slaveholding should not be subject to church discipline because both ideas lacked biblical warrant. Whereas Hodge favored slavery's eventual abolition and encouraged the church's speaking out against the cruelty of Southern slave laws, however, Thornwell believed slavery beneficial to both slaves and their owners and therefore left its continuance or elimination totally in the hands of civil authorities. Their debates on other matters often reached the level of heated, even exasperated, exchanges. Each defended his position as genuine Presbyterianism that protected the denomination from diverting from its historic roots. Their differences in ecclesiology covered a wide range of topics: the *jure divino* stature of church polity, the spirituality of the church, the role of elders and pastors, and subscription to the Westminster Confession. These matters came to the fore in several General Assemblies over several decades.[2]

As Old School Presbyterians, both Hodge and Thornwell opposed the tendency of American denominations to take on the characteristics of nineteenth-century culture in their polity. Hodge took up the cudgels for Presbyterian polity in several ways. He began lecturing on church government in 1845 because of Samuel Miller's decline in health.

Subsequently he delivered an address, "What Is Presbyterianism?," which the Presbyterian Board of Publication printed as an eighty-page tract in 1855. Hodge also contributed to Presbyterian polity in the many *PR* articles reporting the proceedings of the General Assemblies.[3]

Both men espoused a *jure divino* theory of Presbyterianism, which asserted that the New Testament established principles of church government. They believed that God established in Scripture the form of government that should direct the church in its functions. The two men differed sharply, however, on the application of that theory. Hodge summarized his view of ecclesiastical polity in three general principles in "What Is Presbyterianism?": "1. That the people have a right to a substantive part in the government of the Church. 2. That presbyters who minister in word and doctrine, are the highest government officers of the Church, and all belong to the same order. 3. That the outward and visible Church is or should be, one, in the sense that a smaller part is subject to a larger, and a larger to the whole. It is not holding one of these principles that makes a man a Presbyterian, but his holding them all."[4] At this very fundamental level of what constitutes Presbyterianism, Thornwell disagreed. He rejected Hodge's three principles as not being uniquely Presbyterian. Congregationalists shared the practice of participation of people; parity of the clergy occurred in other evangelical churches; and Rome asserted the unity of the church. Therefore, Thornwell stated in his definition what he called the distinctive Presbyterian view of the church: "the government of the Church by parliamentary assemblies, composed of two classes of Elders, and Elders only, and so arranged as to realize the visible unity of the whole Church."[5]

Several issues arose out of the differences between the two men's views that led Hodge to characterize Thornwell's view as "high church Presbyterianism": whether ruling elders should participate in imposition of hands in ordaining ministers, whether ruling elders should be included in quorums for presbytery meetings, and whether the ministries of the church should be conducted by boards or committees. While these matters may sound esoteric to contemporary ears, they precipitated considerable debate as to what constituted Old School ecclesiology. Hodge and Thornwell became the leading advocates of the Northern and Southern attempts to delineate Presbyterian polity. In all these matters Hodge's position carried the day in various General Assemblies, but Thornwell's perspective survived in the Southern church.

The first issue emerged in the 1842 General Assembly when a unanimous vote opposed elders' laying on hands during the ordination of ministers. The action passed without debate, but the matter did not die there. The Synod of Kentucky subsequently approved the right of elders to participate in ordination. A minority objected, which led to an overture coming before the 1843 Assembly to consider the matter again. Thornwell and R. J. Breckinridge of Kentucky squared off in extended debate against Hodge, Miller, and others. To the Southerners, the elder was the equivalent of a biblical presbyter, not a lower class than the clergy. On the basis of 1 Timothy 5:17, Thornwell believed two classes existed within the one office of presbyter. Neither was higher or lower than the other. Ruling elders shared the same ruling function with the teaching elder, but not the teaching function. Since both were elected rulers and represented the people in governing the church through its various courts, both should participate in recognizing the call to ministry, just as they both participated in cases before the presbytery, synod, and General Assembly.

Participation by elders, therefore, was nothing less than necessary for Presbyterian polity. Since the presbytery carried out ordinations, both elders—ruling and teaching—must participate in the rite of ordaining. In light of Hodge's opposition to this view, Thornwell stated his position in the form of an irony: "It is remarkable . . . that the officers whose presence is rendered unnecessary [by rejecting elders' laying on of hands] are precisely the officers whose sole business it is to rule."[6]

Hodge, on the other hand, objected to demands that ruling elders participate in ordination. He conceded that his opponents' case seemed "plausible." Their logic rested on a syllogism: since presbyteries consisted of ministers and ruling elders and since presbyteries possessed power to ordain, therefore elders should participate in that rite.[7] Hodge objected to that logic, however, for several reasons. First and foremost, he opposed allowing elders to participate based on the definition of *presbytery* as "a body of ministers regularly convened, in which ruling elders have a right to deliberate and vote as members."

The difference between ministers as members and elders as delegates carried immense weight as he finished his definition: "The ministers are the standing, constituent members, the elders, members only as delegated, for a particular meeting, and for the special purpose of deliberating and voting." Hodge called this definition "the leading principle" for deciding the issue. Delegates were no more members of the presbytery than corresponding members—visiting ministers who also attended meetings. The constitution also made it clear that "the work of ordination belongs to ministers," which was borne out in works by other contemporary writers, whom Hodge quoted. Thus, when speaking of members of the presbytery engaged in ordaining, "the language is of necessity confined to those members who are in the ministry." As for duties of the office, Hodge stated that "ordination to the ministry is . . . as much a peculiar function of the ministry as preaching is . . . Ordination is an act of executive power, which does not pertain to the ruling elder." Finally, the tradition of the church spoke against the practice. While not bearing the authority of Scripture, the practice of the church in the past ought to give innovators pause to change its procedures. Those who framed the Westminster Directory handed down the procedure for ministerial ordination. If they had intended a difference in practice, they would have included it in the Directory. He stated, "No case of lay ordination, or of an ordination in which ruling elders participated, has been produced or . . . can be produced in the history of any Presbyterian Church." He added with a touch of sarcasm, "Surely it is rather late in the day to begin to teach the whole Presbyterian world what are the first principles of their own system."[8]

Hodge prevailed as the assembly voted 183–9 against changing the rite of ordination, and the following year the General Assembly reaffirmed the action by declaring that elders could not participate in laying on of hands. The Southern perspective, though defeated soundly, flourished years later. At the founding of the Southern Presbyterian Church in 1861, the views of Thornwell, Breckinridge, and Robert Lewis Dabney of Virginia became the cornerstone of Southern Presbyterian polity. When the Presbyterian Church in the United States adopted its *Book of Church Order* in 1879, it advanced the standing of elders by providing for their participation in ordaining ministers.

Ultimately, whether "late in the day" or not, Hodge's position also gave way on this point in the Northern church as well.

A second polity dispute between the Northern and Southern wings of the Old School arose at the 1843 assembly. This one focused on whether the quorum required for presbytery meetings should include ruling elders or only ministers. Unlike Hodge, who limited the term *member of presbytery* to ministers, Thornwell argued that since both pastors and ruling elders represent the biblical term *presbyter*, double representation in all church courts not only was necessary but distinguished Presbyterian polity from other forms of church government. An implication of parity of elders meant that both ministers and elders not only must be necessary for presbytery meetings, but should also be included in quorums required for those meetings.[9]

Hodge's position regarding the quorum rested on his discussion of the previous item on the docket—the definition of a presbytery. He repeated that a presbytery was a "body of ministers who are its standing members." The Directory required three ministers as a quorum to conduct business. Thus, for Hodge, *members* referred only to ministers; ruling elders were distinguished as *delegates*. Hodge believed that since ministers constituted the presbytery, "they are the permanent members of the body; in that body each session has a right to be represented by one elder. This, we consider the plain meaning of our Book. Elders have a right to come, and it is very important they should come, but they are not compelled to come, nor is their presence necessary to the constitution of the body." Citing what he perceived to be the original intent of the framers, he said that if the authors of Presbyterian polity intended to introduce "the novel idea that there could be no presbytery, without ruling elders, they would doubtless have said, 'Three ministers and at least one ruling elder, shall be necessary to form quorum.' " For Hodge, the fact that they did not do so spoke for itself. Unless the constitution explicitly required their presence, ruling elders should not be included in the quorum for a meeting. As for the Southern complaint that Hodge's position undervalued the role of elders, Hodge argued that the "influence of a man in our judicatories depends far more on his personal qualifications than on his station." In fact, Hodge asserted that ruling elders often wielded more influence on the floor of the assembly than ministers. His last lines in this section of his report stated: "The value of the office of ruling elder, we hold to be inestimable; but it depends upon his being a ruling elder, with rights, duties, and privileges distinct from those of the minister; on his being, in the ordinary sense of the word, a layman and not a clergyman." Again, the lines were clearly drawn between Northern and Southern views of the ruling elder. Hodge's position carried the day, but with a smaller plurality of 83–35.[10]

As in the case of ruling elders' participating in ordaining ministers, the 1879 *Book of Church Order* in the Southern church also adopted the Thornwellian position regarding quorums at presbytery meetings. It required three ministers belonging to the presbytery and at least one elder. Though still not requiring a parity of representation, it moved in that direction. The distinction between Southern and Northern conservatives clearly comes to light in the Hodge–Thornwell debates. Thornwell's positions on the elder question, though defeated soundly in both instances, eventually became distinctive of Southern Presbyterianism. For Thornwell, both preacher and elder shared the office of presbyter. Both were clergymen and both were laymen. They both equally represented the people and God in their office. The parity of all presbyters must be preserved. Thus Thornwell took umbrage at both decisions, which he believed undercut the ruling elder.

A third ecclesiastical issue separated the Northern and Southern Old Schoolers and came to a head in the 1860 General Assembly. The Old School stood united in opposing voluntary societies as the means by which the church should educate its ministers and carry out foreign and domestic missions. The groups differed sharply, however, over the constitutionality of boards to carry out these tasks. Thornwell viewed the boards of the church as unconstitutional and pressed for committees to replace them. Hodge reported that Thornwell's ecclesiology entailed "radically different views . . . of the nature and powers of the church." His speeches at the assembly "were very long and very ardent." He traced the origin of the church's boards to the wrongful influence of Congregationalists, who attempted to introduce voluntary societies to carry on various ministries of the church. Resisting the use of external, independent societies to perform its mission, the denomination under the leadership of men such as Hodge and other Old Schoolers appointed its own boards to engage these tasks. Thornwell opposed the appointment of boards as the appropriate means to fulfill the church's mission because the Bible did not command them. Pressing the *jure divino* view of church polity, Thornwell insisted that Scripture established a form of church government that permitted no alteration from its principles. Thornwell's strict interpretation of the *jure divino* view of church government averred that the church could do only what the Bible expressly commands: "We must be able to plead a 'Thus saith the Lord' for every organization or agency which we employ in carrying on the work of the church." The church had "no discretionary power to create a new church court, or judicatory, or anything to stand in the place of or to perform the duty which belongs to the church of God's creation and ordination." Since Christ gave the church "its officers, courts and laws" by which to carry out the church's mission, the church could not appoint or delegate to another body the responsibility of carrying out that work. Because of his high view of the church, Thornwell argued that boards possessed an unauthorized autonomy with their own officers, committees, and agendas. He feared that boards would become large and unwieldy and by concentrating power in the hands of a few individuals in the Northeast would not represent the church as a whole. Therefore, he proposed that ministries be carried out by committees, which would be smaller and more responsive to the church's needs because of their close relation to the General Assembly, which alone possessed authority to govern the church.[11]

Hodge agreed that God established the polity for the church in Scripture and that the term *jure divino* appropriately described the Presbyterian view of church government over against Episcopal and Congregational models. Hodge contended, however, that from the beginning Presbyterians did not simply respond to Congregationalism when it rejected voluntary societies. Instead, following its constitutional mandate to train and sustain ministers, the church formed its own committees, which eventually expanded into the Boards of Domestic Mission, Foreign Missions, Education, Publication, and Committee of Church Extension as the church and its ministries enlarged. He proceeded to dispute Thornwell's interpretation of *jus divinum*. For Hodge, every church—not just Presbyterians—that argued for *jus divinum* "was content to claim divine authority for the essential elements of their system, while they claimed a discretionary power as to matters of detail and modes of operation." He then upped the wattage of debate with the comment, "The great principles of Presbyterianism are in the Bible; but it is preposterous to assert that our whole Book of Discipline is there." He adopted similarly strong language when he labeled Thornwell's theory "utterly impractical and suicidal." If the church followed Thornwell's interpretation, numerous procedures and institutions that had become fixtures in the church would be eliminated for the simple reason that the Bible said nothing about Sunday schools, academies, colleges, and theological seminaries, all of which were governed by boards. To Thornwell's proposal that committees replace boards, Hodge responded that committees suffered from the same problem as boards in that the Bible does not command them either: "It is not only revolting, but ridiculous, to say that the Bible forbids a Board and commands a Committee." Hodge concluded that either could be inferred from Scripture. Making these matters of debate he declared "utterly unreasonable." The assembly agreed with Hodge overwhelmingly in its vote to continue boards 234–56, but some changes were adopted in the organization of the boards that reflected Thornwell's concerns.[12]

We have already seen that the two men disagreed on how to interpret the spirituality of the church in the issue of slavery. At the 1860 General Assembly, both men affirmed the church to be a purely spiritual body. They held that the church and state constituted two separate entities and that neither should intrude into the other's affairs. The 1859 General Assembly broached the issue of colonization and Thornwell objected, saying that the spirituality of the church meant that it is "exclusively a *spiritual* organization, and possesses none but *spiritual power* . . . She has nothing to do with the voluntary associations of men for various civil and social purposes that were outside of her pale." The church's great aim consisted of delivering souls from sin, not of "becom[ing] entangled with the kingdoms and the policy of this world." While Christians as individuals may and ought to participate in philanthropic ventures, "the church, as such, [should] keep to her specific task." Hodge demurred. He agreed that the church's task was to preach the gospel, but that it was also to educate and was "called of God to set forth and enjoin upon the consciences of men the relative duties of parents and children, of magistrates and people, of masters and slaves." While the church may not meddle in policy, "if the state . . . violates the Sabbath . . . or legalizes piracy, or concubinage, or polygamy . . . if in short it does anything directly contrary to the law of God," then "the church is bound to make that law known, and set it home upon the conscience of all concerned." In support of this view, Hodge cited the church's defending the morality of the American Revolution, denouncing cruelty of slave laws, and denouncing persecution of Christians in Switzerland in 1830. He summarized the historical stance of the church by saying, "[The church] has never been afraid to denounce what God forbids, or to proclaim in all ears what God commands."[13]

In his treatment of "Province of the Church" at the 1860 General Assembly, Hodge followed up his report of the previous assembly by arguing that Southerners took the church's spirituality to an extreme. Southerners claimed "that the church was bound to restrict her deliverances to her own members, and to matters under her control; and that organizations outside of her pale, however objectionable or praiseworthy, could be neither recommended nor objected to; and the action of the state, however inconsistent with the word of God, could not be testified against." Hodge flatly rejected this view, which he said effectively "put[s] a muzzle over [the church's] lips, and forbid[s] her exercising one of her highest and most important prerogatives." If Thornwell's view prevailed, all statements ever issued by the church over moral and spiritual implications regarding "Bible Societies, Colonization, Temperance, Slavery or the Slave-trade" would have to be recanted. To remain silent in the face of events bearing enormous moral significance would be intolerable. In the end, the church reached another compromise resolution, which stated on the one hand that the General Assembly "disclaim[ed] all right to interfere in secular matters" and on the other that it "assert[ed] the right to bear testimony in favour of truth and holiness and against all false doctrines and sins."

Hodge expressed satisfaction with the unanimous acceptance of the compromise resolution.[14]

The spirituality of the church continued to be a major bone of contention within the Old School denomination. While it fairly simmered in the 1860 General Assembly, it would boil over in the following year, resulting in further division within American Presbyterianism. The Old School would divide as the country divided—between North and South. Hodge would be profoundly saddened by both ruptures and freely vent his grief.

28

Subscription to the Westminster Confession of Faith

The Adopting Act of 1729 put into place the Presbyterian church's criteria for ministerial subscription. Early debates focused on whether the church's ministry should be tested primarily by ministers' conforming to the objective standard of Reformed doctrine or in addition by the subjective measure of religious experience. The division into the Old and New School churches resulted in large part from theological differences. During the period of separation between the two Presbyterian bodies, earlier points that had separated the two parties, such as the Plan of Union, issues of church government, and cooperation with voluntary societies, faded into the background. Theological differences, however, remained. Charles Hodge remained cautious about a reunion of the two churches. While he did not believe the New School to be rife with heresy, he thought that a spirit of latitude existed among New Schoolers that made them more tolerant of differences than he deemed prudent.[1]

Hodge's view of subscription must be seen against this historical backdrop. As early as 1831, well before the schism in 1837, Hodge argued for the absolute necessity of creeds in order for churches to enjoy "ecclesiastical connexion." While creeds seemed to receive universal commendation by Presbyterians, they divided over how to interpret subscription or assent to those standards of belief. He outlined what he believed to be two extremes that Presbyterians should assiduously avoid:

> On the one hand, there are some, who seem inclined to give the phrase in question [*system of doctrine*], such a latitude that any one, who holds the great fundamental doctrines of the Gospel as they are recognized by all evangelical denominations, might adopt it; while on the other, some are disposed to interpret it so strictly as to make it not only involve the adoption of all the doctrines contained in the Confession, but to preclude all diversity in the manner of conceiving and explaining them. They are therefore disposed to regard those, who do not in this sense adopt the Confession of Faith and yet remain in the Church, as guilty of a great departure from moral honesty. This we think an extreme, and a mischievous one. Because, it tends to the impeachment of character of many upright men, and because its application would split the Church into innumerable fragments.[2]

The issue resurfaced indirectly in the 1858 General Assembly when a resolution arose for the Board of Publication to prepare an official commentary on the whole Bible to direct future General Assemblies. While not defined in terms of subscription, the resolution would effectively serve the same purpose of giving too definite expression than appropriate for the church. Hodge enumerated many reasons against the resolution. It would severely restrict liberty in biblical interpretation. No one scholar or group of scholars was capable of such a massive undertaking. In addition, the confession did not require such a document; and the denomination would inevitably fragment because not even one interpretation of the confession, let alone the entire Bible, existed. He stated in exasperation, "We could not hold together one week if we made the adoption of all its propositions a condition of ministerial communion . . . This is more than all the popes, who ever lived, merged in one would dare to propose."[3]

The dispute over the resolution to produce a commentary prompted Hodge to revisit the issue of subscription in "Adoption of the Confession of Faith" in the last issue of the *PR* that year. He wrote not only in the context of adding to his discussion of the General Assembly resolution but also in relation to the continued division of the Old and New Schools in the North. He conceded that he had little new to add to what he had written in 1831. He used the ordination question "Do you sincerely receive and adopt the Confession of Faith of this church, as containing the system of doctrine taught in the Holy Scriptures?" He used as analogies examples from other traditions. Just as Jesuits must affirm the Roman Catholic system of doctrine and Anglicans subscribe to the Church of England's Thirty-nine Articles, so Presbyterians subscribed to the Westminster Confession "in [its] plain, historical sense" as a "system of doctrine" as distinguishing Presbyterianism from all other systems.[4]

Hodge stressed that ministerial candidates therefore did not have the liberty to interpret the confession in any other way than it had been understood in the past. Thus the confession stood distinct in its integrity over against other systems of doctrine, such as Pelagianism and Unitarianism, which had their own peculiar doctrines. Hodge proceeded to demonstrate that Presbyterians had labored diligently to form the Adopting Act of 1729, which allowed scruples, but only about doctrines not "essential and necessary." He enumerated historical examples that illustrated the church's following these principles and referred readers to chapter 3 of *CHPC* as evidence that "no exception to the Confession of Faith, touching any of the doctrines constituting that system, was ever allowed." The interpretation of "system of doctrine," therefore, did not encompass a vague "substance" of any doctrine, but the specific form in which that doctrine was understood historically. Some men who had entered the Presbyterian ministry by the substance-of-doctrine view turned out to deny imputation of Adam's sin and Christ's righteousness, sinful depravity, and Christ's definite atonement. Hodge concluded that "the very idea of a doctrine is a truth in a specific form, and, therefore, those who do not hold the doctrines of the Confession in the form in which they are therein presented, do not hold the doctrines." The substance-of-doctrine view that Hodge believed characterized New Schoolers, therefore, bore responsibility "more than all other causes combined" for the disastrous schism.[5]

Hodge used the same principles when he addressed the "every proposition" view of Old Schoolers who demanded that ministers subscribe to every doctrine of the confession exactly as it was stated. The every-proposition view erred to the opposite extreme. The confession, because it was a human work, could contain elements that lay outside the "system of doctrine" that the confession claimed to affirm. Thus, he insisted, "it is one thing to adopt the system of doctrine contained in the Westminster Confession, and quite another to adopt every proposition contained in the Confession." For Hodge, the distinction was an important one.[6]

Hodge concluded that if the every-proposition view were declared to be the Presbyterian view of subscription, even "the venerable Dr. Ashbel Green and scores of men among our fathers of like standing" would be deposed from the ministry. He cited his former pastor because Green represented the Old School in its ultra form. He further stated candidly that if such a view prevailed, "we verily believe we should be left almost alone. We [i.e., Hodge himself] are not sure that we personally know a dozen ministers besides ourselves who could stand the test."[7]

With each extreme eliminated, what remained was the concept that *system of doctrine* had a "fixed, historical meaning" that all ministers must affirm when being ordained. The Westminster Standards contained three distinct classes of doctrines: those common to all Christians in the Apostles' and Nicene creeds; those common to all Protestants, separating them from Roman Catholics; and those that belonged to Reformed churches alone, differentiating them from Lutherans, Anglicans, Arminians, and other denominations. A Presbyterian minister, by affirming his ordination vows, "holds in its integrity the system of doctrine contained in the Westminster Confession." Yet again in this issue of subscription to the confession, Hodge distinguished himself from both New Schoolers, who tended to hold a looser view, and more conservative Old Schoolers, who demanded a more restrictive expression. His solution to the dispute, while a via media, left no doubt as to his loyalty to the confession. The confession thereby retained its authoritative role in ministerial subscription, yet was recognized as a human attempt to frame orthodox belief. In simplest terms, Hodge believed that only a middle way avoided extremism.[8]

In the various controversies covered in part 4, Hodge marked off positions that identified him as both a devoted churchman and a moderate Old Schooler. His loyalty to his church and zeal to ensure that it retained its orthodoxy were beyond dispute. The clarity and intensity with which he expressed his views was rivaled by few. He forged his views in the context of General Assembly debates and carefully crafted journal articles. Whether addressing evangelical theology in *WOL* or Roman Catholic baptism, the role of intellect versus feelings in theology, maintaining the highest standards in theological education, Northern versus Southern polity, or strict versus loose subscription, Hodge proved himself a masterly controversialist. He easily earned his reputation as the premier Northern Old School spokesman. While James Henry Thornwell and Robert Lewis Dabney championed Old School Presbyterianism in the South, Hodge knew no equal in the North. That he did so as a moderate added to his reputation for fairness in assembly debates and his *PR* summaries. His efforts also garnered respect for the seminary as it became synonymous with Reformed Calvinism in its traditional form.

PART 5

Interaction with Europe

Charles Hodge's two-year educational venture in Europe left an indelible impression that remained with him for the rest of his career. He owed to his 1826–28 hiatus from seminary teaching a debt for shoring up his educational credentials, instilling confidence in classroom teaching, bolstering his Reformed perspective as it faced opposition to new ideas, and reinforcing his vision to maintain Princeton's goals in the face of competing visions for theological education. He drew on all of these in the following decades of classroom instruction, journal editing, publishing, and service in various courts of the Presbyterian church. As much as he hoped that theological education in Europe might change for the better under the influence of evangelicals such as August Tholuck, Augustus Neander, and Ernst Wilhelm Hengstenberg, Hodge found that theological innovation spread rather than declined on the Continent. He therefore established the regimen of reading theological texts as they came off European presses and especially as they were translated into English. He did not limit his attention to Germany, though he became most exercised over its scholarship; he also monitored theological and ecclesiastical developments in England. Apprehensive that innovations, whatever their origins, would invade all American denominations, he subjected them to the same rigorous examination that he accorded to domestic innovations. His sometimes fierce opposition to European thinking owed not to a desire to score points in speculative debate or to make scholarship an end in itself. Theological scholarship should serve the church, and it did so most directly by the way in which it trained its ministerial candidates. To this end Hodge labored might and main to respond to foreign scholarly works and movements that might influence American pastors and thus potentially divert their denominations from their historic orthodox roots.

29

Anglicanism's Oxford Movement

Charles Hodge's rapt attention to denominational activity and theological education in America during the early decades of the nineteenth century did not prevent him from keeping abreast of the religious situation and theological scholarship abroad. Through his editorship of the *PR*, he monitored all things foreign and domestic. European scholarship representing the leading edge of theological and biblical thought had originally prompted his 1826–28 trip. His intensive study on the Continent only confirmed his concerns, noted briefly in his *Dissertation*, that the momentum of modern thought and especially German scholarship diverged from traditional Reformed orthodoxy. Upon his return, Hodge continually reported trends in American theological education. While European writings obviously influenced American thinkers, Hodge believed that divulging the radical nature of departures from Reformed orthodoxy and their effect on theological students and clergy could impede the progress of liberalism in this country.[1]

In the late 1830s and early 1840s, Hodge came into his own as a major figure in denominational matters and theological education. He used the same skills by which he analyzed developments in America to review foreign works that he believed should come to the attention of fellow Presbyterians. Because of their potential to influence theological educators, their students, and pastors serving in the pulpit, Hodge unleashed a barrage of trenchant reviews in which he referred to the peculiar nature of German theological scholarship over against English and American thought. As already discussed, Hodge candidly admitted his difficulty in understanding the complexities of German philosophy. It would not be an overstatement to say that he was mystified by what he called the German *mind*, a term roughly corresponding to the contemporary term *worldview*.[2] He judged the pantheistic tendencies of G. W. F. Hegel and Friedrich Schleiermacher as incompatible with the Bible's content and the Westminster Confession as a summation of Christian doctrine. Steeped in Common Sense Realism, which had originated in Scotland in the late eighteenth and early nineteenth centuries to offset the skepticism of thinkers such as David Hume, Hodge, like the vast majority of other American Protestant thinkers, preferred the moral rationalism of thinkers such as Dugald Stewart, Thomas Reid, and William Hamilton as the philosophy most compatible with Christian theology.[3] Because of pantheistic tendencies that even Tholuck and Neander admitted dominated their European contemporaries, Hodge greatly preferred the clarity and straightforwardness of what he called the English and American minds over against the German mind.

The first of his reviews of European thought, however, took on a work in his native English—*Tracts for the Times*, a product of the Oxford movement. Composed primarily of professors at Oxford University, the group formed an Anglo-Catholic faction in the Church of England. They claimed a substantial hearing among Anglicans through the publication of tracts, which evolved from their initial form as brief anonymous leaflets into lengthy treatises. John Henry Newman, High Church Anglican priest who gained recognition through his preaching at St. Mary's Church, initiated the tracts in 1833 to oppose objectionable features of Roman Catholicism and Protestant dissenters. Both threatened to displace traditional Anglicanism. Newman and his associates, who moved closer in their sympathies toward Catholicism, sought a recovery of the principles and worship of the early church, which they believed had been lost. They called for another reformation in the Church of England—one different in kind from what had actually occurred on the Continent and in England in the sixteenth century.[4]

Hodge stated his view of the Oxonians' goal in the opening lines of his review of the three-volume second edition *Tracts for the Times* (1837) by characterizing the tracts "as among the most important ephemerical [*sic*] productions of the day." Hodge thereby contended at the outset that the Tractarian movement, being transient in nature, possessed no lasting power. For Hodge, the tracts proposed an alien system of doctrine and practice from that outlined in Anglicanism's charter document, the Thirty-nine Articles of Religion. Though much less detailed than the Westminster Confession of 1648, the Thirty-nine Articles of 1563 constituted the Anglican Church as a Reformed church. To show the Oxford movement's departure from Reformed faith, he quoted the tracts' assertion that "the one catholic and apostolic church . . . [is] the storehouse and direct channel of grace, as a divine ordinance . . . which conveys secret strength and life to every one who shares in it." Hodge called this assertion "the centre of the system around which all the other doctrines revolve and to which they tend." The centrality of the church as the channel of grace carried with it a more intense emphasis on the sacraments and liturgy than in the past. Such a view conflicted with Reformed confessions, which affirmed the true church as "the congregation of faithful men in which the pure word of God is preached and the sacraments are duly administered." Whereas the tracts made the church and its conveyance of grace through an apostolic succession of ordained clergy pivotal, Reformed churches affirmed Christ and justification by faith as their foundation. To the Tractarians, "the church . . . is the great mediator between God and man, the only authorized channel of divine communication." Hodge contrasted John Keble's term *Episcopal grace* with Reformed emphasis on justification by grace through faith.[5]

Hodge cited the tract "Via Media,"[6] which called for a "second reformation" to repudiate "ultra Protestantism," that is, churches that rejected the polity and practices of early Catholicism. Hodge stated that original Reformers of the English church "are represented as having gone much too far in their opposition to Popery; and the Reformers of the foreign churches [those on the Continent] are rejected as either allies or brethren." In briefest terms, Tractarians sought a return to the ancient church. Hodge quoted one author's desire "to die in the faith of the Catholic church before the division of the East and West," that is, before the schism of 1054 that separated the Western Roman and Eastern Orthodox churches. Tractarian writers admitted that Rome erred by increasing the number of sacraments, abusing the use of images, rendering excessive power to the pope, and teaching transubstantiation of bread and wine in the Lord's Supper. They labeled such corruptions "incidental" and of "little importance," however, when compared to Scottish and Continental churches' elimination of the episcopacy and other rites inherited from the early church. Hodge expressed dismay that the Tractarians' ecumenism differed from that of the original English Reformers, who affectionately cited John Calvin's *Institutes* and endorsed the writings of Martin Bucer, Peter Martyr Vermigli, and other Continental figures. It pained Hodge to note that they applauded William Laud, a staunch advocate of episcopacy and opponent of the Puritans during Elizabeth's reign, and denigrated Thomas Cranmer, Archbishop of Canterbury during the reign of Edward VI, who held priests and bishops equal in ecclesiastical status.[7]

Hodge then bore down on the issue of authority. He denied any biblical basis for reverting to traditions: "when a system is advanced of such portentous character and pressed on our belief as the condition of salvation, we must have scriptural reasons." Tract 19 acknowledged the legitimacy of such requests by saying that "the faintest probabilities are strong enough to determine our conduct." As evidence for Episcopal ordination, the author cited Acts 13:2–3, the account of Antioch's setting apart Paul and Barnabas for mission among the Gentiles. Hodge sarcastically stated, "A better specimen for faintness could hardly be selected," and he proceeded to enumerate three reasons why the event did not justify Episcopal ordination: (1) Paul had already ministered in Damascus, Arabia, Jerusalem, Cilicia, and Antioch itself; (2) Paul categorically stated that he received his ministry directly from Christ and not from men; and (3) there was no apostle at Antioch to ordain him. Hodge believed that no tracts offered sufficient justification for Episcopal ordination.[8]

Hodge concluded by summarizing the "system" of the Tractarians. Among his list he cites the following beliefs: (1) the church is "the storehouse and channel of grace"; (2) the sacraments convey grace to recipients; (3) ordained clergy "alone have the awful and mysterious power of conferring the gifts of the Holy Ghost"; (4) believers are "justified in baptism, and for sins committed after baptism, they must do the best they can"; (5) the body and blood of Christ are present in the Eucharist; and (6) the "rule of faith and practice is the written and unwritten word of God, the latter interpreting, limiting, and correcting the former." While these elements alone may not constitute the "popery" that conformed strictly to the decrees of the Catholic Council of Trent of the sixteenth century, for Hodge they did constitute the "popery" that Protestant Reformers rejected. Trent may have propagated more errors than *Tracts for the Times*, but both were "at variance with the scriptures, and with the Reformers, and equally destructive of evangelical religion and liberty of conscience."[9]

Unable to judge precisely from afar the gains of the Oxford movement in England, Hodge nevertheless deduced from the various editions of *Tracts for the Times* that it had gained many adherents. He discerned distinctly different moods in Newman's various prefaces to the three volumes. In the first volume Newman stated that the doctrines being advocated were not widely held. The tone in volumes 2 and 3, however, changed dramatically. Said Hodge, "The preface to the second, rejoices in the great change already produced in public sentiment on these points; and that to the third volume speaks still more confidently." He cited evangelical leaders in England who expressed apprehension at the movement's gains. As for its effect in America, Hodge quoted Episcopal publications lauding Newman's praise of the Virgin Mary and extolling John Keble, one of Oxford's foremost leaders, as "the sweetest spirit of the age."[10]

Both in the Anglican Church in England and the Episcopalian Church in America Hodge detected a "leaven of popery" that had ebbed and flowed in past eras. He expressed concern that the Oxford movement would exercise a powerful influence at the popular level on "sentimental religionists, whose devotion must be kindled through the imagination; and [on] those also, who for any reason, are led to read and reverence the fathers more than the scriptures." Hodge agreed with those who affirmed that if the movement succeeded, "the true Protestants must leave the church." He continued, "Every thing gained at the Reformation is at stake in this controversy, and the duty of separation from Oxford is as imperative as it was three hundred years ago, to separate from Rome." Hodge likened sixteenth-century Protestant resistance to popish arrogance to modern-day ongoing struggles for religious and civil liberty in England and America. He warned that Tractarians who quoted favorably from Archbishop William Laud would inevitably respond in kind to those who opposed their Catholic program, which resembled the Inquisition. Sounding like a latter-day Roger Williams, who had championed Baptist liberty of conscience in his *Bloudy Tenet* in 1644, Hodge maintained, "The principles of these Tracts have never been combined with zeal and power without leading to persecution." The urgency for Anglicans to discern the errors of the Tractarians resembled a similar need in the original Reformation. He stated that "the duty of separation from Oxford is as imperative as it was three hundred years ago to separate from Rome." Hodge closed his review with the hope that opponents would overcome the Tractarian movement so that "the whole body of the Reformed be united in one great brotherhood, as in the days of Cranmer and Calvin."[11]

Hodge wrote this review in 1839 before the appearance in 1841 of Newman's famous Tract 90, which claimed that the Thirty-nine Articles did not oppose Catholic beliefs in purgatory, use of images, relics, invocation of the saints, and even the additional sacraments; rather, they only condemned Roman corruptions. Hodge would clearly have bridled at such an assertion. The Oxford controversy abated when Newman withdrew from the Church of England in October 1845 and joined the Roman Catholic Church. He led an exodus of over a thousand Anglicans, which included over two hundred ministers. Hodge's proposal of separating from Oxford thereby became moot.[12]

Hodge concentrated his critique of the Oxford tracts on several areas. As a matter of historical interest, he viewed the Oxford movement as a retreat from and renunciation of gains made by sixteenth-century Continental and English Reformers. Hodge's ecumenicity shows itself in his acknowledging the kinship between the Continental and English Reformers. While not agreeing with Anglicans' Episcopal ecclesiology, he believed that the Church of England had freed itself from its Catholic roots.[13] The Oxford movement threatened to jeopardize historic Anglicanism's Reformed doctrine and practice. It would survive only if initial gains by *Tracts for the Times* could be successfully blunted. As in other *PR* articles, Hodge acquitted himself as an able controversialist. He distinguished between Tractarian principles of Newman and his colleagues John Keble, Richard Froude, and Bovarie Posey and those of initial Reformers such as Thomas Cranmer, under whose leadership the Anglican Church had emerged in the sixteenth century. Hodge's concern, however, extended beyond the ecclesiastical context in England. The potential for the Oxford movement's regressing into old Catholicism threatened not only the Anglican Church but also its Episcopalian cousin in America. Always eager to acknowledge evangelical kinship with conservative forces regardless of denominational affiliation, Hodge granted that though differences existed between Reformed Presbyterianism and the Anglican communion, he gladly supported every effort to resist the incursion of Roman ideas into any Protestant denomination.

30

German and American Transcendentalism

Charles Hodge's concern for the Oxford movement and its potential for affecting American Episcopalianism was overshadowed by more profound uneasiness with theological and biblical developments in the Christian church in Germany and the continued drift in scholarship toward unorthodox views. They posed a serious threat not only to European evangelical religion but also to theological education in America as they gained a hearing in American seminaries. He expressed his alarm by contrasting what he viewed as substantial departures from Reformed thought. He used the term *mind* to illustrate what he considered the differences between American and English thinking on the one hand and German thought on the other: the *English mind* and the *American mind* as sharply distinguished from the *German mind*. As mentioned earlier, Hodge's expressions correspond roughly to the contemporary expression *worldview*, which depicts diverse perspectives in intellectual pursuits, academic disciplines, cultural practices, moral ethos, and behavioral patterns.

Hodge attempted to master German language through his studies in Europe so that he could keep abreast of advancing scholarship on the Continent. He and others acknowledged that the flow of ideas among the Europeans had reversed its direction. Instead of deism infiltrating from Britain to France and Germany, the intellectual traffic had shifted as German pantheism made its way toward Britain and France.[1]

Hodge therefore addressed the rising hegemony of German pantheism that had burgeoned only further since the late 1820s. The Princeton Plan had identified deism as the most formidable opponent of Reformed thinking, and made its refutation high on the list of the seminary's apologetic requirements in schooling pastors for the ministry.[2] The heydays of deism's supremacy in England and Germany now lay in the past. August Tholuck informed Hodge during their discussions at Halle that the influences of Immanuel Kant had waned before Hodge's arrival. Perhaps Tholuck's assurance of Kantianism's demise explains why, with one exception already cited in notes from Tholuck's lectures, Hodge never referred to the contents of Kant's primary religious work, *RWLRA*. Hodge almost certainly never read the work. It is inconceivable that if he had done so, he would not have included somewhere in his corpus of writings a detailed analysis and refutation of Kant's moralistic recasting of Christianity. Had he read Kant's 1793 deistic work, Hodge, the inveterate advocate and practitioner of traditional Reformed piety, would surely have discussed Kant's categorical rejection of traditional piety as mere superstition and his substituting in its place merely moral activity. By espousing Christianity as a moralistic religion, Kant accepted only moral acts as legitimately religious. He repudiated pietistic practices that he remembered from his youth—prayer,[3] church attendance, hymn-singing, and other forms of worship associated with the Judeo-Christian tradition. Kant denounced the traditional means of grace as attempts to win God's favor by performing acts devoid of morally good conduct. Hodge, in light of his lifelong adherence to Reformed orthodoxy coupled with appropriate worship and pious devotional activity, would not have failed to cite Kant's religious work as an example of the deficiencies of Enlightenment thinking.[4]

Kant's passing from the scene, however, did not presage a return to religious orthodoxy in Germany. As Hodge confirmed during his

European studies, German biblical and theological scholarship continued to develop in a more radical direction. Paul Tillich correctly pointed out in *A History of Christian Thought* that Friedrich Schleiermacher stood at a crucial juncture in Christian theological progress. By the dawn of the nineteenth century, Germany stood almost three hundred years removed from the Reformation. Several movements—Protestant scholasticism, pietism, and deism—had propelled theological thought forward, each with its distinctive emphases. While scholasticism and pietism offered further refinements or correctives to the orthodox theologies of the original Reformers, the resulting changes did not alter Christianity as profoundly as did deism. Many Enlightenment thinkers exhibited the tendency to view deism as the next stage in Christianity's progress toward the ideal religion. By reformulating Christianity in rational terms, they believed that Christianity would evolve into the next higher stage of religious development. Thus, when Romanticism burst onto the scene as a reaction to the rational and classical ideals of the Enlightenment, Schleiermacher confronted a critical decision. Should Protestantism recover its sixteenth-century roots much as the Reformers had reclaimed first-century biblical content? Should Christianity shed Enlightenment emphases much as Martin Luther and John Calvin had demanded that their eras reject medieval corruptions? Tillich claimed that Schleiermacher had chosen correctly when he elected to continue the synthesis mentality of his Enlightenment predecessors by his new synthesis with Romanticism. He did so in his *Speeches on Religion to Its Cultured Despisers* (1799) and his magnum opus, *The Christian Faith* (1821).[5]

Hodge assumed the task of assessing this transmutation of German religion and theological education in four articles, the first appearing in 1839. In each article Hodge not only critiqued the movements in question, but also expressed his concern that they posed a challenge to American religion and theological education. The articles ranged from a discussion of the Germanic roots of New England transcendentalism to a review of the translation of his friend August Tholuck's historical work on the New Testament church, a summation of the "religious state of Germany," and what Hodge labeled "The Latest Form of Infidelity." We will examine each of these against the background of his European studies and his notion of what constitutes proper method and theological content in the education of clergy. The nature of theological education that he encountered in Germany had not diminished with the passing of decades but had further departed from traditional orthodoxy. The latest expression of that development threatened to invade America's educational scene. In each instance, Hodge explained that what prompted him to engage his subjects was the appearance of the works in translation. As the works became accessible to the larger public, he undertook the task of reviewing them to warn of their potential danger to orthodox Christianity.[6]

The first article, entitled "Transcendentalism," reviewed two works by Victor Cousin, professor of philosophy at the University of Paris, and Ralph Waldo Emerson's 1838 espousal of transcendentalism to the senior class at Harvard. Hodge opened by chronicling metaphysical speculation in New England from its inception in Jonathan Edwards to the transcendentalist Ralph Waldo Emerson. He spoke warmly of Edwards as "the greatest of modern Christian metaphysicians" for "his eminently patient and discriminating, and conclusive research." After Edwards, however, New England theology declined precipitously. New England theology deteriorated from Hopkinsianism to Taylorism and then to transcendentalism. Hodge tied the two works of Cousin to Emerson's to show the flow of intellectual traffic from Germany to France to America and specifically the threat that European thought posed to American theological education.[7]

Hodge began his examination with a disclaimer—he professed no expertise in the various systems of German metaphysics. He admitted a clear distinction between two intellectual milieus with the tongue-in-cheek confession that "the Anglo-Saxon *dummheit*, with which Germans charge the English, reigns we fear in us after an inveterate sort." He disclosed a conversation that has often been cited as evidence of a sharp difference between Hodge's orthodoxy and the Romanticism of Schleiermacher. In that conversation, mentioned previously, with an admirer of Schleiermacher Hodge said, " 'But we do not understand his [Schleiermacher's] book.' '*Understand* it!' cried the other, with amazement, 'what then? But do not you *feel* it?' " Hodge then explored the philosophical progression leading up to the systems of G. W. F. Hegel and Schleiermacher. In doing so, he summarized Kant's epistemological and moral thought. In his *Critique of Pure Reason* (1781), Kant affirmed our rational autonomy via the twelve categories of reason, and in *Critique of Practical Reason* (1787), he established man's moral autonomy through the categorical imperative and the postulates of practical reason. Hodge mentioned Kant's *RWLRA*, but he did not explore its contents. He repeatedly referred to charges by Kant's contemporaries that Kant was needlessly obscure, coined numerous technical terms, and on one occasion refused to clarify his writings with the dismissive remark, "I meant what I said, and at the age of near four score, I have something else more important to do, than to write a commentary on my own works." Hodge also summarized Johann Gottlieb Fichte's and Friedrich Wilhelm Joseph Schelling's further developments of German idealism, which by denying a personal God paved the way for the various philosophies of pantheism.[8]

What disturbed Hodge was the ease with which *theologians* accepted Kant's philosophical and religious speculation despite its departure from traditional orthodoxy. He bewailed that "the present generation of clergymen in Germany" and "Christian ministers among ourselves, men of education and piety," had succumbed to the new teaching. They failed to discern the incompatibility between Christian orthodoxy and philosophical speculation produced by German thinkers. Hodge declared himself "filled with amazement" that such "Christian ministers" subscribed to "statements which they do not comprehend, or [gave] the weight of their authority to the conclusions which by the best theologians of Germany are denounced as incompatible with the fundamentals, we say not of Christianity, but of natural religion." By "best theologians of Germany" Hodge had in mind Hengstenberg and his fellow evangelicals.[9]

For Hodge, German philosophy reached its most destructive influence by its blunders into pantheism. He expressed special concern that students who were of the same age as he when he first confronted German thinking firsthand were being seduced by "the enchanted ground of German literature, either in its primitive or its secondary and Gallicized [French] division." In some of the most acerbic comments Hodge ever penned in the *PR*, he warned his readers of the dangers of German thought: "Let us with all the earnestness of disinterested dread caution the young American. Under the disguises of romance and poesy, he will learn to tolerate the hell-born dogmas of the *young Germany*." The German, French, and "mongrel philosophies" were "districts of the same kingdom; alike in arrogance, in nonsense and in impiety." Not surprisingly, those who espoused transcendental thought responded with equal venom to the American and British way of thinking: "The Germans of the Transcendental School complain that we of the Anglo Saxon race are dull, terrestrial, and shallow"—to which he responds that "their defect is equally unfortunate, for no one of them has the faculty for descrying an absurdity as such." Hodge noted that prominent German historian F. C. Baur, for example, openly admitted that German theological systems resembled the heretical Gnosticism of early church history. Such candor only deepened Hodge's revulsion.[10]

Hodge then turned his attention to the influence of German thought on American education: "Every parent and guardian in the land, has an interest in knowing which of our colleges are making experiment of the effects of this philosophy upon the minds of the young men entrusted to their care."[11] As an example of American education's being led astray, Hodge cited Ralph Waldo Emerson's famous "Divinity School Address" in 1838 to Harvard ministerial students. Emerson's address marked the paradigm shift in America from pre-Kantian conceptions of reason to post-Kantian or Romantic transcendental conceptions of reason. Hodge stated that the address contained "the application of the Transcendental Philosophy in the form of instruction to young men, about to go forth as preachers of Christianity." Reflecting his concern for American theological education, Hodge subjected Emerson's sermon to strong criticism. He cited a passage in which Emerson enumerated his reasons for rejecting traditional theological tenets. Emerson listed the previous errors of traditional religion: "The stationariness of religion; the assumption that the age of inspiration is past, that the Bible is closed; the fear of degrading the character of Jesus by representing him as a man, indicate with sufficient clearness the falsehood of our theology." To replace outmoded ideas, Emerson proposed a new task for Christian ministry: "It is the office of a true teacher to show us that God is, not was; that he speaketh, not spake. The true Christianity—

a faith like Christ's in the *infinitude of man*—is lost" (emphasis in original). Emerson plaintively asked, "In how many churches, and by how many prophets, tell me, is man made sensible that he is an infinite soul; that the earth and heavens are passing into his mind; that he is drinking for ever the soul of God?" Emerson believed all people are as inspired as those who authored the books of the Bible and that they need only look within themselves to find truth.[12]

Hodge categorized Emerson's address as "the first fruits of transcendentalism in our country." Transcendentalism originated in New England as a religious, philosophical, and literary movement in the early nineteenth century. It made a significant impact on the intellectual milieu in New England by its opposition to traditional Christian doctrine and especially the Unitarianism taught at Harvard Divinity School. Ironically, Hodge believed the new philosophy rendered the previous dangers of Unitarianism minuscule in comparison. In perhaps the only instance in which Hodge spoke positively of Unitarianism, he declared that despite rejecting the Trinity, Unitarians at least affirmed belief in a personal, transcendent God. Hodge opposed transcendentalism because of its roots in German idealism, which denied basic tenets of Common Sense Realism. Hodge, therefore, gleefully reported that Emerson's address was "offensive to the authorities of the university." A Harvard Unitarian professor attacked the address. In addition, one no less prominent than Henry Ware Jr. disputed Emerson from the pulpit in a sermon, "The Personality of God." Ware's pedigree suited Hodge's purpose perfectly. Not only was he professor of pulpit eloquence at Harvard, he was also the son of Henry Ware, whose election as the Hollis Professor of Divinity in 1805 had signaled Harvard's turning to Unitarianism away from Trinitarianism. To add insult to injury to Emerson's address, Hodge reported that members of the Harvard Divinity School published Ware's attack of Emerson's address shortly thereafter.[13]

Despite initial opposition, such as Hodge's journal article, Emerson promulgated his philosophy further through a series of lectures that received encouragement from French philosopher and educator Victor Cousin. Hodge cited a letter in which Cousin informed Emerson that he would "observe the progress of philosophy in America" and that he hoped that another book he intended to publish would "be useful to America." Hodge stated that although he had read Cousin's works on psychology and history of philosophy when they first appeared, he postponed commenting on them. "We kept silence because we did not wish in any degree to draw public attention to them until evidence was afforded that they were read." Emerson's address therefore confirmed that they had received a hearing. Hodge denounced Cousin's transcendentalism with the ultimate put-down that it was secondhand goods: "if we must have a transatlantic philosophy, we desire to have it in its native robustness and freshness. We do not wish to have it through the medium of French declaimers, or of the French language, than which no tongue is less fit to convey the endless distinctions of the German. We wish to have it before it has undergone two or three transmutations; not from subalterns but from masters." Given the supposedly rarefied air of scholarly discourse, Hodge could hardly have chosen more demeaning terminology for Cousin's position and influence among intellectual elites. German philosophy had already been successfully refuted by "the best men in the country of its origin." The last thing America needed, sniffed Hodge, was a "philosophy which shall conduct our young scholars into the high road to Atheism." More important than his put-down of Cousin, Hodge feared that pantheism would not stop in its advance by infiltrating only Harvard. He worried that New School ideas might not be the only force for Presbyterians to face: "the time may not be far off, when some new Emerson shall preach Pantheism under the banner of a self-styled Calvinism." The mentality of synthesizing Christianity with whatever appeared next in the flow of ideas might eventually affect even the citadels of Reformed thought.[14]

Hodge concluded his review by situating transcendentalism in the broader context of American religious history. He considered the latest developments in New England as more threatening to American theology than previous unorthodox religious beliefs. Although he had long since deplored Unitarianism—the most recent expression of Socinianism and its predecessor Arianism—and rationalistic deism, he unexpectedly deemed both preferable to "the German insanity," which would lead young scholars astray from orthodoxy. In Hodge's opinion, therefore, German philosophy in its pantheistic form proved totally incompatible with the Christian gospel. Its denial of a personal God in favor of vague expressions that failed to distinguish between the Creator and his creation rendered it diametrically opposed to Christian theology. As for how America should ward off the danger posed by German pantheism, Hodge had a ready answer—continue in the "mode of philosophizing which has for several generations prevailed among our British ancestors [Scottish philosophy]." Simply stated, Hodge advocated the continuation of the American and British mind.[15]

In 1846 Hodge reviewed the state of German scholarship in yet another article, "Religious State of Germany." In the former article on Emerson and Cousin, he had focused on radical pantheist views. In this review he concentrated on the diversity of parties within German churches and on controversies between evangelical confessionalists and their opponents over the importance of doctrine and clergy's faithfulness to the Augsburg Confession.[16]

He praised Hengstenberg and his journal *Evangelische Kirchen-Zeitung* for holding fast to conservative views in the face of opposition. Much as Hodge and his Old School colleagues resisted theological innovations in American Presbyterianism, Hengstenberg bemoaned the dearth of sound doctrine in liberal scholarship and its negative influence on German clergy. He insisted that Protestant ministers affirm the central tenets of the Augsburg Confession of 1528, the primary confession of the Lutheran church and one of the founding documents of the Reformation. He lamented the tendency of nineteenth-century scholars to divert from and belittle what had long been the standard of Lutheran orthodoxy. Hodge utilized Hengstenberg's criticism of the German situation to further his own agenda of maintaining Reformed orthodoxy in America. Citing the recurring theme in his reviews, Hodge feared the effect that pantheistic thinking, radical biblical criticism, and disavowing standards governing ministerial communion would have as books became more accessible to a wider audience. "So long as this pantheism is confined to books, which few would read, and still fewer understand, the evil might be bourne [*sic*]. But when it came to be popularized and adopted by pastors in their addresses to the people, it was felt that such men ought no longer to be tolerated in a Christian church." Unorthodox thinking might not have as baneful an effect on the church if it remained isolated within the scholarly community. Hodge, however, feared that theological students and pastors who were exposed to these ideas in their ministerial training would inevitably end up preaching them from their pulpits.[17]

To illustrate the various degrees of accessibility of German writings to the wider public, Hodge noted the disparity between the vagueness of the pantheists and the clarity of those who candidly denied historic biblical truths. He contrasted the "impenetrable system" of Hegel with David Friedrich Strauss's "fluent tongue." Whereas Hegel's writings proved daunting to even the most erudite among German scholars, Strauss's frank denial of biblical content was within reach of every reader. German scholars boldly denounced orthodox views. Hodge referred to another scholar who stated bluntly that it was a sin and foolishness to pretend that the Augsburg Confession actually edified people. The same person "ridiculed the blood of the atonement and confession of sin read every Sabbath from the altar and profanely declared 'We do not fear the wrath of God, and seek no means of propitiation.'" Confronted with such radical denials, especially by pastors, evangelicals such as Hengstenberg called for concerted action. They contended that those who espoused the doctrines of the "Friends of Light" (the most radical group within the church) had actually put themselves outside the boundary of the church. Thus one evangelical protest stated that "we can no longer regard as rightful ministers of this church . . . [those] who in recent times [several names cited] . . . partly in public assemblies, and partly through the press reject the Bible as divine revelation, and the only source and rule of our faith; who boldly deny the divinity of our blessed Lord and Saviour Jesus Christ, and renounce the fundamental doctrines of our evangelical church." Hodge lauded the fact that "such declarations have been signed by upward of a thousand clergymen," which indicated that evangelicalism had experienced somewhat of a resurgence as a result of Hengstenberg's leadership.[18]

Hodge proceeded to distinguish four factions within the German religious context. The evangelical party, led by Hengstenberg, sought to make subscription to the Augsburg Confession a requirement of ministerial communion. Such a requirement paralleled Old Schoolers' insistence on subscription to the Westminster Confession as a prerequisite to Presbyterian ministry. The middle bloc, consisting of Schleiermacher's followers, was divided into two parties. The first was composed of "those who by his influence were brought to Christ, and then from Him, the only true Master, learned the truth." By this statement Hodge at least acknowledged, as colleagues such as Tholuck had years earlier, that some benefits had resulted from Schleiermacher's Christocentrism. The other group associated with Schleiermacher, however, consisted of "mere disciples, who are as anxious to maintain the wood, hay and stubble of their master's system, as the truth which it contains." The gap separating evangelicals and others resulted from the "great latitude . . . allowed in Germany in receiving the symbols of the church." At the other extreme from the evangelicals, the third party called the "Friends of Light" favored radical diversions from traditional doctrine that made them easy targets of Hengstenberg's attacks. Hodge used the term *infidelity* throughout the article to characterize pastors who recited the creeds but did not hold to their traditional interpretation.[19]

The opponents of Hengstenberg, however, refused to be denied, as they launched a counterattack that garnered support from public figures and church authorities alike "to curtail or destroy his influence." A party composed primarily of Schleiermacher's disciples signed a protest against Hengstenberg's journal. Among other allegations, they charged that the journal "stiffly [insisted] on that view of Christianity, which has been inherited from the beginning of the reformation"; that it demanded "slavish adherence to the letter of the Augsburg confession"; and that it made the authority of the Augsburg Confession similar to the pope's demanding acceptance of Catholic dogma. To allegations that his journal aggressively attacked the other parties, Hengstenberg replied that he had always respected Schleiermacher. As a matter of fact, he had penned an article against Schleiermacher only after being provoked by a vicious attack in which he thundered against the evangelicals: "The ground is heaving beneath our feet, and miserable worms are crawling out from religious crevices, who regard all speculation, beyond the circumvallation of the ancient letter [the Bible], as satanic." Hengstenberg believed this remark grounds for a response.[20]

Evangelicals justified their protest further by affirming that the confessionalism they sought merely continued what the church had always required of its ministers: "the church party strive[s] for nothing more than to have it acknowledged that no man should be a minister in the church who does not receive the fundamental articles of the faith." Hengstenberg, for example, took umbrage at the comparison of confessional allegiance to Catholics' adherence to papal decrees. Hodge argued for Hengstenberg's respect for biblical authority: "[Hengstenberg] does not maintain that he arrived at his present conviction fortuitously, without the aid of the church, her confession and especially her hymns. He refers with gratitude to what he owes to the Augsburg Confession, when it came to him, in the time of his awakening faith, as a guide through the labyrinth of various and apparently conflicting views which his unassisted study of the Bible had not enabled him to master; and with no less gratitude to the strength derived from the hymns of the church in times of temptation and conflict." Evangelicals' allegiance to confessional orthodoxy bore no resemblance to bowing to an ecclesiastical system such as Catholicism. Instead, by stating evangelical doctrine, Hengstenberg only upheld principles from the Protestant Reformation. He cited Luther's answer to Desiderius Erasmus when the latter questioned the necessity of doctrinal subscription. Charges regarding disturbances over doctrine, said Luther, should be leveled not at those who "adhere to God's word but to those who oppose it." Christ's deity, virgin birth, resurrection, and ascension constituted fundamental truths that could not be compromised. By rejecting them, liberals compromised the gospel itself.[21]

Schleiermacher's divergence from traditional doctrine had an apologetic goal. The climate of opinion of the Enlightenment, especially Kant's severe recasting of knowledge as limited to the phenomenal realm and religion to the moral realm, demanded a reconstrual of the nature of religion. Instead of religion as rational as manifested by doctrinal belief or religion as moral as expressed in the will, Schleiermacher relegated religion to the entirely separate realm of intuition or feeling. Hodge positioned Schleiermacher at a crucial juncture in the history of ideas: he "came on the stage [when] the whole sphere of knowledge was filled with error. Into that sphere religion could not enter and live." Religion in general and Christianity in particular could not survive under these conceptions. Because of attacks on its truth claims, Christianity found itself vulnerable to oral and written assault from biblical critics and theological innovators who denied key biblical doctrines. The situation demanded a new apologetic, which Schleiermacher deftly adapted from Germany's Romantic movement. He "sought for [Christianity] a refuge in the dark chamber of feeling, and nobly laboured to guard it from all assaults." While saving religion from the errors of rationalism was laudable as a goal, Schleiermacher's definition of religion as feeling changed Christianity from resting on the objective truth of the gospel to resting on the subjective experience of the believer. Hodge summarized the result: "This theory . . . performed the welcome service of getting rid at one stroke of confessions of faith and of leaving an open field for individual development." Such a method separated what in Hodge's opinion should always remain conjoined—the object of faith and the experience of faith itself. Schleiermacher's view sundered that relation. Without the foundation of objectively true and fixed doctrine, the church could make no progress. Because the true basis of religion was feeling, doctrine was "merely the imperfect, and necessarily faulty form in which that feeling expresses itself." In Schleiermacher's view, correct feelings, not correct doctrine, determined the legitimacy of any religion.[22]

Schleiermacher believed such a reconstrual of religion necessary for Christianity to progress against the onslaught of modern thought. Confessionalists such as Hengstenberg and Hodge were cast as enemies of progress for not participating in efforts to meet the challenges of new movements, such as Romanticism. Only as Christianity accommodated to cultural change could the church hope to survive in the nineteenth century. Hodge countered with exactly the opposite strategy: the church must progress, but not in the way that Schleiermacher and other moderns proposed. Genuine progress in Christianity did not rest on the fresh experiences of each generation of believers alone, though Hodge in his piety left considerable room for the role of experience. Piety must rest on something firm. Progress in Christianity could not occur on Schleiermacher's terms, for whoever based religion on individual experience could not make progress. Hodge summarized, "Progress in any science is possible only because one man stands on the shoulders of those before him. He who rejects the acquisitions of former ages [the historical confessions], and insists on beginning everything anew, must always be at the beginning. And he who regards all the labour of the church for eighteen hundred years as establishing nothing is just where Hermas[23] was in the first century. If he denies the possibility of fixed doctrine conformed to truth, if doctrine in its very nature is the transient form of feeling, the flower which to-day is, and to-morrow is cast into the oven, he makes progress an impossibility."[24]

Hodge's treatment of German scholarship thus followed the same pattern as his assessment of the Oxford movement. In his view, what was coming out of Germany had not improved since his two-year stint almost forty years previously. The theological and biblical perspectives had become even more liberal and more widespread in the meantime. Since German thinking was always more progressive, representing the vanguard of modern thought, Hodge believed that clear and forthright assessments needed to be made lest it infiltrate American thinking. To mix a metaphor, if the very fortress of the Reformation could be moved from its firm foundation, Hodge determined to see to it that radical scholarship would not move evangelical thought in America from its moorings.

31

Revisiting an Old Friend

Of all of Charles Hodge's evaluations of European scholarship in the *PR*, the most intriguing review examines Augustus Neander's *History of the Planting and Training of the Christian Church by the Apostles*. The review deserves special attention because of the number of factors influencing Hodge's estimation of the book. Foremost, the book in question was written by one of his closest friends during his 1826–28 visit to Europe.[1] Second only to his friendship with August Tholuck, his relations with Ludwig and Otto von Gerlach and Neander remained the most intimate and congenial of all the acquaintances Hodge made in Germany. Even though these men belonged to the mediating party in theological scholarship, Hodge found a common evangelical piety central to maintaining their bond as they stood their ground against the more radical scholars. Hodge also acknowledged the high level of scholarship exhibited in Neander's work. His appreciation of their friendship and common commitment to Christian piety shines through as he calls attention to the strengths of Neander's detailed exploration of New Testament material.

The nuances of Hodge's review, however, reflect changes that had occurred since the European visit. Hodge's own field of study had shifted from biblical languages to systematic theology. As a systematic theologian, Hodge now confronted a more delicate situation resulting from differences in their respective theological milieus. Biblical studies and systematics had each developed its own autonomy in Europe following the Enlightenment model of scholarship. Scholars such as Neander came under no compunction to relate their findings to confessional standards. This occasioned for Hodge a difficulty in his efforts to locate Neander's position in the broad spectrum of nineteenth-century theological discourse. His friend's study probed biblical material and specifically biblical history. Though not a historian, Hodge believed that all topics of Christian studies should coalesce when scholars conducted research in their respective fields. Thus, whether pursuing biblical, historical, or theological topics, scholars in their conclusions should exhibit a unity of truth consistent with confessional statements. Hodge struggled painfully to remain positive about the work of one of his closest allies who refused to be identified with radically new ideas. Yet because Neander's views occupied a mediating position, they were not fully consistent with orthodox confessions of either the Lutheran or Calvinist mold. Hodge struck a somewhat moderate pose in his review—praising the brilliance and highest level of research while expressing strong reservations about the method and conclusions of Neander's book.

Throughout the almost thirty-page review, Hodge walked a fine line between extolling the excellence of scholarship underlying Neander's presentation and identifying weaknesses in method, precision of expression, and subsequent conclusions. He began with an outline of Neander's education and accomplishments. Converted from Judaism, he had studied under prestigious teachers and eventually taught at the universities at Halle and Berlin. Hodge noted Neander's monographs on Bernard of Clairvaux, the Gnostics, and Chrysostom as well as lectures on theology. In addition, Hodge applauded his friend's "childlike simplicity" in his private life and that "his days and nights are spent in a devotion to profound study, such as would appal [*sic*] an American scholar." Despite these factors, which endeared the author to Hodge, he voiced profound frustration in pinpointing Neander's position theologically. He made several passes in his attempt to position Neander's views. On the one hand, Neander was "a friend of the gospel and an opposer to Neology." He flatly opposed deism, which occupied one end of the theological continuum, while expressing "repugnance and horror" at the "high-flying, transcendental, visionary, arrogant, pantheistic philosophists." As for where he had stood among his associates during Hodge's studies in Europe, Hodge used Tholuck as a reference point. Neander would "be at a place more remote from our own ground." Finally, he placed Neander between the "blunt negations of rationalism, and the positive daring of Hengstenberg." The position of Ernst Wilhelm Hengstenberg, as leader of German evangelicals, of course most closely resembled Hodge's own confessional position.[2]

Most significantly, Hodge claimed that Neander's method in studying the New Testament negatively affected his scholarly conclusions. In Hodge's opinion, Neander was "little concerned to reconcile apparent discrepancies in the New Testament teaching, by any reference to an analogy of faith." By "analogy of faith" Hodge meant that Scripture was to be interpreted by itself; one did not need to turn to something external. Any one passage of the Bible was to be interpreted by the whole of Scripture. Lack of concern in exhibiting the unity of truth in the New Testament became evident in Neander's interpretation of historical facts. Princetonians placed great store in biblical facts and how they served as indispensable fodder for systematic theology. Even though Neander's text surveyed the apostolic material historically, since God providentially directed historical events and inspired the accounts of those events, Hodge believed that his conclusions should demonstrate their compatibility with some identifiable creed, confession, or tradition. Neander showed little inclination to interpret biblical content within any known doctrinal system.[3]

To take an obvious example, Hodge knew from their many conversations that Neander's favorite doctrine—Hodge called it his "darling tenet"—was the universal priesthood of believers. He made this key element in Martin Luther's theology a touchstone in all his writings. Yet Neander failed to make the connection between this biblical principle and any historical tradition. He gave the impression that "no established system, philosophical or theological," underlay his scholarship. Hodge could not help but contrast Neander's method with his own: "Thus zealous for spiritual rather than visible religion, for piety rather than logical precision, and for generals rather than particulars, it is not surprising that Neander should consider venial the aberrations of errorists and even of heretics, and that his own statements should contain many things which strike us, of a more rigid school, as perilously latitudinarian." His characterization of his own position as "rigid" illustrates that Hodge did all in his power at the outset of the review to be as congenial as possible.[4]

Having acknowledged the distance between Neander and himself, Hodge then fleshed out the implications of their differences. Neander's treatment of facts illustrated the peril of failing to identify his findings with any theological or philosophical system. Hodge, as did his colleagues at Princeton, loved facts as integral to their adherence to the Westminster Standards and the tenets of Scottish philosophy. Facts as objective in nature were indispensable not only for defending biblical truth, but as the ontological foundation for dogmatic theology. Thus Hodge could only lament, "There is no writer known to us in whom the disposition to methodize particulars, and round off a theory, is more apparent." He continued, "Though a historian, it is remarkable that he seems never content with the bare statement of an event. His histories are not objective. A fact—as a fact—is nothing to him. No point of a narrative is valued, until it can be brought into some curve which he hastens to determine." Thus, when Neander explored texts, he rendered equal attention to heretical views as to orthodox systems. "Each creed is *totus teres atque rotundus* [altogether rounded and circular]." Though Hodge did not explicitly say so, Neander's failure to identify his interpretation of apostolic teaching left one with the impression that his interpretation verged on being the autonomous conclusion of Neander himself. While Hodge found biblical exposition and hermeneutics in the Princeton tradition readily compatible with classic creeds and confessions, he was pained to see his friend's inability or unwillingness to labor under the same or at least similar assumptions. Hodge thought every biblical scholar, historian, and theologian should identify his views with some identifiable tradition or system.[5]

Hodge drew the consequence of his friend's historical method: "[Neander] gives us materials for a conclusion, rather than the conclusion itself." Neander did not reach the conclusion that the materials warranted. Rather than state or imply a final truth on the various subjects studied, the matter in question remained more or less open. Neander's book did not blatantly fall outside the boundaries of orthodoxy. In fact, Hodge praised the book for being "as a whole . . . a learned, candid and truly fascinating book. It throws new light on an old subject. It takes us over a familiar but inexhaustible field, with a new guide of incomparable abilities." Such a method proved totally compatible with German scholarship as representative of the Berlin method of theological education. It exhibited originality and brilliance throughout. But it also displayed the Berlin method as produced by an Enlightenment institution. The Berlin model treated theological truth as always developing. By rejecting the notion of final truth, theology operated under the same epistemological principle as all other disciplines in the university's curriculum. The scholarship should exhibit *Wissenschaft*—scientific research. By this method all topics remained open to correction and subject to further development. Hodge could not have expressed Neander's scholarship any more clearly than he did in the following statement: "His [Neander's] motto is *free development*. It seems to be a part of his nature, to have no capacity for seeing anything in insulation. All objects of his mind are *in fluxu*. He regards every fact as a transition-point from one state of things to another." Hodge's comments demonstrate his concern about how Neander's contribution as a biblical scholar would prove compatible with traditional systematic theology as opposed to the contributions it might offer to biblical theology.[6]

Hodge then examined the shortcomings of Neander's treatment resulting from the Enlightenment method. While his scholarship did not manifest radical ideas characteristic of the rising liberalism, it did demonstrate "the German tendency to tamper with inspired statements." He cited Neander's treatment of Pentecost in Acts 2, Peter's vision at Joppa, and Paul's Damascas road conversion as examples. While Hodge believed his friend to be a supernaturalist, Neander unexpectedly attempted "to explain the wonderful phenomena [the apostles' speaking in tongues, Peter's vision, and Paul's conversion] on psychological principles." This interpretation in principle "shut out miracles, in whole or in part." The supposed miracles of the book of Acts recorded not objective supernatural phenomena but the "inward mental state" of the apostles and the "inward transaction in Paul's mind." While undoubtedly biblical characters' internal experiences were profoundly affected, Hodge would insist that the events in question were ontologically objective in nature and not just products of the apostles' minds.[7]

Neander's treatment of theological topics fared no better in Hodge's opinion. Instead of conclusions that might engender a clear, unified system of theology, Neander's treatment of apostolic epistles manifested what Hodge found most troubling in Schleiermacher's preaching—a vagueness and lack of precision. Many great doctrines, he said, are "shadowed here:—but only shadowed. We attempt to seize the definite logical assertion, and it eludes our grasp. The mind of the author seems incapable of viewing any one truth with a clear bounding demarcation. . . . Familiar ideas meet us at every step, but so hazy is the medium, that we dare not assure ourselves of the recognition. One who had learned them previously might have his knowledge refreshed here; but he could not learn them here for the first time, with any distinctness." Hodge longed to see the names of Luther, Calvin, and even Socinus and Arminius and their respective interpretations of the biblical passages, but they did not appear. Neander's method, Hodge concluded, "leads him to understate the plain significance of the text."[8]

Hodge's rather harsh criticism of Neander reveals the differences between the emerging discipline of biblical theology in Germany in which scholars attempted to distance themselves from the strictures of traditional dogmatics. Hodge readily acknowledged that Neander steered clear of heretical opinion. While Neander did not explicitly express Arian conclusions, Hodge wished that Neander would show himself more explicitly an Athanasian! Hodge can be faulted for demanding that Neander's work approximate a systematic theology because he failed to use traditional terms such as *Trinity* and *hypostatic union* to affirm the full deity and humanity of Christ. After all, these terms did not appear in church history until after the period under

Neander's examination. Hodge acknowledged that he placed severe demands on Neander. He did so by comparing his friend's work with that of Protestant scholastics such as Francis Turretin, whose work Hodge used as a text in his Princeton courses. Hodge readily admitted a "thousand faults" of men like Turretin: "they are stiff, they are prolix, they are technical, they are intolerant and austere, they are scholastic in their distinctions, but they have one great merit—they always let us know what they mean." He praised the "intellectual habitude" of men such as Turretin, Richard Baxter, Jonathan Edwards, and William Paley, all of whom avoided the deficiencies of German scholarship and exemplified the virtues of the British and American minds.[9]

Hodge concluded the review rather tersely by justifying his public criticism of his friend's work. He repeated his admiration of Neander's scholarship and reminded his readers that he never opened a work by the distinguished German without benefiting from its content. His respect for Neander, however, could not forestall a compulsion to review the book and its flaws. Hodge professed that he wrote for only one reason: the book appeared in print in translation and thus was easily available to American students and pastors. As long as Neander's work remained inaccessible to the American public because of its availability only in German, Hodge had felt no compunction to review it. But, he continued, "now that it has appeared in a translation, from the press of a popular and enterprising publisher, we have seen no way to escape from our conviction." Hodge's concern stemmed from his zeal to maintain theological orthodoxy as the basis for ministerial training in America. He feared the negative effect that Neander's scholarship might have on American pastoral education. As in the case of the Oxford movement's potential harmful effect on American Episcopalians and a similar injurious outcome of transcendentalism on Harvard's ministerial students, Hodge also foresaw the possible deleterious consequences of Neander's work on students and pastors within his own denomination. Therefore, though conflicted about whether to remain silent or to subject Neander's work to criticism, the appearance of Neander's history in English prompted him to engage the work critically.[10]

PART 6

Mature Presbyterian Theologian

The 1860s and 1870s witnessed Charles Hodge's mature years in service to the seminary, the Presbyterian church, and the wider evangelical community. His denomination had been divided since the schism of 1837, and the country endured the devastations of the Civil War from 1860 to 1865. Hodge grieved over both and addressed each schism with heartfelt opinions. Utilizing the journal he had begun while still in his twenties, he expressed his deep convictions on both reunions and their consequences. He produced his theological magnum opus—his three-volume *ST*—and added to his considerable reputation as a controversialist by addressing the greatest scientific issue of the nineteenth century: biological evolution. His lifelong attraction to science and its advancements did not deter him from presciently recognizing the inherent dangers of applying scientific method beyond its appropriate boundaries. Finally, he celebrated the zenith of his academic career, his jubilee in 1873. These contributions rounded out Hodge's diverse service to American ecclesiastical and intellectual life.

32

A Nation and Church Divided and Reunited

Debate over the spirituality of the church mentioned in chapter 3 surfaced again at the 1860 and 1861 General Assemblies. While the former controversy involved Northern Old Schoolers versus Southern Old Schoolers, disputes in the 1860s pitted Northern Old Schoolers against each other. Whereas fissure had developed in the ranks between Philadelphia and Princeton in 1837 over theological tolerance and its consequences, division in the 1860s entailed the spirituality of the church, patriotism, and ministerial communion. In 1861 Hodge articulated in its most categorically accurate form the doctrine over which he and James Henley Thornwell had differed earlier.[1] It occurred in the context of perhaps the most contested issue within American Presbyterian history since the Adopting Act of 1729—political and ecclesiastical loyalty. When the Old School Assembly convened in Philadelphia on April 12, 1861, hostilities had already erupted at Fort Sumter, South Carolina. Because of secession of Southern states, the number of delegates from the South was greatly diminished. The Old School had remained together since the 1837 schism despite deep differences over slavery. Hodge expressed the view of most Northern Old Schoolers, who strongly disapproved of the South's rebellion, calling it unjustified. He wrote in the April 1861 edition of the *PR* that division in the country should not intrude into the church. Despite political differences, the church should maintain its spiritual unity. "We are prepared to say, that notwithstanding this deplorable state of things, we are bound to hold together as a church, because the grounds of difference, important as they are, do not relate to the divinely appointed terms of Christian or ministerial communion."[2]

Hodge's foreboding notwithstanding, the issue of unity—ecclesiastical and political—erupted at the assembly and catapulted the denomination to the center of national attention. On May 18 Gardiner Spring, pastor of New York's Brick Church and son of a Revolutionary officer, called for a day of fasting and prayer in response to the recent outbreak of war. He proposed a committee "to inquire into the expediency of making some expression of their devotion to the Union of these States, and their loyalty to the Government."[3] Hodge, sensing that the tide of Northern patriotism would divide the Old School church, attempted to defuse the issue that unleashed a fierce debate over whether the church should declare fidelity to a particular government a requirement of ministerial communion. He led the faction that proposed an alternative expression of patriotism that would not require ministers to take an oath of allegiance and would therefore not result in Southern defection from the church. An intense five-day marathon of debate punctuated with applause from the crowded church followed. Heated exchanges over resolutions and counter-resolutions captured the attention not only of the media but also of the White House. Telegrams flowed in and out of the assembly over the advisability of the church's declaration of political loyalty. Hodge reported that a member of the President's Cabinet had said, "The best you [referring to the Old School assembly] can do for the union is to keep unbroken the unity of your Church."[4]

The telegrams in support of Hodge's claim, presented to an unbelieving Spring, could not impede the Northern patriotic groundswell. Delegates in the overheated political atmosphere felt pressure from their presbyteries to make a pronouncement on the part of the denomination. Though Spring's initial proposal was defeated by a majority report probably written by Hodge, the minority report on the resolution carried on the floor of the assembly. It stated: "That this General Assembly, in the spirit of that Christian patriotism which the Scriptures enjoin, and which has always characterized this church, do hereby acknowledge and declare our obligation to promote and perpetuate, so far as in us lies, the integrity of these United States, and to strengthen, uphold, and encourage the Federal Government in the exercise of all its functions under our noble Constitution." On this issue the church proved to be as divided as the rest of the country. A resounding vote, yet one reflecting the absence of Southern delegates to the assembly, passed the resolution 156–66. The only forces pleased with the outcome were New School Presbyterians.[5]

Hodge and several others issued a protest, objecting vigorously to the resolution while affirming the spiritual task of the church: "We, the undersigned, respectfully protest against the action of the General Assembly in adopting the minority report of the Committee on the State of the Country. We make this protest, not because we do not acknowledge loyalty to our country to be moral and religious duty, according to the word of God, which requires us to be subject to the powers that be; nor because we deny the right of the Assembly to enjoin that and all other like duties on the ministers and churches under its care; but because we deny the right of the General Assembly to decide the political question, to what government the allegiance of Presbyterians, as citizens, is due, and its right to make that decision a condition of membership in our church." It continued by stating an obvious view that the resolution decided a political issue that divided the country. Many Presbyterians believed that they owed their primary allegiance to states and that in such circumstances the assembly "pronounces or assumes a particular interpretation of the Constitution. This is a matter clearly beyond the jurisdiction of the Assembly."[6]

Hodge equated the inappropriateness of this resolution to one that would require the singing of "The Star-Spangled Banner" at the Lord's Supper! It represented a departure from General Assembly precedence, which in the past had refused to make anything a condition of ministerial fellowship other than what Scripture or the Westminster Standards required. Just as the denomination had refused to make alcohol consumption and slaveholding a matter of discipline, it should maintain its integrity by resisting the temptation to speak on such a matter not defined or commanded by the Bible. The unity of the church hung in the balance, especially since Southern members of the Old School did not attend the assembly. Spring's resolutions would "diminish the resources of the church . . . [and] greatly weaken its power for good and expose it to the danger of being carried away more and more from its true principles by a worldly or fanatical spirit."[7]

Opponents of Hodge's protest issued a strident, point-by-point response. Yet Hodge remained unconvinced. He reminded delegates that two years previously the assembly had spoken out against an extreme example when advocates of the church's spirituality argued that the church could not address the issue of colonization of blacks. Since the 1860 General Assembly had passed a resolution on the church's spirituality, Hodge concluded, "As this resolution was unanimously adopted, we ought to be of one mind as to the principle, however we may differ in its application." The church must teach the duty of submission to powers of government, but as in innumerable examples regarding royal succession throughout European history, the church had no authority deciding such matters. Closer to home, during the struggle for American independence, the Church of England had not issued a mandate of loyalty to King George: "Had any such attempt been made, the American Presbyterians would doubtless have said that the church had exceeded its powers, that it was not her province to decide on the political questions at issue, that we must be allowed to determine those matters for ourselves on our responsibility to God." Aghast at the assembly's action, though a thoroughgoing patriot, writing on many occasions on the state of the country, Hodge firmly believed that the church had overstepped its bounds.[8]

As subsequent events unfolded, no one exceeded Charles Hodge in his despair over the crisis of the Civil War and his conviction of the paramount importance that the states remain united. He believed in the moral legitimacy of the federal government's responsibility to restore that union. But the responsibility of private conviction was not the same as the corporate responsibility of the General Assembly. "If the doctrine of secession is the true, then the Presbyterians in South Carolina are bound to renounce allegiance to the Federal Government. If it is wrong, they are in rebellion, and may, and ought to be treated accordingly by the state, but not by the church." As in his previous debates with Thornwell, he argued that whenever a matter is moral, the church must address it. On the other hand, whenever "the thing is in its own nature indifferent, *so far as the church is concerned*, [a person] may act according to his conscience." Thus a secessionist may be punished legally by the state and be held morally guilty by God, but the church may not discipline him. Therefore, although Hodge, an ardent patriot, personally felt very strongly about the necessity of maintaining the union, the assembly had no right to compel Old School Southerners to change their political loyalty. The Old School church would suffer the consequences of loss of members and prestige because of its passage of the Spring resolutions. The major figures who benefited from their passage were New Schoolers, who "could not repress their joy that our time for separations and disaster had come."[9]

Hodge foresaw the consequences of the Spring resolutions for the Old School church. In the months following the assembly, forty-seven Southerners broke their ties with the Northern church, and in December 1861 they formed the General Assembly of the Presbyterian Church in the Confederate States. The two factions would not unite again until over a century later.

If Hodge was disappointed by the action of the General Assembly at the outset of the Civil War, he was equally dismayed by the Northern church's treatment of the Southern church at the war's conclusion. The 1865 assembly met in Pittsburgh inflamed with a spirit of retribution not only for the past conflict but also for President Abraham Lincoln's assassination a month before.[10] The majority determined to impose severe sanctions on Southern pastors and churches as prerequisite for readmission into the denomination. They branded secession "an atrocious rebellion against the government of the United States, for the perpetuation of slavery" and the withdrawal of the churches in 1861 "a schism." Restoration of pastors and churches would be granted only after they "give evidence of repentance for their sin and renounce their error." Pastors must be examined as to whether they held slavery to be a "Divine institution" or "an ordinance of God." In addition, the assembly instructed the Board of Domestic Missions to treat the South as a missionary territory. These measures became known as the "Pittsburgh orders."[11]

Although he did not attend the assembly, and the Pittsburgh orders eventually became a dead letter, Hodge lodged a strong criticism in his annual summary similar to what he wrote regarding the Spring resolutions. In both instances the church court had overstepped its bounds. In requiring repentance and confession over slavery and secession, the church had incorrectly intruded into political affairs and thus violated its spiritual task. He also probed what had inclined the church to make such a serious mistake. Just as he had argued in his *CHPC* that group psychological excitements rendered the awakenings no longer religious in nature, so he contended that the assembly had been animated by popular political sentiments rather than legitimate ecclesiastical principle. He wrote, "In all popular assemblies, in times of public agitation, we may expect violent language and extreme measures." Such outbreaks of strong patriotic feelings infected all denominations, not just Presbyterians. But the existence of such widespread phenomena did not justify the extreme measures levied against the South. With pride Hodge claimed that "an axiom of our Presbyterianism [is] that the General Assembly can make no law to bind the conscience." That is, it could not add to or detract from "the constitutional terms of ministerial or Christian fellowship." If the assembly could proscribe slavery and demand political loyalty, it could also "make their deliverances on temperance, colonization, or any other subject." By issuing the Pittsburgh orders, the assembly had clearly contravened its own precedents. As in the case of the Spring resolutions, the Pittsburgh orders therefore violated a prized Presbyterian principle. The orders illegally presumed to bind man's conscience. Hodge concluded: "We are bound by our ordination vows to promote the peace and unity of the church, to endeavour to bring into harmony and Christian fellowship, both external and inward, all who agree with us in the adoption of the same faith and discipline . . . Whatever therefore tends to alienation and division is contrary to the spirit of the gospel. On this ground we are persuaded a very general objection to the action of the Assembly on the state of the country will be entertained, as well as very profound regret."[12]

While few of his contemporaries could compete with Hodge's patriotism as well as his ecclesiastical allegiance, he maintained a clear distinction between patriotic loyalty and religious commitment. Both entailed convictions that powerfully motivated behavior in two prominent realms of human existence. By insisting that the two remain separate, Hodge did not create a dualism between the two as if they constituted antagonists for human loyalties. Consistent with much of the Reformed tradition, Hodge viewed church and state as institutions created by God to order human affairs in their respective realms. Each contributed good to the betterment of mankind. Each, however, could also intrude wrongly into the other's sphere of influence. In controversies over major issues in his denomination, such as these two in 1861 and 1865, Hodge more frequently than not bested those who took up opposing positions. In these two instances, therefore, he found himself at odds with the majority of his fellow Presbyterians. As in disputes with opponents outside Presbyterianism, Hodge used his journal to articulate his views in detail.

In one other major controversy within his denomination over reunion, Hodge also found himself in the minority, and in this case a very small one. While the division of the two Old School Presbyterian churches was not healed, in the 1860s a movement for the reunion of the Old and New Schools in the North gained momentum. In 1862 the Old School made an unexpected overture when the General Assembly ended its twenty-five-year policy of nonrecognition of the New School by proposing an exchange of delegates to explore bringing an end to the schism. By the middle of the nineteenth century, matters that had originally precipitated schism no longer existed: revivalism, slavery, the Plan of Union, differences in form of government, and cooperation with voluntary societies. A single yet decisive question, however, remained in many Old Schoolers' minds, including Hodge's—theological differences between the two factions. Even on that front, however, an effort by the New School to substantiate its orthodoxy after the excision and schism lessened the antagonism between the two groups. In August 1837, members of the New School met in Auburn, New York to answer categorically Old School charges of doctrinal laxity. The Auburn Declaration resulted from the meeting. The framers of the document intended to state the "true doctrines" of the New Schoolers over against the "errors" charged against them in the "Old School Testimony and Memorial" of that year. The declaration listed sixteen alleged errors and refuted each point by point by stating the "true doctrine" actually affirmed by New Schoolers. The declaration established an orthodox theological framework that New Schoolers would exploit to their advantage as the movement gained steam for reunion.[13]

Parties weighed in on the issue, ranging from those fervently favoring reunion to those adamantly opposed. Hodge sided with the latter. Negotiations between the Old and New School progressed in the mid-1860s. The assemblies of 1866, both of which met in St. Louis, formed committees to pursue how to manage such an undertaking. Though the majority clearly considered reunion in the best interest of the two churches, Hodge remained opposed. His son explained that his father's hesitancy stemmed from his innate conservatism. He said that his father before the schism in 1837 had been "constitutionally a conservative and spontaneously resisted all change; because he did not believe the evils prevalent to be as imminent nor as dangerous as represented by the ultra Old School men." He regarded the extreme methods employed by the Philadelphia men to sever ties to be unconstitutional. Rather than the brash method of exscinding presbyteries, he favored utilizing Presbyterian polity to bring about a resolution without rending the church in two. Decades later, when the movement emerged to end the division, Hodge again exhibited the same conservatism. Once the schism had occurred, and the two parties developed distinctive identities over the next several decades, he saw no compelling reason to end the separation. While holding no animus to New Schoolers, he believed that continuance of two separate denominations was justified.[14]

Hodge expressed his views in his yearly account of the 1868 General Assembly, where the issue of reunion predominated. The original resolution affirmed, among other requirements, subscription to the doctrinal and ecclesiastical standards of the Westminster Confession, the equality of ministers and churches after the reunion, consolidation of records and boards of the two factions, and the necessity of avoiding causes that had originally divided the church. As in the 1837 schism, debate swirled around the issue of theological orthodoxy. Two amendments to the resolution to unite elicited the most spirited exchanges. The first, proposed by Henry Boynton Smith, professor at Union Seminary in New York, stated, "It [is] understood that this Confession is to be received in its proper historical—that is the Calvinistic or Reformed—sense." Smith proposed this phrase, which reprised Hodge's statement at the 1867 General Assembly. Further inflaming the discussion, however, Phineas Gurley, graduate of Princeton Seminary and former chaplain of the U.S. Senate, proposed another amendment, which appeared to conflict with Smith's: "It is also understood that various methods of viewing, stating, explaining, and illustrating the doctrines of the Confession, which do not impair the integrity of the Reformed or Calvinistic system, are to be freely allowed in the united church as they have hitherto been allowed in the separate churches." While Hodge might have been expected to favor Smith's and oppose Gurley's, in the final analysis he opposed both.[15]

Hodge did not believe New Schoolers were heretical, but he contended that historically the New School had held to a latitudinarian view of subscription. Instances such as the trial, appeal, and—in Hodge's opinion—lack of resolution of the Albert Barnes case supported his concerns.[16] On the other hand, we have already seen that Hodge believed that some doctrinal liberty should exist in confessional subscription and that a person could be a consistent Calvinist while disagreeing with the confession on nonessentials. Hodge and others who opposed reunion believed that New Schoolers had established a pattern of leniency in doctrinal matters. Hodge wrote in the *PR*, "The question . . . is not what the New-school ministry believe, but what they tolerate." Old and New parties held a different view on what was essential to the integrity of the confession. Hodge therefore believed that Old School principles would be sacrificed if New School disciplinary procedures were permitted. Gurley's amendment by allowing theological views previously sanctioned by the New School would nullify the unity of the church.[17]

Hodge delivered a brief speech on the matter that ended: "What do we want? We ask for the adoption of the Confession of Faith and catechisms, pure and simple. [Thus he opposed Smith's amendment.] When a man is asked what original sin is, we wish him to give the answer of those standards. Our New-school brethren say they have adopted them since 1837. Then make this your simple basis, and adopt Mr. Humphrey's amendment, and I am for union." (Edward Porter Humphrey, former moderator of the assembly and later president of Amherst, had proposed the amendment: "No form of doctrine heretofore condemned by the General Assembly of either body shall be deemed consistent with the system of doctrine taught in our common standards.") Humphrey's amendment was tabled by a vote of 155–80. Hodge considered this an indication that views other than traditional Old School views would be tolerated in the future, and he reiterated his concern that the proposed basis for reunion lay "under a great cloud of uncertainties and ambiguities. It is far from certain what is sent to [the two assemblies], and requires a sober second thought." Truth be told, Hodge and fifty-three colleagues like Humphrey actually favored reunion with the Southern Old School, which they believed more theologically aligned with their position than the New School North.[18]

Hodge did not attend the 1869 General Assembly in New York and therefore could not write his annual summary of its proceedings. The July issue of the *PR*, however, carried three related articles: a summary of the proceedings, written by fellow Princetonian Lyman Atwater, a defense of the reunion by Philadelphia minister G. W. Musgrove, and Hodge's rejoinder "The New Basis of Union." In one speech, a delegate, Dr. Thomas H. Skinner of Union Theological Seminary, defending the orthodoxy of all Presbyterian seminaries, said, "The drift . . . in the teachings of the ministry of the New School body is not in a separate channel from ours, but in the same broad, deep channel. In fact, they *out-Princeton* Princeton itself"! Delegates' testimonies affirmed overwhelmingly that theological difficulties no longer posed an obstacle to reunion and that the two branches of Presbyterianism ought to join together again.[19]

Hodge remained unconvinced. His son reported that he spoke and wrote publicly and privately "on every occasion that was afforded him." Every year from 1865 to 1869 he wrote articles in the *PR* on topics of union and reunion. He sided with the dwindling number of those opposed to the reunion by signing a protest at the 1868 assembly. In "The New Basis of Union," composed after the 1869 assembly, he reiterated his reasons for opposing the reunion. In a brief five pages he encapsulated his concerns as presbyteries prepared to vote. He acknowledged that the terms of union ("our acknowledged standards," "our common standards," "simple standards") were preferable to those previously submitted. Whatever the impending vote, everyone "should not only submit, but endeavor to carry [the reunion] out in good faith; and do his best to render it successful." He heralded the Pauline and Augustinian heritage of the Old School. Maintaining the purity of the Reformed faith in the future lay in the hands of those entrusted with preserving the gospel. He asserted that "fidelity to this strictness is of incalculable greater importance to the cause of Christ than any increase in numbers, wealth, or power." If history was any teacher, however, the Old School and New School had differed in their use of the Confession—the New School being tolerant of positions that the Old School would not accept. Thus Hodge posed the question, "What is to be the character of the united church? Is it to be strict, as the Old School has hitherto been, or tolerant, as the New School?" Despite his opposition, Hodge conceded that "it is exceedingly painful to stand aloof" from the momentum in favor of reunion that characterized the mood of the 1869 assembly. While he dissented from the majority, he said, "We earnestly pray that, should the union be consummated, it may produce not only a great efficiency, but also of the power of religion and zeal for the truth. If the truth be lost, all is lost. Our numbers, wealth, and influence will avail us nothing."[20]

Hodge's son wrote of his father's vote: "And after the majority of his most thorough sympathizers, seeing the event inevitable, had capitulated in order to secure the most favorable conditions possible, he wavered not a hair's breadth, but rode nine miles to meet the Presbytery in Cranberry, on October 5th, 1869 with the 'anthrax malitiosissimus' on the back of his neck, for the purpose of casting his final vote against it."[21] The two churches voted overwhelmingly to reunite. The New School presbytery vote was unanimous (113–0) and the

Old School vote nearly so (128–3). Hodge found himself in a distinct minority. His campaign against reunion and failure to join even his "sympathizers" as the outcome for reunion seemed "inevitable" probably sealed his reputation for rigid, Old School orthodoxy. While he clearly distanced himself from the strictest Old School party in 1837, his polemical articles in the *PR* and refusal to join the movement to reunite Presbyterians may have done more to offset his otherwise more moderate stance in other controversies. There would, however, be further opportunities for Hodge to demonstrate that his allegiance to Old School orthodoxy did not prevent him from contributing to the larger evangelical context.[22]

33

Reformed among Evangelicals

On October 2, 1873, the Evangelical Alliance convened a conference in New York. The alliance, formed in 1846, consisted of about eight hundred delegates representing fifty evangelical churches from European countries and the United States. Focusing on Christian fellowship and unity, previous meetings had been held in London (1851), Paris (1855), Berlin (1857), Geneva (1861), and Amsterdam (1867). The alliance made no claim to be a union of churches. Its members were merely allies who sought to encourage the essential unity of evangelical Christianity throughout the world regardless of denominational differences or geographical contexts. In addition to European nations and the United States, representatives from "heathen countries" in the form of missionaries and converts also attended. The official record of the proceedings stated, "All branches of the one Evangelical church were represented by clergymen and laymen, distinguished by various peculiarities, yet rejoicing to feel that they were one in Christ Jesus." About one hundred presenters read essays on virtually every theological, religious, and moral question of the age to thousands of attendees.[1]

A myriad of symbols commemorated the historic occasion. The motto of the alliance emblazoned at the front of the meeting hall read, "Unum Corpus Sumus in Christo" ("We Are One Body in Christ"), and another motto signifying its basic principles accompanied it: "IN NECESSARIIS UNITAS; IN DUBIIS LIBERTAS; IN OMNIBUS CARITAS" ("UNITY IN NECESSARY THINGS; LIBERTY IN QUESTIONABLE THINGS; IN ALL THINGS CHARITY"). An array of symbols of unity filled the auditorium. America's national motto, *E Pluribus Unum* ("Out of Many, One"), hung from the ceiling. Surrounding the mottos at the front, the names of prominent Reformers and theologians—Martin Luther, John Calvin, John Wycliffe, Jonathan Edwards, John Knox, John Bunyan, and John Wesley—illustrated that despite the diversity of traditions and differences in doctrine, their common evangelical convictions united them. Further imagery of the ecumenical nature of the gathering was evident in the Greek name for *fish*, ιχθυς, the emblem used by Christians to identify themselves in the early persecutions of the church. At the back of the hall, the letters α and ω, the first and last letters of the Greek alphabet that Jesus applied to himself in the book of Revelation, hung on the gallery, and on the other sides of the gallery hung flags of attending nations alternating with the American Stars and Stripes. A. A. Hodge called the 1873 meeting "one of the memorable events in the history of American Christianity."[2]

Typical of such conferences, each day's activity consisted principally of addresses that explored the goals, beliefs, and achievements of evangelicalism around the world. Participants read essays to emphasize the motto of the alliance—those matters on which evangelicals shared common beliefs. Dr. James McCosh, president of Princeton, attended with Charles Hodge, along with other faculty. McCosh read a paper in the philosophical section of the conference entitled "Religious Aspects of the Doctrine of Development," and Dr. Arnold Guyot, also a Princeton faculty member, presented "Cosmogony and the Bible; or, The Biblical Account of Creation in the Light of Modern Science." Other papers focused on biblical criticism, modern infidelity, and the condition of Christianity in various parts of the world.

The meeting proved a significant opportunity for Hodge—like that offered by the Sunday-School Union in publishing *WOL*—to contribute to an audience larger than his Presbyterian following and exceeding even American evangelicalism. He delivered the opening prayer for the ten days of meetings in which he embraced the ecumenical nature of the gathering. He began the prayer, "Come Holy Spirit, come! Descend in all Thy plenitude of grace. Come as the Spirit of reverence and love. Aid us, O God, in the discharge of the duties on which we are about to enter. We have assembled here from almost all parts of the world. We come to confess Thee before men; to avow our faith that God is, that He is the Creator, Preserver, and Governor of the world." Hodge's essay, the first in a series of twelve on "Christian Union," afforded him the opportunity to set the tone of the entire conference by affirming the basic principles of the Evangelical Alliance. Others addressed topics such as "Communion of Saints," "Spiritual Unity Not Organic Unity," "Christian Union and Denominational Distinctions," and "The Lord's Supper in Relation to Christian Union."[3]

In broad strokes, Hodge built on the foundation of his opening prayer to outline the premises of evangelical union. The unity of individual believers rested on their oneness in Christ, a unity from before the foundation of the world. This mystical union lay "below our consciousness." Believers, united to Christ by the Holy Spirit, manifested "the sameness of their spiritual life or religious experience. Convicted of their sins, believers acknowledge in common their forgiveness in Christ, sing the great hymns of the ages and manifest a mutual love of one another."[4]

In addition to the unity of individual Christians, Hodge said, churches or congregations also manifested Christian unity by acknowledging each other's legitimacy as churches. Churches manifested an external unity so that believers who moved from place to place could say, "A Christian in one place is a Christian in all other places, and is entitled to be so regarded and treated." Spiritual unity took precedence over external unity. While all churches manifested spiritual unity and were therefore true churches, they could legitimately differ and part company over doctrine without being schismatic. Hodge distinguished the true church to which all genuine churches belong.[5]

Hodge then broached the difficult issue of unity despite denominational differences. If his first two points were valid, Hodge reasoned, "the first duty of denominational churches to each other is mutual recognition." Just as individual Christians and congregations acknowledged others, so must denominations. "We are not at liberty to give any definition of a Christian which shall exclude any of the true followers of Christ; so we are not at liberty to give any definition of a church which shall exclude any body which Christ recognizes as a church by his presence." The second duty that denominations owed one another was "intercommunion." He said, "The terms of Christian fellowship . . . are prescribed by Christ, and are the same for all churches. No particular church has the right to require any thing as a term of communion which Christ has not made a condition of salvation." Finally, a third duty of denominations was "the recognition of each other's sacraments and orders." The validity of sacraments rested not on the virtue of those administering them. Their legitimacy depended "first on that being done which Christ has enjoined; second on its being done by a church or by its authority; third on its being done with the serious intention of obeying the command of Christ." If all these were present, "the sacraments of one church are just as valid as those of another."[6]

Hodge concluded his address by summarizing results of genuine Christian unity:

> If the principles above stated be correct, it is of the last importance that they should be practically recognized. If all Christians really believe that they constitute the mystical body of Christ on earth, they would sympathize with each other as readily as the hands sympathize with the feet or the feet with the hands. If all churches, whether local or denominational, believed that they too are one body in Christ Jesus, then instead of conflict we should have concord; instead of mutual criminations we should have mutual respect and confidence; instead of rivalry and opposition we should have cordial co-operation. The whole visible Church would then present an undivided front against infidelity and every form of Antichristian error, and the sacramental host of God, though divided into different corps, would constitute one army glorious and invincible.[7]

A disclaiming footnote appeared at the bottom of Hodge's essay that was published after the conference. Hodge wrote—obviously in the aftermath of the meetings—"No speaker on the floor of the Alliance was understood to speak for any one but himself. The Alliance was in no wise committed by any thing he said." Hodge expressed his views of the church's unity as one of many attempts to forward the cause of the Evangelical Alliance. He did not write as if speaking authoritatively on behalf of the alliance. He continued by saying of himself, "This he did freely, although fully aware that many Episcopalians, Presbyterians, Congregationalists, and Baptists dissented more or less from some of the principles which he advanced." The footnote ended with the following poignant comment: "It is with surprise, therefore, as well as with regret, that he learns that some of his brethren were grieved by what he said, especially on the subject of Christian communion." Thus Hodge expressed surprise that his attempt at ecumenicity should occasion such offense.[8]

How incongruous that Hodge's address, intended as a keynote opening for the entire conference on the nature of the alliance's unity, should come under criticism! *LCH* noted that a Baptist editorial insisted that Hodge in his address "overlooked the claims of courtesy, propriety and justice." Baptist opposition to Hodge's exposition of communion ironically reprised the symbol of Reformation disunity in the sixteenth century when Martin Luther and Ulrich Zwingli failed to agree on the Lord's Supper at the 1529 Marburg colloquy. Hodge responded to the criticism he received in the November 1 issue of the *Presbyterian*. He reminded readers that other speakers had expressed their own views just as he had: "I find that every other member of the Alliance acted on the same principle that I did—expressing his own sentiments without intending to commit anybody else. Some of our scientific brethren expressed views on the Mosaic account of the creation, and of the modern theory of 'development' [evolution] from which others dissented. No one took offence at this. Others again advocated the propriety of the Union of Church and State. We Americans were not thereby offended." As in previous differences over confessional subscription decades earlier in his own denomination, Hodge assumed an irenic stance. He defended the right of evangelicals to differ from one another by saying, "An Evangelical Alliance conducted on the principle that every member must agree with what every other member says, it seems to me must be a failure." Just as no single Presbyterian theologian could author *the* authoritative commentary on the Bible or even the Westminster Standards, so evangelicals of all types should allow for legitimate differences on minor matters (as the motto of the Alliance clearly stated!). Hodge praised the gathering in New York and expressed his gratitude for the honor of being a presenter. He closed by writing poignantly, "Your brother in the bonds which no difference between Baptists and Pedo-baptists can sunder."[9]

In addition to addressing the sessions on unity, Hodge also attended sessions on theological issues where he heard messages by two Princeton friends, James McCosh, president of the college, and Arnold Guyot, professor of geology and physical geography. McCosh read a paper, "Religious Aspects of the Doctrine of Development," supporting a theory of evolution in which God directed the process by which acquired characteristics are passed to produce new species. McCosh argued that rather than attacking evolution, religious thinkers might better direct their efforts to support a theistic evolution. Hodge listened intently and posed the following question during the discussion: "I don't stand here to make a speech at all. I rise simply to ask . . . one question. I want [the Rev J. C. Brown, who responded positively to McCosh's presentation] to tell us what development is. That has not been done. The great question which divides theists from atheists—Christians from unbelievers—is this: Is development an intellectual process guided by God, or is it a blind process of unintelligible, unconscious force, which knows no end and adopts no means? In other words, is God the author of all we see, the creator of all the beauty and grandeur of this world, or is unintelligible force, gravity, electricity, and such like? This is a vital question, sir. We can not stand here and hear men talk about development, without telling us what development is." Having posed the issue, Hodge left the conference and set himself the task of answering his own question as it pertained to Darwin's great work. To that effort we turn in the next chapter.[10]

34

Science under Scrutiny

Princetonians loved science. Protestants as a whole were fascinated with progress in empirical studies in the decades preceding the Civil War. As in all other subjects in the seminary curriculum, Archibald Alexander established the intellectual framework on science that would prevail at Old Princeton. Alexander's first article in the *PR*, "The Bible, A Key to the Phenomena of the Natural World," asserted the premise that would drive all Princetonian opinions on science: the compatibility between the results of scientific investigation and biblical teaching. By affirming the harmony between science and theology, he launched Princeton's commitment to champion the integrity of theological orthodoxy and the scientific enterprise. Likewise, Samuel Miller in his *Retrospect* proudly summarized advances in eighteenth-century science. Princeton's goal throughout the nineteenth century, therefore, was twofold: to be scientific in its theological method using a plenarily inspired Bible and to demonstrate the harmony between Christian truth and scientific findings.[1]

As John Stewart has pointed out, Charles Hodge's enthrallment with science had its roots in his earliest Philadelphia environment. His family's ties to Benjamin Rush, eminent physician and later professor at the University of Pennsylvania, his father's medical practice, his brother Hugh's pioneering work in gynecology, and Charles's own initial desire to follow his brother into the field of medicine stimulated Charles's fascination with science. After his change to biblical and theological ideas prompted his intellectual development abroad, his continuing interest in nature and the ability of science to unearth its order and structure spurred him to further his knowledge. While in Europe, in addition to attending lectures within his field, he exploited opportunities to broaden his vista of the natural world in both Paris and Germany. He eagerly anticipated attending Alexander von Humboldt's lectures and then filled his journal pages with detailed notes.[2]

Throughout his editorship of the *PR*, Hodge commissioned a plethora of articles to satisfy the intensifying desire of many Presbyterians to absorb as much scientific information as possible, especially in light of burgeoning scientific reappraisals of long-held beliefs about astronomy, the geological record, the age of the earth, the unity of the human race, and the origin of species. He cultivated friendships with conservative scientific scholars in these fields to keep the journal's readership apprised of the latest developments in natural studies. The *PR* articles spanned many disciplines: the natural sciences, such as astronomy, geology, chemistry, biology, and zoology, as well as nascent social sciences, such as psychology and anthropology, and what they deemed false sciences, such as phrenology.

Mark Noll and David Livingstone summarize interests that drove Hodge to publish so many articles on scientific matters. Confessionally, he and his colleagues worked from the premise that God not only had created the cosmos, but maintained it by his providential, sovereign will. While Scripture provided the primary witness to creation and providence, modern science by its empirical method afforded another access to the knowledge of God and his creation. While not a textbook on science, the Bible spoke truthfully on whatever subject it explored. Hodge also had an apologetic interest. Immanuel Kant was not the only thinker who desired to uphold Newtonian physics against threats posed by David Hume's skepticism. Scientists in several disciplines contested long-held views by hypothesizing about the age of the earth, the unity of mankind, and the development of species. Hodge and his cadre of like-minded scientists wrote confidently and found an eager Christian audience, who expected carefully reasoned answers or confirmations in response to the latest scientific developments. Rather than being simplistic responses, Hodge's articles demonstrated a breadth of reading on both sides of the issues. Finally, Hodge labored among the forefront of evangelicals who sought to maintain the traditions of American cultural life against potential inroads that proponents of science might make through faulty use of science. Princetonians considered themselves guardians not only of American civilization but of truth and civilization in general. By training pastor-scholars and keeping Presbyterian laity informed, they informed a formidable educational phalanx on the conservative side in the rising culture wars.[3]

With these factors in mind, Hodge undertook his task with the same vigor he expended on articulating Reformed theology. Much as the charter of the seminary at its founding identified deism as a worldview that theological students must be prepared to refute, so Hodge singled out novel scientific theories and conclusions that threatened religious orthodoxy. Hodge's most significant contribution to the rising dispute between science and religion lay in his attempts to fashion a rapprochement between the two fields. Ironically, Hodge published his perspective on the unity of scientific and biblical truth the same year Charles Darwin published *On the Origin of Species*. Hodge's article on the unity of the race in 1859 opposed polygenetic theory that the various races had descended from separate creations simultaneously with their different characteristics, attributes, and abilities. Confessionally, apologetically, and as a guardian of American traditions, Hodge insisted on the unity of the race descending from Adam and Eve. The grand biblical theme of redemption rested on the historicity and unique origin of Adam and Eve. A polygenetic perspective called into question foundational Mosaic and Pauline views. Hodge considered as nonnegotiable the unique origin of the human race and the connection between Adam's sin, which plunged the race into sin, and Christ as the second Adam, whose death on the cross provided redemption for God's elect. By maintaining the historical connection between the first and second Adams, Hodge reprised the concerns he had raised when he opposed the New School views of Albert Barnes in the 1820s.[4]

The majority of the article exposed problems in the polygenetic view of Louis Agassiz, prominent Harvard paleontologist and geologist. Hodge's most basic concern, however, lay in advancing the dialogue between science and religion and specifically maintaining the role of theology in public discourse. Much as Friedrich Schleiermacher had had to argue for the place of theology in Berlin University's post-Enlightenment curriculum to ensure that religion was not excluded from the realm of intellectual discourse, so Hodge foresaw the growing popularity of science marginalizing religion from the realm of ideas in America. To this end he stated, "It is not our intention to write a zoological treatise. We are simply testing the correctness of a definition." Hodge did not expect to contribute to the field of science, a matter in which he lacked credentials to do so. He was not trained in that field, nor did he claim any expertise as a scientist. He knew, however, that reputable scientists disagreed with Agassiz's polygenesis. Hodge intended to make those voices heard in a wider public. He framed the discussion so that religion and science could work harmoniously in the furtherance of truth. Therefore, he sought merely to define the role of each. Correctness of definition, in Hodge's opinion, occupied the place of primacy not only in theology but also in science, for whoever controlled definition controlled the method and outcome of the discussion.[5]

He began by stating the premise of all his writings on science: "theology and science overlap in many points with one another. Science takes cognizance of man; his origin, prerogatives, and powers. So does theology. The philosopher has no right to warn the theologian off of this ground as a trespasser; and the theologian has no right to put the philosopher under an interdict. Both have their rights." Science and religion differed, however, in their methods of approach—science worked by induction in the realm of nature; theology was formed by induction within God's revelation. Each field erred when its practitioners demanded the exclusive right to interpret nature. While theologians came under reproach for narrow-mindedness by appealing to revelation, Hodge accused scientists of being equally guilty when they "ignore all facts which do not fall within their own department," that is, they "form their theories without any regard to moral and religious truths." Far from being anti-scientific, therefore, Hodge maintained his respect for inductive method and what it could uncover in nature, for induction functioned as his modus operandi in systematic theology.[6]

In his article on the unity of the human race, he affirmed, without citing sources, a principle that became known as "God's two books": the book of nature and the book of Scripture.[7] Hodge believed that science and the Bible, each correctly interpreted, could never contradict each other: "The church is willing to meet men of science on equal terms . . . The church will stand by her convictions founded on something surer than consciousness, even the power of God (1 Cor. 2:5), and let science prove what facts it can, assured that God in nature can never contradict God in the Bible and in the hearts of his people." While science's role consisted of supporting its findings by correctly using facts, the church must interpret the Bible "under the guidance of the facts of science." Cases in point in theology were instances when the church changed its teaching of a geocentric universe to a heliocentric universe and from a literal seven twenty-four-hour view of creation to a process that occurred over long periods of time. Hodge believed that science had indisputable evidence that led him and many other theologians to alter their interpretation of Genesis 1 in both of these instances.[8]

Having made such a concession, Hodge addressed errors that both science and religion must avoid. The church, conscious of its fallibility in interpreting the Bible and changing its view of the cosmos, must caution men of science to not too hastily demand a change in understanding the Bible. "Instead of pouncing on such facts [that are 'apparently hostile' to received religious views] and parading them as if in triumph . . . they should be slow to admit them and withhold their sanction until the evidence admits of no contradiction or doubt." Aware of a growing momentum to use science to foster unbelief, Hodge demanded that people so inclined recall "the vast difference between facts and theories. The former, and not the latter are authoritative." The church changed its view of the cosmos when Copernican theory was confirmed with factual support from Galileo's and Tycho Brahe's observations. Asserting a complementarity between scientific and religious facts,

Hodge urged that scientific fact must not be the sole determiner of truth. One must also consider religious fact. Although Hodge sensed that this would be an uphill struggle and many would interpret his efforts as naive in the extreme, he believed the effort must be made.[9]

The epitome of Hodge's efforts to achieve some reconciliation between science and religion appeared in *WID*.[10] Most reviewers cite his words at the end of the book: "What is Darwinism? It is atheism." Often overlooked is the full statement. The sentence above is preceded by: "We have thus arrived at the answer to our question" and followed by: "This does not mean, as before said, that Mr. Darwin himself and all who adopt his views are atheists; but it means that his theory is atheistic, that the exclusion of design from nature is . . . tantamount to atheism." Hodge framed his conclusion as a result of probing Darwin's etiology—his insistence that evolution of species had developed without purpose or design. Evolution had occurred by natural selection, a purely natural process by which animal species and eventually humans emerged as a result of changes involving survival of the fittest. Humans had originated not from an immediate creation by God, nor from a process directed or ordered by God. No purpose or design had ordered the development leading to the formation of biological, animal, and human life.[11]

Definition, therefore, stood foremost in Hodge's mind. Noll and Livingstone note that Hodge did not argue on the basis of biblical exegesis but almost solely on the philosophical question of definition. Darwin's entire scheme resulted from the total absence of design or purpose in evolutionary development, a principal concern for theology and philosophy up to that time. Without purpose guiding the processes leading to species' full development, the entire discussion excluded God and substituted a purely natural cause within an autonomous nature. Thus, according to Noll and Livingstone, *WID* was nothing but an extended treatment of definition, an apologetic argument *to* design rather than the frequently used apologetic argument *from* design. The reason for such detailed treatment lay in Hodge's belief that whoever had the predominating view in the ensuing discussion would exercise the more dominant cultural influence. Hodge therefore foresaw the cultural debate moving beyond the harmony of science and religion as means of explaining reality to science as the exclusive interpreter of nature. If the secular advocates of science had their way and science became autonomous rather than a discipline harmonized with Christian thought and ethics, it threatened to frame all knowledge in entirely this-worldly terms.[12]

Unity of mankind—the topic of Hodge's article—proved, therefore, to be another case in point for Hodge's complementarian view. In Hodge's opinion, scientists had clearly documented that varieties exist within the human race. Races differed in conformation, color, size, and mental aptitudes, and races lived in vastly different environments. In light of these facts, Hodge admitted that "a plausible argument" might be posed for polygenesis—that the separate races had originated and developed independently of one another and had not descended from a single source. While plausible, however, polygenesis was not the only possible interpretation of the facts. The Bible explicitly posed another interpretation, and reputable scientists had mustered evidence in support of the Bible's teaching on the unity of mankind. More importantly, he argued, polygenesis proved thoroughly detrimental to Christianity, for it "subverts the great doctrines of the common apostasy and redemption of the race, and is opposed to the universal faith of the church." While seemingly unimportant to many, the unity of the human race provided an overarching explanation for more than origin of the races. It accounted for the universal existence of human sinfulness, and it foreshadowed a redemption for human sin through the work of Christ on the cross.[13]

Undoubtedly Hodge's work constituted a polemic, calculated to refute a major attack on the traditional view of human origins. Little noticed, however, is Hodge's detailed attempt to forge a peace between the opposing forces of science and religion. Not unlike Hodge's moderation as an advocate of Old School thinking in its dispute with New Schoolers, Hodge sought still another center, as it were, this time not within extremes of his denomination but on the much larger stage of public discourse. After delving into arguments on both sides of the question of evolution,[14] Hodge probed the emerging alienation of science and religion. In perhaps his best attempt in analyzing facts and their interpretation, Hodge edged toward a more presuppositional epistemology than in any of his other writings. He prefaced his treatment thus: "[These] remarks we would fain to make in a humble way irenical. There is need of an Irenicum [a means to establish peace between two warring parties], for there is an antagonism between scientific men as a class and religious men as a class." While not everyone on either side acknowledged the virtue of establishing a peace, Hodge believed the effort absolutely necessary. Seeking such a rapprochement between the two concurred with his views of education discussed earlier. Presbyterians had every reason to foster harmony between the two fields, since they viewed all truth under the rubric of unity. With the a priori notion that truth rested on God's revelation, whether in nature or the Bible, conflict between disciplines in the vast array of intellectual studies, when conducted appropriately, was impossible.[15]

As part of his argument, Hodge used the German term *Wissenschaft*, "scientific study," the central focus of Berlin theological education. In this view, human knowledge should result from sustained, disciplined study. Just as theological education of pastors rested on serious, prolonged training in a carefully regimented curriculum designed to produce pastor-scholars, study in the sciences should be subject to standards of scientific inquiry. Rather than follow German usage to forestall any claim of final truth, Hodge proposed the term as a way of ordering all knowledge into a meaningful unity. The scientist studied the material order, while the metaphysician studied the mind. If only knowledge received through the senses was allowed, then other sources of knowledge were excluded by presupposition. Hodge stated categorically that herein lay the "main root of the trouble" of the alienation of science and religion. "The tendency . . . of a mind addicted to one kind of evidence to become more or less insensible to other kinds of proof is undeniable." Hodge clearly perceived an incipient if not maturing positivism at work in which only that apprehended by the senses could finally be defined as knowledge. In fact, those who yielded to the positivism of science tended to deny not only God but also the mind and even the self because they were not perceived by means of scientific methods.[16]

A second cause of science's alienation from religion stemmed from a failure to distinguish facts and explanations or theories from those facts. Besides pointing out the lack of facts from the fossil record to support Darwin's theory, Hodge went so far as to say that facts are "sacred." By his adherence to facts, he did not mean that facts are brute facts—that they possess the power of themselves to demonstrate a truth. He reminded readers, "It is to be remembered that the facts are from God, the explanation from men; and the two are often as far apart as Heaven and its antipode." Resorting to hyperbole, Hodge stated that since human explanation changed "almost as often as phases of the moon," people would do well to avoid accepting every new theory—and in this case Darwin's theory of evolution. Hodge alleged that the "facts" used by evolutionists to further their new theory did not differ from what scientists had long known about nature. The shift in their interpretation, therefore, was, he said, merely "a subjective one." The danger of such a remarkable change in interpretation was "that scientific men give the name of science to their explanations as well as to the facts. Nay, they are often, and naturally, more zealous for their explanations than they are for the facts. The facts are God's, the explanations are their own." In these statements, Hodge may have come as close as he did in any of his epistemological utterances to a presuppositionalist orientation on the interplay between facts and their interpretation.[17]

The third cause of the alienation of science and religion was the tendency on the part of scientists who departed from previous practice of conceiving them as mutually compatible. Rather than envisioning a harmony between the two disciplines, they tended to disparage scholars who were not themselves a part of the scientific community if they questioned scientific findings. Such scientists, Hodge contended, had a propensity to stigmatize religious people as "narrow-minded, bigots, old women, Bible worshippers, etc." Thus English biologist Thomas Huxley, frequently called "Darwin's Bulldog" as the English naturalist's most ardent defender, established his Irenicum by affirming science's antipathy to all things religious. He conceived science as an independent, autonomous discipline. In an unexpected use of the term, Hodge likened Huxley and his coterie as modern-day "Pharisees" who needed rebuking as much as those of the first century did. Other bases for an Irenicum were likewise bound to fail when elitist adherents denounced anyone not a scientist who attempted to interpret natural data without the Darwinian paradigm. While scientists and other professionals such as lawyers and physicians might naturally consider their fields sacred and immune from opinions of outsiders, Hodge denied that any discipline could claim independence from the broad ranks of scholarship: "no department of human knowledge is isolated. One runs into and overlaps another." Thus, for Hodge, harmonization not only guaranteed the continued close relationship between science and religion, but also fully promoted scientific advance. Far from being obscurantist in its attitude toward science, religion encouraged scientific enterprises. The two did not, however, proceed autonomously.[18]

Hodge concluded that no Irenicum would come about until these errors were addressed. He believed that given the growing intransigent claims of some scientists, the primary burden lay with men of science, who must accept responsibility for several actions. Men of science must "recognize practically, and not merely in words, that there are other kinds of evidence of truth than the testimony of the senses. They must come to give due weight to the testimony of consciousness and to the intuitions of the reason and conscience. They must cease to require that deference due to established facts to be paid to their speculations and explanations. And they must treat their fellow-men with due respect." Hodge's Irenicum therefore set the bar as high for scientists as Huxley's and Haeckel's did for theologians. As the debate heightened in intensity, the question emerged whether a consensus was possible among disputants on either side of the debate, let alone a harmonious settlement between Darwinians and anti-Darwinians. The multiplication of publications by proponents on both sides of the evolution question and differences within the Darwinist and Christian camps only aggravated the alienation further. Proponents on the Darwinian side debated what constituted Darwinism. And Christians haggled over whether Darwinism could be tamed by synthesizing development and divine providence—what would become popular as "theistic evolution."[19]

Hodge feared that acceptance of Darwinian ideas coupled with the isolation of science from its Christian roots would foster the growth of antagonistic philosophies such as materialism. He made several references to materialism in his critique. He cited French philosopher Baron Paul d'Holbach, Ernst Haeckel, and Ludwig Buchner as among its advocates. Hodge concluded his analysis of Huxley's and Haeckel's elitist Irenicum with the following critical judgment: "a man in order to be entitled to be heard on the evolution theory must be willing to renounce his faith not only in the Bible, but in God, in the soul, in a future life, and become a monistic materialist." Not only would religious ideas no longer play a role in public discourse, but doctrinaire utterances of science would become the new dogma replacing the traditional dogmas of religion.[20]

That Hodge possessed a broader perspective of science than simply opposing Darwinism becomes obvious when one considers his treatment of science in *ST*.[21] The term *science* appears seventy-eight times in his three-volume work. Most remembered was his assertion of theology as a science in his seventeen-page definition.[22] More important for Hodge's larger view of science and its methods is his fifty-three-page analysis of materialism in chapter 3, "Anti-Theistic Theories." Not only did Hodge treat the materialism of ancient Greek philosophers and speculations of eighteenth-century philosophers, he examined the root of what would become the social sciences. Hodge called French philosopher Auguste Comte, who founded the discipline of sociology, "the author of the 'Positive Philosophy,'" which alleged that the senses were the only true source of knowledge and that "hence nothing exists but matter. There is no mind distinct from matter; no such thing as efficiency; no causes, whether first or final; no God; no future state of existence for man." Positivistic reductionism eliminated all claims to knowledge not rooted in sensory experience.[23] In Comte's view, "theology and psychology are, therefore, banished from the domain of science." Hodge meant by this the traditional views of theology and psychology. Positivists such as Comte still used the term *psychology*, yet it no longer meant "study of the soul" but reduced all things human to mere matter.[24]

Hodge used the term *social science* only once in *ST*.[25] Yet he clearly foresaw the implications of subjects such as psychology and sociology coming under the influence of materialist philosophy. To illustrate the reductionist nature of Comte's positivism, Hodge cited several passages from *Philosophie Positive* that would reduce analysis of the mind to mere physiology. Comte wrote: "Positive Philosophy regards all phenomena as subjected to invariable natural laws. Our business is,—seeing how vain is any research into what are called causes, whether first or final,—to pursue an accurate discovery of these laws, with a view to reducing them to the smallest possible number." Treating all human behavior—willing, thinking, choosing, and so on—as a result of purely natural "laws" had significant ramifications. Comte wrote, "If we regard these functions [of the mind] under their statical aspect,—that is if we consider the conditions under which they exist,—we must determine the organic circumstances of the case, which inquiry involves it with anatomy and physiology. If we look at the dynamic aspect, we have to study simply the exercise and results of the intellectual powers of the human race, which is neither more nor less than the general object of Positive Philosophy." Human thought, choice, and all other capacities, by this line of reasoning, were comprehended as a result of natural law.[26]

Hodge further pointed out "the presumptuous character" of positivism in its predictions for the field of sociology. He questioned its claims to be a science like the natural sciences. To make his point, he cited meteorology as an example: scientists had difficulty even in predicting the weather. Because of the number and complexities of causes that influenced the weather, meteorologists could not guarantee their forecast of the wind for even the next forty-eight hours, let alone the direction of the winds a year hence.[27] The inadequacy of meteorology to function as a science, however, paled in comparison with the difficulty in predicting human behavior. Hodge continued, "The causes which determine human action in the individual and in society, are far more complex and inscrutable than those which determine the state of the weather. Yet Comte assumes to have reduced Sociology to a science, vying with mathematics in certainty." Hodge was incredulous that Comte could make the following claim: "I will venture to say . . . that Sociological science, though only established by this book, already rivals mathematical science itself, not in precision and fecundity, but in positivity and rationality." Comte stopped short of affirming sociology's power of prediction, which lay at the heart of the natural sciences. He nevertheless affirmed for sociology the highest rationality. Positivism represented the arrival of the highest stage in human development. Human existence had begun with the primitive, religious stage in which all things were understood in light of the supernatural. Such was mankind in its childhood. Humans then developed in the youth of the race into the higher metaphysical stage in which reason usurped the place of authority. Finally, mankind's adulthood was manifested in the highest, positivist stage in which science by its power of demonstration assumed control over human destiny.[28]

In assessing the practical applications of positivism, which Hodge called "very serious," he asserted the final outcome of the social sciences: "Positivism claims the right of absolute and universal control over all human affairs; over education, politics, social organization, and religion." Hodge foresaw that "science" would develop from a means by which to know the world to the means of controlling the world. Comte claimed the scientific elitism of Haeckel and Huxley when he wrote incredulously, "Can it be supposed that the most important and the most delicate conceptions, and those which by their complexity are accessible to only a small number of highly prepared understandings, are to be abandoned to the arbitrary and variable decisions of the least competent minds?" Hodge concluded from Comte's presumption, "This argument is conclusive. If social life, the acts of men, are as much and as certainly determined by physical laws as material changes, those who have ascertained these laws are entitled to control all other men."[29]

Hodge's assessment and critique of the social sciences may have been even more important than his treatment of Darwinism. Taken together, his criticisms of Darwinism and the materialistic tendencies of the new social sciences alerted evangelicals to contemporary efforts to free science from its previous relationship with traditional religion. In his treatment of Hodge's attacks on the "deformities" of science, Ronald Numbers documented the *PR*'s articles on the rise of pseudosciences such as phrenology, mesmerism, and materialistic physiology. Hodge's controversy over polygenesis illustrates his suspicion of anthropology. Not only did polygeneticists' new theory contradict biblical teaching regarding the human race, but claiming exclusive right to interpret data supporting their theory precluded others from offering a different perspective.[30] This elitist special pleading hardly looked like genuine science as practiced in the past. In pointing out the influence of materialism on the new sciences, Hodge alerted readers to a method he had experienced firsthand in his own discipline of theology during his studies in Germany.

Hodge's additional remarks on Comte and positivism in his *ST* reveal that he foresaw what lay ahead in the further development of what he called pseudoscience. Although he retained a high estimation of modern science and scientists' ability to identify natural laws, Hodge also anticipated the potential for the misuse of science when pseudoscientists replaced theistically based science with a so-called science based on a materialistic worldview. With his positivistic outlook, Comte's predilection to reduce human existence merely to what could be quantified represented a clear misuse of science. As important as empirically identifiable data might be, for example in what physiologists could gain from studying the brain, to reduce human thought exclusively to quantifiable data excluded man's unique qualitative attributes necessary for understanding mankind's equally real religious, ethical, and aesthetic experience. The latter aspects of human experience stood at the center of the traditional view that human beings were uniquely created in the image of God. The Christian worldview that alone offered the motive for modern science—a meaningful world created and ordered by God with human beings as the crown of creation, worthy of being studied as such—was in danger of being jettisoned in favor of a totally new perspective that would change not only the face of science but man's perception of himself. Proponents of the new social sciences, therefore, were self-consciously adopting a new basis for science that would free them from the moral strictures inherent in a theistic worldview. Not without reason did Hodge use the warfare metaphor in *WID*. After analyzing Haeckel's Irenicum, he wrote, "Religion is a system of knowledge, as well as a state of feeling. The truths on which all religion is founded are drawn within the domain of science, the nature of the first cause, its relation to the world, the nature of second causes, the origin of life, anthropology, including the origin, nature, and destiny of man. Religion has to fight for its life against a large class of scientific men. All attempts to prevent her exercising her right to be heard are unreasonable and vain." Hodge therefore viewed proponents of new scientific theories as issuing a new dogma. They were being as doctrinaire in their assertions as any previous theologians had been in the past. While wishing for an Irenicum, Hodge foresaw only further conflict between the two sides in their understanding of the natural world and man's place in it.[31]

35

Fifty Years and Counting

While in Europe, Charles Hodge witnessed the celebration of Professor August Hermann Nehemeyer, chancellor of the University of Halle, for his fifty years of academic service. The practice of celebrating professors' careers extending so many years was called a jubilee, named after the Jewish tradition that proclaimed liberty in various ways for the land and the people every fifty years for God's covenant faithfulness.[1] In his European journal Hodge reported the trappings of the chancellor's jubilee—the grandeur of the setting, names of attending scholars from various European universities, congratulatory addresses in Latin and German, and presentations of a bust of the recipient and a porcelain vase from the king.[2]

On April 23, 1872, the first such academic celebration on American soil occurred in Princeton as colleagues, friends, and visiting dignitaries gathered to honor Charles Hodge's fifty years of teaching. Seventy alumni appointed by the board of directors of the seminary labored for over a year to honor Hodge's signal contributions to the school and American Presbyterianism. Four years earlier his responsibilities for the *PR* had been relieved somewhat when Lyman Atwater became coeditor of the journal. Hodge fully retired from his "ball and chain" in 1871. He was still shepherding his *ST* through the publication process when he wrote to his longtime friend John Johns of his disappointment that Johns could not attend because of his responsibilities as Episcopalian bishop. Hodge penned a humorous rebuke, "Why can't you visit some of your churches before the 22nd, so as to be free a few days after that date? A bishop is not worth the mentioning if he cannot do what he pleases."[3]

The widely recognized honor bestowed on Hodge was evidenced by Princeton retailers' closing their shops for the occasion. Four hundred former students from as far as Texas, Colorado, and California attended, representing almost every graduating class in the history of the seminary. Delegates including faculty from a wide variety of colleges and seminaries joined with representatives from American and European churches to form an impressive assembly. The throng crowded every pew as well as available standing room of the First Presbyterian Church. Hodge's family attended in force—his wife, children, grandchildren, and brother Hugh, who had succumbed to blindness.[4]

Dr. Henry Boardman of Philadelphia, with whom Hodge had exchanged correspondence on seminary and denominational matters for decades, spoke on behalf of the board of directors. After applauding Princeton's legacy to that point in time, Boardman concentrated on Hodge's unique contributions: "But what honor, beloved Brother, has God put upon you! For fifty years you have been training men to preach the glorious gospel of the grace of God to their fellow-sinners. The teacher of teachers, your pupils have become professors in numerous Colleges and Seminaries at home and abroad. Not to speak of one or two thousand pastors, who are exerting an ameliorating influence upon this nation more potent than that of an equal number of men belonging to any other calling, you are helping, through your students, to educate a great body of Christian ministers, not a few of whom are to be employed in laying the foundations of Christianity in pagan lands."[5]

Hodge observed the proceedings while inclined on a couch out of sight of the gathered crowd. When he came forward to respond, the audience rose spontaneously to greet him. Hodge attempted to deflect attention from himself by focusing his remarks on the seminary. Exhibiting yet again his long-ingrained conservatism, he extolled the "law of fixedness and transmissibility of types [that] pervades all the works of God." He likened the fixed character of the order of nature and the continuity of nations' and states' histories as a result of the original contributions of their founders to the unique character of Princeton Seminary inherited from its original professors, Archibald Alexander and Samuel Miller. While their learning and native abilities had earned them respect, their "character and principles" bore even greater importance. Displaying his ecumenicity appropriate to the gathered audience, he continued, "There are different types of religion even among true believers." He cast a wide net to capture figures who had exemplified the evangelical tradition throughout church history. Like Princeton, other traditions and schools, "the religion of St. Bernard and of John Wesley, of Jeremy Taylor, and of Jonathan Edwards, although essentially the same, had in each case its peculiar character. Every great historical Church has its own type of piety." Thus, all evangelical traditions manifested distinctive features, but they also held a common bond in their piety and doctrines.[6]

As evidence of evangelical commonality among all Christians despite their diversities, Hodge referred to the note written by Augustus Neander when he left Berlin: "Ουδεν εν εαυτω, *nothing in ourself*, εν Κυριω παντα, *all things in the Lord*, ω μονω δουλευειν δοξα και ξαυγμα, *whom to serve is a glory and a joy*." He offered a brief panegyric on the seminary's retaining of the great truths initially taught by his predecessors. He also reiterated his favorite characterization of the *PR* and the school: "I am not afraid to say that a new idea never originated in this Seminary." Proof lay in its reverence for the Bible and its storehouse of truths. He concluded by reminding his audience that he shared with alumni who had come to honor him an affection for their alma mater. The nearby graves of his predecessors reminded all those present of the seminary's heritage: "The memory of these men constitutes the aureole which surrounds the brows of Princeton, a glory which excites no envy, and yet attracts all eyes."[7]

An abundance of speeches and congratulatory letters followed Boardman's address—some fifteen in all. Henry B. Smith, theologian at

Union Seminary in New York, probably spoke for many when he said that "at least five hundred speeches" were not made! Clearly, no effort was spared to honor a professor who had taught twenty-seven hundred students—more than had attended any other American seminary.[8]

At the close of the day, a reception at Hodge's home was held, attended by friends from all over the world. Inscribed over the doors of his house, the dates 1822–72 reminded all in attendance of Hodge's jubilee. He wrote in his journal: "April 24th. The apex of my life. The Semi-centenary Anniversary of my connection with the Seminary as Professor. The day, by the blessing of God, was fine, and the celebration a wonderful success. The attendance of Alumni very large; delegations of other institutions numerous, and of the highest character; the congratulations from all at home and abroad of the most gratifying kind, altogether affording an imposing and most affecting testimony of the unity of faith, and of common love to the same gospel, and to our common God and Saviour Jesus Christ."[9]

Within a year of his jubilee, Hodge lost his brother. In February 1873, Hugh suffered a chill during a severe cold spell while visiting patients late into the evening. He returned home, and apparently unaffected, he retired to bed. In the night, however, his son, also a doctor, heard him fall and found him unconscious. Administration of artificial respiration some thirty to forty times permitted his children to visit his bedside before he died. Due to his own ill health, Charles could not join them. Finally Hugh succumbed to a heart attack. Deeply saddened at the unexpected loss, Hodge wrote to his friend Johns, "We are left like two trees standing almost alone. The fewer the dearer. My brother's death was entirely unexpected. He was perfectly well, and far stronger than I am." Days later Charles learned of the deaths of two other friends who had been his classmates at both the college and the seminary.[10]

Hodge received an additional honor shortly after the celebration of his jubilee. The General Assembly of that year consisted of many of his past students as well as former members of the New School who traveled a good distance to attend the annual meeting. They expressed a desire to see Hodge, especially in the aftermath of his jubilee. The original plan called for Hodge to travel to the assembly, but an incapacitating attack of bronchitis forced a change in events. The assembly, in a magnanimous gesture, adjourned for a day on Wednesday, May 28, from its meeting in Baltimore to pay a visit en masse to Hodge in Washington, DC. Hodge happened to be visiting his brother-in-law, General David Hunter, a routine he followed each May for many years. Delegates gathered in the Capitol Rotunda, where after several short addresses they heartily sang the Doxology. The delegates went to the White House and then to the grand dining room of Willard's Hotel for a dinner arranged by the churches in DC. As on similar occasions when his feelings could get the best of him, Hodge showed signs of deep emotion and accepted the collective congratulations warmly.[11]

A Life Lived to the Full

After his semicentennial and as Hodge advanced in age, concern grew over how to assist him in his workload and eventually find a replacement. A committee of the board of directors approached Hodge in 1874 about the possibility of appointing his son to the chair of history of doctrine with the intent that A. A. would help lighten his father's labors and upon Charles's death replace him. Hodge rejected the proposition. In yet another reference to the Plan of the Seminary, he stated that it lacked any provision for two professors in systematics. In addition, he believed that since A. A. was prospering in his current position as professor of systematic theology at Western Theological Seminary near Pittsburgh, he should remain there.[12]

Three years later, however, deterioration of his health led him to change his mind. He wrote to Boardman that because of weakness he had not attended either the chapel or the Sunday afternoon conferences. He also had not taken his yearly May trip to Washington the previous year. He concluded that he should relinquish his teaching responsibilities at the seminary, and he offered to the committee of the board either the resignation of his professorship altogether or the acceptance of the previous offer of assistance. In a rather formal letter to his son, Hodge enumerated six considerations regarding A. A.'s appointment. He concluded, "The question whether you are the best available man to fill the place here, is for our Directors to decide. Their decision, however, is subject to a veto from your 'inner consciousness,' if your conscience constrains you to exercise it. 'Commit your way to unto the Lord, and He will direct your steps.' "[13]

Consequently, A. A. Hodge was inaugurated as associate professor of didactic theology on November 8, 1877 in Princeton's First Presbyterian Church. He assumed the responsibility for the middler class in theology, while his father retained the senior class and lectured the junior class on the Epistles. At the conclusion of the academic year, Hodge relinquished the Department of Didactic Theology to his son. A. A. Hodge continued the Princeton theology through his dynamic preaching, teaching, and writings. Hodge's son was remembered for a gift his father lacked: vivid illustrations of theological truths and practical application of biblical teaching for everyday life.[14]

Charles's ministry in the seminary continued, but with reduced activity because of the decline in his physical stamina. He gave his last presentation in the Oratory on April 14, 1878, almost sixty years after he had given his first student speech. A week later he ministered and participated in communion for the final time. He attended his last service of public worship by speaking at a friend's funeral in New York. Although succumbing to increasing weakness, he attempted to retain his regimen of spending the day in the chair of his study. Of that chair he spoke affectionately: "This old chair and I have been growing to fit each other for forty years." On June 19, in the middle of Commencement Week at the college where he had prepared for his lifelong ministry, he died. Resolutions by the Presbytery of New Brunswick, the board of the seminary, trustees of his college, alumni of the seminary, and various boards on which he served honored his passing. And as in the case of his jubilee, all shops in the town where he lived most of his life were shuttered for business.[15]

Legacy

The death of Charles Hodge brought to an end a lifetime of service to his seminary, his church, and the larger religious and cultural scene in America. In a sense, however, the Princeton theology with which his name has since been synonymous was just beginning its hegemony in

American Presbyterianism. Struggles over doctrine and practice within the Presbyterian church that characterized the New School–Old School debates flared in the modernist–fundamentalist controversies of the early twentieth century. Hodge's successors—A. A. Hodge, Benjamin B. Warfield, and J. Gresham Machen—played principal roles in continuing Princeton's heritage in the face of advancing liberalizing forces that eventually led to a broadening denomination.[16]

On the occasions when Hodge spoke of what Princeton represented, he sought to deflect attention from his accomplishments. Remarks such as those he made at his jubilee were not those of false humility. Instead he feted those who had preceded him, whether immediately in mentors such as Alexander and Miller or remotely in sixteenth-century Reformers or, more distantly still, in the church father Augustine, the apostle Paul, and ultimately the Lord of whom he spoke so fervently. The Old School theology fashioned from this varied background he taught his family in daily devotions, instilled in the pastor-scholars graduating from the seminary, broadcast widely through the *PR*, and actively demonstrated through his preaching and labors in various committees and courts of the church. While he himself did not sense the call to the pastorate, he taught thousands who would assume pastoral roles in his denomination.

He had championed Calvinism—both its theology and piety he had learned from the Westminster Confession ministered by his mother and pastor. Comfortable with his New Side / confessionalist roots and temperamentally conservative by nature, he retained his spiritual and intellectual roots as he encouraged a denomination and the wider evangelical churches to do the same. Cognizant of both his intellectual and spiritual strengths and weaknesses, he sought to exploit the former and repair the latter. Hodge illustrated a religious life not because of reasons that might immediately come to the popular mind—because the subjects he taught were theology and biblical courses; because he kept devotional diaries; because he taught for over fifty years at a seminary; because he read the Bible privately or preached publicly; because he defended Calvinism as it was fading in its influence in American ecclesiastical settings; because he wrote yearly accounts of his denomination's General Assembly or numerous other activities usually associated with religion. Rather, Hodge personified a religious life well lived in the classical meaning of the word *religion*. The English term is derived from the Latin *religare*, which means "to bind or commit." Richard John Neuhaus noted that religion does not refer to specific acts that are "religious" in nature and therefore identify some people as religious while others are not. Because all people in their innermost being are committed to something, whether they acknowledge it or not, there are no *areligious* people. Everyone, consciously or unconsciously, orders life according to what he or she is bound or committed to. Thus, all people are religious, not just those who perform acts that are intrinsically religious in nature as opposed to other activities that are areligious or secular in nature. Religion, therefore, is not just one among other facets of life, such as political, economic, social, familial, and leisure activities. Rather, it is the commitment of the heart that informs all other dimensions of life.[17]

Hodge never unpacked the word *pious*, the term he used most frequently to characterize those whose theology and piety reflected what he considered a truly biblical way of life. If for no other reason, his little manual written for the Sunday-School Union must be remembered as capturing a holistic pious or religious life. He may well have fallen prey to the popular conception of religion used above. Thus, for example, Princetonians distinguished between the classroom and the Sunday afternoon conferences. The former's purpose was to feed the mind and the latter's to feed the heart. But as Hodge's life is taken as a whole, he manifested the principle that his religion was not simply a part of his life but of a single piece. It involved the entirety of his life, not just one aspect among others. His commitment to the God of Reformed theology manifested itself regardless of the activity he engaged in. It governed his devotion to his family and deeply informed the warm letters to his wife and affection for his children. It motivated his venturing to Europe to better himself for his teaching responsibilities. It drove him to write almost frenetically in his journal and to compose his prodigious three-volume *ST* as well as his concise layman's *WOL*. It permeated his intense debates over voluntary societies, Presbyterian polity, support of infant baptism, and critique of conversion-driven revivalism, but it also informed his views of slavery, patriotism during the Civil

War, and interest in all things medical and scientific. It informed his view of knowledge itself, for which he has drawn much criticism. But regardless of how much he utilized Common Sense philosophy or insisted on inductive fact-gathering, those never usurped the final authority of biblical revelation. He tempered his view of reason by appealing to more than rationalistic evidences; in fact, he gave greater weight to internal evidences and the work of the Holy Spirit in the heart. He might have identified Friedrich Schleiermacher's subjectivism as the *bête noire* of modern thinking. But he situated Schleiermacher in heaven, and Hodge's own life exemplified the God-consciousness that Schleiermacher emphasized as the heart of theology. His strongly emotional nature also suffused his correspondence and surfaced when appropriate in even his most rigorous intellectual debates.[18]

Hodge never articulated a presuppositional apologetic similar to later Reformed Dutch thinkers. But like Benjamin Warfield, who followed him in the twentieth century, he contributed significantly to identifying the underlying systems that drove modern theology and changes in science. Hodge, like those who preceded as well as those who followed him, considered modernism a deformation, and probably a temporary one at that. The Plan of the Seminary required a solid effort against deism so that pastors could successfully refute it. Hodge fought pantheism, and his successors labored against other forms of modernism with the same intent. If earlier deists viewed their constructions as the next stage of the development of Christianity, Princetonians viewed them as temporary in nature, something to be countered and eventually overcome. They believed that development of doctrine consisted not of finding new truth but in further clarifying truth already revealed. Hodge seemed fully convinced that, given time and careful scholarship, conservatives could prevail. Such thinking fueled the later fundamentalists in their battles with modernism. Warfield, for example, would follow Hodge's lead of reviewing German literature. He never wrote a systematic theology that might displace Hodge's work. Arguably, Warfield's most neglected contribution to twentieth-century Reformed theology was volume 10 in the Oxford collected works, *Critical Reviews*. In them, with remarkable similarity to Hodge's reviews in the *PR*, Warfield painstakingly unpacked the scholarship originating from European writers. He revealed the naturalistic biases that underlay their theological innovations. If Schleiermacher and his cohorts sought to reconfigure Christianity on a noncognitive level to prevent the faith from being criticized, the Princetonians welcomed the opportunity to answer any and all challenges that modern unbelief might muster. Like Hodge, Warfield and Machen insisted that modern doctrines rose not from careful examination of the Bible but from imposing modern, alien perspectives upon the texts.[19]

A man of the center, Hodge fashioned his career as professor, scholar, and churchman by attempting to forge a via media between extremes. Only those more conservative than he, however, ever seriously questioned his commitment to Reformed orthodoxy and polity. Though living in the shadow of a gifted brother in his youth, he found in biblical and theological studies a calling that piqued his interest, fed his piety, and drove him to succeed. Although initially lacking confidence in his intellectual prowess, augmented by doubts of even members of his family, he never flagged in intensity to overcome deficiencies.

A two-year immersion in European culture tested his fervently held beliefs and convictions. He constantly found ways to benefit from exposure to attitudes and milieus when they differed sharply from his own. A cadre of European friends, whose piety he shared though having differences in theology, ensured that his sojourn would bolster his confidence. When he returned, he resumed a ministry that spilled over from the confines of the relatively new seminary into his denomination and, thanks to an industrious journal, to American intellectual discourse. Nothing escaped his journal's notice, and while Hodge was not personally contentious by nature, he took up the cudgels of controversial debate in an age when aggressive discourse sharpened people's sensitivity to issues differing as sharply as abolitionism, social reform, revivalism, education, a politically sundered nation, a divided church, baptismal practices, and modern science. He enabled a church not only to maintain its spiritual footing doctrinally as others sought an innovative Calvinism but also to retain its essential spiritual mission when parties diverted it into a political agenda contrary to the church's calling.

Gregarious by nature, Hodge owed much to the support of faculty and those outside the familiar confines of his rural community that trained him for ministry. Instruction throughout his life served only to reinforce habits of mind and heart, which he never relinquished. Though one of the country's foremost controversialists, he garnered the respect not only of an appreciative Reformed audience but also of those with whom he disagreed.

In pursuit of his goal to maintain Reformed theology as it was beginning to wane in American life, Hodge occasionally ventured into territories outside of his training—sometimes with beneficial results, sometimes with deleterious effects. In history, for example, he found that in writing his denomination's constitutional history, he had to correct former misconceptions. Following good Common Sense principles—examining the facts as manifested in primary source documents—he found that research led him to conclusions very different from his former opinions. Though it cast a momentary shadow upon a long-standing relationship with his mentor, Hodge doggedly stood by his guns.

While the term *New Side–Old School Presbyterian* might seem a contradiction if not an impossibility in principle, Charles Hodge managed to exhibit the best that each faction could offer in its heyday. Unabashed in his enthusiasm for sound orthodoxy coupled with Reformed piety, as churchman, theologian, controversialist, and writer on all matters of interest, he lived and worked as one of the nineteenth century's most influential Presbyterians.

Notes

Part 1: Roots

1. Robert Ellis Thompson, *A History of the Presbyterian Churches in the United States* (1895; repr., Eugene, OR: Wipf and Stock, 2003), 1.

Chapter 1: New Side Confessionalist

1. *LCH*, 1–3. Extended treatment of Hodge's life appears in numerous passages in both volumes of *PS*. Shorter but substantial biographical accounts appear in Mark A. Noll, "Introduction," in *The Way of Life*, by Charles Hodge (New York: Paulist Press, 1987); John W. Stewart and James H. Moorehead, "Introducing Charles Hodge to Postmoderns," in *CHR*, 1–41; *MTC*, 1–14.

2. *LCH*, 5–7. Hodge's extensive genealogical account appears in *CHP*, box 1, folder 8. The Hodge Papers at Princeton University are formidable in size; the collection consists of twenty-seven boxes—13½ linear feet.

3. The terms *New Light* and *Old Light* are used to identify defenders and opponents of the First Great Awakening associated with George Whitefield and Jonathan Edwards. Leonard Trinterud claims that *New Light* originated in Ireland as a term of opprobrium leveled by the subscription party on their opponents. It gained negative connotations when those so dubbed lapsed into Arianism. By calling the awakeners *New Lights*, the Old Lights "sought to attach to them the name of heresy and the reputation of being opposed to any true Presbyterianism." Leonard J. Trinterud, *The Forming of an American Tradition* (Philadelphia: Westminster Press, 1949), 42, 169. Princetonians sometimes used the term to refer to the College of New Jersey, later renamed Princeton. Archibald Alexander used the term *New Light* in his account of the founding of the Log College, which was the antecedent to Princeton College. *Biographical Sketches of the Founder, and Principal Alumni of the Log College: Together*

with an Account of the Revivals of Religion, under Their Ministry (Princeton, NJ: J. T. Robinson, 1845), 54. In the autobiographical section of *LCH*, Charles Hodge also used *New Light* to describe the College of New Jersey. *LCH*, 20. Thus Princeton, which descended from both the Log College and the College of New Jersey, originated as a New Light institution. Historians have used the terms *New Side* and *Old Side* to describe the factions involved in the Presbyterian phase of the First Great Awakening. The terms *Old Side* and *New Side* identified the presbyteries of Philadelphia and New Brunswick after the schism that resulted over the revival in 1741.

4. *LCH*, 2–3. Further discussion of differences between the New Side and Old Side appears in Trinterud, *The Forming of an American Tradition*, chaps. 6–10; *LSAP*, chaps. 1–2; E. Brooks Holifield, *Theology in America: Christian Thought from the Age of the Puritans to the Civil War* (New Haven, CT: Yale University Press, 2003), 93–101; Sydney E. Ahlstrom, *A Religious History of the American People*, 2nd ed. (New Haven, CT: Yale University Press, 2004); Mark A. Noll, *America's God: From Jonathan Edwards to Abraham Lincoln* (New York: Oxford University Press, 2002).

5. *LCH*, 2–3. Conventicles originated first among pietists in Germany under the leadership of Phillip Jacob Spener in the seventeenth century. As pietist practices spread to other countries, England passed conventicle acts in 1664 and 1670, which prohibited illegal meetings in private houses for worship by more than five people other than those prescribed by the Book of Common Prayer. The Toleration Act of 1689 finally rescinded the anti-conventicle acts. Cf. Dale Brown, *Understanding Pietism* (Grand Rapids: Eerdmans, 1978); Ted Campbell, *The Religion of the Heart: A Study of European Religious Life in the Seventeenth and Eighteenth Centuries* (Columbia, SC: University of South Carolina Press, 1991); F. Ernest Stoeffler, *The Rise of Evangelical Pietism* (Leiden: Brill, 1965).

6. D. G. Hart has explored confessionalism as a forgotten element in American denominational life. Because revivalism exercised such a dominant role in defining American religion, Hart contends that the confessional strands in Lutheranism, Presbyterianism, and Episcopalianism have suffered from mistreatment and neglect by historians. *LSAP*, 49–50.

Chapter 2: Early Religious Experience

1. My initial interest in Hodge was spurred by the alleged lack of attention to the affective dimension. *Piety and the Princeton Theologians* attempted to correct previous studies of Princetonians that claimed that rationalism so dominated their thought that they virtually eliminated subjective emphases from their theology. This study broaches the issue using different criteria of pietism and confessionalism. Others have debated whether Hodge ever effectively integrated dichotomous elements in his writings. This study is intended to extend this discussion forward. Cf. W. Andrew Hoffecker, *Piety and the Princeton Theologians: Archibald Alexander, Charles Hodge, and Benjamin Warfield* (Phillipsburg, NJ: Presbyterian and Reformed, 1981); Mark A. Noll, ed., *The Princeton Theology, 1812–1921: Scripture, Science, and Theological Method*

from Archibald Alexander to Benjamin Warfield (Grand Rapids: Baker, 1983); *WOL*; David Wells, ed., *The Princeton Theology* (Grand Rapids: Baker, 1989); *PS*, vol. 1. A recent and reliable attempt to interpret Hodge in this matter is Mark A. Noll, "Charles Hodge as an Expositor of the Spiritual Life," in *CHR*, 181–216.

2. The income resulted from commerce on the Arch Street wharf. As the war approached, commerce was suspended, thus cutting off revenue from Hodge's grandfather's docks and warehouses. Hodge gives an indication of the early wealth of his family by recalling that Andrew Hodge as a "successful merchant . . . possessed one of the only six carriages then in the city [Philadelphia]." *LCH*, 3.

3. *LCH*, 9–10. Charles's affection for his mother appears in the way he began and closed his letters. "Dear Mother" was often replaced with more endearing words of greeting: "My Dear Mother," "My Dearest Mother," and "My Dear Mamma." While he most frequently closed his letters with the simple words "Your son," he also used phrases such as "My dear mother's affectionate son," "I am ever, my dear mother, your affectionate Charles," "I remain, dear mother, your son," and "Your loving son." Hodge displayed similar familial affection in letters to his brother, using "My dear brother," "Your affectionate brother," and "Your loving brother." Reflective of Hodge's affection for his mother, William McLaughlin in describing evangelicalism in the nineteenth century stated that virtually every collection of sermons from that period included at least one on "The Christian Home" and another that extolled the glories of "Motherhood." William G. McLaughlin, *The American Evangelicals, 1800–1900: An Anthology* (New York: Harper, 1968), 17–19.

4. *LCH*, 13. Hodge would later recall the benefits of being catechized, and that memory would buttress his confrontation with New School Presbyterian piety.

5. The old measures stood in contrast to "new measures" adopted by revivalists in the Second Great Awakening of the nineteenth century. See John Williamson Nevin's critique of new measures in his *Anxious Bench* as described in part 4 below.

6. *PS*, 1:106. In his *ST* Hodge devoted chapter 20 in volume 3 (pp. 466–709) to "The Means of Grace." Hodge's comment on the role of the Bible in Christian nurture reflected his own background: "True religion prevails in any community, in proportion to the degree in which the young are instructed in the facts and indoctrinated in the truths of the Bible . . . Where the young are from the beginning imbued with the knowledge of the Bible, there pure Christianity abides; and where they are allowed to grow up in ignorance of divine truth, there true religion languishes and loses more and more of its power. Such is the testimony of experience." Ibid., 3:470.

7. The *Princeton Review* had several titles in its history. It began as *Biblical Repertory*, then *Biblical Repertory and Theological Review*, *Biblical Repertory and Princeton Review*, and finally *Princeton Review*.

8. Archibald Alexander, "Dr. Green's Lectures on the Shorter Catechism," *PR* 2 (1830): 299–300. Alexander provided a brief history of catechizing, from the patriarchs in the Old Testament to its use in the New Testament and Origen's catechetical school at Alexandria. While Hodge studied in Europe, he took extensive notes on August

Tholuck's perspective on method of theological instruction in his *Encyclopedia of Theology*, which supported the Princeton method of teaching theology by recitation. Under the topic "Value of Oral Instruction," Tholuck enumerated advantages of catechetical instruction. The teacher "can be satisfied that the student really understands him and the powers of the student are better exercised and the subject is brought more intimately before his mind and made his own." By the catechetical method, "all misapprehensions can be best prevented by questions directed to the students." The method "enables the student to accept [the teacher's] instructions," and "the attention of the hearer is also better secured." Tholuck concluded: "All these considerations give the catechetical method decided preference over all others for all those whose minds are not already cultivated and developed." Tholuck's remarks mirror rather remarkably Hodge's experience under the guidance of his mother and pastor and reflect the tedium of the classroom recitation at Princeton. He also elaborated on the lecture ("oral") method, which he believed built on the catechetical. While catechism had the advantage of focusing on particular points, lectures expanded on those points. Lectures enabled students to see the connectedness of ideas and establish the habit of reflection, thus bringing the various parts of a theological system into an integrated whole. Notes, "*Encyclopedia of Theology* by August Tholuck, Halle, 1827," in Hodge Papers, Princeton Theological Seminary.

9. Alexander, "Dr. Green's Lectures," 299–300.

10. Ibid., 304–5.

11. *LCH*, 13.

12. Ibid.

Chapter 3: From Philadelphia to the College of New Jersey

1. Hodge recounted his being particularly affected by an Irish Swedenborgian named Taylor, who eschewed drilling students in rote memorization in favor of gathering his students around a map and expatiating on a country's topographical features, ancient ruins, population, manners and customs, and prominent historical figures. "He would linger around the battle-fields, describe the conflicts, taking part vehemently with one side against the other. He was an enthusiast, and infected his pupils with his spirit." *LCH*, 12. Taylor's enthusiasm joined with attention to detail is reflected in Hodge's journal of his years in Europe and his voluminous letter-writing.

2. Varnum Lansing Collins examines curriculum and entrance requirements from the college's origin to the end of the nineteenth century. He notes that the trustees abruptly raised the standards for admission in 1819 by adding proficiency in several more classical works, geography, and English grammar. Princeton was the first American college to list grammar and added geography only a year later than Harvard required it. Varnum Lansing Collins, *Princeton* (New York: Oxford University Press, 1914), 291–305. Hodge relates an incident in 1842 of a random meeting in the train station at Philadelphia with the tutor who had examined him in 1812. Upon finding out Hodge's identity, the man said, "O! Pshaw! I thought he was an old man." *LCH*,

22. Thomas Jefferson Wertenbaker, *Princeton, 1746–1896* (Princeton, NJ: Princeton University Press, 1946), treats curriculum and entrance requirements as they developed under various administrations. Wertenbaker criticizes Princeton's admitting students such as Hodge to advanced standing because it led to accepting less qualified students as freshmen. Thus, more students entered Princeton as sophomores than as freshmen, the latter requiring remedial instruction. As late as 1825, out of a total student body of 107 at Princeton, only 6 were freshmen. Dr. James W. Alexander complained of the low standards: "Let the standard of college attainments be elevated far above the present degree. Let the servile work of learning to read Latin and Greek be kept to the schools. . . . I would have the students learn in college the higher branches of education—the higher mathematics if his taste let him pursue it, the philosophy of the mind, ethics, natural law, political economy and the classics." John Hall, ed., *Forty Years' Familiar Letters of James W. Alexander, Constituting, with Notes, the Memoir of His Life* (New York: Scribner, 1870), 9, quoted in Wertenbaker, *Princeton*, 162. Wertenbaker's history of Princeton draws heavily upon James Maclean's two-volume *History of the College of New Jersey* (Philadelphia: J. B. Lippincott & Co., 1877).

3. Protestant scholastic Francis Turretin's voluminous *Insitutio Theologiae Elencticae* (1679–85) functioned as the theological text at Princeton Seminary from its founding until Hodge published his three-volume *ST* in 1871–73.

4. *LCH*, 25–30. Wertenbaker contrasts the weakness of academic leadership provided by Green with the progressive proposals by Lindsley, which if followed would have greatly enhanced the quality of Princeton's education. Wertenbaker's perspective of "Princeton's Nadir" becomes evident in his statement that only the "secularizing of Princeton," the lessening of denominational control and meeting the needs of the nation, altered the curricular offerings and substantially influenced graduates to select other vocations. Wertenbaker, *Princeton*, 162–65, 182. Hodge lamented his lack of foreign languages profoundly, and it played a significant role in his decision to study abroad after his graduation from seminary.

5. *LCH*, 32–33. Despite his general silence on these matters, Hodge continued to rely heavily on his mother's approval. According to *LCH*, his mother had "required" him to return to Philadelphia after his graduation to bolster his knowledge and recover his health, which had suffered from his exertion to excel in his classes. He mentions his delay in writing to her, a procrastination that seems in part due to his anxiety about receiving her consent to attend seminary. Ambivalence marks the letter's content. On the one hand, he says, "And here my dear mamma, I leave myself entirely at your disposal." On the other, he strongly states that another year of general reading (perhaps suggested by her?) would only postpone his inevitable enrollment. *LCH*, 41–43. Years later Hodge noted his thirtieth birthday in his journal written during his two-year sojourn in Germany. In several sentences he expressed his piety and the lack of his accomplishments and could not resist tying both to the remembrance of his mother: "This night thirty years ago I was born. Thirty years of love and mercy. Thirty years of sin. Thirty years and nothing done. Oh my God, from my soul I pray thee, grant

me thy Holy Spirit that if permitted yet longer to live, it may be to more purpose . . . Bless, O God, my dear, precious mother, who thirty years ago, first rejoiced over me." "Journal," 96. Hodge's "Journal" is available online: http://scdc.library.ptsem.edu /mets/mets.aspx?src=hodgeeurojournal&div=0.

6. Wertenbaker, Maclean, and Collins provide details of student unrest over campus policies, regulations, and food that gave rise to vandalism, use of explosive "crackers," and other incidents of mischief. *LCH*, 26; *PS*, 1:38.

7. Letter to Hugh Hodge, February 15, 1815, in *CHP*, box 9, folder 1.

8. Richard Robert Osmer, *Confirmation: Presbyterian Practices in Ecumenical Perspective* (Louisville, KY: Geneva Press, 1996), 126. Osmer distinguishes the "Nurture/ Development Trajectory" of Old School Presbyterians characterized by continuity between baptism, instruction, and admission to the Lord's Supper and the "Crisis/ Nurture Trajectory" of New Schoolers in which conversion stands alone as a dramatic change of life. Nurture in this model follows rather than precedes conversion, since the individual is assumed to have no previous understanding in the faith and therefore needs to be catechized. Ibid., 125–33. Osmer cites Eric Hadan, *The History of the Use of the Shorter Catechism in the Presbyterian Church in the United States of America* (Kansas City, KS: Central Seminary Press, 1941).

9. The autobiographical material in *LCH* moves from depicting the spiritual tone at the college under Green and Archibald Alexander, which Hodge describes with the comment "Those were memorable days," to the comments of the revival in 1814–15. Of the revival, Hodge states that half the student body "gave to their fellow-men, in their after life, every evidence of having become true believers during this revival." He lists the names and churches that they later served. A. A. Hodge inserts a paragraph telling of his father's profession of faith and joining the church as part of "that wonderful revival of religion . . . one of the most memorable in the whole history of the town." *LCH*, 30.

10. Ibid. D. G. Hart mentions "Old World Presbyterian" extreme reticence in speaking of one's religious experience as a primary feature of confessionalism. He cites Old Side minister John Thomson's refusal to make questions into a person's experience—such as a revivalist conversion—a test of one's faith and a criterion for ministerial communion. *LSAP*, 32–42.

11. Letter of January 23, 1815, in *CHP*, box 7, folder 1. Prayer meetings erupted at various venues on campus and spread throughout the community, with the result that people who "instinctively followed each other last winter in mischief . . . are led in the same manner this season to good." Despite the possibility that students simply followed the crowd, she concludes, "It is very probable that after the effervescence subsides, there will be a good number who will experience a radical change." Ibid.

12. Arthur Thomas calls the Virginia revivals that extended from 1787 to 1837 "the forgotten phase of the Second Great Awakening." Leaders such as John Holt Rice, who led revivals at Hampden-Sydney Academy (later Union Theological Seminary) and organized the First Presbyterian Church in Richmond, preached a Calvinist-based

revivalism. Others held revivals on college campuses, aiming their appeals at prominent figures such as lawyers, intellectuals, writers, and other professionals. While emotional outbursts occurred, preachers urged restraint and took precautions to ensure that order prevailed. This type of revivalism received support from Princetonians and other Old Schoolers even as they severely criticized revivals in other venues for their excesses and divergences from theological orthodoxy. Arthur D. Thomas, "Reasonable Revivalism: Presbyterian Evangelization of Educated Virginians," *JPH* 61 (1983): 316–34.

Chapter 4: Following the Plan

1. Hodge's close friends John Johns and Philip R. Fendall shared first honors, and Charles shared second honors with Alexander Wortz. *LCH*, 38.

2. Forced by circumstances to be a generalist, Alexander attempted to acquaint himself with sources from the Greek and Latin church fathers through the Enlightenment. James Alexander mentions by name the prominent modern figures Descartes, Leibniz, Wolff, and Voetius, as well as authors in both the established Anglican Church and "nonconformist divines" up to New England Hopkins and Emmons in the American scene. James W. Alexander explained in the biography of his father: "[Alexander] gave the biography of eminent opponents, clear analysis of their systems, and refutation of their reasons. What might be considered by some an inordinate length of time, was devoted to the cardinal differences, such as the controversy with Deists, Arians, Socinians, Pelagians, Arminians, Papists and Universalists; all being made to revolve around the Calvinistic system, which upon sincere conviction, he had adopted." James W. Alexander, *Life of Archibald Alexander: First Professor in the Theological Seminary at Princeton, New Jersey* (New York: Charles Scribner, 1854). See also discussion below on the "Plan of the Seminary."

3. Letters of January 11, 1817, December 13, 1917, in *CHP*, box 7, folder 1. Apropos of his mother's estimate of Charles's academic ability, Hugh commented on his brother's aptitude for seminary work: "Now he began to discover considerable facility in acquiring knowledge, although he was not much of a student." Despite his being "very much pressed" in his studies, Hodge engaged in activities such as "The Musical Association of Princeton," which met once each week. Members of his family remember his singing hymns in his study, and Hodge claimed hymnody as a treasure of the church as well as a potential basis for theology. Hodge's tight schedule, sunny disposition, and need for external impulses to prevail are reflected in the following comment: "My duties are so numerous and constant that there is not an hour in the day in which I feel at liberty to attend to what is foreign to my present pursuits. I am happy that such is the case, being persuaded that it is necessary *for me* to be pressed forward, in order to do all I am able to accomplish." Letter of March 22, 1817, in *CHP*, box 7, folder 1.

4. The most obvious testimony to Hodge's extensive associations and the character of his friendships is his vast correspondence (including many letters to Johns), words of greeting delivered at the celebration of his semicentennial as professor, and the tributes collected upon his death.

5. Maclean wrote a two-volume history of the university. During his school years he shared classrooms with men who became influential figures in law, the judiciary, the Congress, the ministry, and missionary efforts around the globe. Hodge enumerated his classmates in *LCH*, 34–36. Hodge's sixty-year friendship with Johns was "singular, and in the experience of either of them, had no rival of its kind." Ibid., 52. The relationships with Johns, McIlvaine, and leaders in other denominations, including churches in foreign lands, fostered an ecumenical perspective that broadened Hodge's theological contacts outside his Presbyterian background. When Hodge presented greetings at the annual meeting of the Protestant Episcopal Evangelical Societies decades later, he mentioned the bond that had united him with Johns and McIlvaine since the 1815 revival at Princeton and their sharing the same classroom at the seminary. Ibid., 509–30, 588–616.

6. Ibid., 47. Although Alexander exerted the most sustained and pervasive influence, Hodge benefited from other professors as well, especially Samuel Miller, the second professor of the seminary, who taught church history and polity. Miller's wide-ranging *A Brief Retrospect of the Eighteenth Century: Part First; in Two Volumes: Containing a Sketch of the Revolutions and Improvements in Science, Arts, and Literature, during That Period* (New York: T. and J. Swords, 1803) kept Princeton's vision from being narrowly theological. Hodge learned from Miller that a minister of the gospel ought to avoid provinciality by cultivating awareness across the spectrum of cultural developments—history, philosophy, the sciences, literature, and the arts. Cf. Anita Schorsch, "Samuel Miller, Renaissance Man: His Legacy of 'True Taste,'" *JPH* 66, 2 (Summer 1988): 71–87.

7. *BH*. Pertinent sections of the "Plan of the Seminary" appear as appendage 1 in *PS*, vol. 1. The Plan is also available online: www.digital.library.ptsem.edu and www.books.google.com/books.

8. The primary author of the Plan, Ashbel Green, in concert with Alexander and Miller, pressured the General Assembly until it finally acquiesced in founding the school in 1812. Cf. Mark A. Noll, "The Founding of Princeton Seminary," *WTJ* 42 (1979): 72–110. Citing the Plan as an influence on Hodge's life is justified by the significant correlation between the Plan's intent of producing ministers with clearly defined characteristics and the qualities of Hodge's life manifested in his letters and diaries.

9. The eight articles are "Of the General Assembly," "Of the Board of Directors," "Of the Professors," " Of Study and Attainments," "Of Devotion, and Improvement in Practical Piety," "Of the Students," "Of the Library," and "Of the Funds." The seriousness with which the Plan was to be taken is illustrated by Section 7 of Article II: "At the commencement of each stated spring meeting, the whole plan of the Seminary shall be distinctly read before the board of directors."

10. *BH*, 37, 40. The inclusion of the American Education Society as a potential source of funds indicates that Princeton's dispute over voluntary societies had not reached its peak. *BH* also states that before 1838, support from Female Cent Societies, one among many voluntary societies in the early nineteenth century, aided indigent students.

11. Arguably, the Plan mandates the "Athens" model of theological education in contemporary discussions of seminary education. The Athens model stresses *paideia*, the formation of the student's character in the process of appropriating revealed wisdom. The counterpart is the "Berlin" model, which emphasizes theological education as *Wissenschaft*, disciplined theological study, combined with professional education for ministry. Cf. *BAB*. David Kelsey maintains that no genuine synthesis is possible in these two models. The discussion that follows shows that Princeton nevertheless attempted in some way to mediate the two models.

12. *BH*, 18. Princeton's emphasis on learning the original languages of the Old and New Testaments reflects John Calvin's Genevan Academy. For Calvin's emphasis on biblical languages, see John Currid, *Calvin and the Biblical Languages* (Fearn, Ross-shire, UK: Christian Focus, 2007).

13. *BH*, 18. Glenn T. Miller notes that America's early seminaries established their curriculums with apologetic aims in mind. The requirement regarding deism reflected evangelical concerns that deists prominent in the initial history of the country, such as Thomas Jefferson and Thomas Paine, had deliberately distanced themselves from traditional Christianity. In addition, parading the Goddess of Reason in France showed the extremes of deism. *PAI*, 19, 26.

14. *BH*, 19–20. Reflecting concern for students' behavior, Samuel Miller published what might be called a handbook for ministerial behavior in his *Letters on Clerical Manners and Morals Addressed to a Student in the Theological Seminary at Princeton, N.J.* (New York: G. & C. Carvill, 1827).

15. *BH*, 21–23. One could hardly envision a charter document for a seminary more consistent with the Westminster Confession and catechisms than the "Plan of the Seminary."

16. "Certain Evils in the Seminary," in *CHP*, box 6, folder 18. See chapter 16 for Hodge's assessment of the temperance movement.

17. See *BAB*, 6–11. Although Princeton never explicitly affirmed the Athenian model by name, seminary education at Princeton clearly bore more resemblance to this Athens model than the Berlin model, which is described in the next chapter. Glenn T. Miller noted that Calvin's naming his Genevan school an "academy" illustrated his humanist background and Calvin's emphasis on studying the original languages of the Bible. *PAI*, 13. David Calhoun notes that Alexander and Miller, because of their years in ministry, better modeled how pastors should preach than did others, such as Hodge, who had no previous pastoral experience. *PS*, 1:92–99, 373–74.

18. "Dr. Spring on the Power of the Pulpit," *PR* 20, 3 (1848): 470–71.

19. Ibid., 476–77. In a footnote Hodge cited a report from the American Tract Society documenting that 106 students from 17 seminaries utilized their vacation to visit 42,644 families, distributed 10,021 volumes to destitute households, and handed out 712,000 tracts. They also attended or spoke at 931 meetings. He also reported activities in behalf of the American Sunday-School Union and other voluntary societies.

20. Ibid., 479.

21. Ibid., 482–84.

22. Ibid., 485. Spring's criticism may be viewed as an early criticism that would grow in intensity against the overemphasis of intellectual preparation and a lack of practical theology at Princeton. Calhoun notes that practical theology was Princeton's weakest part of the curriculum. Alexander and Miller, as former pastors, best exemplified the balance that Spring's criticism sought. Beginning in the 1880s, vast changes occurred as seminaries deemphasized the original languages and electives began to edge out previously required courses. Benjamin B. Warfield defended the Plan in the 1920s and spoke on students' need for spiritual culture in seminary life. Students complained of a lack in practical courses. *PS*, 1:91–100, 372–74; ibid., 2:215–16, 265–68.

23. Presbyterians, Congregationalists, and Episcopalians were noted for emphasizing an educated ministry, whereas Baptists and Methodists focused more on the spiritual qualification of pastors. For a detailed discussion of the relative decline of the former denominations and the rise of the latter in the nineteenth century, see Roger Finke and Rodney Stark, "The Upstart Sects within America," in *The Churching of America 1776–1990: Winners and Losers in Our Religious Economy* (New Brunswick, NJ: Rutgers University Press, 1992), 55–116.

Chapter 5: Fledgling Ministry

1. Mark Noll points out that many denominations suffered extreme shortages of pastors during the early national period, not just Presbyterians, in "The Founding of Princeton Seminary," *WTJ* (1979): 72–110. Alexander initially offered the position to Hodge's close friend John Johns, who "was always first—first everywhere, and first in everything," but Johns turned it down in favor of ministering in the Episcopal Church. *LCH*, 63–65.

2. Hodge also took advantage of his relocation to Philadelphia to attend lectures on anatomy and physiology at the University of Pennsylvania. Throughout his life he took great interest in scientific and medical subjects and became an informed layman capable of intelligent discussion on a wide range of issues. *LCH*, 66, 68. Cf. Ronald L. Numbers, "Charles Hodge and the Beauties and Deformities of Science," in *CHR*, 77–102.

3. Hodge preached in the mornings first at the Falls of Schuylkill and later at Cohocksink, a mission station, and at the United States Arsenal at Frankford in the afternoons.

4. The diary is lodged in *CHP*, box 1, folder 13, but is accessible in its entirety in Charles D. Cashdollar, "The Pursuit of Piety: Charles Hodge's Diary, 1819–1820," *JPH* 55 (Fall 1977): 267–83. Nine entries appear in *LCH*, 72–74. The original consists of fifteen pages written on both sides, each side recording a different Sabbath. The page numbers in the following notes are from Cashdollar's article.

5. Ibid., 270, 274, 278–79.

6. The words *piety* and *feeling* appear with equal regularity throughout the journal. Together they appear some thirty times.

7. Ibid., 270, 272.

8. Ibid., 280.

9. Ibid., 271, 275, 279–80. D. G. Hart's recent study of John Williamson Nevin provides a portrayal of Nevin's spiritual life that is strikingly similar to Hodge's. Nevin's early religious training resembled Hodge's. Each grew up in a confessionalist covenantal family, sustained rigorous catechetical instruction, experienced a revival conversion, and subsequently struggled with paroxysms of doubt and guilt from not being able to live up to his own unrealistic spiritual expectations. Nevin, however, successfully emerged from his spiritual quagmire when he perceived the conflict between two disparate pieties in the Presbyterian heritage, the "New England Puritanic theory" associated with New Side revivalism and "the old proper Presbyterian theory of the seventeenth century" in the confessionalist tradition. In reflecting on the nuances that separated the older churchly Presbyterianism and the revivalist strand, Nevin stated in his autobiography that Princeton Seminary bore the blame for his spiritual vacillation: "Our teaching was not steadily and consistently in one direction. . . . So it was that I found myself in a sort of strait between these two systems, and knew not how to adjust the one rightly with the other in my religious life." D. G. Hart, *John Williamson Nevin: High Church Calvinist* (Phillipsburg, NJ: P&R Publishing, 2005), 50.

10. Cashdollar, "The Pursuit of Piety," 269.

11. Cashdollar contends that the diary demonstrates in large part why Hodge ended up in the seminary classroom and not in the pastorate. Because Princetonians placed such a premium on piety, daily spiritual experience exceeded conversion as the litmus test for one's calling as a pastor. Leaving the spiritual confines of Princeton, many graduates found maintaining the intense piety demanded by the Plan virtually impossible and thus questioned the validity of their call. Because his failures outnumbered his successes as a preacher of piety in 1819–20, Hodge resorted to the classroom, where he felt more comfortable. Ibid., 267–70, 281. Cashdollar's views on Hodge's vocation, however, fail to take into account that before his ten-month stint as missionary preacher, Alexander had already broached the possibility of Hodge's joining the faculty. On May 6, 1918, before his missionary endeavors, Alexander asked Hodge to consider teaching at the seminary. Alexander instructed Hodge to pursue his Hebrew study and to be open to joining the faculty. *LCH*, 65–66. Hodge's thinking on his future work was so unsettled at this time that he pondered a career in medicine by attending lectures on anatomy and physiology. Ibid., 68.

12. Two interesting parallels can be cited that bear similarities to Hodge's struggles to maintain his New Side piety, one from his own time and another from the twentieth century. As mentioned above, John Williamson Nevin, Hodge's classmate at Princeton, experienced similar paroxysms of spiritual highs and lows. D. G. Hart describes Nevin's piety in *John Williamson Nevin: High Church Calvinist.* Nevin grew up in a confessionalist environment with strong emphasis on catechetical instruction within a covenant family and communal discipline using the traditional means of grace—daily prayer and Bible reading, weekly corporate worship, and participation in the Lord's

Supper. But at Union College, Nevin came under the influence of New Side piety in the form of a revival conversion experience like Hodge's. Hart describes Nevin's experience following his conversion: "Instead of taking comfort from the objective promises of the gospel, Nevin thought that he should constantly examine himself to see how well he was progressing." Ibid., 46. Hart cites Nevin's autobiography: "What could the result of such painful autopsy be (this everlasting studying of symptoms, this perpetual feeling of the spiritual pulse) other than the weakening of faith, the darkening of hope, and the souring of that most excellent grace of charity itself?" John Williamson Nevin, *My Own Life: The Earlier Years* (Lancaster, PA: Historical Society of the Evangelical and Reformed Church, 1964), 4. Hart concludes that at Princeton Seminary, Nevin noticed a strong internal tension between the New Side piety of Alexander and the churchly piety of Samuel Miller. Also, twentieth-century Anglican apologist C. S. Lewis's youthful struggles with his nightly prayers show a striking similarity to Hodge's and Nevin's spiritual struggles. Lewis describes his attempts to experience "realizations" (cf. Hodge's "impressions")—to "*feel* what he was praying" (emphasis added)—each evening: "I set myself a standard. No clause of my prayer was to be allowed to pass muster unless it was accompanied by what I called a 'realization,' by which I meant certain vividness of the imagination and the affections. My nightly task was to produce by sheer will power a phenomenon which will power could never produce, which was so ill-defined that I could never say with absolute certainty whether it had occurred, and which, even if it did occur, was of very mediocre spiritual value. If only someone had read to me old Walter Hilton's [fourteenth-century English mystic in *Guide to Perfection*] warning that we must never in prayer strive to extort 'by maistry' what God does not give! But no one did; and night after night I endeavored to pump up my 'realizations.'" C. S. Lewis, *Surprised by Joy: The Shape of My Early Life* (New York: Harcourt, 1955), 62. In another essay Lewis distinguished between experiences of "looking at" and "looking along." He distinguished between cognitively thinking about pain or love and experiencing pain and being in love: "You get one experience of a thing when you look along it and another when you look at it. Which is the 'true' or 'valid' experience? Which tells you most about the thing?" "Meditation in a Toolshed," in *God in the Dock* (Grand Rapids: Eerdmans, 1970), 213. Lewis also made the following comment on reading devotional guides to stimulate the religious affections: "For my own part, I tend to find the doctrinal books often more helpful in devotion than the devotional books . . . I believe that many who find that 'nothing happens' when they sit down, or kneel down, to a book of devotion, would find that the heart sings unbidden while they are working their way through a tough bit of theology with a pipe in their teeth and pencil in their hand." "On the Reading of Old Books," in ibid., 205. Both Lewis and Nevin resolved the issue of their inner spiritual conflict. Nevin did so by consciously choosing to adhere to his confessionalist roots. Lewis did so by acknowledging the balance between "looking at" and "looking along." Hodge seems to have recognized the pitfalls of an overly introspective piety but never verbalized that resolution to the extent that Nevin and Lewis did.

Chapter 6: Expanding Vistas

1. Letter of July 10, 1820, in *CHP*, box 9, folder 1. Hodge would supplement his salary by supply preaching in churches throughout the presbytery. *LCH*, 76.

2. On the panorama he witnessed from the top of the State House, he remarked, "Our eyes rested on what is thought the finest prospect in America. Boston, Charlestown and Cambridge were all below us; the harbor, with its many islands, and the broad ocean full in view, altogether forms a combination of the beautiful and grand, which makes the Bostonians willing to enter into a competition with the admirers of the Bay of Naples." Letter of October 9, 1820, in *LCH*, 78.

3. Hodge's consistency in these matters is borne out in all his correspondence. A. A. Hodge's footnote describes Taylor as "author of the modification of New England Theology, called 'Taylorism,' against which the polemic guns of the *Princeton Review* were trained for forty years." *LCH*, 79. Hodge focused on the inadequacies of Taylor's views on regeneration in *ST*, 3:12–14.

4. Hodge adds the following evaluation of Kirkland: "[Kirkland] is entirely free from anything which would indicate that he believes, what those around him believe"—a remark implying that Kirkland differed from the dominant Unitarian theological milieu of Harvard. Letter of October, 25, 1820, in *CHP*, box 7, folder 1.

5. Ibid. Hodge continues: "He told me he had lost at least three years by taking a wrong course at first. I am persuaded that it would be the best thing I could do to spend a year with such a man. But it is impossible. I will write to him, however, and see him as often as I can." Ibid. Hodge did not pursue this course. Instead he decided to get even more firsthand instruction by studying abroad. Although Hodge later challenged Stuart's interpretation of Romans, especially on the federal headship of Adam, he continued to hold Stuart in high esteem.

6. Letters of October 9, 25, 1820, in *CHP*, box 9, folder 1.

Chapter 7: Fledgling Professor

1. Letter of November 21, 1820, in *CHP*, box 9, folder 1.

2. Letter of December 19, 1821, in *CHP*, box 9, folder 1.

3. *LCH*, 86.

4. Letter of January 1, 1822, in *CHP*, box 9, folder 1.

5. Letter of January 19, 1822, in *CHP*, box 9, folder 1.

6. Hodge and other Princetonians never understood plenary inspiration to mean that the Holy Spirit dictated the words of the Bible but that the biblical authors drew from their own cultural setting and vocabulary when writing.

7. *Dissertation*, 23–24, 27. Hodge's views reflected the Athens model of theological instruction discussed above as *paideia*. Instruction should not only inform the intellect but also shape the behavior or piety of the student. Instructors must also teach conforming with this model. For a brief discussion of "disengaged reason," see Michael Payne, "Philosophy among the Ruins: The Twentieth Century and Beyond," in *Revolutions in*

Worldview: Understanding the Flow of Western Thought, ed. W. Andrew Hoffecker (Phillipsburg, NJ: P&R Publishing, 2007), 336, 345.

8. Ibid., 7, 15, 38. Ernest Sandeen argues in "The Princeton Theology: One Source of Biblical Literalism in American Protestantism," *Church History* 31, 3 (1962): 307–21, that Hodge's son and B. B. Warfield introduced the notion of inerrancy in 1881. Randall Balmer refutes Sandeen's claim in "The Princetonians and Scripture: A Reconsideration," *WTJ* 44 (1982): 352–65. Hodge's remarks support Balmer's contention.

9. *Dissertation*, 14, 40.

10. Ibid., 39, 41–42, 48–49.

11. Ibid., 41–42.

12. Ibid., 44–45, 47, 49. Cf. Thomas H. Olbricht, "Charles Hodge as an American New Testament Interpreter," *JPH* 52, 2 (Summer 1979): 117–33. Olbricht traces the development of Hodge's views from his seminal reflections in his *Dissertation* to the expansion of those ideas under August Tholuck in Europe (which we will study in part 2) to his mature exegetical thought as manifested in his commentaries on Pauline writings.

13. *Dissertation*, 49–51.

14. Letter of April 2, 1822, in *LCH*, 89. Hodge expressed profound desire for his future as he unburdened himself to Alexander as the General Assembly drew near: "I would prefer being here [at Princeton] with the smaller salary, to any other situation with the largest, that the country affords." Letter of May 6, 1822, in ibid., 91.

15. Ibid., 94.

16. Letter of April 15, 1822, in *CHP*, box 9, folder 1. A. A. Hodge noted in *LCH* that Hugh published articles in medical journals. He wrote two famous larger works, "Diseases Peculiar to Women" (1860) and a text on obstetrics (1863). He also wrote a number of "introductory lectures," one of which bears mention. A. A. wrote, "One of these on criminal abortion, after being reprinted several times, was published with some additions under the title of 'Foeticide.'" *LCH*, 540. On the latter issue the 1869 General Assembly adopted a resolution condemning infanticide as "a horrible crime" and as something being practiced "to an alarming extent." The resolution continued, "This Assembly regards the destruction by parents of their own offspring before birth with abhorrence, as a crime against God and against Nature." Pastors were enjoined to be "no longer silent or tolerant of these things." "The General Assembly of 1869," *PR* 41, 3 (1869): 414–16.

17. In a letter to Hugh, Charles said that the cost of building the house was $3,500–4,000. Given Hodge's penchant for keeping meticulous financial records, the surprising feature about this figure is its inexactness. One could safely say without too much exaggeration that Hodge kept track of every dime's expenditure when he set his mind to it. *CHP*, box, 9, folder 4, contains thirteen account books written in exquisite penmanship, which contrasts sharply with the scrawl in most of his correspondence. Hodge's obsession with keeping records and historical mementos is perhaps best illustrated by his saving his arithmetic papers from his schoolboy years.

18. A. A. Hodge omits any reference to his birth in *LCH*.

19. Letter of December 25, 1825, in *CHP*, box 7, folder 1. In his genealogical record, Hodge traced Sarah's family tree back to Franklin. *CHP*, box 1, folder 4.

20. *LCH*, 99.

21. The journal appeared first as a massive 608-page volume. In the introduction Hodge stated its purpose of filling a field then unoccupied in American theological studies. It would make "information contained in expensive and rare volumes" and published previously only in European languages available to students who would otherwise not have access to them. Hodge also restated the theme in his *Dissertation*, that biblical criticism as a discipline is not inimical to orthodoxy but has been so reconstrued by "the most celebrated writers on these subjects" who held "loose theological opinions." Theological error preceded errors in biblical studies. Theological error of English, French, and German deists made errors in biblical criticism possible. Therefore, Hodge envisioned that the journal would enable orthodox students to reclaim biblical criticism for the cause of Christian truth. *PR* 1, 1 (January 1825): iii–iv.

22. *LCH*, 99.

23. Letter of August 29, 1826, in *CHP*, box 9, folder 2. Hodge added in a September 14 letter that Alexander and Patton fully supported his proposal, and that earlier in his career Patton had benefited from a similar course of action. Hodge's confession of leaving his Greek behind him after college and spending all his time with "other concerns" may remain a temptation to theological students in all eras, since they usually take the languages early in seminary and may not be required to use them in subsequent courses unless advanced biblical exegetical courses are built into the curriculum!

24. Letter of July 18, 1826, in *CHP*, box 9, folder 2.

25. Letter of September 25, 1826, in *CHP*, box 9, folder 2. The appointment of Nevin marked one of several times their paths intersected. Nevin, having studied Hebrew under Hodge, graduated from Princeton just before his appointment. Later in their careers, sharp differences marred their originally amicable relationship. For additional comment on Nevin's years at Princeton and his later conflicts with Hodge, cf. D. G. Hart, *John Williamson Nevin: High Church Calvinist* (Phillipsburg, NJ: P&R Publishing, 2005).

Part 2: Broadened Abroad

1. Chapter 6 in *LCH* on Hodge's study leave abroad ("From his Departure for Europe October, 1826, to his Return to Princeton, September, 1828") occupies an impressive ninety-eight pages. The chapter is supported by numerous letters between Hodge and his family, faculty, and friends and his extensive "Journal" of 183 pages, which is cited at great length in *LCH*. In addition to comments by various sources on Hodge's experience (Noll, Stewart, Calhoun, et al.), see Jacob N. Beam, "Charles Hodge's Student Years in Germany," *Princeton University Library Chronicle* 3 (1947): 103–14; B. A. Gerrish, "Charles Hodge and the Europeans," in *CHR*, 129–58.

Chapter 8: Separation from Family

1. *PAI*, 107.

2. Archibald Alexander wrote sketches of the founder, William Tennent, and those whom he taught in *Biographical Sketches of the Founder, and Principal Alumni of the Log College: Together with an Account of the Revivals of Religion, under Their Ministry* (Princeton, NJ: J. T. Robinson, 1845).

3. David Calhoun explores Tennent's accomplishments in "The Log College," in *Colonial Presbyterianism: Commemorating the 300th Anniversary of the First Presbytery in America*, ed. S. Donald Fortson (Eugene, OR: Wipf and Stock, 2007), 49–61. Other American colleges that sent their professors abroad established the precedent for Princeton's supporting Hodge's venture to Europe. Edward Everett, professor of Greek at Harvard, spent four years in France, England, and Germany; he earned a PhD at Göttingen in 1817. Hodge met Everett during his trip to Boston in 1819 immediately after Everett's return. Robert Bridges Patton (Yale 1817) also studied at Göttingen. Eventually he became the first Princeton faculty member to receive a German doctorate. Bowdoin College also sent Henry Wadsworth Longfellow in 1826 to study languages and literature in Europe in preparation for teaching at Bowdoin and Harvard. Both Everett and Patton strongly influenced Hodge to embark abroad. Jacob N. Beam, "Charles Hodge's Student Years in Germany," *Princeton University Library Chronicle* 3 (1947): 104–5.

4. Letter of March 24, 1827, in *CHP*, box 13, folder 17.

5. Letter of July 21, 1827, in *CHP*, box 17, folder 63. Miller also took advantage of Hodge's presence in Germany to enhance his teaching of church history. Miller added in his letter: "I would like to know what work on Ecclesiastical History is now considered as the most popular and interesting in Germany; in what manner this branch of knowledge is generally taught in the Universities in Germany—whether by *lecture* or *textbook*—and if the latter what book is most frequently employed for this purpose." (Emphasis in original.)

6. No recent full-scale study of Miller exists. His influence at Princeton and on Hodge was nonetheless significant. Miller's son Samuel published a biography of his father: *The Life of Samuel Miller, D.D., LL.D., Second Professor of the Theological Seminary of the Presbyterian Church at Princeton, New Jersey* (Philadelphia: Claxton, Remsen and Haffelfinger, 1869). Cf. also Gilbert Chinard, "A Land Mark in American Intellectual History: Samuel Miller's *A Brief Retrospect of the Eighteenth Century*," *Princeton University Chronicle* 14 (Winter 1953): 55–71; Jacob Susskind, "Samuel Miller's Intellectual History of the Eighteenth Century," *JPH* 49 (1971): 15–31; Anita Schorsch, "Samuel Miller, Renaissance Man: His Legacy of 'True Taste,'" *American Presbyterians* 66, 2 (Summer 1988): 71–87.

Chapter 9: Maintaining Family Connections

1. Indeed, besides his repeated sense of sorrow for abandoning his wife and children and justifying his prolonged absence, Hodge expressed his concern to his brother that

Sarah's financial needs be met: "with respect to my dear wife I have only one request to make and that is that she may be spared any embarrassment about pecuniary concerns." Letter of December 21, 1826, in *CHP*, box 9, folder 2.

2. Letters of November 1, 1826, November 11, 1826, in *CHP*, box 8, folder 3. All correspondence was written on sheets of paper approximately 9½ × 16 folded in two and again in thirds with the address written on the back. They were sealed with wax, creating a 3 × 5-inch parcel. Pages were filled to within a quarter-inch of the edge to make maximum use of the sheets. Hodge advised Sarah to "get some bank paper which is very thin & consequently light. Send me several sheets written as closely as possible." He also advised her to "fill your paper completely and write small."

3. Letter of September 30, 1826, in *CHP*, box 8, folder 3.

4. Letter of October 2, 1826, in *CHP*, box 8, folder 3.

5. Hodge also used correspondence with his wife to fulfill his fatherly responsibilities to his children. He addressed young Alexander directly to offer praise and instruction: "My dear son. Your Father still loves you as much as ever. He prays every day for the dear Saviour to make you a good boy, & to bless you & your dear sister. You must pray for your Father for the dear Saviour loves to hear little children pray. You must love Mother & be very obedient . . . I know you love your sister & always give her part of every thing you have . . . I hope you will learn very fast that you may read the good Bible & write without Mama's guiding your hand." Letter of November 18, 1826, in *CHP*, box 8, folder 3.

6. Ibid.

7. Ibid.

8. "Sarah Bache Hodge," in *CHP*, box 8, folder 1. Years later, Sarah wrote from Danville, Kentucky, that Mary had delivered a son. She sewed a lock of the baby's hair into the margin of the letter. *CHP*, box 8, folder 3.

9. *LCH*, 227.

10. The cover page of Hodge's "Journal" contains the simple inscription "Charles Hodge Halle March 7, 1827." But the second page reads: "A long Letter to my Dear Sarah." He thus intended the "Journal" to supplement the many letters he wrote. While Sarah may have found the majority of entries interesting, one wonders whether she would think the detailed notes of Alexander Humboldt's lectures on physical science that Hodge took during the latter part of his stay in Berlin very fascinating! Notes on Humboldt's lectures begin in December 1827 and become more predominant until they occupy most of the concluding pages. Hodge probably used the "Journal" (letter to "Dear Sarah") to record his notes because he could not bear to waste the paper. He was coming to the end of his stay in Europe, and many blank pages remained. So he filled them with notes from Humboldt's lectures!

11. He began a letter to his mother, "I believe it's your turn to be addressed at the head of my letter." Letter of December 4, 1827, in *CHP*, box 7, folder 2.

12. Letter of December 28, 1826, in *CHP*, box 8, folder 1. His rapid grasp of French owed much to his staying with a family who spoke only French.

13. *LCH*, 106.

14. Letter to Archibald Alexander, in *LCH*, 109.

15. Ibid., 105–13. Marquis de Lafayette, a general in the revolutionary army and friend of George Washington, visited Princeton in the fall of 1824. In a gala celebration, Lafayette received a doctor of laws degree, which Princeton granted in absentia in 1790. Hodge was serving on the faculty during Lafayette's visit.

Chapter 10: Student, Conversationalist, Cultural and Ecclesiastical Observer

1. Letter of March 11, 1827, in *CHP*, box 8, folder 1. Hodge appreciated Tholuck's facility with English, since Hodge found German much more difficult than French. In a little over a year, however, he attained sufficient proficiency to engage in both writing and conversing with his newfound colleagues. Occasionally he conceded that his summary of a sermon or lecture was deficient because he was unable to comprehend its content fully.

2. Notes, "*Encyclopedia of Theology* by August Tholuck, Halle 1827," Special Collections, Princeton Theological Seminary, n.p.

3. Common Sense Realism was the lingua franca of early-nineteenth-century American theologians. When John Witherspoon became the sixth president of the College of New Jersey, he inculcated Scottish philosophy into the curriculum as the foundation of intellectual pursuit. Princeton Seminary under Archibald Alexander adopted the principles of Common Sense philosophy in the seminary's theological and apologetic classes, and Hodge followed suit. The following works are most helpful in expositing Princeton and Hodge's philosophical perspective: Peter Hicks, *The Philosophy of Charles Hodge: A 19th Century Evangelical Approach to Reason, Knowledge and Truth* (Lewiston, NY: Edwin Mellen Press, 1997); *RRPM*; Ligon Duncan III, "Common Sense Realism and American Presbyterianism: An Evaluation of the Impact of Scottish Realism on Princeton and the South" (MA thesis, Covenant Theological Seminary, 1987). Briefer expositions appear in Mark A. Noll, ed., *The Princeton Theology, 1812–1921: Scripture, Science, and Theological Method from Archibald Alexander to Benjamin Warfield* (Grand Rapids: Baker, 1983), 30–33; *PS*, 2:413–15; E. Brooks Holifield, "Hodge, the Seminary, and the American Theological Context," in *CHR*, 123–28.

4. Other mediating theologians included Isaac August Dorner of Berlin and Adolf von Harless of Erlangen. For discussions of the mediating school, see Donald Wayne Riddle, "The Background of Modern Historical Study of Christianity," *Church History* 4, 3 (September 1935): 203–13; Donald G. Dawe, *The Form of a Servant: A Historical Analysis of the Kenotic Motif* (Philadelphia: Westminster Press, 1964).

5. Lecture 7, "Conflict of Faith with Infidelity," in "History of Theology in 18th Century by August Tholuck, June 1827," Hodge Papers, Princeton Theological Seminary. Notes on Tholuck's *Wissenschaffliche Dogmatik* consisted of twelve booklets, all in German. "Lecture Notes Taken while in Germany," in *CHP*, box 2, folder 10. Hodge later showed his deep respect for his friend by publishing

his work "History of Theology in the Eighteenth Century by Dr. August Tholuck, Professor of Theology in the University of Halle; Translated from the German by the Editor," *PR* 4 (1828): 9–57. Hodge also took extensive notes on Ernst Wilhelm Hengstenberg: "Introduction to Old Testament," "Job," and "On Prophecy," in *CHP*, box 2, folder 1.

6. "Journal," 9–14.

7. Ibid., 6–7, 14, 18. John Stewart commented that the paradigmatic differences between Hodge's and Schleiermacher's theology were rooted in Hodge's use of Scottish Realism, "a philosophical tradition utterly foreign to Schleiermacher." *MTC*, 27.

8. Ibid., 164.

9. Cf. *RWLRA*, bk. 4. In further notes on Tholuck's Lecture 7, "Conflict of Faith with Infidelity," a reference notes *RWLRA*, but Hodge does not discuss its contents.

10. "Journal," 22, 27. Hodge has been frequently criticized for the easy way in which he identified his own views with those of the Bible and for not recognizing how his own interpretations of history, theology, and biblical interpretation were shaped by his American context. Cf. Mark A. Noll, "Charles Hodge as an Expositor of the Spiritual Life," in *CHR*, 205–16. Hodge's description of the place of baptism and the raising of covenant children appears below in chapter 17.

11. "Journal," 31–32. Hodge's view of the Lord's Supper emphasized its memorial nature.

12. Ibid., 36. Hodge also commented on the various forms of Jewish piety in Germany, noting the differences between those who were "generally infidels" (probably Reformed Jews) and the Hasidim, whose rabbis "are infallible, work miracles, give absolution, etc." Among his wide-ranging comments evaluating various religious groups, he noted the extreme poverty of the Jews, that they were "miserably filthy and offensive when not raised much above the ordinary level by wealth." As to their character, however, he believed they were "more moral than either the Catholics or Protestants of Poland." Ibid., 53.

13. Ibid., 60. A. A. Hodge omitted his father's reference to Tholuck's views on Romans 5 from *LCH* perhaps so as not to highlight a difference between the two friends on a point of such importance to Hodge in later theological polemics.

14. Ibid., 65. Hodge had earlier recorded in his journal that Tholuck borrowed much from the prevailing "philosophical spirit," which considered "matter as only a different modification of spirit, the essence of both being the same." *LCH*, 119.

15. Hodge commented that his awe of the German scholars when viewed from afar was lost upon meeting them in person. Of Gesenius he said, "From the other side of the Atlantic these men seemed something out of the ordinary. But here whatever their minds may be their bodies are made of clay." He was flabbergasted that Germans studied "in complete disabile [*sic*]." He wrote to Sarah that Tholuck wore no cravat or suspenders and that his shirt "had not seen the wash tub for many days." Letter of March 1, 1827, in *CHP*, box 7, folder 2.

16. "Journal," 18–19.

17. Ibid., 61–62. Cf. W. Andrew Hoffecker, "Beauty and the Princeton Piety," in *Soli Deo Gloria: Essays in Reformed Theology: Festschrift for John H. Gerstner*, ed. R. C. Sproul (Nutley, NJ: Presbyterian and Reformed, 1976), 118–33, for an expanded view of Hodge's view of beauty. Perhaps the most curious entry of his cultural experiences describes his visit to an insane asylum in Pirna, where a physician showed him "the means of amusement and cure they had devised for their patients. The latter are various bathing establishments, chairs, and beds, which can be set in rapid rotary motion, the quickness and duration of the motion being proportioned to the state of the patient." "Journal," 67.

Chapter 11: Berlin—The Reigning Center of Nineteenth-Century German Culture

1. Letter to Sarah Bache Hodge, November 4, 1827, in *CHP*, box 8, folder 4; notes on Lachmann's lectures, in *CHP*, box 2, folder 1.

2. *LCH*, 151.

3. Tholuck referred to Gerlach as "the Wesley of Berlin." *LCH*, 199.

4. "Journal," 22, 72–74.

5. Ibid., 102, 141–42.

6. The account of Silesia appears in ibid., 94. Reflective on his son's alteration of the journal, when Hodge wrote *CHPC* (see below in chapter 20), he would cast such phenomena associated with excesses of American awakenings in a very negative light.

7. "Journal," 89–90, 119–20.

Chapter 12: A New Model in Theological Education

1. *LCH*, 160–61 (emphasis in original). Less than a month later Alexander repeated his warning: "it will be worthwhile to have gone to Germany to know that there is but little worth going for. It will at any rate place you on a level with the other *traveled* literati of this country. But whatever you may gain of literature and knowledge of the world, I hope and pray that you may not lose any thing of the love of the truth and spirituality of mind." And on October 30 Alexander wrote an encouragement and caution: "I rejoice that you live in an infected atmosphere, without being yourself infected. May God preserve you." Ibid., 161.

2. "Journal," 164–65.

3. Ibid., 49.

4. Ibid., 136.

5. As in chapter 4, my primary source for the shift in theological education is *BAB*. The material found here relies on David Kelsey's discussion of the Berlin model. Ibid., 12–27.

6. The quotation is from Daniel Fallon, *The German University* (Boulder, CO: Colorado Associated University Press, 1980), cited in *BAB*, 13.

7. *BAB*, 12–14. Immanuel Kant articulated this new double standard for academic research in the field of religion in *RWLRA* (1791). Privately a church could require

a pastor or scholar to adhere to its confessional standard. The pastor was obligated to hold fast to the church's creed in catechizing, teaching, and preaching. But Kant insisted that publicly, a scholar or pastor must have "complete freedom, indeed even the calling, to impart to the public all of his carefully considered and well-intentioned thoughts concerning mistaken aspects of that symbol, as well as his suggestions for the better arrangement of religious and church matters." Kant drew a clear line between public life and private religion based on the dualism affirmed in his *Critique of Pure Reason.* As moderns progressed in their rational inquiry and their religion became increasingly rational, that is, they ceased in the "perpetuation of absurdities," this double standard of truth would become increasingly unnecessary. *RWLRA*, xxxiii, 7–10, 12, 103.

8. A detailed discussion of Hodge's assessment of Schleiermacher and European scholarship appears in B. A. Gerrish, "Charles Hodge and the Europeans," in *CHR*, 129–58.

9. *BAB*, 22–24. Terrence N. Tice probes Schleiermacher's views on theological education as *Wissenschaft* and professional in "Schleiermacher on the Scientific Study of Religion," in *Friedrich Schleiermacher and the Founding of the University of Berlin: The Study of Religion as a Scientific Discipline*, ed. Herbert Richardson (Lewiston, NY: Edwin Mellen Press, 1991), 45–82. Tice's summation reflects Schleiermacher's distinctive views of theology, which Hodge expressed difficulty in understanding upon hearing him lecture and preach: "in sum, and in Schleiermacher's words: 'This is the distinctive domain which I would assign to religious, alone and in its entirety. . . . Your feeling is your piety, with two qualifications: first, insofar as that feeling expresses the being and life common to you and to the universe in the way described, second, insofar as the particular moments of that feeling come to you as the operation of God within you mediated through the operation of the world upon you. The details that make up this category consist neither of your knowledge nor of its objects, neither of your works and deeds nor of the various spheres of conduct. They consist simply of your experiences of receptivity and the influences upon you of all that lives and moves around you accompanying and conditioning those experiences. These and only these are the exclusive elements of religious—all of them.' Study these!"

10. *BAB*, 22–24. Burton J. Bledstein explores the professionalism that characterized German education and its subsequent influence in American culture. He asks, "Why did Americans, with their evangelical impulses, entrepreneurial habits, and suspicions of Old World privileges and central governments favor German higher education?" He concludes that Americans adopted the German method that emphasized specialization to augment what was viewed as deficient in their American education. *The Culture of Professionalism: The Middle Class and the Development of Higher Education in America* (New York: Norton, 1976), 309–18.

11. On more than one occasion Hodge puzzled over the way in which theological students in the new theological environment in Germany reasoned theologically over against his American students schooled in Scottish philosophy. On February 5, 1828,

he reported a heated discussion (he called it a "logomachy"—a meaningless battle of words) "whether the *justitia vitae* of a Christian was really or only figuratively a *sacrificium*." Hodge summarized his assessment of the debate: "This gave me occasion to remark the effect on their minds, of the universal attention to philosophy required of the students in Germany. They were acute and discriminating, but amazingly deficient in plain, healthy good sense." When at the end of the debate a pious soldier offered the straightforward comment, "I have nothing but my sinful, hateful self to give. Shall I call *that* an offering, when the Bible calls Christ an offering?" Hodge noted approvingly, "His good sense and warm Christian feeling made him see more clearly and express more forcibly the true merits of the case, than all the speculating theologians present." "Journal," 127–28.

12. Bledstein probes the phenomenon of "career" replacing "calling" among American ministers: "The profession of the ministry had entered a competitive society in which unrestrained individual self-determination undermined traditional life styles. No longer did Americans feel the restriction imposed by a 'calling' in which dependent man subordinated himself to the summons of an autonomous God who had determined the station in which every man could work most diligently for the public good and avoid idleness." *The Culture of Professionalism*, 174. Bledstein discusses the professionalism of the ministry in ibid., 173–76, 197–98, 200, 208–9, 226–27.

13. "Call to the Ministry" (n.d.), in *CHP*, box 6, folder 1. Hodge presented his views in outline form in one of the regular Sunday conference addresses. Since the church is the body of Christ, it has the task of recognizing people who possess gifts of ministry. "The right to teach supposes the ability to teach, as much as the eye supposes the power of vision." The evidences of a call to ministry consist of regeneration, "intellectual qualifications (including ability, knowledge, and orthodoxy)," spiritual qualifications ("high appreciation of the office, a strong desire for it from proper motives, a willingness to go anywhere and to submit to everything in the discharge of its duties, a sense of responsibility or obligation, so that we can say, 'Woe is me if I preach not the gospel!' "), and "bodily qualifications; good health and the necessary gifts of utterance." "Call to the Ministry, September 28, 1856," in *Princeton Sermons: Outlines of Discourses, Doctrinal and Practical, Delivered at Princeton Theological Seminary on Sabbath Afternoons* (London: Thomas Nelson, 1879), 310–11.

14. "Journal," 82.

15. The most extended attempt to interpret Schleiermacher's method appeared in *ST*. At the outset of that work, Hodge delineated three methods of doing theology: speculative, inductive, and mystical. He used Schleiermacher's theology as a prototype of the third. As a measure of his respect, he discussed Schleiermacher's views on virtually every theological topic. He included more citations in his index for Schleiermacher than he did for either Augustine or Calvin. His discussion on method occupies pages 1–17 of volume 1.

16. Hodge in his famous footnote in *ST*, 2:440: "When in Berlin the writer often attended Schleiermacher's church. The hymns to be sung were printed on slips of

paper and distributed at the doors. They were always evangelical and spiritual in an eminent degree, filled with praise and gratitude to our Redeemer. Tholuck said that Schleiermacher, when sitting in the evening with his family, would often say, 'Hush, children; let us sing a hymn of praise to Christ.' Can we doubt that he is singing those praises now? To whomsoever Christ is God, St. John assures us, Christ is a Saviour."

17. *LCH*, 188.

Chapter 13: Assessing the Sojourn in Europe

1. Scottish Presbyterian Charles A. Salmond in a memoir of the two Hodges commented on Charles's study abroad and the differences between theological education in Princeton and Germany. Interestingly, Salmond had also left his native Scotland to study under Albrecht Ritschl in Göttingen for the same reason that Hodge left America—to profit from the latest German scholarship. Subsequently in 1877, however, Salmond also spent a year in Princeton to gain what was old from "that ancient Seminary, as antiquity is measured in America." Salmond never regretted his additional study at Princeton. He stated straightforwardly that Germans could likewise benefit from "mingling for a time in American society." He added that "the student can hardly fail to be impressed and personally stimulated by contact with the earnest religious life of Christian America, which is a kind of thing that German theology, whatever its excellencies are, seems little calculated to produce or foster." Salmond's comments reflect his recognition of the differences between the two countries' approach to theological education. Charles A. Salmond, *Princetoniana: Charles and A. A. Hodge with Class Notes and Table Talk of Hodge the Younger* (New York: Scribner and Welford, 1888), 13–14. Salmond sat under Hodge's teaching at Princeton in 1878 and commented on his stumbling over a question on the sacraments. Ibid., 46.

2. Hodge's most visceral response during his trip was occasioned by his visit to Voltaire's room in the palace Sans Souci in Potsdam. Upon viewing the bed and table "in *statu quo*," he wrote to his wife that "it made me almost sick to look around me. For of all men who ever lived he most excites my bad feelings." Letter of April 18, 1828, in *CHP*, box 8, folder 4.

3. Letter of April 5, 1828, in *CHP*, box 13, folder 17.

4. Letter of April 6, 1828, in *CHP*, box 7, folder 2.

5. Letter of August 16, 1827, in *CHP*, box 13, folder 17. Alexander added that because of his advancing age, he looked forward to preparing for another world: "I think before very many years you will be senior Professor in this Institution, and I am afraid you will see trouble."

6. A few years after his return from Europe, Hodge reviewed Hengstenberg's commentary on Daniel as an example of sound scholarship. While the lion's portion of the article summarized Hengstenberg's point-by-point refutation of Germans' criticisms of the book of Daniel, Hodge opened and closed the review with high praise for the German evangelical. Calling Hengstenberg "a young but very learned and devout professor in the Berlin University," Hodge remarked, "It is as pleasing as it is novel, to

read books so strongly marked with all that learning and acuteness which constitute the glory of the German literati, yet having for their object the defence of revelation, and savouring throughout of evangelical religion." Hodge lauded Hengstenberg for piercing the subtle "pseudo-theology of modern German critics." To offset the errors of modern scholarship, Hengstenberg exposed their false premises and applied his considerable learning to defend traditional views of Daniel. While one might cite orthodox works from England or America, how much better, Hodge averred, to find in Hengstenberg "that champions for the truth should arise in the very midst of its assailants, armed with their armour, skilled in their devices." "Hengstenberg on Daniel," *PR* 4, 1 (1832): 48, 71.

Part 3: Moderate Old School Presbyterian

1. A study of Princeton Seminary's students and the school's rise to prominence in American education appears in Peter Wallace and Mark Noll, "The Students of Princeton Seminary, 1812–1929: A Research Note," *American Presbyterians* 72, 3 (1994): 203–15. The disparity between 500 having attended and only 132 having graduated reflects the fact that the majority of students did not complete seminary education in the early nineteenth century as a result of factors such as lack of financial resources, sickness, and even early deaths. Ibid., 204.

2. *LCH*, 203. Paul K. Conkin cites Hodge, Nathaniel Taylor, and Horace Bushnell as primary representatives of moderate—or what he calls "the uneasy center" of—Reformed theology in America in its maturity. *UCRC*, 210–49.

Chapter 14: Newfound Confidence

1. *LCH*, 203. While his lecture presented a positive view, in a letter to August Tholuck written shortly after his return, Hodge turned more critical of the American scene and particularly its public figures: "Although I feel as deeply as ever the great advantages which our ecclesiastical liberty confers upon us, and think that we have great reason to rejoice in the general prevalence of truth and piety in most sections of our country, I am now aware to a greater degree, than formerly, of the evils which attend even the best system. Our worldly men are more worldly even than yours. Religion being no more concern of the State, they do not even pay it the formal regard which in your country it receives as a part of one general secular establishment. Everything depends with us on public opinion, and this will, in the main, be right as long as vital piety be prevalent to the extent it is at present." Ibid., 210–11.

2. Ibid., 203–4. For evangelicalism's influence, see Paul K. Conkin, "The Age of Evangelical Hegemony," in *UCRC*, 114–46; Nathan O. Hatch, *The Democratization of American Christianity* (New Haven, CT: Yale University Press, 1989).

3. *LCH*, 203–4.

4. Ibid.

5. Ibid., 207–8, 210–11. In one of his first letters to Tholuck, he enthused, "I look back to my sojourn in Germany with feelings of unmingled pleasure . . . I love the German character, as exhibited in Christians, quite as much as though I were myself a German, and cannot pass a German immigrant in the street without feelings of interest I experience for no other people." Ibid., 207. Glenn T. Miller notes that Hodge kept a picture of Tholuck in his study to "inspire deeper investigation." *PAI*, 27.

6. *LCH*, 208, 211, 218. While in Germany, Hodge purchased a copy of the Qur'an for the library and an exposition of Kant's philosophy. Letter to Hugh Hodge, January 29, 1827, in *CHP*, box 13, folder 1. Interestingly, in light of their previous disagreements over Reformed theology, Tholuck requested that Hodge furnish him with "the most current work in America for or against predestination, together with a historical review of its advocates and opponents." Apparently Hodge's willingness to stand alone as he and his friends debated predestination had piqued Tholuck's curiosity to probe the matter further! *LCH*, 216.

7. Auburn originated in Geneva Presbytery of western New York in 1818. It functioned across denominational lines with Congregationalists to provide an educated clergy for America's frontier and foreign missions. In 1939 in the Great Depression, it moved to New York City, where it shared the campus of Union Theological Seminary. In the South, Union Seminary opened in Hampden-Sydney, Virginia, in 1823 and later moved to Richmond, where it became a Southern Old School rival to Princeton under the leadership of Robert L. Dabney. In 1860 Hodge pressured Dabney to join him at Princeton, but Dabney refused, claiming that Princeton already possessed teaching wealth and that his staying in Virginia would strengthen the South. Western Seminary, whose roots extended back to two classical academies in the 1780s, began in 1827 to furnish ministers for the rapidly opening territories along the Ohio River. Columbia Seminary, founded in Georgia but moving to Columbia, South Carolina, in 1830, developed a Southern Old School perspective with James Henley Thornwell as its most prominent leader. Hodge would spar with Thornwell on the floor of General Assembly over polity matters. In the West, Old Schoolers founded Lane Theological Seminary in suburban Cincinnati in 1829. Lyman Beecher, a Congregationalist turned Presbyterian, served as president and edged the school toward the revivalism of the Second Great Awakening. Within a few years of its founding, the school became embroiled in a dispute over slavery. McCormick Theological Seminary, initially named Indiana Seminary, was established in Hanover, Indiana, in 1830. Cyrus H. McCormick, zealous Old School layman and inventor of the reaper that transformed American farming, played a key role in moving the seminary to Chicago. Finally, Union Seminary in New York started in 1836 as a New School institution (The New York Theological Seminary) but remained independent. Before it became the nemesis of Princeton and the hotbed of evangelical liberalism in the late nineteenth century, Henry Boynton Smith, its most able theologian, interacted with Hodge over the reunion of Old and New Schools after the Civil War. D. G. Hart and John R. Muether discuss the proliferation of seminaries as indicative of the struggle to define Presbyterian identity. *SABC*, 104–8.

8. *LCH*, 207.

9. Mark Noll notes that Hodge's grandson, William Berryman Scott, Princeton University paleontologist, testified to his grandfather's optimistic bearing and kindly disposition: "It is the fashion nowadays to decry the Calvinistic theology and to paint its professors as gloomy and austere fanatics. Whatever may be true of other communities, I can truthfully say that never, in any part of the world, have I met such sunny, genial, kindly and tolerant people as my Grandfather and his children. He stands in my memory as the ideal of a perfect saint and gentleman, in whom I could see no flaw. The whole community revered and honoured him, but I can give no conception of the position which he held, or of the selfless, unconscious way in which he held it. He never talked of himself." *CHR*, 210.

10. A. A. Hodge's treatment of his father's ailment occupies pages 234–39 in *LCH*. Hodge regularly reported his progress or lack thereof in letters to his physician brother. David Calhoun identifies his affliction as "probably a chronic rheumatoid condition." *PS*, 1:277, 462n2. In responding to a request from Hodge's close friend Henry A. Boardman, A. A., after examining his father's numerous letters to family members, gave a detailed account of his father's ailment. Letter of March 1871, in *CHP*, box 14, folder 23.

11. Letter of July 21, 1829, in *CHP*, box 9, folder 2.

Chapter 15: A Prodigious Journalistic Venture

1. Cf. Mark A. Noll, *America's God: From Jonathan Edwards to Abraham Lincoln* (New York: Oxford University Press, 2002), 3–18. American evangelical voluntary societies were based on European groups that furthered Sunday schools, Bible and tract distribution, missionary activities, and other social causes in the late eighteenth century. See R. J. Morris, "Voluntary Societies and British Urban Elites, 1780–1850: An Analysis," *Historical Journal* 26, 1 (1983): 95–118.

2. Although the *PR* rightly gained the reputation for supporting Old School views, Hodge remarked in a letter to his brother regarding the 1837 schism, "The *Repertory* will not be made a party concern I am persuaded. Its conductors would rather see it die." Letter of July 26, 1837, in *CHP*, box 11, folder 4. Mark Noll narrates the history of the journal and those who submitted the majority of the articles in "The Princeton Review: 1825–1921," *WTJ* 50, 2 (1988): 283–304. E. Brooks Holifield includes the *PR* "among the most learned periodicals in America." *Theology in America: Christian Thought from the Age of the Puritans to the Civil War* (New Haven, CT: Yale University Press, 2003), 16.

3. *LCH*, 247–48. In his "Retrospect," Hodge stated the original purpose of the journal: "It was designed to render accessible to American readers some of the fruits of the mature learning of English and German scholars." Of his editorship he said, "Although the labouring oar was still in one pair of hands," the contributions "had the sanction of a number of gentlemen who had the confidence of the public" who "read and canvassed . . . all contributions touching delicate or difficult questions." "Retrospect," 2.

4. *PAI*, 108.

5. William Hutchison, *The Modernist Impulse in American Protestantism* (Cambridge, MA: Harvard University Press, 1976), 199.

6. "Retrospect," 3. Regarding the breadth of vision in the *PR*, a rough analysis of articles written from the 1830s to the 1880s yields the following topics and estimated number of articles on each (excluding biblical and theological topics): biography (19); education (66); fine arts (20); history (30); Indian affairs (8); international affairs (43); linguistics (12); literature (27); philosophy (101); public affairs, politics (70); present age (18); psychology (17); Sabbath (10); science (57); slavery (16); temperance (13); world religions (3); worldview (12).

7. "Retrospect," 14–15. Glenn T. Miller states that Princeton's carefully conceived Plan of the Seminary and the extent to which it was followed enabled Princeton to be "the only American theological institution to teach a consistent theological position for more than two generations." *PAI*, 107. Hodge's interaction with Schaff and Nevin is discussed in greater detail in part 4.

8. Mark Noll underscores the breadth of the journal as perhaps most exemplified by James Waddell Alexander, who wrote on "everything . . . everyone . . . and nearly every place"—a claim that Noll substantiates by listing eight to fifteen examples in each category! "The Princeton Review," 292.

9. "The Princeton Review on the State of the Country and of the Church," *PR* 37, 4 (1865): 657. Contents of the *PR* from 1830 to 1882 are available online: http://quod.lib.umich.edu/m/moajrnl/browse.journals/prin.html.

Chapter 16: Old School–New School Rivalry

1. Robert Ellis Thompson, *A History of the Presbyterian Churches in the United States* (1895; repr., Eugene, OR: Wipf and Stock, 2003), 126; E. H. Gillett, *History of the Presbyterian Church in the United States of America*, vol. 2 (Philadelphia: Presbyterian Publication Committee, 1864), 216. E. Brooks Holifield traces the differences between New and Old Schools under the titles "Calvinism Revised" and "'True Calvinism' Defended," in *Theology in America: Christian Thought from the Age of the Puritans to the Civil War* (New Haven, CT: Yale University Press, 2003), 341–94.

2. While Hodge is most remembered for his three-volume *ST*, the breadth of his vision is best explored in the pages of the *PR*. A. A. Hodge believed that the *PR* represented his father's most significant contribution to the church. Thus he organized chapters in the biography around the articles that his father wrote, and he devoted extensive coverage to the most important entries. The articles are listed in the following chapters of *LCH*: chapter 7 (1829–39) in pages 260–71; chapter 9 (1840–51) in pages 332–41; chapter 10 (1851–61) in pages 400–421; and chapter 11 (1861–72) in pages 460–62, 466–71, 491–501.

3. For documents illustrative of the Old School–New School controversy, see Maurice W. Armstrong, Lefferts A. Loetscher, and Charles A. Anderson, eds., *The Presbyterian Enterprise: Sources of American Presbyterian History* (Philadelphia: Westminster Press, 1956), 146–71.

4. The intention of the Plan of Union was to reduce rivalry between the two denominations, both of which adhered to Reformed theology. Rather than duplicate efforts by establishing separate congregations in a given area as the denominations expanded into the frontier, founders of the Plan urged a system by which churches could function together in advancing the gospel. Ironically, the Plan of Union resulted in greater benefits to Presbyterians than to Congregationalists. More churches organized under the Plan followed Presbyterian polity than Congregational. Congregational presence, however, opened the potential for New England theology, a modified Calvinism, to infiltrate the Northwest. On the Plan of Union, cf. *SABC*, 102–4, 116, 122–23, 125–26, 134; Randall Herbert Balmer and John R. Fitzmier, *The Presbyterians* (Westport, CT: Praeger, 1994), 47–49; *UCRC*, 160–63; Thompson, *A History of the Presbyterian Churches in the United States*, 72, 116–18, 142.

5. Hodge's first dispute over voluntary groups occurred as early as 1829 over the American Education Society's lending financial resources to ministerial candidates. Hodge contended that this policy, which New Schoolers accepted, made the candidate an object of charity because the money was merely a loan that must eventually be repaid. Instead, Hodge argued, whenever a person "devotes his whole time and talents to the service of any community, *at its request*, it is obligatory on that community to provide for his support." When candidates finished their training under the society's policy, they began ministry "burdened with debt" and labored in a vocation where they could ill afford it. "Retrospect," 4–6.

6. David F. Wells documented that the state lotteries proliferated so rapidly in the early nineteenth century that one editor lampooned state legislatures as existing for the purpose of creating lotteries. By 1826, Maryland alone was allowing no fewer than eleven legal lotteries, which sold tickets ranging from $5 to $50 each. Thus a voluntary society formed in 1833 in Pennsylvania to work for their elimination. Wells also surveyed sermons that denounced the evils of profanity, Sabbath-breaking, and intemperance. "American Society as Seen from the 19th Century Pulpit," *BS* (April–June 1987): 130.

7. The "great eight" voluntary societies were organized over a sixteen-year period: the American Board of Commissioners for Foreign Missions (1810), the American Education Society (1815), the American Bible Society (1816), the American Colonization Society (1816), the American Sunday-School Union (1817), the American Tract Society (1826), the American Home Missionary Society (1826), and the American Temperance Society (1826). An indication of the enormity of their success is the fact that in the 1830s the combined budgets of the largest societies equaled the expenses of the United States government. Cf. Martin Marty, *Righteous Empire: The Protestant Experience in America* (New York: Dial Press, 1970); Timothy Smith, *Revivalism and Social Reform: American Protestantism on the Eve of the Civil War* (New York: Harper, 1965); *UCRC*, 137–46; *PS*, 1:239–41.

8. "Voluntary Societies and Ecclesiastical Organizations," *PR* 9, 1 (1837): 112. Hodge originally stated the criteria for Presbyterian participation in voluntary societ-

ies in his previous year's review, "The General Assembly of 1836," *PR* 8, 3 (1836): 429. Of peripheral interest regarding voluntary societies is the fact that the American Colonization Society, the first national organization to confront the difficult issue of slavery, held its initial meeting at Princeton in 1816. The purpose of the society was to encourage owners to free their slaves and then to assist freed blacks. Unfortunately, the means the society proposed to fulfill that mission was the ill-advised and ill-fated solution of sending blacks to colonize and evangelize Africa. Most of the seminary faculty and student body attended the first meeting of the society. *PS*, 1:329.

9. "Retrospect," 17–19.

10. "The General Assembly of 1843," *PR* 15, 3 (1843): 462, 464, 466. The temperance issue resurfaced at later General Assemblies. In 1869 a resolution on total abstinence produced lengthy debate. Hodge reiterated that while he himself favored abstinence, the assembly correctly refused to call all alcoholic consumption sinful because scriptural warrant was lacking. "The General Assembly of 1869," *PR* 41, 3 (1869): 411–14. Hodge also addressed the issue of temperance in "The Temperance Question," in *The Church and Its Polity*, ed. William Durant and A. A. Hodge (New York: Thomas Nelson and Sons, 1879), 224–31.

11. "A Plea for Voluntary Societies and Defence of the Decisions of the General Assembly of 1836 against the Strictures of the Princeton Review and Others," *PR* 9, 1 (1837): 112.

12. Hodge thereby defended Presbyterian polity as a via media in connectional church government between Episcopal polity on the one hand, in which ascending courts entailed a hierarchy of spiritual rule from parishes to dioceses and archdioceses (and in Roman Catholicism ultimately the papacy), and at the other extreme Baptist or independent polity, which denied any formal connection between churches. Ibid., 114, 116.

13. Ibid., 120. The secretary in question, Dr. Absalom Peters, came under attack by many Old Schoolers for furthering his society at the expense of the Board of Domestic Missions. Cf. James H. Moorehead, "The 'Restless Spirit of Radicalism': Old School Fears and the Schism of 1837," *JPH* 78, 1 (2000): 29–30.

14. "Retrospect," 8. Hodge argued extensively for a Presbyterian Board of Foreign Missions in his 1836 review of the General Assembly. The previous assembly had authorized its formation as reasonable and expedient. While some in the church favored the use of voluntary societies, a significant portion of the church desired an ecclesiastical board. Hodge cited other denominations, especially the Moravians, for their zeal as a church for missions. When the New Schoolers defeated the proposal for an ecclesiastical board, Hodge lamented that "it effects a radical revolution in the whole church. It not only cuts off the Boards of Education, all ecclesiastical seminaries, and gives up the control of all the affairs of the church, beyond mere matters of discipline, to voluntary associations. And by whom are these voluntary associations controlled? By moneyed men." "The General Assembly of 1836," 438.

15. Ibid., 429–30.

16. "Retrospect," 9–15. For the changes in American Calvinism in the first half of the nineteenth century, see Mark A. Noll, "Americanization of Calvinism," in *America's God: From Jonathan Edwards to Abraham Lincoln* (New York: Oxford University Press, 2002), chaps. 12–15; Holifield, "Calvinism Revised" and " 'True Calvinism' Defended," in *Theology in America*, 341–94.

17. "Retrospect," 10–15.

18. "Stuart on Romans," *PR* 5, 3 (1833): 382–83. Stephen J. Stein examines the heated exchange between Hodge and Stuart in "Stuart and Hodge on Romans 5:12–21: An Exegetical Controversy about Original Sin," *JPH* 47 (1969): 340–58.

19. "Stuart on Romans," 392, 414. Hodge also stated that ironically Stuart actually made the case for imputation in his exegesis without actually using the word in his discussion of verses 15–18. Stuart's treatment of Paul's argument, therefore, was open to the charge of being inconsistent and contradictory. Hodge wrote prolifically on the subject of imputation in the *PR*. Cf. "Inquiries Respecting the Doctrine of Imputation," *PR* 2, 3 (1830): 425–72; "The Christian Spectator on the Doctrine of Imputation," *PR* 3, 3 (1831): 407–33; "The First and Second Adam," *PR* 32, 2 (1860): 335–76.

20. Cases involving Barnes dragged out for several years. Hodge wrote to his mother after the 1828 General Assembly that though Barnes held the support of many in the denomination, Hodge trusted the select committee to study the charges because they were "thoroughgoing men." Letter of May 28, 1828, in *CHP*, box 8, folder 4.

21. Charges were brought against Barnes in the Philadelphia Presbytery in 1830, and the matter eventually appeared before the 1831 General Assembly. The assembly acquitted Barnes but admonished him for unguarded statements. *SABC*, 118–20; Noll, *America's God*, 302–3; *PS*, 1:242. Taylor's theological reformulation of Calvinism owed to his coming under the influence of Enlightenment humanism in which he failed to distinguish between natural and moral inability. Cf. *RRPM*, 20, 22.

22. "Notes, Explanatory and Practical, on the Epistle to the Romans, Designed for Bible-Classes and Sunday Schools. By Albert Barnes," *PR* 7, 2 (1835): 286–87. Kant rankled at the fact that his *RWLRA* (1793) did not pass censorship under Prussian ruler Friedrich William II that favored pietist orthodoxy. Theodore M. Greene, "The Historical Context and Religious Significance of Kant's *Religion*," introduction to *Religion within the Limits of Reason Alone*, by Immanuel Kant, translated by Theodore M. Greene and Hoyt H. Hudson (New York: Harper & Row, 1960), xxxii. See chapter 31 below for a similar complaint that Hodge lodged against Augustus Neander's monograph in 1844 on the teaching of the New Testament apostles.

23. "Notes on Romans," 290.

24. Ibid., 299, 302.

25. Ibid., 319, 326. In addition, Hodge states later in his review that Barnes "greatly mars" Romans 8:18–23. Hodge refers readers to his previous review of Stuart and other articles in the *PR* on the subject; he cites other theologians' defense of the term; he rejects the Catholic doctrine of infusion of righteousness; and he shows its indispensability to account not only for our fallen human nature but for the doctrine of justification.

26. Ibid., 327, 339–40.

27. *SABC*, 120.

28. The assembly refused that year to address one contentious issue separating Old and New Schoolers—slavery. A committee proposed that because the issue "would tend to distract and divide our churches, and would, probably in no wise promote the benefit of those whose welfare is immediately contemplated," the assembly should take no action. A counter report proposed that slavery be considered a sin and slaveholding subject to censure. The assembly compromised by postponing the issue indefinitely by a vote of 154–90. "The General Assembly of 1836," 440–41.

29. Ibid., 458, 466.

30. Ibid., 470, 473, 475–76.

31. For his commentary on Romans, see *LCH*, 271–79; *PS*, 1:196–98.

32. *LCH*, 272.

33. A recent analysis of Hodge as an exegete is David Kelsey, "Charles Hodge as Interpreter of Scripture," in *CHR*, 217–45. Kelsey's most instructive comment is that Hodge utilized the tools of biblical criticism but also held that Scripture itself possesses a unity of thought: "Hodge interpreted Scripture not only within the horizons of textual criticism, the cultural and historical context of the authors and the original readers, and the authors' personal and literary styles; he also interpreted within the horizon of Scripture construed as a certain type of unified whole that teaches truths." Ibid., 233.

34. Warfield began his summary by recounting Hodge's manner of reciting. After opening each class with prayer, he would open "his well thumbed Greek Testament—on which it was plain that there was not a single marginal note—look at the passage for a second, and then throwing his head back, and closing his eyes, begin his exposition. He scarcely again glanced at the Testament during the hour, the text was evidently before his mind, verbally, and the matter of his exposition thoroughly at his command. In an unbroken stream it flowed from subject to subject, simple, clear, cogent, unfailingly reverent." Benjamin B. Warfield, "Dr. Hodge as a Teacher of Exegesis," in *Selected Shorter Writings of Benjamin B. Warfield*, vol. 1, ed. John E. Meeter (Nutley, NJ: Presbyterian and Reformed, 1973), 437–38.

35. Ibid., 438.

36. Ibid.; Francis L. Patton, "Charles Hodge," *Presbyterian Review* 6 (1881): 356. Monod's comment appears in *LCH*, 278.

37. Warfield, "Dr. Hodge as a Teacher of Exegesis," 439.

38. *LCH*, 271–72.

39. Ibid., 274, 276. Hodge complied with Alexander's suggestion that he make his commentary accessible to a wider readership than scholars by concluding each chapter with two sections. The first, "Doctrine," expounded the doctrinal content of the passage. More to the point, "Remarks" drew the practical implication of the passage. For example, on Romans 5:12, which was so important for Hodge's view of the fall, Hodge commented: "We should never yield to temptation on the ground that the sin to which we are solicited appears to be a trifle (merely eating a forbidden fruit)

or that it is but ONCE. Remember, the ONE offence of one man. How often has a man, or a family, been ruined for ever by ONE sin!" Charles Hodge, *A Commentary on the Epistle to the Romans* (Philadelphia: Grigg & Elliot, 1835), 298.

40. Ibid., 271–72.

Chapter 17: Old School Nurture vs. New School Revivalism

1. Cf. *PS*, 1:222–29; *SABC*, 109–13.

2. Richard Robert Osmer, *Confirmation: Presbyterian Practices in Ecumenical Perspective* (Louisville, KY: Geneva Press, 1996), 129.

3. Sunday schools eventually eclipsed catechism instruction as the primary means of Christian education. Initially, however, Presbyterians supported the Sunday school movement, which originated under Robert Raikes in Britain in 1780. Sabbath schools emerged as part of the burgeoning voluntary societies on the American scene in the early nineteenth century. As Old School concern grew over potential harm that voluntary societies posed to Presbyterian doctrine, enthusiasm cooled. Cf. Robert F. Lay, "New School Missionaries and Old School Presbyters on the Indiana Frontier: The Case of Samuel Newbury," *JPH* 77 (Winter 1999): 225–36.

4. Charles G. Finney, *Lectures on Revivals of Religion* (Boston: C. H. Pierce, 1848), lecture 1. Cf. Iain H. Murray, *Revival and Revivalism* (Carlisle, PA: Banner of Truth, 1994), chap. 9; Whitney R. Cross, *The Burned-over District: The Social and Intellectual History of Enthusiastic Religion in Western New York, 1800–1850* (New York: Harper, 1950), chaps. 9–10.

5. Hodge subjected Finney's views to strong yet not vitriolic criticism in "Finney's Lectures on Systematic Theology," *PR* 19, 2 (1847): 237–77. Hodge stated that Finney's work was not so much a theology but a philosophy in which from certain postulates or first principles a merely rational deductive system followed. The result was a religion that was essentially moral in nature. Beginning with the premise of moral free will, Finney had developed a philosophical framework in which "the scriptures are throughout recognized as a mere subordinate authority. They are allowed to come in and bear confirmatory testimony, but their place is altogether secondary." Ibid., 275.

6. "Neglect of Infant Baptism," *PR* 29, 1 (1857): 73–101.

7. Hodge cited several sources for this view: (1) the Westminster Confession: "The visible church . . . consists of all those throughout the world that profess the true religion with their children"; (2) the Larger Catechism: "The universal church consists of all those persons, in every nation, together with their children"; (3) Form of Government: "A particular church consists of a number of professing Christians with their offspring"; and (4) Scripture passages: "your children . . . are holy" (1 Cor. 7:14); and "of such [children] is the kingdom of God" (Luke 18:16 KJV). Even Old School rival James Henley Thornwell argued that children were not under discipline of the church. He distinguished between professing and nonprofessing members. He denied that all members of the church were subject to discipline because only those who professed faith in Christ fell under the church's government. Thornwell's syllogism

was: "Members of the Church are the proper subjects of discipline: Only those who voluntarily profess their faith in Christ are members of the Church: Therefore, only those who thus profess their faith are the proper subjects of discipline." Hodge used two analogies in support of the old doctrine: in the Old Testament every Hebrew child was subject to the laws of the theocracy, and in modern politics every Englishman and American was subject to laws of the state "without any personal and voluntary profession of allegiance." If the old doctrine was not retained, Presbyterians would be guilty of "abandoning ground to the Independents and Anabaptists." "Infant Members Subjects of Discipline," in *The Church and Its Polity*, ed. William Durant and A. A. Hodge (New York: Thomas Nelson and Sons, 1879), 215–18.

8. "Neglect of Infant Baptism," 77–80. Robert Ellis Thompson notes that "Puritan individualism" and New England "independent conception of the church" conflicted with historic Presbyterianism. By seeking "a regenerate church-membership," they "introduced the fashion of speaking of the adult communicants as the only 'members of the church,' and of treating its baptized children as outside pagans, exempt even from its discipline." *A History of the Presbyterian Churches in the United States* (1895; repr., Eugene, OR: Wipf and Stock, 2003), 88.

9. Ibid., 84, 86. Hodge contrasted the sharp decline in baptisms among Presbyterians with the stable number of infant baptisms among Episcopalians. While stability in Episcopalian continuance of infant baptism might only signify that denomination's belief that baptism was a "saving ordinance" (i.e., a belief in baptismal regeneration), it illustrated that Episcopalians remained more consistent with their paedobaptist beliefs than Presbyterians. Ibid., 89.

10. Ibid.

11. Ibid., 91. In the language of twenty-first-century American educational debates, Hodge was arguing for a nineteenth-century version of "no child left behind"!

12. In a separate but related matter, Hodge also addressed the issue of baptism of infant children of nonprofessors. A. A. Hodge included a letter that his father had written to a neighbor who was not a communicating member of a church yet requested Hodge to baptize his children. Profession of faith by parents was essential to baptizing infants because of the nature of promises made in the sacrament. While the father might want to have his child baptized, Hodge said, "no minister could in this view of the case, conscientiously administer the ordinance unless the parents (or one of them) were prepared intelligently to make the profession and incur the responsibility which it necessarily involves." *LCH*, 399.

13. Thompson, *A History of the Presbyterian Churches in the United States*, 93, 95–96, 99.

14. "The Church Membership of Infants," *PR* 30, 2 (1858): 350–51.

15. Ibid., 351.

16. Ibid., 366.

17. Ibid., 369, 372–73. In a lengthy footnote, Hodge explored the Lutheran idea of presumptive regeneration, which he rejected in favor of presumptive election. When

Presbyterians baptized infants, "it is not their vital union with Christ, nor their actual regeneration by the Holy Ghost, that is presumed, but their election. This is no more than is done when we baptize an adult, or when he is received to the Lord's table. We presume he is one of the elect. Whether he is so or not, we cannot tell; but he belongs to the class which, by the command of Christ, we are required so to regard and treat." Ibid., 376.

18. Ibid., 389.

19. Ibid.

20. *LCH*, 453. In *LCH* his son wrote of the purpose of the conferences: "Here in the most effective manner they sought to build up Christian men rather than form accomplished scholars and to instruct them on the wisest methods of conducting their future work of saving souls and edifying the Church of Christ." Ibid.

21. Charles Hodge, *Princeton Sermons: Outlines of Discourses, Doctrinal and Practical, Delivered at Princeton Theological Seminary on Sabbath Afternoons* (London: Thomas Nelson and Sons, 1879), iii. A large portion of the preface written by A. A. was repeated verbatim in *LCH*, 453–56. What Hodge contributed publicly he also practiced privately in his home. His children remembered his leading family morning devotions consisting of prayer, repeating the Apostles' Creed, and a profession of faith in the Trinity. Before his lameness prevented his doing so, Hodge paced in his study while singing hymns that appealed to the emotions. *LCH*, 227.

22. A. A. wrote one of the most astounding comments of any Princetonian when describing Alexander's presentations: "a solemn hush fell upon us, and we felt not as those who listen to a teacher, but as those who are admitted to approach, with the shoes from off their feet, to gaze in and listen through an opened window to the mysterious workings of a sanctified soul under the immediate revelations of the Holy Ghost." Ibid., 457.

23. *Princeton Sermons*, vii.

24. A more detailed examination of Hodge's devotional writings and preaching appears in W. Andrew Hoffecker, *Piety and the Princeton Theologians: Archibald Alexander, Charles Hodge, and Benjamin Warfield* (Phillipsburg, NJ: Presbyterian and Reformed, 1981), 81–94.

25. The best summaries of Hodge's integration of the objective and subjective elements in the Christian life—although differing in their emphases—are Mark A. Noll, "Charles Hodge as an Expositor of the Spiritual Life," in *CHR*, 181–216, and *RRPM*, 44–48.

26. "The Theology of the Intellect and That of the Feelings," *PR* 22, 4 (1850): 642–74; "Prof. Park's Remarks on the Princeton Review," *PR* 23, 2 (1851): 306–47; "Professor Park and the Princeton Review," *PR* 23, 4 (1851): 674–95.

27. "Discourses on Christian Nurture," *PR* 19, 4 (1847): 502, 509–10, 515, 518.

28. Ibid., 519, 521.

29. Ibid., 523–24.

30. Ibid., 526, 530–31. Bushnell differentiated his "supernaturalism" from "super-supernaturalism" of theologians such as Edwards. According to Bushnell, Edwards's view was "the *ictic* theory" in which God descended from "beyond the fixed stars" to work

regeneration: "Hanging . . . every thing [i.e., regeneration] thus on miracle, or a pure *ictus Dei*, separate from all instrumental connexions of truth, feeling dependence, motive choice, there was manifestly nothing left but to wait for the concussion." Ibid., 532. Bushnell's argument seems to resemble Friedrich Schleiermacher's distinction between his "mystical" view of the atonement over against the "magical" view of the Reformed tradition.

31. "Charles Hodge as an Expositor of the Spiritual Life," 187.

Chapter 18: Abolitionism vs. Gradual Elimination of Slavery

1. Cf. David Calhoun, "The Church and the Country," in *PS*, 1:323–32. Of particular interest are references to the Princetonians' lament that Presbyterians ministered primarily to moderate to wealthy Americans and neglected ministry to the poor.

2. *Minutes of the General Assembly of the Presbyterian Church in the United States of America . . . AD. 1789–1820 Inclusive* (Philadelphia: Presbyterian Board of Publication, 1847), 692.

3. The debate over slavery at Princeton did not reach the fever pitch that erupted at other seminaries, such as Lane Seminary in Cincinnati. The Lane board action prohibiting abolitionist meetings led over forty students, the "Lane Rebels," to withdraw and eventually enroll at Oberlin College, which became a veritable hotbed of abolitionism. Hodge argued that the Princetonians stood in opposition to "fanatical parties." One extreme advocated "immediate and universal emancipation." And the other "no less fanatical" faction said that "one class of men may rightfully keep another in ignorance and degradation, in order to keep them in bondage." He continued, "The old school Presbyterians have been the great conservative body . . . They have stood up as a wall against the flood of abolitionism, which would have overwhelmed the church and riven asunder the State." "Emancipation," *PR* 21, 4 (1849): 586.

4. Hodge has come under sharp criticism for his views on slavery, most recently in Allen Guelzo's essay "Charles Hodge's Antislavery Moment" in *CHR*. A. A. Hodge's biography makes no reference to slavery's existence in Princeton or that Hodge, his family, and associates at the seminary owned slaves. Guelzo explores these matters in detail. He has contextualized Hodge's views by pointing out that although Hodge lived in a northern state, slavery still existed in New Jersey in the early decades of the nineteenth century. The state passed an emancipation law in 1804 that made it a "free state," but no exact timetable had been established for slavery's elimination. In addition, both the college and the seminary drew a significant number of students from the South, which would make them favorable to slavery. Taken together, these factors indicate that Hodge was influenced by his times. Guelzo's analysis adds weight to the judgment that Princeton Seminary and Hodge, in particular, were late comers to the rising tide of moral criticism against the South's peculiar institution. *CHR*, 299–325.

5. "Slavery," *PR* 8, 2 (1836): 275. Mark A. Noll summarized Hodge's exegetical method in "The Bible and Slavery," in *Religion and the American Civil War*, ed. Randall M. Miller, Harry S. Stout, and Charles Regan Wilson (New York: Oxford University Press, 1998), 43–73. "The specifically hermeneutical stance adopted by [Hodge]

was a tacit abandonment of biblical literalism. [Hodge] took for granted that the Bible must be an interpreted book, and that the meaning of its words must be conditioned by other realities . . . [viz.] the fuller context of the Scriptures themselves." Ibid., 60. Hodge's position as centrist has been most cogently presented by Peter Wallace, "The Defense of the Forgotten Center: Charles Hodge and the Enigma of Emancipationism in Antebellum America," *JPH* 75, 3 (Fall 1997): 165–77; and *MTC*, 67–110.

6. "Slavery," 278.

7. "West India Emancipation," *PR* 10, 4 (1838): 603.

8. "Slavery," 270, 279–80.

9. Ibid., 275, 277. Hodge's case would have been stronger if he had more thoroughly differentiated different kinds of slavery so as to expose evils underlying American slavery. In support of the idea that slavery is not inherently sinful was Old Testament slavery, which was often an economic measure to enable people to free themselves from debt. Indentured servitude, therefore, differed substantially from slavery rooted in manstealing and fostered by the brutal slave trade in the modern era.

10. "The General Assembly of 1846," *PR* 18, 3 (1846): 426; *Commentary on the Epistle to the Ephesians* (New York: Robert Carter & Brothers, 1858), 369.

11. "Slavery," 293; "Abolitionism," *PR* 16, 4 (1844): 575, 578; "Emancipation," 587.

12. "Slavery," 303; "West India Emancipation," 608; "Abolitionism," 575; "The General Assembly of 1846," 425–26; *Commentary on Ephesians*, 369.

13. "West India Emancipation," 617–44; "Emancipation," 592.

14. "Emancipation," 588.

15. "Abolitionism," 575; "The General Assembly of 1846," 426.

16. "Slavery," 510. In "Abolitionism," Hodge made a similar argument about the unjust ways in which Southern laws stood in contrast to biblical principles: "all those laws which are designed to restrict the master in the discharge of the duties, which flow from his relation to his slaves; which forbid his teaching them to read, or which prohibit marriage among them, or which allow of the separation of those who are married, or are otherwise in conflict with the word of God, are wicked laws; laws which do not find their justification in the admission of the right of ownership in the master, but are in direct contravention of the obligations which necessarily flow from that right." "Abolitionism," 578.

17. "Emancipation," 605. See also "West India Emancipation," 608, 612–13; "The General Assembly of 1846," 424–25. In this regard, slavery was, like polygamy, permitted in the Old Testament but eventually to be prohibited because it was morally inferior to monogamy.

18. "Abolitionism," 581. Hodge also seems to have naively accepted the report of a slaveowner from South Carolina as representative of others in the South when he said that his slaves could both read and write. Stewart argues that the General Assembly in the 1840s proceeded on the assumption that slavery should be handled on a regional basis. Ibid., 575; *MTC*, 79.

19. "Slavery," 302. Hodge's analogy of the mason is reported in *PS*, 1:327.

20. "The Princeton Review on the State of the Country and of the Church," *PR* 37, 4 (1865): 641–43.

21. Ibid., 646.

22. Ibid., 647.

23. "Abolitionism," 580.

24. Archibald Alexander, *A History of Colonization on the Western Coast of Africa* (Philadelphia: William S. Martien, 1846), cited in *PS*, 1:483n27.

25. "Emancipation," 595, 600–601.

26. "The Princeton Review on the State of the Country and of the Church," 639. Hodge was most disturbed.

27. Stewart mentions instances in which Hodge faced criticism from sources other than American abolitionists and proslavery Southerners. In 1835 two English clergymen spoke disparagingly of America after their visit and made exaggerated statements about slavery. Hodge responded in "Reed and Matheson: The Narrative," *PR* 7, 4 (1835): 623–25. *MTC*, 74. *LCH* narrates Hodge's response to his friend William Cunningham, leader of the Free Church of Scotland. When Presbyterians from Canada, Scotland, and Ireland critiqued Hodge's middle-of-the-road approach, Hodge wrote testily: "It is the want of sense as much as the want of justice, manifested in such effusions [from Scottish Presbyterians] and in the proceedings of your emancipation societies that tries our patience." *LCH*, 359.

28. In the twentieth century, Hodge's reputation has suffered from being misrepresented in historical assessments of his era. Just as Hodge came under unbalanced criticism for rationalism in theological method, others have cast him as unambiguously proslavery, despite his careful attempts to distinguish his position otherwise. While even Hodge's favorable critics acknowledge inconsistencies and at times naiveté in his views of slavery, emancipation, and the status of blacks, others have treated him rather cavalierly. The most notable treatment has been Larry Tise, *Proslavery: A History of the Defense of Slavery in America, 1701–1840* (Athens, GA: University of Georgia Press, 1987). Tise inexcusably classified Hodge as proslavery. He cited two of Hodge's articles that appeared in a compendium, E. N. Elliott, ed., *Cotton Is King and Proslavery Arguments* (Augusta, GA: Pritchard, Abbott & Loomis, 1860), 349–80, which grouped Hodge with ardent proslavery views. The editor of *Cotton Is King*, however, intentionally omitted two sections in which Hodge rebuked Southerners for their refusal to elevate "slaves to the stature of freemen" and Hodge's assertion that "slaves are not of a different race from their masters." Tise, by failing to mention these significant omissions, presents Hodge in a negative light. As our treatment has stressed, Hodge labored might and main to distinguish his position from those of the proslavery South.

Chapter 19: Schism of 1837

1. *LCH*, 290.

2. More than forty years ago, George M. Marsden published the first major study of evangelicalism: *The Evangelical Mind and the New School Presbyterian Experience:*

A Case Study of Thought and Theology in Nineteenth-Century America (New Haven, CT: Yale University Press, 1970). Not until 2004 did a comparable examination of Old School Presbyterianism appear in Peter Wallace's Notre Dame PhD thesis, " 'The Bond of Union': The Old School Presbyterian Church and the American Nation, 1837–1861." Both works explore the origin, development, and significant contributions of primary figures involved, but Wallace's work is more extensive in its detail.

3. Documents relating to the 1837 schism, including the "Old-School Testimony and Memorial" of 1837, the exscinding acts, and a New School claim of the unconstitutional nature of the exscinding acts appear in Maurice W. Armstrong, Lefferts A. Loetscher, and Charles A. Anderson, eds., *The Presbyterian Enterprise: Sources of American Presbyterian History* (Philadelphia: Westminster Press, 1956), 153–64.

4. Hodge had met Nathaniel W. Taylor during his 1820 visit to New England. Since that time, Taylor had fulfilled the academic promise that Hodge had discerned in him by establishing a distinguished ministry and teaching career at Yale. Viewing traditional Calvinism as a hindrance to revivalism and the progress of religion, Taylor revised Calvinism beginning with his 1828 address to Congregational clergy, "*Concio ad Clerum*: A Sermon: On Human Nature, Sin, and Freedom." Taylor developed a system that did not deny but critically altered key doctrines, such as original sin and God's sovereignty. The Princetonians viewed this "New Divinity" or "New Haven Divinity" as deeply injurious to Calvinism.

5. Samuel Hopkins (1721–1803) was a Congregational minister whose theological system, known as "consistent Calvinism" and the "New Divinity," revised the Reformed view of original sin. Nathaniel Taylor's New Haven Theology further refined Hopkins's views.

6. *LCH*, 289–90. Other sources that stress Hodge's mediating or centrist position in his career at Princeton are *UCRC*; *MTC*; Peter Wallace, "The Defense of the Forgotten Center: Charles Hodge and the Enigma of Emancipationism in Antebellum America," *JPH* 75, 3 (Fall 1997): 165–77. James Moorehead in "The 'Restless Spirit of Radicalism': Old School Fears and the Schism of 1837," *JPH* 78, 1 (Spring 2000): 19–33, traces issues leading to the schism and names extreme Old Schoolers Breckinridge's and Junkin's fears of radicalism as primary factors leading to schism. Moorehead mentions Princeton briefly (only Samuel Miller by name) as a mediating group between extremes.

7. "Retrospect," 19, 21. In his assessment of the abrogation of the Plan of Union, Hodge exhibited a remarkable range of awareness of legal matters by citing Chief Justice Marshall on points of law and cases from Georgia, Kentucky, New York, and New Hampshire. "The General Assembly of 1837," *PR* 9, 3 (1837): 450–60.

8. *LCH*, 306. In describing the character of various leaders in the Old School–New School controversy and the 1837 schism, Robert Ellis Thompson depicts Hodge as manifesting "a Johannine character" and Princeton as representing "the moderate party" on the eve of the schism. *A History of the Presbyterian Churches in the United States* (1895; repr., Eugene, OR: Wipf and Stock, 2003), 127.

9. "Retrospect," 21. Ironically, less than a century later, similar circumstances arose in the fundamentalist–modernist controversy. Several times the denomination went on record in affirming "fundamentals," which modernists labeled in essence "extra-constitutional" in the 1924 Auburn Affirmation. Bradley J. Longfield, *The Presbyterian Controversy: Fundamentalists, Modernists, and Moderates* (New York: Oxford University Press, 1991).

10. "Retrospect," 22. In a letter to his brother, Hodge accused the Philadelphia men, including his former pastor, Ashbel Green, of "splitting the Old School portion of the church," which would leave the denomination "completely in the power of the New School men, give them the command of the Seminaries, Boards and Education and Missions." Hodge also divulged that as the result of an article in the *PR*, the Philadelphia Synod had "passed a vote which amounts to a formal declaration of want of confidence in the Seminary. They propose transferring their patronage to Pittsburgh, or to found a new institution." *LCH*, 306.

11. "A Plea for Voluntary Societies and Defence of the Decisions of the General Assembly of 1836 against the Strictures of the Princeton Review and Others," *PR* 9, 1 (1837): 146.

12. "Retrospect," 22–23. By using the example of imputation, Hodge recalled the Barnes controversy in 1830, when the Presbytery of Philadelphia had censured Barnes. Regarding subscription to the Westminster Confession, Hodge remained consistent in maintaining that what was needed was not subscription to every point of the confession, as some demanded, but subscription to the confession as a system of truth.

13. The Princeton men were again divided over whether to publish a note stating the difference of opinion among themselves. Some held that a blanket statement of approval by the conductors of the *PR* was necessary to sustain the momentum of Old School action. Hodge felt otherwise; he insisted that it would be improper to imply a unanimous approval if it did not exist. "Retrospect," 28–29.

14. Letter of July 26, 1837, in *CHP*, box 10, folder 3.

15. "Retrospect," 27.

16. Letter of June 11, 1837, in *CHP*, box 10, folder 3.

17. "The General Assembly of 1838," *PR* 10, 3 (1838): 457.

18. The New School formed its own assembly at the rear of the church and then moved to another location. *SABC*, 125–26.

19. "The General Assembly of 1838," 458.

20. Ibid., 460–63. The term *Presbygational* emerged later in the nineteenth century to describe the amalgamation of Presbyterian and Congregational churches.

21. Letter of February 28, 1839, in *CHP*, box 14, folder 23.

22. Ibid.

23. Letter of March 27, 1839, in *CHP*, box 14, folder 23. The proceedings of the initial trial as well as the appeal are found in Ashbel Green, *The Case of the General Assembly of the Presbyterian Church in the United States of America, before the Supreme Court of the Commonwealth of Pennsylvania, Impartially Reported by*

Disinterested Stenographers; Including All the Proceedings, Testimony, and Arguments at Nisi Prius *and before the Court in Bank, with the Charge of Judge Rogers, the Verdict of the Jury, and the Opinion of Chief Justice Gibson. The Whole Compiled and Prepared for the Press by the Rev. D. W. Lathrop* (Philadelphia: A. McElroy, 1839).

24. Letter of March 27, 1839, in *CHP*, box 10, folder 1.

25. Ibid., folder 23.

26. *LCH*, 320.

27. Letter of March 27, 1839, in *CHP*, box 10, folder 1.

28. Letter of February 28, 1839, in *CHP*, box 14, folder 23.

Chapter 20: Revisionist Historian

1. David Calhoun, "Plan of the Seminary," in *PS*, 1:423–24. Commenting on Hodge's responsibility as narrator, Archibald Alexander set the bar high for Hodge's responsibility as a competent historian: "You are writing a history which will probably connect your name with the orthodox Presbyterian name as long as it lasts; and you are not at liberty to depart one iota from what appears to you to be a correct statement of facts, and correct judgment on them. If other persons take a different view of either, that is no reason you should change anything in deference to them." *LCH*, 281.

2. Letter of March 28, 1839, in *CHP*, box 14, folder 23.

3. Letter of January 29, 1839, in ibid.

4. *LCH*, 279; Letter of October 12, 1838, in *CHP*, box 10, folder 3; *CHPC*, 1:iii–iv.

5. *CHPC*, 1:9. In his narration of the 1741 schism that divided the denomination, Hodge identified the two sides as the New Brunswick Presbytery and the Philadelphia Presbytery.

6. Ibid., 1:9, 12–13. On the range of opinions about the variety of forms of early Presbyterianism and the Adopting Act of 1729, cf. Randall Herbert Balmer and John R. Fitzmier, *The Presbyterians* (Westport, CT: Greenwood Press, 1993), 25–27; Maurice W. Armstrong, Lefferts A. Loetscher, and Charles A. Anderson, eds., *The Presbyterian Enterprise: Sources of American Presbyterian History* (Philadelphia: Westminster Press, 1956); S. Donald Fortson, "The Presbyterian Creed: Old School / New School Reunion and Confessional Subscription" (PhD diss., Westminster Theological Seminary, 2003), 24–29, 298–301; Leonard J. Trinterud, *The Forming of an American Tradition: A Reexamination of Colonial Presbyterianism* (Philadelphia: Westminster Press, 1949), 38–52; Bryan F. LeBeau, *Jonathan Dickinson and the Formative Years of American Presbyterianism* (Lexington, KY: University of Kentucky Press, 1997), 45–63; Charles Augustus Briggs, *American Presbyterianism: Its Origin and Early History* (Edinburgh: T&T Clark, 1885), 216–21; *SABC*, 40–59; Charles G. Dennison and Richard Gamble, *Pressing toward the Mark: Essays Commemorating Fifty Years of the Orthodox Presbyterian Church* (Philadelphia: Committee for the Historian of the Orthodox Presbyterian Church, 1986).

7. *CHPC*, 1:12.

8. Hodge then went over the top by countering Congregationalists' claims: "It would be much nearer the truth to say, that Presbyterians have been the basis of several denomi-

nations. Half the population of the country would now be Presbyterian, had the descendants of Presbyterians, in all cases, adhered to the faith of their fathers." Ibid., 1:60.

9. Ibid., 1:84, 87, 90. Hodge also probed disputes over the synod's power from 1705 to 1729 in which Jonathan Dickinson and others influenced by New England Congregationalism had objected to powers of synod intruding into congregations and presbyteries. A compromise resulted: "that when any matter is determined by a major vote, every member shall either actively concur with, or passively submit to such determination; or if his conscience permit him to do neither, he shall, after sufficient liberty modestly to reason and remonstrate, peaceably withdraw from our communion, without attempting to make any schism." The final result was that "the decisions of Synod were to be binding on all those who could obey them with a good conscience." Ibid., 1:124.

10. Ibid., 1:129, 133–34, 139.

11. Hodge defended Thompson in a lengthy footnote as "a really good man." He wrote that "it is a pleasure and honour to be allowed to vindicate his memory." Ibid., 1:135–37.

12. Ibid., 1:144.

13. Ibid., 1:145.

14. Ibid., 1:183. As David Calhoun has pointed out, Hodge's position here was his strongest statement on subscription. Calhoun probes Hodge's various articles on subscription and concludes that they illustrate his moderation on the issue of subscription. On the one hand, Hodge rejected the New School, who adopted a "latitudinarian view," which demanded only acceptance of the essential doctrines of Christianity and would not distinguish Presbyterians from other evangelical denominations. But he also rejected Old Schoolers who held a more rigid view that allowed no diversity in interpreting the confession. *PS*, 1:399, 493.

15. *CHPC*, 1:200.

16. Ibid., 1:201.

17. Ibid. Hodge also cited the synod as mandating that presbyteries should examine ministers yearly concerning their ministerial tasks, which included among others preaching the confession, pressing sinners for conversion, encouraging congregations to use the means of grace in pursuing their sanctification, and catechizing and instructing the youth. Failure to perform these duties would result in censure. Ibid., 1:202.

18. Hodge availed himself of the widest range of sources as he interpreted these decisive events—official records of the synod, historical works, biographies, and sermons, treatises, memoirs, and pamphlets from both advocates and opponents of the revivals. Ibid., 2:iii–v.

19. Ibid., 2:v. He added that "the reader will find no conclusions in the following pages materially different from those to which Mr. Tennent had arrived in 1749," referring to Tennent's later retractions of his earlier censoriousness.

20. Ibid., 2:12, 39, 54. Hodge also credits Dickinson with exemplary behavior.

21. Hodge frequently wrote to his brother for medical advice and to inform Hugh of the physical ills of his family. In preparation for this section of the book, Hodge

wrote to his brother about the medical evidence that might exist about "certain nervous disorders, such as epilepsy, hysteria, etc. . . . I want to put it in my History of the Pres. Ch. 'You don't say so!' Yes I do . . . It is a very difficult and interesting subject, & I want light upon it." Letter of July 25, 1839, in *CHP*, box 10, folder 4. In a subsequent letter he expanded on his request: "You seem to think I meant to penetrate very far into the Labarynth [*sic*] of medico-metaphysical speculations about nervous disorders. You need not be apprehensive on that score. A single page will probably embrace all that I have to say, but to write that page, I should like to read a volume or two." He then asserted that emotional phenomena had frequently accompanied times of religious excitement. He stated, "I am persuaded that [such outbursts] are nothing but one form of an *infectious* nervous disease, generated by strong impressions on the imagination and lively emotions. If so they have nothing to do properly speaking with religion, and instead of being encouraged or tolerated, as they almost always have been by good men, to the great injury of religion, they ought by all means to be guarded against and suppressed as much as epilepsy or hysterics." Hodge narrated an incident involving one of the seminary students, who had suffered an attack "after a long walk in the sun" of "violent involuntary laughing and was followed by jerking of the arms, & vehement stamping with the feet which four or five attendants could not restrain. The attack left him very weak, & he went to his friends since which I have not hear [*sic*] fr. him." Letter of August 15, 1839, in *CHP*, box 10, folder 4.

22. *CHPC*, 2:59, 65–66, 80. To Hodge's credit, though he castigated Edwards and Whitefield at length, he reserved his strongest denunciation for New England revivalist James Davenport, upon whom Edwards had also heaped criticism for outlandish behavior. Hodge also did not acknowledge Edwards's *Distinguishing Marks of the Work of the Spirit*, in which Edwards listed emotional outbreaks as not necessarily a sign of genuine revival.

23. Ibid., 2:91.

24. Ibid., 2:133. Hodge conceded that Edwards had later condemned the evils that attended the awakening in New England and that Tennent had issued a strong retraction of his earlier "excessive heat of temper" and "spiritual fooleries." Ibid., 2:92. The intensity of Tennent's denials rivaled his earlier claims of the necessity of investigating and condemning lack of spiritual life in supposedly unconverted ministers. He repudiated the view that anyone could judge another person's spiritual state: "I know of no passage of the Bible that proves converting grace, or the church's judgment of it, to be a term of Christian communion, of divine appointment." Ibid., 2:94.

25. Ibid., 2:101. Strangely enough, Hodge actually ended the chapter by reminding his readers of the "great good which was then accomplished [by the revival]. In many places there was little of these evils [here he mentions New Jersey and Virginia]. And in many other places the soundness of the doctrines taught, the experience detailed, and the permanent effects produced, abundantly attest the genuineness of the revival. To the Presbyterian Church, particularly, it was the commencement of a new life, the vigour of which is still felt in all her veins." Ibid.

26. Ibid., 2:108–9.

27. Ibid., 2:111. Cf. *PAI*, 85–89; Robert Ellis Thompson, *A History of the Presbyterian Churches in the United States* (1895; repr., Eugene, OR: Wipf and Stock, 2003), 85–88.

28. *CHPC*, 2:121, 123, 140.

29. Ibid., 2:180, 207.

Chapter 21: To Publish or Not to Publish

1. Hodge's weakness as a historian is probed by James Turner, "Charles Hodge in the Intellectual Weather of the Nineteenth Century," in *CHR*, 41–61. Hodge's historical dispute with John Williamson Nevin is found below in chapter 26.

2. *LCH*, 281.

3. Some of Alexander's letters during Hodge's studies in Germany read like revival-meeting statistics of events in Trenton, New York, and Princeton. For a fuller discussion of Alexander's religious experience and conversion, cf. W. Andrew Hoffecker, *Piety and the Princeton Theologians: Archibald Alexander, Charles Hodge, and Benjamin Warfield* (Phillipsburg, NJ: Presbyterian and Reformed, 1981), 2–9.

4. Letter of January 21, 1840, in *CHP*, box 14, folder 23.

5. Ibid.

6. Letter of September 12, 1838, in *CHP*, box 14, folder 23.

7. Ibid. Alexander examined Gilbert Tennent's revivalist legacy in *Biographical Sketches of the Founder, and Principal Alumni of the Log College: Together with an Account of the Revivals of Religion, under Their Ministry. Collected and Edited by A. Alexander* (Princeton, NJ: J. T. Robertson, 1845). He wrote this account after the publishing of Hodge's *CHPC*. While acknowledging Tennent's abusive treatment of ministers and other serious mistakes, Alexander insisted that Presbyterianism had stood in great need of an awakening in the eighteenth century, which from a human point of view Tennent deserved recognition for bringing about. Alexander did, however, refer readers to Hodge's work. "They who desire to see a lucid view of the ecclesiastical transactions of that period, are referred to Dr. Hodge's 'Constitutional History of the Presbyterian Church,'" to which he immediately added: "or they may go to the fountainhead, by consulting the 'Records of the Transactions of the Synod,' recently given to the public, by the 'Board of Education.'" Ibid., 57. This latter remark may be Alexander's thinly veiled retort to his protégé about the use of primary sources. After all, Hodge insisted that he had come to radically different conclusions from his previous views of the revivals because of what he found in original documents!

8. Letter of January 21, 1840, in *CHP*, box 14, folder 23.

9. Ibid.

Part 4: Old School Controversialist and Churchman

1. A synopsis of the major controversies in Hodge's career appears in E. Brooks Holifield, *Theology in America: Christian Thought from the Age of the Puritans to*

the Civil War (New Haven, CT: Yale University Press, 2003), 377–89. Mark A. Noll outlines the major themes that characterized Princeton and Hodge's part in articulating them in *The Princeton Theology, 1812–1921: Scripture, Science, and Theological Method from Archibald Alexander to Benjamin Warfield* (Grand Rapids: Baker, 1983), 25–45. See also E. Brooks Holifield, "Hodge, the Seminary, and the American Theological Context," in *CHR*, 103–28; James Turner, "Charles Hodge in the Intellectual Weather of the Nineteenth Century," in ibid., 41–62; Bruce Kuklick, "The Place of Charles Hodge in the History of Ideas in America," in ibid., 63–76. Each essay explores Hodge's contributions to religious controversies as well as the larger American context.

Chapter 22: Changes

1. Letter of March 29, 1846, in *CHP*, box 11, folder 4.
2. Letter of December 3, 1846, in *CHP*, box 11, folder 4. Faculty colleague Dr. William M. Paxton in a memorial tribute described Hodge's emotional tie with his son upon his departure to India: "No one who was present will ever forget an impromptu address which he delivered in the First Church, in Princeton, about the time his son sailed as a missionary to India. His fatherly affection working in unison with his religious feeling, awoke him to a power of pathos which thrilled the whole assembly with a wonderful impulse." *LCH*, 601. Given Hodge's predilection to preparing what appeared to be "impromptu," the remarks for his son's departure had probably been well planned in advance! Going to the mission field in the nineteenth century entailed great uncertainty about one's future. Hodge may well have been thankful that his son went to the Far East, since many missionaries who went to Africa shipped their goods in caskets because so many died from diseases that necessitated their return to America for burial.
3. Letter of January 31, 1846, in *CHP*, box 11, folder 4.
4. *LCH*, 367.
5. Ibid., 384–85.
6. Ibid., 385. Paul C. Kemeny examines Princeton's Presbyterian heritage and Woodrow Wilson's revisionist efforts in the twentieth century to distance the college from its evangelical roots in "Princeton University, Secularization Theories, and Revisionist History: A Review Essay," *JPH* 75, 2 (1997): 71–83.
7. *LCH*, 386. Hodge's polemic against scientism, discussed in part 5, was one of his last contributions to American intellectual life. The quote from Kemeny comes from *Princeton in the Nation's Service: Religious Ideals and Educational Practice, 1868–1928* (New York: Oxford University Press, 1998), 31. Kemeny cites other contributions of Hodge in education in ibid., 28, 48, 56, 62.
8. J. A. Alexander, a child prodigy who had learned the basics of Latin, Hebrew, and Greek by the age of ten, breezed through Princeton, followed Hodge's footsteps by visiting with August Tholuck in Europe, and returned to become Hodge's assistant in 1834. Unlike Hodge, who struggled with languages, Alexander could read twenty-

four and was fluent in seven. He was the natural choice to succeed Hodge in the field of biblical languages. Cf. *PS*, 1:198–203.

9. Warfield witnessed Hodge's exegetical efforts in the classroom because in addition to his appointment in theology, Hodge continued to lecture on the Pauline Epistles as part of his teaching responsibilities.

10. *LCH*, 322–23. Ironically, I vividly remember what elicited the greatest outburst of laughter in one of my PhD classes in the late 1960s. The discussion of the seminar focused on identifying the resources for doing systematic theology. One participant offered sarcastically, "Some people believe it ought to be the Bible!"

11. Ibid., 363.

12. Letter of December 25, 1849, in *CHP*, box 11, folder 6. Exactly a month later, Hodge remembered what he had written to her when he was abroad: "Pleasure without you is no enjoyment." Letter of January 25, 1850, in *CHP*, box 12, folder 1.

13. Letter of December 16, 1850, in *CHP*, box 12, folder 12. Hodge disclosed to his brother the value of condolence letters he had received after Sarah's death, but he confessed them "powerless." He received many and appreciated them but confessed that he never read any of them a second time.

14. Letter of October 22, 1851, in *CHP*, box 12, folder 12.

15. *LCH*, 382. Hodge also wrote a note on October 13, 1851 after Alexander called him to his bedside and said, "Now my dear son, farewell, you will not see me again. I consider it one of my greatest blessings that I have been able to bring you forward." "Miscellaneous Material," in *CHP*, box 6, folder 27.

Chapter 23: An Evangelical Theology

1. In his introduction to *WOL*, Noll provides the details of its printings, costs, and extensive distribution both domestic and foreign.

2. *WOL*, 53, 55. Hodge's apologetic method demonstrates Archibald Alexander's influence and the method that continued at Princeton throughout the nineteenth and early twentieth centuries. The Princeton apologetic began by authenticating the Bible as the Word of God and then proceeded to attest its witness to major doctrines of Reformed theology. Princeton is frequently remembered for its apologetic use of external evidences. All the major figures, however, stressed the superiority of internal evidences. Paul Helseth probes the moral dimension of reason as the heart of Princetonians' use of right reason. Whereas Enlightenment figures emphasized reason as primarily speculative and cognitive in nature, Hodge and his fellows at Princeton stressed reason in its moral dimension. Helseth points out that *WOL* focuses on man's ability to "reason rightly." Helseth in his thoroughly researched analysis of the mind of Old Princeton has provided a compelling corrective to the way in which Hodge and his colleagues understood the various human faculties. As Helseth summarized Hodge's view: "His reason was subject to God; his will was subject to his reason; his affections and appetites to his will; the body was the obedient organ of the soul" and "his moral perfection in which he resembled God, included knowledge, righteousness and holiness." *RRPM*, 44.

3. *WOL*, 82, 178, 235.

4. Ibid., 191, 202–3.

5. Ibid., 204, 209.

6. *LCH*, 329.

7. Ibid., 330.

8. The following are the articles in the debate: Park, "The Theology of the Intellect and That of the Feelings," *BS* (July 1850): 533–69; Hodge, "The Theology of the Intellect and That of the Feelings," *PR* 22, 4 (1850): 642–74; Park, "Remarks on the Princeton Review," *BS* (January 1851): 135–80; Hodge, "Prof. Park's Remarks on the Princeton Review," *PR* 23, 2 (1851): 306–47; Park, "Unity and Diversities of Belief even on Imputed and Involuntary Sin: With Comments on a Second Article in the Princeton Review," *BS* (July 1851): 594–647; Hodge, "Professor Park and the Princeton Review," *PR* 23, 4 (1851): 674–95. The detailed exchanges between Hodge and Park over eighteen months illustrate the significant impact of religious journals in the nineteenth century. The last two exchanges expanded beyond the original debate over intellect and feelings to focus on the protracted Augustinian and anti-Augustinian controversy over imputation of original sin and the atonement in creeds and confessions throughout church history.

9. "The Theology of the Intellect and That of the Feelings," 650. Mark Noll points out that the two professors did not always convey each other's views in the best light. Both claimed to represent a conservative side of their respective denominations—Park to Congregationalism and Hodge to Presbyterianism. Despite this caveat, Hodge's points in the dialogue illustrate not only his polemical method, but also his insistence of intellect and feelings as cohesively related in genuine Christian experience. Mark A. Noll, ed., *The Princeton Theology, 1812–1921: Scripture, Science, and Theological Method from Archibald Alexander to Benjamin Warfield* (Grand Rapids: Baker, 1983), 186–87.

10. "The Theology of the Intellect and That of the Feelings," 651, 654.

11. Ibid., 652.

12. Ibid., 660. As noted above, the unity of the soul in Princeton theology, including Hodge's, is the determining element in Paul Helseth's thesis. Helseth effectively demonstrates that, all criticisms of Princeton notwithstanding, the epistemology of Old Princeton theology was not baldly rationalistic.

13. Regarding creeds and hymns, Hodge also stated, "If we wish to get the real faith of a people, that faith on which they live, in which intellect and heart alike acquiesce, go to their hymns and forms of devotion. There they are sincere. There they speak what they know to be true; and there consequently their true creed is to be found." Ibid., 667.

14. Ibid., 665–66, 668. Decades later, expressing the same correlation between mind and heart, Hodge stated in his *ST* the true theological method: "The true method in theology requires that the facts of religious experience [Christianity as a way of life] should be accepted as facts, and when duly authenticated by Scripture be allowed to

interpret the doctrinal statements of the Word of God [Christianity as propositional]. So legitimate and powerful is this inward teaching of the Spirit, that it is no uncommon thing to find men having two theologies,—one of the intellect, and another of the heart. The one may find expression in creeds and systems of divinity; the other in their prayers and hymns. It would be safe for a man to resolve to admit into his theology nothing which is not sustained by the devotional writings of true Christians of every denomination." *ST*, 1:16–17.

Chapter 24: Christian Education

1. *PAI*, 99–121. The quotation appears on page 108.
2. "The General Assembly of 1843," *PR* 15, 3 (1843): 412–14.
3. "The General Assembly of 1844," *PR* 16, 3 (1844): 445–48. Hodge's comment critical of earlier attempts to lower standards for ministerial training probably reflected his negative views of New Side ministerial education, which he discussed in *CHPC*.
4. "The General Assembly of 1845," *PR* 17, 3 (1845): 426, 429–30, 432. Decades later, in 1871, Hodge addressed the issue of support of seminary students and pastors in "Preaching the Gospel to the Poor," *PR* 43, 1 (1871): 83–95. Reflecting his own impoverished home life, his early missionary work in Philadelphia, and his persistent emphasis on adequately supporting pastors and seminary students, Hodge made a strong plea for alleviating the plight of the poor. He considered Christ's command to preach to the poor as being readily fulfilled by Roman Catholics, Methodists, and Scottish Presbyterians. But he said that "the Presbyterian Church in this country is not the church of the poor. . . . We as a church, are not doing, and never have done, what we were bound to do in order secure [*sic*] the preaching of the Gospel to the poor." He blamed the deficiency on the Presbyterian system of making each congregation responsible for supporting its pastor. Instead, Hodge argued that support of ministry was the job of the whole church. Since the poor tended to go "with their own class," Hodge called for a system used in Glasgow, Scotland: establish churches with "free seats" (no pew charges) and support a policy used decades earlier (in which he had participated) of sending itinerant missionaries "going from place to place within a given district, and even preaching the Gospel from house to house." They would preach "in destitute places, for six months, or a year, or for a longer period." "Preaching the Gospel to the Poor," 86–94. Thus, out of his own experience and present need, combined with a sensitivity to poverty and concern for supporting seminary students and the larger ministry of the church, Hodge urged a change in his church's polity that would increase its effectiveness in evangelism and education.
5. "The General Assembly of 1846," *PR* 18, 3 (1846): 434–35. Paul Kemeny mentions Hodge's and his son's views of religion in the public schools in the chapter "Education and Religion in the Nation's Service, 1868–1888," in *Princeton in the Nation's Service: Religious Ideals and Educational Practice, 1868–1928* (New York: Oxford University Press, 1998), 28.
6. "The General Assembly of 1846," 436–38.

7. Ibid., 438–39.

8. Thomas J. DiFilippo, *Stephen Girard, The Man, His College and Estate*, 2nd ed. (1999). Available online: http://www.girardweb.com/girard/chapter2.htm. Hodge's assessment that Girard College represented a harbinger of the direction of American education proved prescient as the nineteenth century progressed. Cf. D. G. Hart, *Defending the Faith* (Grand Rapids: Baker, 1994), 30–31, 138–39, 180n20, 194n52.

9. "The General Assembly of 1846," 440–41.

10. "The General Assembly of 1847," *PR* 19, 3 (1847): 425–26. The following year, the General Assembly passed similar resolutions encouraging parochial schools. "The General Assembly of 1848," *PR* 20, 3 (1848): 429–30.

11. "The General Assembly of 1850," *PR* 22, 3 (1850): 459. Robert Ellis Thompson discusses Presbyterian efforts in education and attributes the decline in interest in parochial schools to pressure of other matters and the resignation of Cortlandt van Rensselaer as secretary of the Board of Education in 1860. *A History of the Presbyterian Churches in the United States* (1895; repr., Eugene, OR: Wipf and Stock, 2003), 197–99.

12. "The General Assembly of 1850," 463.

13. "The General Assembly of 1853," *PR* 25, 3 (1853): 472. In 1855 the assembly resolved that "although the public schools are far from being what they ought to be in respect to religious teaching, yet, instead of the withdrawal of Presbyterians from the support of the public system, the General Assembly recommends the putting forth of earnest efforts, wherever practicable, to improve its condition, especially by keeping in the public schools the Bible, as the great text-book of human instruction." "The General Assembly of 1855," *PR* 27, 3 (1855): 477.

14. "The General Assembly of 1850," 464–65. In 1851 the assembly resolved that the practice of requiring a pledge in the early stages of education was "not conducive to the best interests of the candidates, or of the Church." Hodge also added the remark that pledges were "a hurtful snare" and that the only pressure or bias upon a candidate should be "the influence of the Spirit and providence of God." "The General Assembly of 1851," *PR* 23, 3 (1851): 544.

15. "The General Assembly of 1850," 465–67. As in the previous two matters, the 1851 assembly provided that funds not be limited to theological students, but that they also become available for "promising young men of moral character" regardless of their vocational plans. Hodge also added the comment that receiving aid should not be considered something derogatory: "there is nothing more derogatory to a young man being educated by the Church for the ministry, than there is in his being educated by the State for the army." "The General Assembly of 1851," 546.

16. "The General Assembly of 1851," 537.

17. Ibid., 539.

18. Ibid., 540.

19. Ibid. Though Hodge did not mention European scholars, by adopting curricular modifications such as these, Princeton would avoid practices illustrated by Immanuel

Kant and Friedrich Schleiermacher. Kant thoroughly repudiated Old Testament Judaism in *RWLRA* as merely a primitive precursor to Christianity, and Schleiermacher demonstrated a similar dislike by the fact that he taught all the courses in theology at the University of Berlin except the Old Testament.

20. "The General Assembly of 1851," 540–41. Hodge could just as well have referred to himself, since his career and writings flowed over into all parts of the seminary curriculum. His initial field was biblical languages. This not only prepared him to teach biblical courses but equipped him to publish commentaries on various New Testament books. In addition, he wrote major works on history (*CHPC*) and polity (*The Church and Its Polity*). His assumption of his mentor's duties in theology and his habit of preaching regularly meant that he could teach courses in those areas as well.

21. In the latter decades of the 1800s, theological education in America experienced winds of change. One of the prominent voices for reform of the curriculum appeared when Charles W. Eliot, president of Harvard, used the pages of the *PR* in 1883 to call for a renovation of theological education akin to the European model. Some seminaries began to eliminate Hebrew as a requirement and add electives that would effectively crowd out traditionally required courses. Hodge's successors attempted to maintain the Princeton model in the face of calls for dramatic alteration to theological education. Benjamin B. Warfield and J. Gresham Machen argued forcefully for the traditions of Princeton as found in the Plan of the Seminary. Cf. *PS*, 2:264–69. While sympathetic to professors' defense of Princeton's earlier standards, David Calhoun stated that the seminary had "lost something of Alexander's and Miller's [he also includes Hodge in a subsequent sentence] ability to teach and model for the students the skills of ministry." Ibid., 2:269.

Chapter 25: Relations with Roman Catholicism

1. *LCH*, 348.

2. "The General Assembly of 1845," *PR* 17, 3 (1845): 444, 447–48, 451.

3. Ibid., 457. Paul K. Conkin cites Hodge's moderation on theological issues dividing Protestants and Catholics as a key evidence that Hodge was part of "the uneasy center" of Reformed Christianity in the first half of the nineteenth century. Though Hodge spoke vehemently against what he considered Catholicism's semi-Pelagian views of salvation, baptismal regeneration, purgatory, the Lord's Supper, and other doctrines, he frequently mentioned Catholicism's concurrence on key Christian doctrines such as the Trinity, the deity of Christ, and his atoning death. *UCRC*, 228–29.

4. "The General Assembly of 1845," 463–65. In addition to his comments above in chapter 24, footnote 4, about Rome's reaching out to the poor, Hodge stated that the church's obedience to Christ's command to aid the poor depended on "the principles which underlie its organization and modes of action." He used contemporary Catholicism to illustrate his point: "The Roman Catholic countries . . . do reach the poor. In Roman Catholic countries, as in France, in Spain, in Italy, the poor are in the church. They are all baptized in the name of Christ. They are all confirmed. They all

participate in the ministrations of the priesthood. They crowd the sanctuaries, even when the houses of worship are forsaken by the educated and rich. This one thing the Romish Church does do." Although he immediately chastised Rome for its "false doctrines and superstitions," Hodge's enumeration of baptism, confirmation, sacraments, and church attendance well summarized Old School practices he treated in other contexts. "Preaching the Gospel to the Poor," *PR* 43, 1 (1871): 84. Interestingly, he alleged that based on the criterion of reaching the poor, Prussia "must be regarded as the most thoroughly Christian nation in the world" and the United States "one of the most irreligious." Ibid., 85. He applauded the Methodists as followers of John Wesley as the most successful of American denominations to fulfill Christ's commands. And he lamented that "the Presbyterian Church . . . is not the church for the poor." Ibid., 86.

5. "The General Assembly of 1845," 466. A. A. Hodge interprets his father's position as follows: "the great body of people constituting the Roman Catholic Church do profess the essentials of the true Christian religion, whereby many of them bear the image of Christ, and are participants of His fellowship." *LCH*, 340.

6. "The General Assembly of 1845," 470. Hodge addressed similar issues in "Is the Church of Rome a Part of the Visible Church?," *PR* 18, 2 (1846): 320–44. He responded to the question by advancing the same illustration used in the article on baptism: "It is said we give up too much to the papists if we admit Romanists to be in the church. To this we answer, Every false position is a weak position. The cause of truth suffers in no way more than from identifying it with error, which is always done when its friends advocate it on false principles. When one says, we favour intemperance, unless we say that the use of intoxicating liquors, is sinful; another, that we favour slavery, unless we say slaveholding is a sin; and a third, that we favour Popery unless we say the church of Rome is no church, they all, as it seems to us, make the same mistake and greatly injure the cause in which they are engaged . . . It is a great mistake to suppose that Popery is aided by admitting what truth it does include. What gives it its power, what constitutes its peculiarly dangerous character, is that it is not pure infidelity, it is not the entire rejection of the gospel, but truth surrounded by enticing and destructive error." Ibid., 343–44.

7. Letter to Pius IX, Bishop of Rome (1869), in *CHP*, box 6, folder 3, pp. 1–3.

8. Though Hodge does not explicitly state as much, he may have had in mind French bishop and theologian Jacques-Benigne Bossuet's *History of the Variations of the Protestant Churches* (1688). Bossuet originated the apologetic position that contrary to Protestant claims, the Catholic Church did not corrupt ancient beliefs that thereby necessitated the Reformation. Rather, Protestants were the true innovators. By their doctrines and practices, the Reformers and their followers departed from what the church had always believed. They showed themselves to be both heretics by deviating from long-received teachings and schismatics by withdrawing from Catholic communion.

9. Letter to Pius IX, Bishop of Rome, 4–6.

10. *Syllabus of Errors*, along with all other papal encyclicals, can be accessed online at www.papalencyclicals.net.

11. "Is the Church of Rome a Part of the Visible Church?," 320.

Chapter 26: Internecine Controversy: Mercersburg

1. James Hastings Nichols, ed., *The Mercersburg Theology* (New York: Oxford University Press, 1966); D. G. Hart, *John Williamson Nevin: High Church Calvinist* (Phillipsburg, NJ: P&R Publishing, 2005); Sydney E. Ahlstrom, *A Religious History of the American People* (New Haven, CT: Yale University Press, 1972), 615–21; E. Brooks Holifield, *Theology in America: Christian Thought from the Age of the Puritans to the Civil War* (New Haven, CT: Yale University Press, 2003), 467–81; *PAI*, 282–83.

2. "Schaff's Protestantism," *PR* 17, 4 (1845): 626.

3. Ibid., 627. Hodge expressed his appreciation for Schaff's distinguishing the foundational elements of Protestantism by sardonically commending them to New Schoolers for their edification!

4. Ibid., 631–32.

5. Ibid., 634–35.

6. Ibid., 636. Schaff's flirting with German idealism threatened to afflict Reformed thinking with the same errors characteristic of Protestant liberalism later in the nineteenth century.

7. Ibid. Schaff responded to Hodge's seminary with a sharp quip. As Schaff walked arm-in-arm with Hodge and Henry Ward Beecher at a meeting of the Evangelical Alliance at Princeton College, as reported by Schaff's son, Schaff "thanked God he had come on the excursion if for no other reason than that he would thenceforth know one dry place to flee to at the next deluge"! David S. Schaff, T*he Life of Philip Schaff: In Part Autobiographical* (New York: Scribners, 1897), 274.

8. The quotation from Nevin's autobiography appears in Hart, John Williamson Nevin, 47.

9. Cf. Whitney R. Cross, *The Burned-over District: The Social and Intellectual History of Enthusiastic Religion in Western New York, 1800–1850* (New York: Harper, 1950). James Hastings Nichols states that agreement between Nevin, Hodge, and Horace Bushnell on the revivals' "poisonous effect" on infant baptism made it a "three-cornered discussion." *Romanticism in American Theology: Nevin and Schaff at Mercersburg* (Chicago: University of Chicago Press, 1961), 238–44. The quotation is on page 240.

10. Keith W. Clements, *Friedrich Schleiermacher: Pioneer of Modern Theology* (Minneapolis: Fortress Press, 1991), 221.

11. "Doctrine of the Reformed Church on the Lord's Supper," *PR* 20, 2 (1848): 227–77. Hodge included "Mysticism" as a major category in his *ST*, 3:922. He discussed the subject in its philosophical use, in Schleiermacher's theology, and in various movements throughout church history. Interestingly, Hodge added a note about the two-year delay in reviewing the book that reflects his self-esteem and his family's view of his work ethic. Hodge lamented, "We do not suppose other people are quite as bad, in this respect, as ourselves." "Doctrine of the Reformed Church on the Lord's Supper," 227. Many studies have probed the debate between Hodge and Nevin in great detail. For accounts of the interaction between Hodge and Nevin,

see Keith A. Mathison, *Given for You: Reclaiming Calvin's Doctrine of the Lord's Supper* (Phillipsburg, NJ: P&R Publishing, 2002), 129–55; Nichols, *Romanticism in American Theology*, 88–92, 94–101, 103–5; Hart, *John Williamson Nevin*, 127–37, 188–90; Peter J. Wallace, "History and Sacrament: John Williamson Nevin and Charles Hodge on the Lord's Supper," *Mid-America Journal of Theology* 11 (2000): 171–202; B. A. Gerrish, *Tradition and the Modern World: Reformed Theology in the Nineteenth Century* (Chicago: University of Chicago Press, 1978); Holifield, *Theology in America*, 385, 478–79.

12. The Consensus Tigurinus was written by John Calvin and Heinrich Bullinger in 1549 specifically to unify Reformed churches on the sacraments; the Heidelberg Catechism (1563) was composed by Zacharias Ursinus and Caspar Olevianus as a confessional document commissioned by Frederick III, Elector of the Palatinate; the Second Helvetic Confession was written by Heinrich Bullinger in 1536 as a confession of the Swiss churches and was eventually widely recognized as one of Reformed Christianity's foremost confessions.

13. "Doctrine of the Reformed Church on the Lord's Supper," 245–46, 259, 265. The confrontation between Hodge and Nevin as a conflict within the Reformed tradition is discussed by Gerrish, *Tradition and the Modern World*, 60–66.

14. An excellent account of the Lord's Supper and the controversy between Hodge and Nevin appears in Mathison, *Given for You*, 152–55. I am dependent on Mathison's summary and analysis for what follows.

15. Gerrish, *Tradition and the Modern World*, 64.

16. In his original monograph Nevin wrote that the Puritan view had no mystery—no more than in "a common fourth of July celebration"! John Williamson Nevin, *The Mystical Presence and Other Writings on the Eucharist* (Philadelphia: J. B. Lippincott, 1846), 119.

17. Mathison, *Given for You*, 152–55.

18. Ibid., 155. James Hastings Nichols wrote of Nevin's refutation of Hodge: "As an historical monograph it remained without a rival in English until the twentieth century." *Mercersburg Theology*, 246.

19. *ST*, 3:19–20, 204; 2:446, 447ff.

20. George H. Shriver, "Passages in Friendship: John W. Nevin to Charles Hodge," *JPH* 58, 2 (1980): 116–20.

21. Nevin hereby castigates Hodge for refusing to publish Nevin's attempt to state his views in favor of articles written by a virtually illiterate member of the German Reformed Church simply because Voringham opposed Nevin.

22. Ibid. (emphases in original). To Shriver's knowledge, the letter had never been published before. Shriver lamented Nevin's obscurity in contrast to Hodge's fame because Nevin's contributions were "more profound." Shriver depicted Nevin as a "bridgebuilder" between European and American theological scholarship. Hodge, states Shriver, "was more preoccupied with defending a strict, scholastic Reformed theology rather than attempting synthesis or incorporation." Shriver consistently cast

Hodge in an unfavorable light because "Nevin had attempted to hang on to a revered friend, and in old age he was left with a worthless shell." Ibid., 117, 119.

23. *ST*, 3:655 (explanatory note). As a side note, yet significant in light of Shriver's harsh portrayal of the incident, Shriver seemed so intent on casting a negative light on Hodge—which in this instance appears clearly to be justified—that he did not mention Hodge's attempt to temper—however weakly—his former criticism. Thus, ironically, in light of Shriver's omission, he deserves the same censure that Nevin initially leveled at Hodge! Shriver does reluctantly concede, "The respect and esteem between the two continued to the end. Some years before his death Dr. Hodge made it convenient to visit Lancaster [before or after 1872?], and he was heartily received as a guest in Dr. Nevin's family." Shriver, "Passages in Friendship," 119. Most probably, the visit occurred after Hodge published his third volume.

24. *ST*, 3:655.

25. The *British Quarterly Review* states that Hodge possessed an affinity for polemical discourse, as represented by his "collision[s]" with Moses Stuart, Albert Barnes, Edwards Amasa Park, John Nevin, Philip Schaff, and Horace Bushnell, which are featured in this study. *LCH*, 257. Ironically, however, A. A. Hodge apparently offered another olive branch to Mercersburg's theologian when Nevin died in 1886. D. G. Hart comments that because of Nevin's low profile in American religion, Hodge's son was the only figure of some repute who spoke at Nevin's funeral. Hart states, "When Hodge spoke in the Lancaster church he mentioned that Nevin was one of the Presbyterian Church's few great theologians and one of the greatest three or four citizens of the Commonwealth of Pennsylvania." Hart, *John Williamson Nevin*, 226.

Chapter 27: Old School North vs. Old School South

1. Cf. James Henley Thornwell, *The Collected Writings of James Henley Thornwell* (Richmond, VA: Presbyterian Committee of Publication, 1871).

2. My predecessor at Reformed Theological Seminary, Jackson, Mississippi, Dr. Albert H. Freundt, founding professor of church history, was a longtime student of Southern Presbyterian polity. His essay "The Southern Presbyterian Polity of James Henley Thornwell" distinguishes the differences between the two Old School positions of Thornwell and Hodge on church polity. I have depended heavily on his material in the following paragraphs. His essay is posted online at www.geocities.com/afreundt /thornwell.html.

3. Hodge intended to publish a fourth volume to his *ST* to include the subject of ecclesiology, but declining health thwarted that hope. The Rev. William Durant, a student of Hodge, synthesized a vast amount of material in the *PR* articles on ecclesiology—some articles are included in toto—with his teacher's approval. A. A. Hodge reviewed Durant's labor and gave his commendation that the arrangement and discussion of themes accurately reflected his father's treatment. *The Church and Its Polity by Charles Hodge* was published by Thomas Nelson in 1879.

4. *What Is Presbyterianism?* (Philadelphia: Presbyterian Board of Publication, 1855), 6–7.

5. James Henley Thornwell, *Collected Writings*, vol. 4 (Richmond, VA: Presbyterian Committee of Publication, 1889), 267, quoted in Freundt, "The Southern Presbyterian Polity of James Henley Thornwell," n.p.

6. Thornwell, *Collected Writings*, 4:69. The role of ruling elder has been a volatile topic in American Presbyterian history. Despite Hodge's reputation on the topic that emerged out of the preceding conflict, his senior colleague, Samuel Miller, wrote more extensively on it. In 1821 he published *An Essay on the Warrant, Nature and Duties of the Office of the Ruling Elder, in the Presbyterian Church* (New York: Jonathan Leavitt, 1821), which received widespread praise for resurrecting the biblical basis for the office of ruling elder and making it a distinctive feature of Presbyterian polity. Ironically, earlier in his career, Miller had actually supported the practice advocated by the Southerners, but he eventually changed his view, partly as a result of the Congregational advocacy of elders' role in the voluntary societies and lay preaching, which he viewed as an intrusion into the duties of ministers. Cf. *PS*, 1:296–301. In 1835 he published *Presbyterianism the Truly Primitive and Apostolical Constitution of the Church of Christ* (Philadelphia: Presbyterian Board of Publication, 1835), in which he contended against the Episcopal claims of Catholicism that Presbyterian government was "more primitive and apostolical in its whole constitution of *doctrine, worship, and order*, than any other Church now on earth." Quoted in *PS*, 1:302.

7. "The General Assembly of 1843," *PR* 15, 3 (1843): 438.

8. Ibid., 439–40, 443.

9. Freundt, "The Southern Presbyterian Polity of James Henley Thornwell," n.p.

10. "The General Assembly of 1843," 437, 447, 449–50.

11. "The General Assembly of 1860," *PR* 32, 3 (1860): 515, 517. The 1854 General Assembly had previously broached the constitutionality of boards versus committees. Hodge concluded his report of that assembly by saying that objection to boards because "the Scripture know nothing of [them was] . . . the *jus divinum* theory in its dotage." "The General Assembly of 1854," *PR* 26, 3 (1854): 561. Hodge also penned an extensive refutation of Thornwell's *jus divinum* view of church government in the same issue in which he covered the 1860 General Assembly: "Presbyterianism," *PR* 32, 3 (1860): 546–67.

12. "The General Assembly of 1860," 518–19. Hodge did not report the most colorful exchange between himself and Thornwell that has made its way into most accounts of their debates. He reported that Henry Boardman summarized Presbyterian standards and "the modest and moderate language therein employed, as utterly inconsistent with extreme high-church doctrine." Ibid., 520. This comment alludes to Hodge's charge that Thornwell's *jure divino* view constituted "hyper—hyper—hyper—high-church Presbyterianism!," to which Thornwell retorted with an equally quotable put-down that Hodge's views were "no—no—no Presbyterianism, no—no—no

Churchism!" John B. Adger, "The General Assembly of 1860," *Southern Presbyterian Review* 13, 2 (1860): 380.

13. "The General Assembly of 1859," *PR* 31, 3 (1859): 607–8, 615–16, 618.

14. "The General Assembly of 1860," 540–41.

Chapter 28: Subscription to the Westminster Confession of Faith

1. See chapter 32 for Hodge's views on the reunion.

2. "Remarks on Dr. Cox's Communication," *PR* 3, 4 (1831): 520–21. S. Donald Fortson explores the various instances in the denomination's history from the Adopting Act of 1729 to the Old / New School Reunion that Hodge addressed on the issue of subscription in "The Presbyterian Creed: Old School / New School Reunion and Confessional Subscription" (PhD diss., Westminster Theological Seminary, 2003). Also see S. Donald Fortson and David Calhoun, *The Presbyterian Creed: A Confessional Tradition in America, 1729–1870* (Eugene, OR: Wipf and Stock, 2011).

3. "The General Assembly of 1858," *PR* 30, 3 (1858): 561.

4. "Adoption of the Confession of Faith," *PR* 30, 4 (1858): 670, 672.

5. Ibid., 678–80.

6. Ibid., 680–81.

7. Ibid., 686.

8. Ibid., 690.

Chapter 29: Anglicanism's Oxford Movement

1. B. A. Gerrish, "Charles Hodge and the Europeans," in *CHR*, 129–58, offers a sympathetic account of Hodge's interaction with European thinkers. Gerrish, however, downplays Hodge's European studies—as have most other historians—because they occurred at the inception of his career when his ideas were merely taking shape. The focus of this study demonstrates the importance of viewing his German experience as foundational to his labors not just upon his immediate return in 1828 but through the remainder of his teaching and writing. Continuities that permeated all areas of Hodge's life and thought suggest that while development occurred in his thought, his core beliefs remained remarkably constant. He expressed that continuity in his famous claim that a new idea never developed at the seminary. He wanted that continuity safely instilled in Princeton's graduates. A primary theme in this study is that Hodge intended to ensure that the seminary would inform its graduates of all developments of modern scholarship—both positive and negative—without their being taken in by its radical conclusions.

2. Immanuel Kant coined the term *worldview* in 1790. It quickly captured the attention of scholars in early-nineteenth-century Europe. While the term survives in many scholarly circles as a way of identifying the particularities of diverse cultures and schools of thought, the term has elicited both support and critique as a result of incursions made by the rise of postmodernism. For extended discussion of the concept—its

history and impact on various scholarly fields—see David K. Naugle, *Worldview: The History of a Concept* (Grand Rapids: Eerdmans, 2002).

3. Not only did Princetonians adapt Scottish philosophy, but Common Sense Realism so pervaded theological discussion that one could speak of it as the lingua franca of American philosophy in the first half of the nineteenth century. The transcendentalists discussed below are the most obvious exception to this generalization.

4. One of the Oxford movement's leaders, John Keble, went so far as to accuse England in his sermon "National Apostasy," delivered on July 14, 1833, of verging on wholesale apostasy similar to Israel's apostasy under Samuel. Keble warned of apostasy's imminence because English leaders and the people of England threatened to divert from the traditional apostolic church. For a sympathetic contemporary account of the movement, see Richard William Church, *The Oxford Movement: Twelve Years 1833–1845* (New York: Macmillan, 1891). Church was Dean of St. Paul's Church, London.

5. "Oxford Tracts," *PR* 10, 1 (1838): 84, 87–88.

6. Ironically, the term *via media* figured prominently in Princetonians' attempts to distinguish their ideas from other positions that they considered more radical than their own.

7. Ibid., 90, 92, 94–95.

8. Ibid., 102. Hodge cites Tract 45 for criticizing the Reformation's discarding of tradition and making the Bible "the sole document both for ascertaining and proving our faith. . . . Even if Episcopacy were not at all mentioned in scripture, 'it would be our duty to receive it' on the ground of tradition." Ibid., 113.

9. Ibid., 116.

10. Ibid., 117.

11. Ibid., 118–19.

12. Newman defended his defection from Anglicanism as well as his belief in the Roman church as the one true church in his autobiographical *Apologia Pro Sua Vita* (1864).

13. For further comment on Hodge's ecumenicity, especially with historic Anglicanism, see his remarks on the occasion of his semicentennial celebration of his professorship in part 6 below.

Chapter 30: German and American Transcendentalism

1. B. A. Gerrish, "Charles Hodge and the Europeans," in *CHR*, 132.

2. Article IV, Section 1, "Of Study and Attainments," mandated that students develop a working familiarity with original languages so that they could correctly exposit Scripture and become "sound biblical critic[s]." The Plan mandated next that students "read and digest" original writings "relative to what has been called the deistical controversy," which would qualify them as "defender[s] of the Christian faith." Interestingly, this provision comes second in the Plan, preceding the requirement to

"support the doctrines of the Confession of Faith and Catechisms." David Calhoun, "Plan of the Seminary," in *PS*, 1:423–24.

3. Hodge does mention Kant's disparaging remarks about prayer in *ST*, 3:695: "Kant, although a theist, regards all as unphilosophical enthusiasts who assume that God hears or answers prayer." The language resembles Kant's exact expression in *RWLRA*, but Hodge's footnote cites a biographical work on Kant, not *RWLRA* itself. Hodge's penchant for citing sources to illustrate his points renders likely the fact that he remained unfamiliar with Kant's book. Only seven references to Kant appear in the index of *ST*, and none of them refer to *RWLRA*.

4. Cf. *RWLRA*, 179–90, for Kant's discussion of the supposed means of grace: "prayer," "church-going," "initiation" (baptism), and "the oft-repeated ceremony" (communion). Kant not only recast Christianity into a religion of morality but in the process rejected, among others, the doctrines of the historical fall, original sin (which he replaced with the term "radical evil"), miracles, and Christ's substitutionary atonement and resurrection from the dead. A religion within the limits of reason could never comprise such beliefs.

5. Paul Tillich, *A History of Christian Thought: From Its Jewish and Hellenistic Origins to Existentialism* (New York: Simon and Schuster, 1967), 386–87.

6. We earlier examined Hodge's review of Ernst Wilhelm Hengstenberg's commentary on Daniel as an example of successful refutation of German biblical scholarship. In that review he cited the reasons for liberalism's plausibility—"confronting us boldly with a long array of lexicons, and grammars, expositions, illustrations, and critical apparatuses." Their success in presenting a plausible case for unbelief rested on "breaking up the surface of a subject . . . by clouding the general view, and confining the attention to detached particulars, by means of minute discussion and the parade of accuracy even in minutiae." Hengstenberg broke through the German subtleties by exposing their false views of particulars. "Hengstenberg on Daniel," *PR* 4, 1 (1832): 69–70. Hodge's service to evangelical scholarship by reviewing works such as Hengstenberg's has its later parallel in B. B. Warfield's extended reviews of German theology in the twentieth century. Cf. W. Andrew Hoffecker, "Benjamin B. Warfield," in *Reformed Theology in America: A History of Its Modern Development*, ed. David Wells (Grand Rapids: Baker, 1985), 60–86.

7. "Transcendentalism," *PR* 11, 1 (1839): 38.

8. Ibid., 43, 50.

9. Ibid., 57–58.

10. Ibid., 78, 86–87.

11. At this point Hodge inserted a footnote containing the famous quote of Heinrich Heine, "Pantheism is the public secret of Germany." Ibid., 95.

12. Ibid., 95, 97. Bruce Kuklick opened his essay on Hodge's role in nineteenth-century intellectual life by stating that scholars have recently attributed to Emerson the status of an original thinker—"a sage or seer"—in American philosophy. "The Place

of Charles Hodge in the History of Ideas in America," in *CHR*, 63–76. Kuklick then posed the question, "How does Hodge, a contemporary of Emerson's, fit in to these ongoing reappraisals?" Unfortunately, Kuklick does not answer his own question, but instead focuses on Jonathan Edwards, Scottish Realism, and advances in science. Hodge most assuredly responded to Emerson, as the following treatment demonstrates.

13. "Transcendentalism," 98. Hodge also reported that "in one of our public papers, a severe rebuke of Mr. Emerson . . . was attributed to another of the Professors of the university." Ibid. Unitarian minister Jonathan Sinclair Carey offered a surprised analysis of Princeton and Harvard's concurrence in opposing Emerson's transcendentalism in " 'For God or Against Him': Princeton Orthodoxy and Transcendentalists," *American Presbyterians* 64, 4 (1986): 243–58.

14. "Transcendentalism," 99, 101. In 1840 Hodge took similar umbrage to a claim that Kant and Cousin were "two of the greatest philosophers of the age." On the one hand, Kant deserved the title because he did "destroy one system, and introduce another, which had its day." Cousin, however, merited no such distinction, for he neither tore down nor constructed something new: "He has merely transfused into French a weak dilution of German doctrines." "The Latest Form of Infidelity," *PR* 12, 1 (1840): 71.

15. "Transcendentalism," 101.

16. Though Hodge mentioned Catholicism only in passing, he noted that Johannes Ronge led a liberal German movement within the Roman church similar to the Protestant "Friends of Light" mentioned below. In objecting to the errors of Rome, Ronge and his followers espoused deviant views of the Bible and traditional views of Christ. Thus the proliferation of unorthodox views was not limited to German Protestantism. "Religious State of Germany," *PR* 18, 4 (1846): 514–46.

17. Ibid., 527. The followers of Hengstenberg called themselves "The Church-minded" and "Friends of the Confession." Their opponents labeled them "Pietists," "The Strict Orthodox," and "Church Magazine Party," which identified them with Hengstenberg's journal. Ibid., 531.

18. Ibid., 528.

19. Ibid., 529–30. Tholuck had earlier revealed to Hodge that Schleiermacher's Christocentrism had resulted in conversions of people to Christianity.

20. Ibid., 530–31.

21. Ibid., 534, 536, 538. Defending "fundamentals" would become uppermost in the Princeton agenda at the end of the century as the seminary became embroiled in the fundamentalist controversy. Cf. Bradley J. Longfield, *The Presbyterian Controversy: Fundamentalists, Modernists, and Moderates* (New York: Oxford University Press, 1991).

22. "Religious State of Germany," 538–39.

23. Hermas was the early church father whose epistle consisting of visions, mandates, and parables proved popular for a time but was ultimately rejected as canonical. Interestingly, nineteenth-century historian Philip Schaff characterized Hermas's work

as "a book for the time, but not for all times." *History of the Christian Church*, vol. 2 (Grand Rapids: Eerdmans, 1976), 690.

24. "Religious State of Germany," 538–39.

Chapter 31: Revisiting an Old Friend

1. In 1832 Hodge had ended his review "Hengstenberg on Daniel" with the optimistic words, "We may indulge the hope that when a few more Hengstenbergs and Tholucks have arisen, the victory, even in the schools of Germany, will be confessedly upon the side of truth." *PR* 4, 1 (1832): 71.

2. "Neander's History of the Planting of the Church," *PR* 16, 2 (1844): 156.

3. Ibid., 157.

4. Ibid.

5. Ibid., 157–58. Immanuel Kant's distinction between the scholar and the priest becomes evident here. Pastors are accountable that their views accord with received confessions and creeds of the church. They must adhere to standards mandated by their respective churches. Scholars, on the other hand, must remain free to examine, discuss, and point out discrepancies as a result of their scholarly pursuits.

6. Ibid., 158.

7. Ibid., 159. Hodge's argument resembles the point made by Langdon Gilkey in his famous essay "Cosmology, Ontology and the Travail of Biblical Language," *Journal of Religion* 41, 3 (1961): 194–205. Though intended for a far different audience in the twentieth century, Gilkey criticized works such as G. Ernest Wright's *The Acts of God* for using language about biblical events that sounded orthodox. Yet because authors such as Wright denied the historicity of such acts as Moses' confrontation with God at the burning bush and the objective opening of the Red Sea in the Jews' exodus from Egypt, one might rightly ask what exactly was the content of those "acts."

8. "Neander's History," 173. In support of Neander's vagueness regarding the person of Christ, Hodge claimed that the formulas Neander employed could easily be affirmed of Sabellius, the third-century priest whose modalist view was denounced in the Trinitarian controversy of the early church.

9. Ibid., 182–83.

10. Ibid., 183.

Chapter 32: A Nation and Church Divided and Reunited

1. Hodge had called the Southern view something that surely raised the hackles of Thornwell: an "innovation."

2. "The Church and the Country," *PR* 33, 2 (1861): 327.

3. "Minutes of the General Assembly, 1861, vol xvi, 303," quoted in Lewis G. Vander Velde, *The Presbyterian Churches and the Federal Union, 1861–1869* (Cambridge, MA: Harvard University Press, 1932), 45. Vander Velde gives extensive treatment to the Gardiner Spring affair and Hodge's unsuccessful attempt to thwart the church's

committing itself to the federal government. Ibid., 46ff. D. G. Hart and John R. Muether also detail the events that unfolded on the floor of the assembly that occasioned great controversy in the political arena. *SABC*, 147–50.

4. Vander Velde, *The Presbyterian Churches and the Federal Union*, 60.

5. "The General Assembly of 1861," *PR* 33, 3 (1861): 545–46. Hart and Muether cite a New School newspaper that likened the 1861 Old School internecine conflict to the 1837 schism that had divided the denomination. The editorial stated sarcastically, "The excision of the rebellious synods of '61 would be a far clearer vindication of the loyalty of the church to the government, than the excision of the four Synods in '37 was of loyalty to the Confession of Faith." *SABC*, 150.

6. "The General Assembly of 1861," 548.

7. Ibid., 550–51. D. G. Hart points out that Hodge not only articulated the spirituality of the church more succinctly and clearly than Thornwell, but also used the Westminster Confession in doing so. Hodge cited chapter 31: "The church can only exercise her power in enforcing the word of God, in approving what it commands, and condemning what it forbids. A man, in the exercise of his liberty as to things indifferent, may be justly amenable to the laws of the land; and he may incur great guilt in the sight of God, but he cannot be brought under the censure of the church." D. G. Hart, "The Spirituality of the Church," in *Rediscovering Mother Kirk: The Case for Liturgy in the Reformed Tradition* (Grand Rapids: Baker, 2003), 55.

8. "The General Assembly of 1861," 559. A sharply different interpretation of Hodge's reasoning is given by Robert Ellis Thompson, who contends that the Hodge protest ignored "the whole history of the church, the teaching of the Confession, and the authority of God's word . . . The Protest implied a condemnation of Knox and of Calvin, of the Golden Assembly of 1638, of the Westminster Assembly of Divines, of the Revolution Assembly of 1690 and the Assembly of Synods of 1772–82. It is impossible to see how Presbyterianism could have perpetuated its existence on either side of the Atlantic if the Kirk had acted on the theories of the Hodge Protest." Robert Ellis Thompson, *A History of the Presbyterian Churches in the United States* (1895; repr., Eugene, OR: Wipf and Stock, 2003), 154.

9. "The General Assembly of 1861," 560–61, 568. Hodge continued to use the *PR* to support the Northern cause throughout the war. As in the case of the court battle in the aftermath of the 1837 schism, Hodge made statements that represented Northern patriotism.

10. Distraught over the nation's civil strife, Hodge expressed profound grief over Lincoln's assassination. His son wrote, "The assassination of President Lincoln, like an earthquake, convulsed his entire nature and broke up his deepest fountain of tears." *LCH*, 482. Hodge's article "President Lincoln" appeared in the same *PR* issue as his report on the General Assembly of 1865.

11. *Minutes of the General Assembly of the Presbyterian Church of the United States of America* (Philadelphia: Presbyterian Board of Publication, 1865), 562–63. The resolution instructed presbyteries of their "imperative duty, in the present circumstances of our country," to examine ministers on the points mentioned above.

12. "The General Assembly of 1865," *PR* 37, 3 (1865): 505, 507–8, 513.

13. The Auburn Declaration appears in Maurice W. Armstrong, Lefferts A. Loetscher, and Charles A. Anderson, eds., *The Presbyterian Enterprise: Sources of American Presbyterian History* (Philadelphia: Westminster Press, 1956), 166–71. The declaration demonstrated New School allegiance to the doctrines of the Westminster Confession.

14. *LCH*, 502. A detailed account of the reunion, *Presbyterian Reunion: A Memorial Volume, 1837–71* (New York: De Witt C. Lent, 1870), can be found online: http://openlibrary.org/books/OL13489884M/Presbyterian_reunion.

15. "The General Assembly of 1868," *PR* 40, 3 (1868): 422–23. Hodge and over fifty other Old Schoolers opposed the Gurley amendment.

16. Hodge's reference to the Barnes case as evidence of New School tolerance raised the hackles of Henry Boynton Smith, who lashed out at Hodge using his journal, the *American Presbyterian and Theological Review*, to issue a biting response to Hodge's claim that the New School still differed substantially from the Old School on theological matters. He threw down the gauntlet by writing, "The [*PR*] has said what, in common courtesy, it must take back." Hodge toned down his rhetoric substantially in the *PR*. But the Gurley amendment only reinforced Hodge's reluctance to support reunion. Reported in George Marsden, *The Evangelical Mind and the New School Presbyterian Experience: A Case Study of Thought and Theology in Nineteenth-Century America* (New Haven, CT: Yale University Press, 1970), 220.

17. "The General Assembly of 1868," 433–34. The New School argument harked back to its claim in 1837 that there "were only certain 'modes of viewing, stating, explaining, and illustrating certain doctrines.'" This argument resurfaced in the subsequent fundamental–liberal controversy in the 1920s. Harry Emerson Fosdick in his famous sermon "Shall the Fundamentalists Win?" delivered at New York's Riverside Church in 1922 argued that the five fundamentals were merely theories of biblical teachings that liberals interpreted differently. Although holding radically different perspectives on the issue in different historical contexts, Hodge and Fosdick made tolerance or lack thereof defining elements of opposing parties within the church.

18. Ibid., 442–43, 451.

19. Skinner's comment was cited by Hodge's junior editor, Lyman Atwater, in "Proceedings of the Late Assemblies on Reunion," *PR* 41, 3 (1869): 430.

20. *LCH*, 504. See "The New Basis of Union," *PR* 41, 3 (1869): 462–66.

21. *LCH*, 504. Hodge had complained to his brother earlier that he had a cold, a pain in his chest, and a boil. When his brother downplayed the seriousness of the latter, Hodge wrote mockingly in reply, "That anthrax malitiosissimus, ferocissimus, execrabilissimus, however, has kept me awake night after night, and tormented me day after day. That you call nothing! . . . What could ever have put it into the head of Job to scrape himself with a potsherd when his body was covered with boils is more than I can understand. I could not touch mine with a feather." He concluded the letter, "I go about as usual, and hope to be able to attend Presbytery 9 miles from here to-morrow." Ibid., 488. Given his physical condition and ecclesiastical burden, the day must have been most unpleasant.

22. Thompson, *A History of the Presbyterian Churches in the United States*, 180–81.

Chapter 33: Reformed among Evangelicals

1. Philip Schaff and S. Irenaeus Prime, eds., *History, Essays, Orations, and Other Documents of the Sixth General Conference of the Evangelical Alliance, Held in New York, October 2–12, 1873* (New York: Harper, 1874), iii, 6.

2. Ibid., 7; *LCH*, 547.

3. Ironically, of course, the topic of the Lord's Supper became the symbol of the original Reformers' inability to display unity at the Marburg colloquy in October 1529.

4. Schaff and Prime, *History, Essays, Orations*, 139. Hodge never completed what he intended—adding a fourth *ST* volume devoted to the doctrine of the church. Yet about 25 percent of the articles in *PR* dealt with the church.

5. Ibid., 141–43.

6. Ibid., 144.

7. Ibid.

8. Ibid.

9. Hodge's article in the *Presbyterian* appears in *LCH*, 550. Regarding Hodge's catholicity, his son wrote that his father had written "in pencil with trembling on one of his 'Conference Papers,' not long before he died, that he believed that the vast majority of the human race were to share the beatitudes and glories of his Lord's redemption." Among all evidences of his ecumenical congeniality, Hodge reserved his warmest words across denominational lines for his classmate and Episcopalian bishop-friend, John Johns. Being separated for the duration of the Civil War, they did not meet again until March 1866 when Johns visited while Hodge was vacationing at the home of his brother-in-law, General David Hunter, in Maryland. In 1874 Hodge expressed his postmillennial optimism of the church mixed with concern about growing infidelity: "I really believe that the world, on the whole, is getting better, and that the cause of Christ is on the advance. Yet at times I am somewhat startled at the decay of faith, or the prevalence of broad-churchism among all denominations and of skepticism among men of the world." Then in words that he could have penned following his sojourn with friends in Europe and his address at the Evangelical Alliance, he wrote, "Evangelical truth appears to be confined very much to true believers, of whom I hope, the number is now greater than during any former period of the history of the world. As long as piety lasts, the truth will last, and not much longer." In their last face-to-face conversation, Johns said to Hodge, "Charley, you have had more influence on my life than any other person I have ever known . . . It is the last time. Let me have a good look at your face, Charley, for we shall never see each other again until we meet in heaven." Ibid., 567–68. Hodge wrote to a friend after Johns died, "I never had such a friend. For nearly sixty-four years we were as intimate and confidential as though we had been born at one birth . . . I feel like the last tree of a forest." They continued corresponding until Johns's death in 1876. Ibid., 567–69.

10. Mark A. Noll and David N. Livingstone, introduction to *WID*, 26.

Chapter 34: Science under Scrutiny

1. Archibald Alexander, "The Bible and the Natural World," *PR* 1, 1 (1829): 102–21. Samuel Miller treats science in four chapters entitled "Mechanical Philosophy," "Chemical Philosophy," "Natural History," and "Medicine," in *Retrospect of the Eighteenth Century* (New York: T. and J. Swords, 1803), 1:9–378. Representative selections on science from Alexander, Hodge, A. A. Hodge, and Benjamin Warfield are found in Mark A. Noll, ed., *The Princeton Theology, 1812–1921: Scripture, Science, and Theological Method from Archibald Alexander to Benjamin Warfield* (Grand Rapids: Baker, 1983).

2. *MTC*, 15–16. In addition to Stewart's appreciative treatment, the following works probe Hodge's preoccupation with science: Ronald Numbers, "Charles Hodge and the Beauties and Deformities of Science," in *CHR*, 77–101; Mark A. Noll and David N. Livingstone, introduction to *WID*, 11–47; Theodore Dwight Bozeman, *Protestants in an Age of Science: The Baconian Ideal and Antebellum American Religious Thought* (Chapel Hill, NC: University of North Carolina Press, 1977).

3. *WID*, 22. For the emergence of the modern culture wars, see W. Andrew Hoffecker, "Enlightenments and Awakenings: The Beginning of Modern Culture Wars," in *Revolutions in Worldview: Understanding the Flow of Western Thought*, ed. W. Andrew Hoffecker (Phillipsburg, NJ: P&R Publishing, 2007), 240–80. For a twentieth-century explanation of the role of Christianity in the origin of modern science, see Alfred North Whitehead, *Science and the Modern World* (New York: Free Press, 1925), 1–19.

4. "The Unity of Mankind," *PR* 31, 1 (1859): 103–49.

5. Ibid., 113. In the twentieth century, C. S. Lewis sought the same end in his brief essay "Meditation in a Toolshed," in *God in the Dock* (Grand Rapids: Eerdmans, 1970), 212–15. For Lewis, the scientific way of "looking at" reality (emphasis on quantitative) had virtually displaced attempts of "looking along" reality (emphasis on qualitative). Neither view, said Lewis, should claim exclusive rights to define the world and man's place in it.

6. "The Unity of Mankind," 106–7. Hodge expressed his fondness for induction in the famous seventeen-page introduction to *ST*. Again, definition emerged as the decisive issue in doing theology. The method (inductive use of biblical facts) and goal (the glory of God) were of paramount importance in maintaining Reformed theology's stature in American religion. He posed induction as the middle way between the rational speculation of the deists and the experiential method of Schleiermacher. For a fuller discussion of Hodge's theological method, see W. Andrew Hoffecker, *Piety and the Princeton Theologians: Archibald Alexander, Charles Hodge, and Benjamin Warfield* (Grand Rapids: Baker, 1981), 55–64, and *RRPM*, 10, 11, 15n43, 149, 150n44.

7. Galileo in "Letter to Grand Duchess Christina" (1615) cited two early church fathers, Tertullian (once) and Augustine (five times), about the compatibility of nature and the Bible. Galileo cited Augustine as saying, "The intention of the Holy Ghost is to teach us how one goes to heaven, not how heaven goes," and "If anyone shall set the authority of Holy Writ against clear and manifest reason, he who does this knows

not what he has undertaken; for he opposes to the truth not the meaning of the Bible, which is beyond his comprehension, but rather his own interpretation, not what is in the Bible, but what he has found in himself and imagines to be there." With his predecessors, Galileo argued that God would never contradict himself in these two books. If a confirmed fact in nature appeared to contradict the Bible, the problem lay not with science nor with what the Bible taught. If science demonstrated its fact, the *interpretation* of the Bible—not the Bible itself—was incorrect. Galileo's letter may be found online: http://www.fordham.edu/halsall/mod/gallileo-tuscany.html.

8. "The Unity of Mankind," 106. Although Hodge changed his mind on the literal seven twenty-four-hour days of creation in Genesis 1, not all evangelicals accepted the teaching of the day-age theory of creation. Stewart cites Samuel Miller's *Retrospect*, in which he made the strongest statement of the compatibility of religion and science: "Never was there a period . . . of the same extent [i.e., the eighteenth century] . . . that the information and the doctrines contained in the sacred volume were so perfectly harmonized with the most authentic discoveries, and the sound principles of science." *MTC*, 19. Obviously, Hodge believed that the optimism of the previous century's acceptance of the compatibility of science and religion came under severe attack in the nineteenth century.

9. "The Unity of Mankind," 107–8.

10. Noll and Livingstone point out the lack of reference to *WID* in *LCH*—"almost terse to the point of silence" because A. A. devotes but one sentence to his father's book: "In 1874 [Charles] published a small book entitled 'Darwinism,' in opposition to the prevailing doctrine of Atheistic Evolutionism." The lack of further comment bears some similarity to A. A.'s omitting part of his father's account of the European revivals. The son did not want to give the wrong impression of his father's estimation of revivals, especially in light of Charles's distancing himself from the revivalism of the eighteenth century. In the case of evolution, the younger Hodge may have been embarrassed at his father's harsh words on evolution because A. A. proved more favorable to evolution than his father. Therefore, A. A. relegated *WID* and his father's involvement in the meeting of the Evangelical Alliance to minority status.

11. *WID*, 156–57.

12. Noll and Livingstone discuss the importance of definition in their introduction to *WID*.

13. "The Unity of Mankind," 106–7. Hodge repeated his views regarding science and the Bible in *ST*. He reaffirmed that there can be no conflict between the teachings of the Scriptures and the facts of science. Both science and theology had been forced to change their views. Scientific theories had been revised in light of ongoing research, and "the Church has been forced more than once to alter her interpretation of the Bible to accommodate the discoveries of science. But this has been done without doing any violence to the Scriptures or in any degree impairing their authority. Many theories have from time to time been presented, apparently or really inconsistent with the Bible. But these theories have either proved to be false or to harmonize with the Word of God, properly interpreted."

14. Hodge's command of the issues becomes evident as he probes the arguments of Darwin's proponents (Alfred Russel Wallace, Thomas Henry Huxley, Ludwig Buchner, Karl Vogt, and Ernst Haeckel) and opponents (Duke of Argyll, Louis Agassiz, Paul Janet, Marie Flourens, Georges Cuvier, Walter Mitchell, and J. W. Dawson).

15. *WID*, 130. While Hodge did not use the metaphor of warfare, by using the term *antagonism* he clearly sensed an impending conflict between science and religion. Later, scientist John William Draper's *History of the Conflict between Religion and Science* (1874) and Andrew Dickson White's *History of the Warfare of Science and Theology in Christendom* (1896) shaped both academic and popular opinion of an inherent conflict between science and religion or theology. White became the first president of Cornell University, founded to foster scientific study.

16. *WID*, 130–31. Hodge was not alone in discerning positivism's negative effects on theology and Comte's role in its advance. Robert Lewis Dabney, Old School theologian at Union Seminary in Virginia, authored an extensive critique in *The Sensualistic Philosophy of the Nineteenth Century, Considered* (New York: Anson, 1875). Cf. Sean Lucas, *Robert Lewis Dabney: A Southern Presbyterian Life* (Phillipsburg, NJ: P&R Publishing, 2005), 81–86, 168–78, 190–91.

17. *WID*, 133. Paul Kjoss Helseth has argued that correctly understanding "right reason" in the Princeton paradigm demonstrates more common ground between presuppositionalists and evidentialists over the issue of facts and their interpretation than previously thought. *RRPM*, 26–33, 88–97.

18. *WID*, 135, 137. Hodge also stated that "Haeckel's Irenicum" (Haeckel, a German zoologist and a strong proponent of Darwinism, originated the phrase *ontogeny recapitulates phylogeny*) was similar to Huxley's: only those well trained in biology may speak of biological matters. He stated, "Only a very few are able to commit themselves to such a discipline." Hodge quoted Haeckel: "*alle Glaube ist Aberglaube* [all faith is superstition]." Ibid., 136.

19. Ibid., 137. Other conservative Christians explored the outcomes of Hodge's extended treatise on definition. The most interesting involved Harvard botanist Asa Gray, a conservative Congregationalist, who became an ardent defender of Darwin. He argued that Darwin's theory did not necessitate atheism, but could be interpreted as a form of natural theology. As David Calhoun has pointed out, Gray was unable through correspondence to convince Darwin that his findings were capable of a theistic interpretation. As Gray forwarded a copy of his review of Hodge's book to Darwin, he wrote, "You will see what uphill work I have in making a theist of you 'of good and respectable standing.'" Darwin remained impassive to Gray's overture to reconsider his views and replied, "I read with interest your semi-theological review, & have got the book, but I think your review will satisfy me. The more I reflect on this subject, the more perplexed I grow." *PS*, 2:17–18.

20. *WID*, 89, 112, 114, 119, 136.

21. Hodge mentioned Darwin in *ST*, which was completed in 1873, and his analysis of Darwinian evolution foreshadowed the content in *WID* (1874). While he mentioned Darwin only twice by name, he broached *evolution* ten times. He used it in contexts

other than simply naturalistic science (e.g., pantheism, *ST*, 1:118, 304, 566). More frequently he referred to its materialistic form. Hodge bemoaned that natural evolution eliminated "all liberty of secondary causes" (ibid., 1:304); excluded any principle of vitalism, the view that living organisms are more than merely their physical/chemical properties (ibid., 1:266); represented living beings as merely the product of matter and force (ibid., 1:275); and explained the world as "the evolution of an unconscious, unintelligent force, which has no design out of itself" (ibid., 1:566).

22. Hodge's definition of theology as a science has received numerous critiques for being wooden and overly rationalistic. Cf. Ernest Sandeen, *The Roots of Fundamentalism: British and American Millenarianism 1800–1930* (Chicago: University of Chicago Press, 1970); John Vander Stelt, *Philosophy and Scripture: A Study in Old Princeton and Westminster Theology* (Marlton, NJ: Mack Publishing, 1978). For an opposing view, see *RRPM*, 58–73; Hoffecker, *Piety and the Princeton Theologians*, 55–64.

23. Charles Cashdollar discusses epistemology as the foundational element in positivism and thus the source of the transformation of theology in the nineteenth century. Hodge's critique of Comte in *ST* was preceded by four articles in the *PR* by Lyman Atwater and Charles Shields. Atwater, a resolute defender of Reformed theology, attacked Comte's philosophy as "blank, avowed, unblushingly Atheism." Shields, former Old School pastor who taught philosophy at Princeton University, eventually received Episcopal ordination and took a mediating approach advocating a reconciliation of science and Christianity. Cashdollar uses Shields's *Final Philosophy* (1877) and *Philosophia Ultima* (1888–89) as an illustration of the transformation of theology resulting from Comtean positivism. Charles D. Cashdollar, *The Transformation of Theology, 1830–1890: Positivism and Protestant Thought in Britain and America* (Princeton, NJ: Princeton University Press, 1989), 111–20, 334–38.

24. *ST*, 1:254. We have already examined Hodge's view of Victor Cousin's *The Elements of Psychology* in the 1856 issue of the *PR*. Almost a decade later, Hodge addressed the issue of psychology in "The Nature of Man," *PR* 37, 1 (1865): 111–35, when he stated, "The Scriptures do not formally teach any system of psychology." Yet the Bible did teach certain truths relating to human consciousness and the relation of man's mental and physical constitution. As in the case of the physical sciences, although not a text for psychology, the Bible stated truths necessary for a correct understanding of human thought and action—the substantial existence of both body and soul and the unitary nature of the soul, which manifested itself in human will, emotions, and intellect. Though Hodge used the term *faculties*, he did not compartmentalize them into a "faculty psychology" typical of some nineteenth-century psychological theory. For expanded treatment of Princeton's unitary view, see *RRPM*, 10, 32, 37, 40, 63.

25. Hodge wrote, "Materialists, as a general thing, are avowed necessitarians. This is not only true of the Positivists, but the doctrine that human action is determined by necessary laws, is the foundation of their whole system of Social Science." *ST*, 1:278.

26. Ibid., 1:255–56. Cashdollar explores positivism's effect on theology and Hodge's opposition to its influence in *The Transformation of Theology*, 115, 179, 188, 277, 332.

27. Hodge drew upon his avid interest in meteorological conditions and the accuracy of weather predictions in making this judgment. One of his lifelong hobbies consisted of recording in his "Memoranda," a book in which he wrote daily, the temperature and direction of the wind as well as other minor matters of personal interest.

28. *ST*, 1:260. Ironically, Hodge stated that Comte used the lowest stage of religion and its manifestation of papal power to illustrate the control that science was capable of exercising. "Papal infallibility was a great intellectual and social advance." Huxley furthered the idea when he called positivism "Catholicism *minus* Christianity." Ibid., 261.

29. Ibid., 260–61.

30. *CHR*, 81–96.

31. *WID*, 138. One of the most perceptive analyses of the pseudosciences or scientism that Hodge feared in the 1860s appeared almost a century later in a seminal study by Albert Hobbs, a rare conservative sociologist. Hobbs labored in obscurity at the University of Pennsylvania before more famous conservative sociologists Robert Nisbet, Ernest van den Haag, Peter Berger, and Will Herberg came onto the scene. Although approaching the subject from a secular point of view, Hobbs critiqued the social sciences for insisting that scientific method be used in areas of study where moral, religious, or aesthetic criteria should predominate. He also accused those guilty of scientism for using the credentials of science to undermine traditional moral views. Hobbs labeled twentieth-century advocates of the social sciences "pedantic prophets" who "offer 'scientific' explanations of human behavior, family adjustment, divorce, and delinquency . . . [They] employ the phrases of science as a screen through which they can launch their attacks on manners and morals. They use the prestige of science as a privileged sanctuary to shelter them from criticism." Hobbs singled out his own discipline, sociology, as well as psychoanalysis as primary practitioners of scientism. Those involved in scientism used the language of science while failing to follow methods of controlled observation and scientific verification, the crux of science. *Social Problems and Scientism* (Harrisburg, PA: Stackpole, 1953), iv, 7–15. Hobbs also exposed the tendentious nature of sociology in *The Claims of Sociology* (Harrisburg, PA: Stackpole, 1951).

Chapter 35: Fifty Years and Counting

1. Leviticus 25 lists the provisions for the Jewish Jubilee.

2. *LCH*, 128–29.

3. Ibid., 511.

4. Ibid., 512. *LCH* details the institutions and churches foreign and domestic that sent representatives to the ceremony. Alumni collected $45,000 to endow the chair in systematic theology in Hodge's honor. In addition, Hodge received a purse of over $15,000.

5. Ibid., 517.

6. Ibid., 519–20. Boardman illustrated Hodge's humility with the metaphor that it "covered him like a 'raiment of needlework.'" Boardman related an instance in which he had attempted to congratulate Hodge for his accomplishments, only to be

rebuked: "Now, stop! All that can be said is, that God has been pleased to take up a *poor little stick* and do something with it. What I have done is as nothing compared with what is done by a man who goes to Africa, and labors among a heathen tribe, and reduces their language to writing. I am not worthier to stoop down and *unloose the shoes* of such a man." Ibid., 608.

7. Ibid., 521.

8. David Calhoun reported the comment by Smith in *PS*, 2:37. By Hodge's death, the number would grow to over three thousand.

9. *LCH*, 530.

10. Letter of March 4, 1872, in *CHP*, box 13, folder 67.

11. *LCH*, 545–46.

12. Ibid., 570.

13. Ibid., 573.

14. Ibid., 574. A. A.'s most notable works were *Outlines of Theology* (1863), *Popular Lectures on Theological Themes* (1887), and "Inspiration," cowritten with Benjamin Warfield, *Presbyterian Review* 6 (1881): 225–60. Cf. *PS*, 2:52, 68–76, 101–4, 467n13.

15. *LCH*, 580, 583–84.

16. Among studies that trace the trajectory of Presbyterianism in the late nineteenth and early twentieth centuries are the following: Bradley J. Longfield, *The Presbyterian Controversy: Fundamentalists, Modernists, and Moderates* (New York: Oxford University Press, 1991); Lefferts A. Loetscher, *The Broadening Church: A Study of Theological Issues in the Presbyterian Church Since 1869* (Philadelphia: University of Pennsylvania Press, 1954); *SABC*, 169–221.

17. Richard John Neuhaus, *The Naked Public Square: Religion and Democracy in America* (Grand Rapids: Eerdmans, 1984), 250.

18. Similar to Hodge's intense emphasis on the subjective aspect of religion, Benjamin Warfield went so far as to brand Schleiermacher's view of religion as the feeling of absolute dependence or God-consciousness as perfectly amenable to Calvinism. Calvinists, however, differed from Schleiermacher by insisting that such a feeling had an objective reference point—God himself. Benjamin Breckinridge Warfield, *Power of God unto Salvation* (Philadelphia: Presbyterian Board of Education, 1903), 238, 243.

19. Benjamin B. Warfield, *Critical Reviews* (New York: Oxford University Press, 1932). Cf. W. Andrew Hoffecker, "Benjamin B. Warfield," in *Reformed Theology in America: A History of Its Modern Development*, ed. David Wells (Grand Rapids: Eerdmans, 1985), 60–86. Machen especially accused liberals of shoddy scholarship; like Hodge, he criticized growing secularization of education. J. Gresham Machen, *Christianity and Liberalism* (Grand Rapids: Eerdmans, 1923), 1–16; D. G. Hart, *Defending the Faith: J. Gresham Machen and the Crisis of Conservative Protestantism in Modern America* (Grand Rapids: Baker, 1994), 84–107; Stephen Nichols, *J. Gresham Machen: A Guided Tour of His Life and Thought* (Phillipsburg, NJ: P&R Publishing, 2004), 171–88.

Select Bibliography

Treatments of Charles Hodge and the theology of Old Princeton have spawned a massive literature. No compilation includes all that Hodge wrote, let alone the vast number of books, articles, and other treatments of his life and thought. What follows are either cited works or titles that might lead those interested in Hodge to works worthy of their attention.

Adger, John B. "The General Assembly of 1860." *Southern Presbyterian Review* 13, 2 (1860): 352–417.

Ahlstrom, Sydney E. *A Religious History of the American People*. New Haven, CT: Yale University Press, 1972.

———. "The Scottish Philosophy and American Theology." *Church History* 24 (1955): 257–72.

Alexander, Archibald. "The Bible and the Natural World." *Biblical Repertory and Princeton Review* 1, 1 (January 1829): 102–21.

———. *Biographical Sketches of the Founder and Principal Alumni of the Log College: Together with an Account of the Revivals of Religion under Their Ministry*. Princeton, NJ: J. T. Robinson, 1845.

———. "Dr. Green's Lectures on the Shorter Catechism." *Biblical Repertory and Princeton Review* 2 (1830): 297–309.

———. *A History of Colonization on the Western Coast of Africa*. Philadelphia: William S. Martien, 1846.

Alexander, James W. *Life of Archibald Alexander: First Professor in the Theological Seminary at Princeton, New Jersey*. New York: Charles Scribner, 1854.

Armstrong, Maurice W., Lefferts A. Loetscher, and Charles A. Anderson, eds. *The Presbyterian Enterprise: Sources of American Presbyterian History*. Philadelphia: Westminster Press, 1956.

Balmer, Randall. "The Princetonians and Scripture: A Reconsideration." *Westminster Theological Journal* 44 (1982): 352–65.

Balmer, Randall Herbert, and John R. Fitzmier. *The Presbyterians*. Westport, CT: Praeger, 1994.

Barker, William S. "The Social Views of Charles Hodge (1797–1878): A Study in Nineteenth-Century Calvinism and Conservatism." *Presbyterion: Covenant Seminary Review* 1 (Spring 1975): 1–22.

Beam, Jacob N. "Charles Hodge's Student Years in Germany." *Princeton University Library Chronicle* 3 (1947): 103–14.

Bledstein, Burton J. *The Culture of Professionalism: The Middle Class and the Development of Higher Education in America*. New York: Norton, 1976.

Bozeman, Theodore Dwight. *Protestants in an Age of Science: The Baconian Ideal and Antebellum American Religious Thought*. Chapel Hill, NC: University of North Carolina Press, 1977.

A Brief History of the Theological Seminary of the Presbyterian Church, at Princeton, New Jersey; Together with Its Constitution, Bye-Laws, &c. Princeton, NJ: John Bogart, 1838.

Calhoun, David B. "The Log College." In *Colonial Presbyterianism: Commemorating the 300th Anniversary of the First Presbytery in America*, edited by S. Donald Fortson, 49–61. Eugene, OR: Wipf and Stock, 2007.

———. *Princeton Seminary*. 2 vols. Carlisle, PA: Banner of Truth, 1994, 1996.

Carey, Jonathan Sinclair. "'For God or Against Him': Princeton Orthodoxy and Transcendentalists." *American Presbyterians* 64, 4 (Winter 1986): 243–58.

Carwardine, Richard J. "The Politics of Charles Hodge." In *Charles Hodge Revisited: A Critical Appraisal of His Life and Work*, edited by John W. Stewart and James H. Moorehead, 247–97. Grand Rapids: Eerdmans, 2002.

Cashdollar, Charles D. "The Pursuit of Piety: Charles Hodge's Diary, 1819–1820." *Journal of Presbyterian History* 55 (1977): 267–83.

———. *The Transformation of Theology, 1830–1890: Positivism and Protestant Thought in Britain and America*. Princeton, NJ: Princeton University Press, 1989.

Chinard, Gilbert. "A Land Mark in American Intellectual History: Samuel Miller's *A Brief Retrospect of the Eighteenth Century*." *Princeton University Chronicle* 14 (Winter 1953): 55–71.

Church, Richard William. *The Oxford Movement: Twelve Years 1833–1845*. New York: Macmillan, 1891.

Clements, Keith W. *Friedrich Schleiermacher: Pioneer of Modern Theology*. Minneapolis: Fortress Press, 1991.

Coker, Joe L. "Exploring the Roots of the Dispensationalist/Princetonian 'Alliance': Charles Hodge and John Nelson Darby on Eschatology and Interpretation of Scripture." *Fides et Historia* 30 (Winter–Spring 1998): 41–56.

Collins, Varnum Lansing. *Princeton*. New York: Oxford University Press, 1914.

Conkin, Paul K. *The Uneasy Center: Reformed Christianity in Antebellum America*. Chapel Hill, NC: University of North Carolina Press, 1995.

Conser, Walter F. *God and the Natural World*. Columbia, SC: University of South Carolina Press, 1993.

Cross, Whitney R. *The Burned-over District: The Social and Intellectual History of Enthusiastic Religion in Western New York, 1800–1850*. New York: Harper, 1950.

Dabney, Robert Lewis. *The Sensualistic Philosophy of the Nineteenth Century, Considered*. New York: Anson, 1875.

Danhof, Ralph J. *Charles Hodge as a Dogmatician*. Goes, Netherlands: Oosterbaan & Le Cointre, 1929.

Davis, Clair. "Princeton and Inerrancy: The Nineteenth-Century Philosophical Background of Contemporary Concerns." In *Inerrancy and the Church*, edited by John D. Hannah, 359–78. Chicago: Moody Press, 1984.

Dennison, Charles G., and Richard Gamble. *Pressing toward the Mark: Essays Commemorating Fifty Years of the Orthodox Presbyterian Church*. Philadelphia: Committee for the Historian of the Orthodox Presbyterian Church, 1986.

Draper, John William. *History of the Conflict between Religion and Science*. New York: D. Appleton and Company, 1874.

Farmer, James Oscar, Jr. *The Metaphysical Conspiracy: James Henley Thornwell and Synthesis of Southern Values*. Macon, GA: Mercer University Press, 1986.

Finke, Roger, and Rodney Stark. "The Upstart Sects within America." In *The Churching of America 1776–1990: Winners and Losers in Our Religious Economy*, 55–116. New Brunswick, NJ: Rutgers University Press, 1992.

Finney, Charles G. *Lectures on Revivals of Religion*. New York: Leavitt, Lord & Company, 1835.

Fortson, S. Donald. "The Presbyterian Creed: Old School / New School Reunion and Confessional Subscription." PhD diss., Westminster Theological Seminary, 2003.

Fortson, S. Donald, and David Calhoun. *The Presbyterian Creed: A Confessional Tradition in America, 1729–1870*. Eugene, OR: Wipf and Stock, 2011.

Freundt, Albert H. "The Southern Presbyterian Polity of James Henley Thornwell." www.geocities.com/afreundt/thornwell.html.

Gerrish, B. A. "Charles Hodge and the Europeans." In *Charles Hodge Revisited: A Critical Appraisal of His Life and Work*, edited by John W. Stewart and James H. Moorehead, 129–58. Grand Rapids: Eerdmans, 2002.

———. *Tradition and the Modern World: Reformed Theology in the Nineteenth Century*. Chicago: University of Chicago Press, 1978.

Gillett, E. H. *History of the Presbyterian Church in the United States of America*. Philadelphia: Presbyterian Publication Committee, 1864.

———. *Lectures on Systematic Theology*. Oberlin, OH: James M. Fitch, 1846.

Gray, Asa. Review of *What Is Darwinism?*, by Charles Hodge. *The Nation* 465 (May 28, 1874): 348–53.

Green, Ashbel. *The Case of the General Assembly of the Presbyterian Church in the United States of America, before the Supreme Court of the Commonwealth of Pennsylvania, Impartially Reported by Disinterested Stenographers; Including All the Proceedings, Testimony, and Arguments at* Nisi Prius *and before the Court in Bank, with the Charge of Judge Rogers, the Verdict of the Jury, and the Opinion of Chief Justice Gibson. The Whole Compiled and Prepared for the Press by the Rev. D. W. Lathrop*. Philadelphia: A. McElroy, 1839.

Guelzo, Allen C. "Charles Hodge's Antislavery Moment." In *Charles Hodge Revisited: A Critical Appraisal of His Life and Work*, edited by John W. Stewart and James H. Moorehead, 299–325. Grand Rapids: Eerdmans, 2002.

Gundlach, Bradley J. "McCosh and Hodge on Evolution: A Combined Legacy." *Journal of Presbyterian History* 75 (Summer 1997): 85–102.

Gutjahr, Paul C. *Charles Hodge: Guardian of American Orthodoxy*. New York: Oxford University Press, 2011.

Hart, D. G. *Defending the Faith: J. Gresham Machen and the Crisis of Conservative Protestantism in Modern America*. Grand Rapids: Baker, 1994.

———. "Divided between Heart and Mind: The Critical Period for Protestant Thought in America." *Journal of Ecclesiastical History* 38 (April 1987): 254–70.

———. "The Divine and Human in the Seminary Curriculum." *Westminster Theological Journal* 65, 2 (Fall 2003): 45–67.

———. *John Williamson Nevin: High Church Calvinist.* Phillipsburg, NJ: P&R Publishing, 2005.

———. *The Lost Soul of American Protestantism.* Lanham, MD: Rowman & Littlefield, 2002.

———. "Poems, Propositions, and Dogma: The Controversy over Religious Language and the Demise of Theology in American Learning." *Church History* 57, 3 (September 1988): 310–21.

———. "The Spirituality of the Church." In *Rediscovering Mother Kirk: The Case for Liturgy in the Reformed Tradition.* Grand Rapids: Baker, 2003.

Hart, D. G., and John R. Muether, *Seeking a Better Country: 300 Years of American Presbyterianism.* Phillipsburg, NJ: P&R Publishing, 2007.

Hatch, Nathan O. *The Democratization of American Christianity.* New Haven, CT: Yale University Press, 1989.

Helseth, Paul Kjoss. "Right Reason and the Princeton Mind: The Moral Context." *Journal of Presbyterian History* 77 (1999): 13–28.

———. *"Right Reason" and the Princeton Mind: An Unorthodox Proposal.* Phillipsburg, NJ: P&R Publishing, 2010.

Hicks, Peter. *The Philosophy of Charles Hodge: A 19th Century Evangelical Approach to Reason, Knowledge and Truth.* Lewiston, NY: Edwin Mellen Press, 1997.

Hobbs, Albert H. *The Claims of Sociology.* Harrisburg, PA: Stackpole, 1951.

———. *Social Problems and Scientism.* Harrisburg, PA: Stackpole, 1953.

Hodge, Archibald Alexander. *The Life of Charles Hodge.* New York: Charles Scribner's Sons, 1880.

———. *Outlines of Theology.* New York: Robert Carter and Brothers, 1863.

———. *Popular Lectures on Theological Themes.* Philadelphia: Presbyterian Board of Publication, 1887.

Hodge, Charles. "Abolitionism." *Biblical Repertory and Princeton Review* 16, 4 (September 1844): 545–81.

———. "Abraham Lincoln." *Biblical Repertory and Princeton Review* 37, 3 (July 1865): 435–58.

———. "The Act and Testimony." *Biblical Repertory and Princeton Review* (October 1834): 505–22.

———. "The Act and Testimony." *Biblical Repertory and Princeton Review* (January 1835): 110–34.

———. "Adoption of the Confession of Faith." *Biblical Repertory and Princeton Review* 30, 4 (October 1858): 669–92.

———. "Biblical Repertory: A Collection of Tracts in Biblical Literature." *Biblical Repertory and Princeton Review* 1, 1 (January 1825): iii–iv.

———. "The Christian Spectator on the Doctrine of Imputation." *Biblical Repertory and Princeton Review* 3, 3 (1831): 407–33.

———. "The Church and the Country." *Biblical Repertory and Princeton Review* 33, 2 (April 1861): 322–76.

———. "The Church Membership of Infants." *Biblical Repertory and Princeton Review* 30, 2 (1858): 347–89.

———. *Commentary on the Epistle to the Ephesians*. New York: Robert Carter & Brothers, 1858.

———. *A Commentary on the Epistle to the Romans*. Philadelphia: Grigg & Elliot, 1835.

———. "Conflict of Faith with Infidelity." In "History of Theology in 18th Century by August Tholuck, June 1827." Hodge Papers, Princeton Theological Seminary.

———. *The Constitutional History of the Presbyterian Church in the United States of America*. 2 vols. Philadelphia: Presbyterian Board of Publication, 1851.

———. "A Discourse on the Latest Form of Infidelity." *Biblical Repertory and Princeton Review* 12, 1 (January 1840): 31–71.

———. "Discourses on Christian Nurture." *Biblical Repertory and Princeton Review* 19, 4 (October 1847): 502–39.

———. *Discourses on Church Polity*. New York: Charles Scribner's Sons, 1878.

———. *A Dissertation on the Importance of Biblical Literature, by Charles Hodge, A.M. Teacher of the Original Languages of Scripture, in the Theological Seminary of the Presbyterian Church at Princeton*. Trenton, NJ: George Sherman, 1822.

———. "Emancipation." *Biblical Repertory and Princeton Review* 21, 4 (1849): 582–607.

———. "*Encyclopedia of Theology* by August Tholuck, Halle 1827." Special Collections, Princeton Theological Seminary.

———. *Essays and Reviews: Selections from "The Princeton Review."* New York: Robert Carter & Brothers, 1857.

———. "Examination of Some Reasonings against the Unity of Mankind." *Biblical Repertory and Princeton Review* 27, 3 (July 1855): 445–67.

———. "Finney's Lectures on Systematic Theology." *Biblical Repertory and Princeton Review* 19, 2 (April 1847): 237–77.

———. "The First and Second Adam." *Biblical Repertory and Princeton Review* 32, 2 (1860): 335–76.

———. "The General Assembly of 1835." *Biblical Repertory and Princeton Review* 7, 3 (July 1835): 440–82.

———. "The General Assembly of 1836." *Biblical Repertory and Princeton Review* 8, 3 (July 1836): 415–76.

———. "The General Assembly of 1837." *Biblical Repertory and Princeton Review* 9, 3 (July 1837): 407–85.

———. "The General Assembly of 1838." *Biblical Repertory and Princeton Review* 10, 3 (July 1838): 457–03.

———. "The General Assembly of 1843." *Biblical Repertory and Princeton Review* 15, 3 (July 1843): 407–69.

———. "The General Assembly of 1844." *Biblical Repertory and Princeton Review* 16, 3 (July 1844): 418–53.

———. "The General Assembly of 1845." *Biblical Repertory and Princeton Review* 17, 3 (July 1845): 428–71.

———. "The General Assembly of 1846." *Biblical Repertory and Princeton Review* 18, 3 (July 1846): 418–56.

———. "The General Assembly of 1847." *Biblical Repertory and Princeton Review* 19, 3 (July 1847): 396–444.

———. "The General Assembly of 1848." *Biblical Repertory and Princeton Review* 20, 3 (July 1848): 403–51.

———. "The General Assembly of 1850." *Biblical Repertory and Princeton Review* 22, 3 (July 1850): 441–83.

———. "The General Assembly of 1851." *Biblical Repertory and Princeton Review* 23, 3 (July 1851): 521–53.

———. "The General Assembly of 1853." *Biblical Repertory and Princeton Review* 25, 3 (July 1853): 450–528.

———. "The General Assembly of 1854." *Biblical Repertory and Princeton Review* 26, 3 (July 1854): 548–80.

———. "The General Assembly of 1855." *Biblical Repertory and Princeton Review* 27, 3 (July 1855): 467–542.

———. "The General Assembly of 1858." *Biblical Repertory and Princeton Review* 30, 3 (July 1858): 533–70.

———. "The General Assembly of 1859." *Biblical Repertory and Princeton Review* 31, 3 (July 1859): 536–618.

———. "The General Assembly of 1860." *Biblical Repertory and Princeton Review* 32, 3 (July 1860): 511–46.

———. "The General Assembly of 1861." *Biblical Repertory and Princeton Review* 33, 3 (July 1861): 511–68.

———. "The General Assembly of 1865." *Biblical Repertory and Princeton Review* 37, 3 (July 1865): 458–515.

———. "The General Assembly of 1868." *Biblical Repertory and Princeton Review* 40, 3 (July 1868): 410–55.

———. "The General Assembly of 1869." *Biblical Repertory and Princeton Review* 41, 3 (July 1869): 401–23.

———. "Hengstenberg on Daniel." *Biblical Repertory and Princeton Review* 4, 1 (1832): 48–71.

———. "History of Theology in the Eighteenth Century by Dr. August Tholuck, Professor of Theology in the University of Halle; Translated from the German by the Editor." *Biblical Repertory* 4 (1828): 9–57.

———. "Infant Members Subjects of Discipline." In *The Church and Its Polity*, edited by William Durant and A. A. Hodge, 215–18. New York: Thomas Nelson and Sons, 1879.

———. "Inquiries Respecting the Doctrine of Imputation." *Biblical Repertory and Princeton Review* 2, 3 (1830): 425–72.

———. "Is the Church of Rome a Part of the Visible Church?" *Biblical Repertory and Princeton Review* 18, 2 (April 1846): 320–44.

———. "Journal of European Travels." Special Collections, Princeton Theological Seminary.

———. "Lecture Addressed to the Students of the Theological Seminary." *Biblical Repertory and Princeton Review* 1, 1 (January 1829): 75–98.

———. "Lectures on Systematic Theology by Charles Finney." *Biblical Repertory and Princeton Review* 19, 2 (1847): 237–77.

———. "The Life of Archibald Alexander." *Biblical Repertory and Princeton Review* 27, 1 (January 1855): 133–59.

———. "The Mystical Presence." *Biblical Repertory and Princeton Review* 20, 2 (April 1848): 227–78.

———. "The Nature of Man." *Biblical Repertory and Princeton Review* 37, 1 (January 1865): 111–35.

———. "Neander's History of the Planting of the Church." *Biblical Repertory and Princeton Review* 16, 2 (1844): 155–83.

———. "Neglect of Infant Baptism." *Biblical Repertory and Princeton Review* 29, 1 (1857): 73–101.

———. "The New Basis of Union." *Biblical Repertory and Princeton Review* 41, 3 (July 1869): 462–66.

———. "Notes, Explanatory and Practical, on the Epistle to the Romans, Designed for Bible-Classes and Sunday Schools. By Albert Barnes." *Biblical Repertory and Princeton Review* 7, 2 (April 1835): 285–340.

———. "Oxford Tracts." *Biblical Repertory and Princeton Review* 10, 1 (January 1838): 84–119.

———. "A Plea for Voluntary Societies and Defence of the Decisions of the General Assembly of 1836 against the Strictures of the Princeton Review and Others." *Biblical Repertory and Princeton Review* 9, 1 (January 1837): 101–52.

———. "Preaching the Gospel to the Poor." *Biblical Repertory and Princeton Review* 43, 1 (April 1871): 83–95.

———. "Presbyterianism." *Biblical Repertory and Princeton Review* 32, 3 (July 1860): 546–67.

———. "Presbyterian Reunion." *Biblical Repertory and Princeton Review* 40, 1 (January 1868): 53–83.

———. "The Princeton Review on the State of the Country and of the Church." *Biblical Repertory and Princeton Review* 37, 4 (October 1865): 627–57.

———. *Princeton Sermons: Outlines of Discourses, Doctrinal and Practical, Delivered at Princeton Theological Seminary on Sabbath Afternoons*. London: Thomas Nelson and Sons, 1879. (Also published as *Conference Papers, or Analyses of Discourses, Doctrinal and Practical, Delivered on Sabbath Afternoons to the Students of the Theological Seminary, Princeton, New Jersey*. New York: Charles Scribner's Sons, 1879.)

———. "Principles of Church Union, and the Reunion of the Old and New-school Presbyterians." *Biblical Repertory and Princeton Review* 37, 2 (April 1865): 271–313.

———. "Principles of Protestantism by Philip Schaff." *Biblical Repertory and Princeton Review* 17, 4 (1845): 626–36.

———. "Prof. Park's Remarks on the Princeton Review." *Biblical Repertory and Princeton Review* 23, 2 (April 1851): 306–47.

———. "Reed and Matheson: The Narrative." *Biblical Repertory and Princeton Review* 7, 4 (1835): 598–626.

———. "Religious State of Germany." *Biblical Repertory and Princeton Review* 18, 4 (October 1846): 514–46.

———. "Remarks on Dr. Cox's Communication." *Biblical Repertory and Princeton Review* 3, 4 (October 1831): 514–43.

———. "Retrospect of the History of the Princeton Review." *Biblical Repertory and Princeton Review*, Index vol. (1871): 1–39.

———. "Slavery." *Biblical Repertory and Princeton Review* 8, 2 (April 1836): 268–305.

———. "The State of the Country." *Biblical Repertory and Princeton Review* 33, 1 (January 1861): 1–36.

———. "Stuart on Romans." *Biblical Repertory and Princeton Review* 5, 3 (July 1833): 381–416.

———. *Systematic Theology*. 3 vols. New York: Charles Scribner's Sons, 1872–73.

———. "The Temperance Question." In *The Church and Its Polity*, edited by William Durant and A. A. Hodge, 224–31. New York: Thomas Nelson and Sons, 1879.

———. "The Theology of the Intellect and That of the Feelings." *Biblical Repertory and Princeton Review* 22, 4 (October 1850): 642–74.

———. "The Tracts for the Times." *Biblical Repertory and Princeton Review* 10, 1 (January 1838): 84–119.

———. "Transcendentalism." *Biblical Repertory and Princeton Review* 11, 1 (January 1839): 37–101.

———. *The Way of Life*. Philadelphia: American Sunday-School Union, 1841.

———. "West India Emancipation." *Biblical Repertory and Princeton Review* 10, 4 (1838): 602–44.

———. *What Is Darwinism? And Other Writings on Science and Religion*, edited by Mark A. Noll and David Livingstone. Grand Rapids: Baker, 1994.

———. *What Is Presbyterianism?* Philadelphia: Presbyterian Board of Publication, 1855.

Hoffecker, W. Andrew. "Beauty and the Princeton Piety." In *Soli Deo Gloria: Essays in Reformed Theology: Festschrift for John H. Gerstner*, edited by R. C. Sproul, 118–33. Nutley, NJ: Presbyterian and Reformed, 1976.

———. "The Devotional Life of Archibald Alexander, Charles Hodge and Benjamin B. Warfield." *Westminster Theological Journal* 42, 1 (Fall 1979): 111–29.

———. "Enlightenments and Awakenings: The Beginning of Modern Culture Wars." In *Revolutions in Worldview: Understanding the Flow of Western Thought*, edited by W. Andrew Hoffecker, 240–80. Phillipsburg, NJ: P&R Publishing, 2007.

———. *Piety and the Princeton Theologians: Archibald Alexander, Charles Hodge, and Benjamin Warfield*. Phillipsburg, NJ: Presbyterian and Reformed, 1981.

Holifield, E. Brooks. "Hodge, the Seminary, and the American Theological Context." In *Charles Hodge Revisited: A Critical Appraisal of His Life and Work*, edited by John W. Stewart and James H. Moorehead, 103–28. Grand Rapids: Eerdmans, 2002.

———. "Mercersburg, Princeton, and the South: The Sacramental Controversy in the Nineteenth Century." *Journal of Presbyterian History* 54 (1976): 238–57.

———. *Theology in America: Christian Thought from the Age of the Puritans to the Civil War*. New Haven, CT: Yale University Press, 2003.

Hovenkamp, Herbert. *Science and Religion in America: 1800–1860*. Philadelphia: University of Pennsylvania Press, 1978.

Hutchison, William. *The Modernist Impulse in American Protestantism*. Cambridge, MA: Harvard University Press, 1976.

Kant, Immanuel. *Religion within the Limits of Reason Alone*. New York: Harper, 1960.

Kelsey, David H. *Between Athens and Berlin: The Theological Education Debate*. Grand Rapids: Eerdmans, 1993.

———. "Charles Hodge as Interpreter of Scripture." In *Charles Hodge Revisited: A Critical Appraisal of His Life and Work*, edited by John W. Stewart and James H. Moorehead, 217–46. Grand Rapids: Eerdmans, 2002.

Kemeny, Paul C. *Princeton in the Nation's Service: Religious Ideals and Educational Practice, 1868–1928*. New York: Oxford University Press, 1998.

———. "Princeton University, Secularization Theories, and Revisionist History: A Review Essay." *Journal of Presbyterian History* 75, 2 (1997): 71–83.

Kerr, Hugh T., ed. *Sons of the Prophets: Leaders in Protestantism from Princeton Seminary*. Princeton, NJ: Princeton University Press, 1963.

Kuklick, Bruce. "The Place of Charles Hodge in the History of Ideas in America." In *Charles Hodge Revisited: A Critical Appraisal of His Life and Work*, edited by John W. Stewart and James H. Moorehead, 63–76. Grand Rapids: Eerdmans, 2002.

LeBeau, Bryan F. *Jonathan Dickinson and the Formative Years of American Presbyterianism*. Lexington, KY: University of Kentucky Press, 1997.

Livingstone, David N., D. G. Hart, and Mark A. Noll, eds. *Evangelicals and Science in Historical Perspective*. New York: Oxford University Press, 2002.

Loetscher, Lefferts A. *The Broadening Church: A Study of Theological Issues in the Presbyterian Church Since 1869*. Philadelphia: University of Pennsylvania Press, 1954.

———. *Facing the Enlightenment and Pietism: Archibald Alexander and the Founding of Princeton Theological Seminary*. Westport, CT: Greenwood Press, 1983.

Longfield, Bradley J. *The Presbyterian Controversy: Fundamentalists, Modernists, and Moderates*. New York: Oxford University Press, 1991.

Lucas, Sean. *Robert Lewis Dabney: A Southern Presbyterian Life*. Phillipsburg, NJ: P&R Publishing, 2005.

Machen, J. Gresham. *Christianity and Liberalism*. Grand Rapids: Eerdmans, 1923.

Maclean, James. *History of the College of New Jersey*. 2 vols. Philadelphia: J. B. Lippincott & Co., 1877.

Marsden, George M. *The Evangelical Mind and the New School Presbyterian Experience: A Case Study of Thought and Theology in Nineteenth-Century America*. New Haven, CT: Yale University Press, 1970.

———. *Fundamentalism and American Culture: The Shaping of Twentieth-Century American Evangelicalism*. New York: Oxford University Press, 1980.

Mathison, Keith A. *Given for You: Reclaiming Calvin's Doctrine of the Lord's Supper*. Phillipsburg, NJ: P&R Publishing, 2002.

McLaughlin, William G. *The American Evangelicals, 1800–1900: An Anthology*. New York: Harper, 1968.

Miller, Glenn T. *Piety and Intellect: The Aims and Purposes of Ante-Bellum Theological Education*. Atlanta: Scholars Press, 1990.

Miller, Samuel. *A Brief Retrospect of the Eighteenth Century*. 2 vols. New York: Burt Franklin, 1803.

———. *An Essay on the Warrant, Nature and Duties of the Office of the Ruling Elder, in the Presbyterian Church*. New York: Jonathan Leavitt, 1821.

———. *Letters on Clerical Manners and Morals Addressed to a Student in the Theological Seminary at Princeton, N.J.* New York: G. & C. Carvill, 1827.

———. *Presbyterianism the Truly Primitive and Apostolical Constitution of the Church of Christ*. Philadelphia: Presbyterian Board of Publication, 1835.

Miller, Samuel. *The Life of Samuel Miller, D.D., LL.D., Second Professor of the Theological Seminary of the Presbyterian Church at Princeton, New Jersey*. Philadelphia: Claxton, Remsen and Haffelfinger, 1869.

"Minutes of the General Assembly, 1861, vol xvi, 303." In Lewis G. Vander Velde, *The Presbyterian Churches and the Federal Union, 1861–1869*. Cambridge, MA: Harvard University Press, 1932.

Minutes of the General Assembly of the Presbyterian Church in the United States of America . . . A.D. 1789–1820 Inclusive. Philadelphia: Presbyterian Board of Publication, 1847.

Moorehead, James H. "AFTERWORD: Where Does One Find the Legacy of Charles Hodge?" In *Charles Hodge Revisited: A Critical Appraisal of His Life and Work*, edited by John W. Stewart and James H. Moorehead, 327–34. Grand Rapids: Eerdmans, 2002.

———. "The 'Restless Spirit of Radicalism': Old School Fears and the Schism of 1837." *Journal of Presbyterian History* 78, 1 (Spring 2000): 19–33.

Morris, R. J. "Voluntary Societies and British Urban Elites, 1780–1850: An Analysis." *Historical Journal* 26, 1 (1983): 95–118.

Murchie, David Neil. "Morality and Social Ethics in the Thought of Charles Hodge." PhD diss., Drew University, 1980.

Murray, Iain H. *Revival and Revivalism*. Carlisle, PA: Banner of Truth, 1994.

Naugle, David K. *Worldview: The History of a Concept*. Grand Rapids: Eerdmans, 2002.

Nelson, John Oliver. "Charles Hodge (1797–1878): Nestor of Orthodoxy." In *The Lives of Eighteen from Princeton*, edited by Willard Thorp. Princeton, NJ: Princeton University Press, 1946.

———. "The Rise of the Princeton Theology: A Genetic History of American Presbyterianism until 1850." PhD diss., Yale University, 1935.

Nevin, John Williamson. *My Own Life: The Earlier Years*. Lancaster, PA: Historical Society of the Evangelical and Reformed Church, 1964.

———. *The Mystical Presence and Other Writings on the Eucharist*. Philadelphia: J. B. Lippincott, 1846.

Nichols, James Hastings. *Romanticism in American Theology: Nevin and Schaff at Mercersburg*. Chicago: University of Chicago Press, 1961.

———, ed. *The Mercersburg Theology*. New York: Oxford University Press, 1966.

Noll, Mark A. *America's God: From Jonathan Edwards to Abraham Lincoln*. New York: Oxford University Press, 2002.

———. "The Bible and Slavery." In *Religion and the American Civil War*, edited by Randall M. Miller, Harry S. Stout, and Charles Regan Wilson, 43–73. New York: Oxford University Press, 1998.

———. "Charles Hodge as an Expositor of the Spiritual Life." In *Charles Hodge Revisited: A Critical Appraisal of His Life and Work*, edited by John W. Stewart and James H. Moorehead, 181–216. Grand Rapids: Eerdmans, 2002.

———. "Common Sense Traditions and American Evangelical Thought." *American Quarterly* 37, 2 (1985): 216–38.

———. "The Founding of Princeton Seminary." *Westminster Theological Journal* 42 (Fall 1979): 72–110.

———. Introduction. In *The Way of Life*, by Charles Hodge. New York: Paulist Press, 1987.

———. *Princeton and the Republic, 1768–1822: The Search for a Christian Enlightenment in the Era of Samuel Stanhope Smith*. Princeton, NJ: Princeton University Press, 1989.

———. "The Princeton Review: 1825–1921." *Westminster Theological Journal* 50, 2 (1988): 283–304.

———, ed. *The Princeton Theology, 1812–1921: Scripture, Science, and Theological Method from Archibald Alexander to Benjamin Warfield*. Grand Rapids: Baker, 1983.

Norton, Andrews. *A Discourse on the Latest Form of Infidelity*. Cambridge, MA: John Owen, 1839.

Numbers, Ronald L. "Charles Hodge and the Beauties and Deformities of Science." In *Charles Hodge Revisited: A Critical Appraisal of His Life and Work*, edited by John W. Stewart and James H. Moorehead, 77–101. Grand Rapids: Eerdmans, 2002.

Olbricht, Thomas H. "Charles Hodge as an American New Testament Interpreter." *Journal of Presbyterian History* 52, 2 (Summer 1979): 117–33.

Osmer, Richard Robert. *Confirmation: Presbyterian Practices in Ecumenical Perspective*. Louisville, KY: Geneva Press, 1996.

Park, Edwards Amasa. "Remarks on the Princeton Review." *Bibliotheca Sacra* 8, 29 (1851): 135–80.

———. *The Theology of the Intellect and of the Feelings*. Andover, MA: Warren F. Draper, 1850.

Patton, Francis L. "Charles Hodge." *Presbyterian Review* 6 (1881): 349–77.

Presbyterian Reunion: A Memorial Volume, 1837–71. New York: De Witt C. Lent, 1870.

Proceedings Connected with the Semi-Centennial Commemoration of the Professorship of Rev. Charles Hodge, D.D., LL.D., in the Theological Seminary at Princeton, N.J., April 24, 1872. New York: Anson D. F. Randolph & Co., n.d.

Riddle, Donald Wayne. "The Background of Modern Historical Study of Christianity." *Church History* 4, 3 (September 1935): 203–13.

Salmond, Charles A. *Princetoniana: Charles and A. A. Hodge with Class Notes and Table Talk of Hodge the Younger*. New York: Scribner and Welford, 1888.

Sandeen, Ernest. "The Princeton Theology: One Source of Biblical Literalism in American Protestantism." *Church History* 31, 3 (1962): 307–21.

———. *The Roots of Fundamentalism: British and American Millenarianism, 1800–1930*. Chicago: University of Chicago Press, 1970.

Schaff, David. *The Life of Philip Schaff: In Part Autobiographical*. New York: Scribners, 1897.

Schaff, Philip. *The Principle of Protestantism*. Philadelphia: United Church Press, 1964.

Schaff, Philip, and S. Irenaeus Prime, eds. *History, Essays, Orations, and Other Documents of the Sixth General Conference of the Evangelical Alliance, Held in New York, October 2–12, 1873*. New York: Harper, 1874.

Schleiermacher, Friedrich. *The Christian Faith*. 2 vols. New York: Harper, 1963.

Schorsch, Anita. "Samuel Miller, Renaissance Man: His Legacy of 'True Taste.'" *Journal of Presbyterian History* 66, 2 (Summer 1988): 71–87.

Shriver, George H. "Passages in Friendship: John W. Nevin to Charles Hodge." *Journal of Presbyterian History* 58, 2 (Summer 1980): 116–22.

Smith, Timothy. *Revivalism and Social Reform: American Protestantism on the Eve of the Civil War*. New York: Harper, 1965.

Stein, Stephen J. "Stuart and Hodge on Romans 5:12–21: An Exegetical Controversy about Original Sin." *Journal of Presbyterian History* 47 (December 1969): 340–58.

Stewart, John W. "AFTERWORD: Bibliography of the Works by and about Charles Hodge." In *Charles Hodge Revisited: A Critical Appraisal of His Life and Work*, edited by John W. Stewart and James H. Moorehead, 335–75. Grand Rapids: Eerdmans, 2002.

———. "Introducing Charles Hodge to Postmoderns." In *Charles Hodge Revisited: A Critical Appraisal of His Life and Work*, edited by John W. Stewart and James H. Moorehead, 1–40. Grand Rapids: Eerdmans, 2002.

———. *Mediating the Center: Charles Hodge on American Science, Language, Literature, and Politics*. Princeton, NJ: Princeton Theological Seminary, 1995.

———. "The Tethered Theology: Biblical Criticism, Common Sense Philosophy, and the Princeton Theologians, 1812–1860." PhD diss., University of Michigan, 1990.

Stewart, John W., and James H. Moorehead. *Charles Hodge Revisited: A Critical Appraisal of His Life and Work*. Grand Rapids: Eerdmans, 2002.

Stuart, Moses. *A Commentary on the Epistle to the Romans*. Andover, MA: Gould and Newman, 1835.

Susskind, Jacob. "Samuel Miller's Intellectual History of the Eighteenth Century." *Journal of Presbyterian History* 49 (1971): 15–31.

Taylor, Nathaniel W. *Concio ad Clerum: A Sermon Delivered in the Chapel of Yale College, September 10, 1828*. New Haven, CT: Maltby and Homan Hallock, 1842.

Thompson, Robert Ellis. *A History of the Presbyterian Churches in the United States*. 1895; repr., Eugene, OR: Wipf and Stock, 2003.

Thornwell, James Henley. *The Collected Writings of James Henley Thornwell*. Richmond, VA: Presbyterian Committee of Publication, 1871.

Tice, Terrence N. "Schleiermacher on the Scientific Study of Religion." In *Friedrich Schleiermacher and the Founding of the University of Berlin: The Study of Religion as a Scientific Discipline*, edited by Herbert Richardson. Lewiston, NY: Edwin Mellen Press, 1991.

Tillich, Paul. *A History of Christian Thought: From Its Jewish and Hellenistic Origins to Existentialism*. New York: Simon and Schuster, 1967.

Tise, Larry. *Proslavery: A History of the Defense of Slavery in America, 1701–1840*. Athens, GA: University of Georgia Press, 1987.

Trinterud, Leonard J. "Charles Hodge (1797–1878): Theology—Didactic and Polemical." In *Sons of the Prophets: Leaders in Protestantism from Princeton Seminary*, edited by Hugh T. Kerr, 22–38. Princeton, NJ: Princeton University Press, 1963.

Turner, James. "Charles Hodge in the Intellectual Weather of the Nineteenth Century." In *Charles Hodge Revisited: A Critical Appraisal of His Life and Work*, edited by John W. Stewart and James H. Moorehead, 41–62. Grand Rapids: Eerdmans, 2002.

Turretin, Francis. *Institutes of Elenctic Theology*. 3 vols. Translated by George Musgrave Giger. Edited by James T. Dennison Jr. Phillipsburg, NJ: P&R Publishing, 1992, 1994, 1997.

Vander Stelt, John. *Philosophy and Scripture: A Study in Old Princeton and Westminster Theology*. Marlton, NJ: Mack Publishing, 1978.

Vander Velde, Lewis G. *The Presbyterian Churches and the Federal Union, 1861–1869*. Cambridge, MA: Harvard University Press, 1932.

Wallace, Peter. "'The Bond of Union': The Old School Presbyterian Church and the American Nation, 1837–1861." PhD diss., University of Notre Dame, 2004.

———. "The Defense of the Forgotten Center: Charles Hodge and the Enigma of Emancipationism in Antebellum America." *Journal of Presbyterian History* 75, 3 (Fall 1997): 165–77.

———. "History and Sacrament: John Williamson Nevin and Charles Hodge on the Lord's Supper." *Mid-America Journal of Theology* 11 (2000): 171–202.

Wallace, Peter, and Mark Noll. "The Students of Princeton Seminary, 1812–1929: A Research Note." *American Presbyterians* 72, 3 (1994): 203–15.

Warfield, Benjamin B. "Dr. Hodge as a Teacher of Exegesis." In *Selected Shorter Writings of Benjamin B. Warfield*, vol. 1, edited by John E. Meeter, 437–40. Nutley, NJ: Presbyterian and Reformed, 1973.

Wells, Charles. "Charles Hodge's Critique of Darwinism: The Argument to Design." PhD diss., Yale University, 1986.

Wells, David F. "Aftermath and Hindsight of the Atonement Debate." *Bibliotheca Sacra* (January–March 1988): 3–14.

———. "American Society as Seen from the 19th Century Pulpit." *Bibliotheca Sacra* (April–June 1987): 123–43.

———. "The Collision of Views on the Atonement." *Bibliotheca Sacra* (October–December 1988): 123–43.

———. "The Shaping of the 19th-Century Debate over the Atonement." *Bibliotheca Sacra* (July–September 1987): 243–53.

———, ed. *The Princeton Theology*. Grand Rapids: Baker, 1989.

———, ed. *Reformed Theology in America: A History of Its Modern Development*. Grand Rapids: Baker, 1985.

———. "The Stout and Persistent 'Theology' of Charles Hodge." *Christianity Today* (August 30, 1974): 10–15.

Wertenbaker, Thomas Jefferson. *Princeton, 1746–1896*. Princeton, NJ: Princeton University Press, 1946.

White, Andrew Dickson. *History of the Warfare of Science and Theology in Christendom*, 2 vols. New York: D. Appleton and Company, 1896.

Whitehead, Alfred North. *Science and the Modern World*. New York: Free Press, 1925.

Woodbridge, John D., and Randall Balmer. "The Princetonians and Biblical Authority: An Assessment of the Ernest Sandeen Proposal." In *Scripture and Truth*, edited by John D. Woodbridge and D. A. Carson, 245–79. Grand Rapids: Zondervan, 1983.

Index of Subjects and Names